The Complete Idiot's Reference Card

Do's and Don'ts of Family History Research

While things may seem overwhelming at times, there really are some simple rules that will help you immensely during your genealogical trek.

- ➤ Do find those letters.
- ➤ Don't let time slip-slide away.
- ➤ Don't ignore your Crazy Aunt Ednas.
- ➤ Do make copies of everything.
- ➤ Do collect all those old photos.
- ➤ Don't let your organization go.
- ➤ Do browse.
- ➤ Do use common sense.
- ➤ Don't be afraid to ask for help.
- ➤ Don't take help without question.
- ➤ Do let your curiosity be your guide.
- ➤ Do respond to correspondence.
- ➤ Don't use computers as filing cabinets.
- ➤ Do treat the Internet as a big index.
- ➤ Don't believe in "generic" genealogy.
- ➤ Do find and use ethnic resources.
- ➤ Do check lesser-known resources.

tear here

alpha
books

Writing Mistakes You Won't Make

➤ Not knowing when to toss your work

➤ Believing great writers don't rewrite

➤ Believing first drafts are finished drafts

➤ Not listening to your internal nitpicker

➤ Forgetting the fine line between fact and fiction

➤ Forgetting your audience

➤ Forgetting that more is less

➤ Straying from your outline

➤ Being too flexible about your format

➤ Being self-indulgent

➤ Stumbling at the start

➤ Being reference sloppy

➤ Forgetting to make forms work for you

➤ Freezing in the end

Watch for These Usual Grammar/Syntax Suspects

➤ Sentence fragments

➤ Run-on sentences

➤ Comma splices

➤ Double negatives

➤ Hidden homonyms

➤ Misspellings and spellcheck

➤ "Wrong words"

➤ It's/Its

➤ Exclamation point use

➤ Passive voice

➤ Comma goofs

➤ Million dollar words

➤ Clichés

➤ Reference/agreement of pronouns

➤ Redundancy

➤ Sentence stuffers

➤ Deflators

➤ Hyper hyperbole

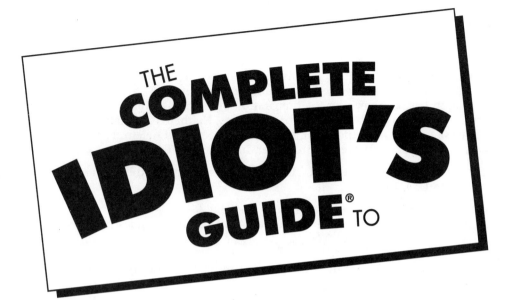

THE COMPLETE IDIOT'S GUIDE® TO

Writing Your Family History

by Lynda Rutledge Stephenson

**alpha
books**

Macmillan USA, Inc.
201 West 103rd Street
Indianapolis, IN 46290

A Pearson Education Company

Publisher
Marie Butler-Knight

Product Manager
Phil Kitchel

Managing Editor
Cari Luna

Acquisitions Editor
Randy Ladenheim-Gil

Development Editor
Alana J. Morgan

Production Editor
Christy Wagner

Copy Editor
Abby Lyon Herriman

Illustrator
Jody P. Schaeffer

Cover Designers
Mike Freeland
Kevin Spear

Book Designers
Scott Cook and Amy Adams of DesignLab

Indexer
Lisa Lawrence

Layout/Proofreading
Terri Edwards
Mary Hunt
Eric S. Miller

Contents at a Glance

Contents

Appendixes

Foreword

Relax. You're not really an idiot. You only feel like one because you've decided to write your family history, but haven't a clue where to start. Begin with congratulating yourself on deciding to make this your goal. Okay, now that the kudos are out of the way, get started by reading this book. There is no magic in this process, only love and determination to accomplish your mission.

Don't let the size of this book overwhelm you. An entertaining read, it covers every aspect of the process, from getting the idea, to explaining terms, to holding the finished product in your hand. You need not be a rocket scientist, only a reasonably intelligent person who can put words together to form sentences on paper.

Trust me. As someone who regularly teaches classes and workshops on writing family histories and autobiographies, I have found that with a little instruction and guidance, anyone can do this. People often surprise themselves. Now it's time for you to do the same. In your hands, you hold the instruction and guidance you need to make your book not only an accurate account of your family, but a great read that will have people turning pages in anticipation.

Filled with personal anecdotes, Lynda Rutledge Stephenson has written a book with a real nuts and bolts, how-to plan for completing your own project. Look to her suggestions not only for finding the facts about your ancestors, but also for making them come alive like the real flesh-and-blood people they were. You can give them each a personality to make them more memorable than a name and a date on a family tree. Make your readers say, "Gee, I wish I had known Aunt Edna." At the same time, you can portray her with such humanity that if Aunt Edna walked through the door, your reader would immediately recognize her.

View this book as a tool to guide you, to teach you, to shine a little light on an otherwise dark path. Learn from it. Grow into the finest writer you can. Imprint this goal upon your heart. Work on it every day to keep your enthusiasm and your creativity at a high level. You have already decided to accept this mission. Don't change your mind now.

Use this book to develop a plan to accomplish your mission. Your own desire and discipline will help you to work that plan and eventually label this a mission accomplished. Always keep your objective in mind and think about how wonderful you'll feel when you can present your book as a gift to the rest of the family.

Imagine the light of gratitude in their eyes. Picture the reaction of older relatives as they relive old memories. Envision the delight of the younger generation when they read about a favorite cousin or about the day they were born. No, the process is not difficult. Your book, totally devoid of any supernatural influence, will weave a web of enchantment that will make everyone think you have magic in your pen. Now, get started.

Joan R. Neubauer

Joan R. Neubauer is the author of *From Memories to Manuscript: The Five-Step Method of Writing Your Life Story* and *Dear Diary: The Art and Craft of Writing a Creative Journal,* as well as numerous other ghostwritten books and articles. She specializes in helping others write their family history or autobiography, while continuing to freelance for magazines across the country. In addition, she maintains a full schedule of teaching classes and workshops for community sponsored programs, writers' clubs, and conferences. She invites you to visit her Web site at www.io.com/~neubauer.

Introduction

I know you.

You're the family member who loves stories.

You're the one who is good with words.

You're the one who remembers the crazy Christmas when Uncle Albert dropped his false teeth into the Jell-O salad, who wonders if the family legend about a great-grand-pa who once wrestled Davy Crockett is true, who has saved every story about your own children's antics in hopes of writing them down some day.

Or perhaps you're the latest family member to embrace genealogy, but the first one to dream of someday creating a family history from all the bits of dusty research information gleaned from across time.

Is that someday today? Since you've made the big step of purchasing this book, I bet it is. Treasure awaits in old documents and grannies' attics, here, there, and everywhere, and it is treasure to share through your gift of writing.

So, what's keeping you from jumping right in? Nothing. With a turn of this page, and with a little help from what I've assembled to guide you, you'll be on your way.

You are joining millions of others who are discovering the joys of digging up their "roots." Every day, the demand is creating more "supply" as new ways of finding and sharing genealogical work appear—from local genealogical libraries and societies to family history magazines to Internet forums and Web sites.

So, there's never been a better time to make your leap into preserving your family history. You'll love it all, from your first genealogical treasure hunt, to interviewing Great Aunt Gertrude to transforming your work into a book to hold in your hand and hand down to generations to come.

How This Book Is Organized

The beauty of any Complete Idiot's Guide is its easy way to deliver a truck-load of information, and so it is with *The Complete Idiot's Guide to Writing Your Family History*. Every last element of this book is designed to make it easy for you to get the information you want and enjoy the experience as you learn.

Notice that, due to the dual nature of our mission, you really have purchased two books in one—the first on beginning a genealogical trek, and the other a writing manual focused on creating your family history in book form. Each of the six sections will guide you through the whole, grand experience, step by step.

Part 1, "Writing Your Family History," leads you through all the big questions of why you want to write a family history, what oral history is and why it's important to save, the magic of "story," and why we are our stories. It also will start you thinking about the very practical ways to shape and mold your work before you begin.

Part 2, "Becoming Your Family's Investigative Journalist," tells you all the ways to track down your family history, what things to look for, where things are hiding, how to find them, and who to interview. In other words, it teaches you to search like a detective, think like an historian, and report like a reporter.

Part 3, "Getting Organized," will keep you from going crazy under the pile of research clogging your extra room as you get serious about all this research. It gives you ways to organize your work, how to correspond in writing during your research, what to do about unusual information you may uncover, and how to know when enough is enough.

Part 4, "Creative Jumpstarts," is a section of exercises to help you make the transition from researcher to writer. It gives you ideas to evoke your memories, lessons in telling a story well—be it yours or others', and prepares you to structure your writing.

Part 5, "Finally, Writing," takes you by the hand and helps you start putting it all on paper. It leads you to "imagine the telling," gives you ideas on beginnings, and then pushes you to finally, finally write until you have a complete manuscript in front of you.

Part 6, "Making Your Writing Sing," tackles the rewriting and editing aspects of your writing process and gives tips on making your work professional instead of amateurish. Then when your manuscript is ready for publication, it offers you advice on how to see it in print.

The appendixes, beyond a glossary of important family history terms, an index, and several sample forms, also offer several different lists for further reading. The lists include books on research help and editing advice, but also magazines, form sources, popular computer programs and established Internet sites.

Extras

Within each chapter are cartoon-illustrated boxes that offer extra, interesting information to add to what you're reading.

Related Facts

These sidebars are chock full of interesting anecdotes and stories that will give you a bigger picture of the task you're undertaking.

A Relatively Good Idea

These sidebars will have plenty of great tips and tricks to keep you going.

The Write Word

These handy little sidebars are there to define any new genealogical or writing terms that we may come across.

'Riting Reminder

Watch out! These boxes will warn you against getting stuck in some of the pitfalls writers tend to fall into!

Deep Thought

These are special boxes designed to keep you in the writing mood. Writers never know when an idea will come or why. But every writer knows how important they are. These ideas are meant to inspire your own. They'll pop up when you least expect them, and probably when you need them the most!

Besides those, at the beginning of each chapter you'll find a box that tells you what to expect, called "In This Chapter." At the end, you'll find tips for "take away" in a segment called "The Least You Need to Know."

Also, depending on whether the chapter is a research chapter or a writing chapter, you'll find at the end of each, either a journal-writing idea called "Journaling Down the Genealogical Trail" or a writing tip called "Progress Report."

Now, one question with three parts before we begin: What's your favorite family story, who's your favorite colorful relative, and what's that family legend begging to be revealed? Keep them in the front of your mind as you read. They will all have their moments in this uniquely personal of all book projects. You are taking the first step on a terrifically fun and potentially enlightening family adventure.

These pages exist to guide you all the way.

Ready, set, turn the page.

xxix

Trademarks

Part 1
Writing Your Family History

Why do you want to write a family history? Could it be that you love the stories your family tells? Those stories are called oral history. Preserving your personal oral history is more important than you know. It is literally "gone with the wind" if you don't. There is a magic to storytelling, and in a very real way, we are our stories. What do I mean? In the next few pages, you'll learn the "why" of writing a family history before we move on to the "how." Think of it as your "deep thinking" foundation for all the work ahead.

What Is a Family History?

"The past isn't gone. It isn't even past."

—William Faulkner

Imagine two different moments in time.

First, imagine it's tomorrow. You are at your granny's house and you are opening her antique camelback trunk. You've wanted to do this since you were a kid, climbing on it while dreaming of finding pirate's treasure inside. Granny didn't talk much about her family; her past had been rock-scrabble hard and to her way of thinking, the past was better forgotten. But she had kept this trunk, and today you rattle off the old lock and open it slowly as the rusty hinges creak and groan.

There, under some moldy old pillows and moth-ravaged quilts, you find a stash of letters bound with a ribbon. Your heart races. Quickly you open the first one, and inside you find a letter from your granny's wild Aunt Lulu who ran off with a traveling salesman to be a flapper in the Roaring '20s. Under that, you find a letter dated 1865 from a Civil War soldier to his sweetheart. Your heart skips a beat—it's a love letter from your great-great-great-granddad to your great-great-great-granny! And what is this piece of paper in the yellowed envelope? It's an obituary for a young man named Virgil Joe, granny's younger brother (you never even knew she had a brother) who died in a farming accident.

You have to take a moment to catch your breath. All of these people might as well be climbing out of the trunk themselves; they have become so suddenly, inexplicably real. Why? Because they wrote something or someone wrote something about them, and the words lasted longer than their mortal bodies. And thankfully, your secretly sentimental granny had made a point of keeping them, so when you were ready, you'd find them.

Imagine, now, that it is 2099. Your great-great-granddaughter opens her granny's Tupperware chest of drawers, and there she finds, under those old-fashioned micro-wave blankets and plastic jumpsuits, these very same letters—along with a special lit-tle book of family history written by you. And now she is the one whose heart skips a beat as she meets you through your written record.

The Write Word

A **family** is a group of people related by blood or marriage and lineage. A **history** is a narrative of events, a story or chronicle, of an interesting past.

This is why you are writing a *family history,* isn't it?

Our lives are the ultimate story, messy in the living but ordered and full of meaning in the telling. Family stories are family history, and good, bad, or ugly, the events of our lives and of those who share our lineage have shaped us.

Where did we come from?

How did we get here?

Why are we here?

Your family history is a series of snapshots, lifeblood moments that can answer such important questions (as well as be a heck of a lot of fun to write).

The Difference Between You and Everybody Else

How would you feel if you really did find such a batch of granny's letters? What an incredible sensation it would be to read your great-great-great-grandmother's most in-timate thoughts circa 1865. The phenomenon would be like travelling in a time ma-chine, wouldn't it? Each letter is like a short story opening a new world. Add the lives of Uncle Virgil Joe and Great Aunt Lulu and those new worlds double. Better yet, these are not only interesting stories, but because they are your family, they are all a part of who you are.

These stories are all as unique as a thumbprint. Wild Great Aunt Lulu's story is one-of-a-kind and undeniably compelling. How could you resist the urge to find out if she ever became a flapper? And what makes Lulu's life unique is exactly the difference between you and everyone else. Her life choices and personality traits, coupled with her moment in time, made her life one-of-a-kind. The same can be said about you. As obvious as that may sound, it's also an incredible truth—each and every life is different from any other ever lived.

Here's the really dramatic part: Great Aunt Lulu told a tiny portion of her unique story to a favorite little niece back on the farm and left a bit of herself to be found. Since there was no one else to tell it but Lulu, no one would ever have heard from her again if she hadn't written and mailed that little snapshot of a particular moment in her life, and that little girl who became your grandmother hadn't kept it. Thank goodness they did. Now you'll never forget her, especially since you have a suspicion that Lulu's dip in your common gene pool may just be where you got your own free spirit or, at the very least, your twinkle toes. So while Lulu's story is unique, it also reverberates with you. That's the way family tales can affect you.

Old family stories give us a fluid feeling of destiny. Living family stories give us a feeling of continuity and even, if we're lucky, understanding. (Prepare yourself—you may finally understand your parents.) Yes, you may have hated that old story your gruff father used to tell about the length of his walk through the snow to his one-room school every day. But just wait—you will be retelling that story one day and laughing affectionately with your children about it, as if doing so was beyond your control.

Crazy Aunt Edna Glue

There's just something irresistible about a story. And the story of your family is in your mirror. In the words of William Faulkner, Nobel Prize–winning author and someone who made a career out of his love/hate relationship with his southern ancestors, "The past isn't gone. It isn't even past."

Sharing stories about your family, past and present, brings people together, acting very much like "family glue." Think back to your last wedding, funeral, or reunion. Odds are someone told that same absurd story about your Crazy Aunt Edna, perhaps with Edna laughing the loudest. To know each other's stories is to connect in a special and specific way. Walking in a cousin's shoes begins by listening to his story. And who doesn't want their story told?

A Relatively Good Idea

Quick! Think of the first repeated family anecdote that comes to mind. It could be funny, it could be tragic, it could be dramatic, it could be deeply boring (at least to you), but it's important. Got it? Jot it down somewhere. We'll come back to it later.

Slip-Sliding Away

Our stories slip away so easily. Imagine, for instance, that instead of finding letters in granny's trunk, you find nothing at all among the quilts and pillows. Granny had pitched those letters long ago, just as you throw away letters from family and friends today, and sadly, granny is no longer alive. Neither you nor that great-granddaughter a century from now will ever hear Lulu's, Virgil Joe's, and that special Civil War couple's stories. And their quiet, wonderful, important parts of history will have vanished as if they never existed.

Important? Yes, important. Personal history is just as important, perhaps more so in a human way, than history "by the textbook."

The Difference Between Great-Granny and Annie Oakley

History is written by the survivors, someone once said. Think about the history classes you took in school. You learned about dead men chosen as the important figures of history by a group of survivors with pens and advanced degrees. But there's a difference between world history and personal history. Personal history is the quiet backbone of each historic epoch. Your history is no less important than John F. Kennedy's, even though nobody may be offering megabucks for the right to write a book on you.

"Yeah, right," I hear you say, after you stop laughing. But it's true, and here's why: Because your life story—added to those of millions of other people—is making the world what it is, as each moment slips into yesterday. We are truly the "real" history and, in tiny, invisible ways, we are creating the eras studied in tomorrow's history classes. Small actions have big impacts, like a ripple effect in a pond.

"Who, Me?"

We affect others, present and future, just by taking up space, just by drawing breath, much less by our deeds. Frank Capra made that point in his movie, *It's a Wonderful Life,* and he made it so well that rare is the American who can channel surf during any Christmas season without getting a dose of that particular morality tale. Remember Jimmy Stewart's character's wish? He wished he had never been born. The rest of the plot involved his guardian angel showing him exactly what the world would be like if he hadn't lived. If you recall, to Jimmy's character's surprise, it wasn't such a lovely place.

With each breath, each action, we are part of history itself. Our lives may not become fodder for Pulitzer Prize–winning biographies, but they are still the stuff of everyone's life story you touch. The same is true for all of your ancestors. I'm not saying that Great-Granny had a life that was as exciting and gender-bending as Annie Oakley. I am saying that Great-Granny (who may have been somebody you'd never want to live in your extra room) without doubt had moments in her life that would literally sing with insight for a great-granddaughter—and that is a guarantee.

"How Did I Get Here?"

"How did I get here?" Try asking a parent that question, and unless he or she is a storyteller, you'll probably get the equivalent of "I brought you here." Ask how that parent got here, you might hear, "My parents brought me here." Ask how *their* parents got here, and you just might get, after a thoughtful pause, "Well, their parents brought them here by covered wagon."

And voilà! Suddenly your family is a part of history, part of the amazing journey that most Americans have taken to become Americans. Yes, your mom may not want to talk about her childhood if it was unhappy, but that is a valued story in itself. Such are the stories of the human spirit, and if there is time, and the moment arises, you may have the honor of hearing her story, partially or completely, a life summed up and thought through, that may give your own existence surprising extra dimensions just because you asked.

And that moment will be powerful. That's the power of oral history.

Gone with the Wind

Family history pretty much relies on oral history. Genealogical searches wouldn't be called searches if the searchers didn't have to comb through old court records, probate wills, and immigration records to know even the tiniest details about their forebears. Happy—bordering on ecstatic—is the genealogist who stumbles upon a letter or a diary full of stories about ancestors. It is an exceedingly rare occasion.

At one time, all history was passed down orally through the telling and retelling to each new generation the stories from generations past. All our fairy tales, all our mythology, all the oldest of our cherished tales were handed down to us through storytelling—oral history. Before the invention of the printing press in 1450 A.D., one of the most important members of any family or social group was the storyteller.

Biblical "begats" are a good example. St. Matthew, in the opening of the New Testament, gives us a peek into that world: "Abraham begat Isaac; Isaac begat Jacob; Jacob begat Judas; Judas begat Phares and Zara of Thamar; Phares begat Esrom; Esrom begat Aram; Aram begat Aminadab; Aminadab begat Naason; Naason begat Salmon; Salmon begat Boaz; Obed begat Jesse; Jesse begat David; David begat Solomon; Solomon begat Reoboam …"

Well, I'm sure you get the picture.

That sort of list was the standard family information given in the Hebrew tradition—which was very much an oral tradition. There's a scene in the old movie *The Bible* in which George C. Scott, a.k.a. "Abraham," is making his son "Isaac" recite just such a list from carved symbols on a heirloom-looking staff. The scene's point was to show the importance of the next generation knowing those "begats."

But St. Matthew's list of "begats" also points out the power of writing things down. For instance, without looking, can you remember one name from the middle of that list? Anyone but a Bible scholar would be hard pressed to name more than the "biggies." But remembering a story about one of them is easy. Tell a tale of David and Goliath and the listener never forgets.

Don't Cry for Aminadab

Without a good story, poor Aminadab is only a very strange-sounding name on a very, very, very old Biblical list. On the bright side, at least he's on a list. That is more than most people who've ever lived can say. His 15 minutes of fame turned out to be several millenniums long and counting—not a bad run on immortality—because his list was preserved due to the fact that his lineage had historical and religious importance to someone with pen and purpose.

No, don't cry for old Aminadab. The average ancient world family's stories were oral history and lost with the last one who didn't make it though the Dark Ages. As some wit defined the Dark Ages, life was dirty, brutal, and short.

With the invention of the printing press, printed words were accessible to everyone—everyone who could read, that is, which eliminated most of the common folk. And who among the common folk felt their stories worthy of the hallowed new printed page? So, sadly, the only family history for the average person was still an oral history, and it could be lost or found only by word of mouth, generation to generation.

Tape Recorder Salvation

Then, on the eighth day, the tape recorder was created and suddenly printed history was under the common person's control. Today any library or bookstore is brimming with oral histories. From Alex Haley's *Roots,* to Studs Terkel's *Hard Times*—which captured short vivid interviews about the Depression—to a group of high school students in Virginia who accumulated several volumes of folk wisdom and oral history tales from mountain people, called *Foxfire.* Even some of our best historical fiction had an oral history format, such as *The Oldest Living Confederate Widow Tells All, Little Big Man,* and *The Autobiography of Miss Jane Pittman.*

Roots, Alex Haley's famous African-American family history, is based on his family's oral history, a set of anecdotal "begats" Haley heard from his granny. "Grandma pumped that story into me as if it were plasma," he once said. A long series of grannies in Haley's family tree had done the very same pumping of family lifeblood into every new generation that finally produced little Alex. He gave the world his family's history—and thousands of people the inspiration to find their own "roots."

Having Our Say by Sadie and Elizabeth Delany, two 100-year-old African-American sisters, is a best-selling memoir of their long lives, and a fascinating peek into a whole century of racial progress. Remarkably, when first approached to put their memories into a book, the sisters didn't believe their life stories were significant enough. But as

Amy Hill Hearth, the reporter who helped them write the book, explained in its preface, "They came to see that by recording their story, they were participating in a tradition as old as time: the passing of knowledge and experience from one generation to the next."

When the latter of the sisters, Sadie, died in 1999, there was a telling quote by a grandniece in her obituary that still amazes me. She said that like so many strangers, she came to truly know her great-aunt by reading the book. Until then, all she knew of Sadie and her life was that she was a retired home economics teacher, and a "sweet aunt who acted far younger than her age."

We no longer live with several generations under one roof. Your granddaddy may or may not have been a raconteur, but if you aren't around to hear his tales, then his stories—and yours, for they are yours, too—are, as Margaret Mitchell would say, "gone with the wind."

The American Way

"Staying put" seems to generate more lasting family storytellers. Perhaps a sense of place nurtures a sense of history and "roots." But this is America and the pioneer blood at the core of this country is always on the move. The odds are high that your ancestors were some part of the westward migration, but you may not know as many colorful tales from that part of the family lore as you'd think.

> **Deep Thought**
>
> **Gone with the Wind**
>
> *Family history relies on oral history, the handing down of anecdotes that makes our ancestors more than old names on yellowed paper. But with just one generation, oral history can be "gone with the wind" of time.*

Just think about it: Times were tough on the roads of this new land where dodging wild animals and hostile conditions was a daily chore. Consider, too, that most people were either illiterate or too tired or too busy trying to survive to write anything down, so their mainly oral stories could be lost in just one silent generation. Often, "go west, young man" was a chance to start over, and fresh starts would, by definition, rarely include sharing memories of "before." One reluctant storyteller and an oral family history could be lost.

My mother was the youngest of seven in an itinerate household of a tenant farmer/traveling salesman/part-time Baptist preacher. By the time her mother had her, she was probably too pooped to tell old stories to her baby girl. By the time I was interested, my mom could only tell me the barest of facts about her mother's early life. All I know is she came to Texas in the back of a horse-drawn wagon with all her brothers and sisters and parents in a turn-of-the-century wagon train of families.

That may have been all there was to tell; there may have been nothing of interest that happened on that never-look-back journey. But pardon me if I don't believe it. Yet I can only imagine now what it must have been like for her then, because any tales worth telling are gone with granny. That is the power and the fragile glory of oral history. An extremely important part of your family history writing mission will be to search and find and save, save, save your own oral history. Your great-grandchildren and all their lineage will thank you.

The rest of your mission? With apologies to baseball, the rest will include your very own genealogical search—a hobby that seems to be becoming America's new favorite pastime.

The Difference Between Family History and Genealogy

Your Cousin Herbert called you the other day. (You didn't know you had a Cousin Herbert.) He is once removed on your father's side, he informs you, and is working on the family genealogy. Then he fills your ear with words like "repository," "archives," "censuses," "deeds," "tombstone surveys," and "necrology."

The Write Word

Genealogy is the descent of a family from an ancestor or ancestors. It can also be defined as the investigation of ancestry and family histories. Genealogists are addicted investigators, happily clogging libraries across the land.

Ooh, you think. That's a bit overwhelming (if not also a touch morbid sounding). Perhaps you would be wasting your time trying to write a family history, since it seems the family already has a very dedicated genealogist on the trail.

The truth? Cousin Herbert may dig up (figuratively, of course) some interesting tidbits of long-gone relatives out on some of the family tree's branches that you could never find for lack of time or expertise. But can the man write? The truth is that Cousin Herbert and you are on somewhat the same path, but in different vehicles, and you may decide that he is a wonderful scout who will add immensely to your effort.

On the other hand, you may wish Cousin Herbert once removed would remove himself again. But even if he can write, he will not be writing your family history. That is your joy and your challenge.

Cousin Herbert, though, is not unusual. *Genealogy* is so popular today that an average town library might easily have a genealogy room set aside for the scores of native lineage hunters. Beyond incurable curiosity, reasons given for diving into dusty old records in search of ancestral facts include …

➤ Finding out why your granny didn't like to talk about your past.

➤ Finding out if your great-great-great uncle really did invent the girdle (or the pencil or the hot dog).

➤ Finding out if your heritage really does include Irish (or Norwegian or Comanche) blood.

➤ Finding out if you really are a descendant of Napoleon (or Cleopatra or Queen Izzie of Lithuania).

➤ Knowing your genetic medical background.

➤ Unlocking the mystery of your engraved silver locket heirloom or that haunting jade vase.

➤ Finding your personal place in history.

➤ Giving you, the budding family history writer, your essential foundation.

Family history may rely heavily on oral history, but like a skeleton to a beating heart, it also relies on a basic genealogical search, the basics of which await you in the pages ahead—as a means to an end, not an end in itself. The two most important differences between researching a genealogy and writing a family history are …

➤ A genealogy is about the search more than the story.

➤ A genealogy is about ancestors more than current family members.

Oh, you will be visiting your share of libraries and cemeteries as you dig deeper into your own genealogy search (much more on that later), but, as a writer, you'll always be in search of the stories to bring dead genealogy facts back to life.

Love Letter to the Future

So what, then, is a family history?

A family history is a series of word snapshots of the people who created you. It is genealogy come alive. It is putting faces on names and flesh

> **Deep Thought**
>
> *You are a Social Security number, a phone number, a fax number, a bank account number, a driver's license number, a credit card number, a number on a sports jersey … and more account numbers than you care to think about. Your stories, though, give you a name.*

> **A Relatively Good Idea**
>
> You are on a *"mission possible"*. Your family history mission, should you choose to take it (and you should) is to …
>
> **1.** Search out and record your family's oral history.
>
> **2.** Research your family's genealogy.
>
> **3.** Write, write, write it all down in a fun way for everybody.

and blood on dates and places. It is "The Life and Times of You and Yours." It is the preserving of personal oral history before it is lost.

It is, in a very wonderful way, a love letter to the future.

The attempt to claim your ancestors is an honorable quest, but the recording of your own family stories is what makes the whole package such a present and future gift. The reward for any writer is discovering your own exclusive vein of gold to mine to your heart and soul's content. The result is a treasure beyond monetary value for your family to "find"—when they are ready.

The Least You Need to Know

➤ Recording family history is like a love letter to future generations.

➤ Oral history will vanish if not preserved.

➤ Personal history is the quiet backbone of world history.

➤ Family history goes beyond genealogy.

➤ Your great-granddaughter will own a Tupperware chest of drawers (and will cherish your family history as gold inside of it).

Chapter 2

Going Beyond Genealogy

In This Chapter

➤ Grasping the magical nature of "story"

➤ The difference between story and memory

➤ The window between world history and your history

➤ Exploring the reasons for writing a family history

What did your ancestors leave you? That is, other than your prominent nose and assorted figure faults?

Aside from such family genes, your ancestors might leave land, money, some yellowed, official papers, or a tombstone to testify that they lived and they died, but rarely do they leave the memories of their lives.

Wouldn't it be wonderful if a requirement for living was to leave behind a recording of it? Think of the size of that library, not to mention the powerhouse of knowledge from all those accumulated sights, sounds, thoughts, and dreams. What are we really but the sum total of our experiences? And yet the remembering stops as soon as our heart ceases to beat. All those years of living done by so many people—yet all we know of them are a few slim facts. It's sad, isn't it? Do you know the antonym the dictionary gives for "memory"? The opposite of memory, it says, is "oblivion."

Stories, Stories, Stories

"My memories? Oh, they're not important," you can almost hear your family members saying through the decades, as if living was only about basic biology, reproducing and then disappearing, the species continued.

While there may be a scientist or two who might believe that, most of us know in our bones and our souls that is not true. Although it may seem, at times, that most of your ancestors hardly left you more than your genes and a bread-crumb trail of their existence, you will also find that a few left a grasp of themselves through family memories. With those memories, they left you the inexpressible feeling of being in a world descended just for you.

How do stories do that? It's a mystery. But they do.

What exactly is a "story"? How do stories work their magic? How can a story be so human and yet so eternal at the same time? The magic is truly what both this book and *your* book are all about. There are some things, however, that we can understand about the magic of "stories." Learning how to grasp the nature of a good story is something any successful family history writer should reach for with both hands and heart. Learning the art of the story is one of the most essential steps for going beyond genealogy. Let's explore that magic.

The Write Word

A **story** is the narrating or relating of an event or series of event, either true or fictitious.

You-Shaped Destiny

What separates us from all other living creatures? One indescribably important thing is our ability to share our life experiences through images encapsulated in the flurry of words we call *stories*.

The Delany sisters, mentioned in the last chapter, who saw a whole century of change, were surprised that anyone would be interested in their family stories—including their own family. But their words, captured at the last moment (considering both sisters were first-time authors after turning 100 years old), placed them and all those who shared their blood and their heritage in a special place. As one thoughtful writer put it, "My father's death marks the end of his story-telling, but not the end of his story." The same is true for you and all your kin. The act of sharing each other through words creates a place in this world that is shaped only for you.

The Write Word

A **pedigree chart** is a visual diagram of your ancestry. Originally a pedigree was used to prove ancestral connection to royalty.

And that act of sharing, dear writer, goes far beyond a name on a family tree, doesn't it? Sure, that's the first place to start—usually with what genealogists call a *pedigree chart*. There's nothing like looking at all those ancestors stretching as far back as you can dig to get a feeling of belonging. But just having a lineage doesn't necessarily make us human or even special. Even dogs can have a "pedigree."

Got Your Mayflower *Pedigree?*

You have to love the term: pedigree charts. The term is a holdover from old genealogical days, which should probably be labeled pre-*Roots* days in genealogical history. That's what almost any genealogical effort seems like since the 1970s. That's when Alex Haley hit a societal and personal nerve by redefining the ancestral search with his phenomenal bestseller, *Roots*. Up to that time, one's pedigree chart was often not so much a search for family, but a search for one's pedigree; status-seekers looking for the bragging rights of being a descendent of royalty or fame.

Since the vast majority of us can't be kin to someone famous (by definition, there aren't enough famous and royal people to go around), even the best of us might not be able to resist a little truth-bending to make a better "story." After all, a prince or duke or hero/heroine always makes any family saga seem more "important." And it's not that hard to get such a family rumor started. (This will be one of the red flags to catch when you, the family investigative journalist, begin to accumulate those family stories. For instance, that story Great Uncle Mortimer keeps telling about being a direct descendent of Geronimo should probably be checked out.)

Bragging Rights

A high school classmate of mine, with whom I always seemed to be in competition of some sort, added a personal note inside an announcement for our reunion, the first communication between us since signing each other's senior yearbook. The note stated he was a collector of documents signed by Declaration of Independence signers and asked, "Are you descended from Edward Rutledge?"

The truth is I'd been imagining that I was somehow related to that Declaration of Independence signer ever since the moment in grammar school when we studied that historic document and I noticed my last name was at the bottom of it. Imagination is a formidable thing for an eight-year-old, and you can believe that I sure did some imagining.

But am I really related to that famous Rutledge? According to my genealogical pedigree chart, my Rutledge ancestor came to America in the bottom of an immigrant boat, and my family oral history suggests it was as an indentured servant, not a scion of a Southern colony. So, sadly for my bragging rights, I guess I'm not kin to any signers of that famous Declaration. (That is, unless Ed had a long-lost cousin unfairly banished from the family fortune who, with courage and intestinal fortitude, disguised himself as an indentured servant in order to come to the New World to claim his share of the family's fortune ...)

Gone to the Dogs

So pedigree charts may hook us up with our lost blue blood or just our place in the great parade of biological life. But the chart still doesn't make us human, does it?

My English Cocker Spaniel Brazos has a champion pedigree chart back to England, so my dog certainly has a better chance at scratching up "royal lineage" in his pedigree chart than I do. But just having a pedigree chart says nothing about what an incredible animal he is, nor does it give even a hint of what he adds to my life. The interesting thing is, however, that I can say the same thing about Baylor, the American Cocker Spaniel who shared my life for 14 years before Brazos. And, as for his pedigree, Baylor came off a Lubbock, Texas, farm.

What makes my dogs special, especially when they are gone, is not their pedigrees but the stories I have of them. With much affection for both animals, they are dogs, and my treasured stories that include them are ones I tell, not ones they have told me.

So, distilled to its essence, to be human is to experience and share our stories, whether it's over the dinner table, at a coffee rendezvous, on a long-distance phone call, or to a stranger on a plane. (And even sometimes, to our dogs.) No matter where we are or what is happening to us, we must tell our story.

Plot of Our Lives

> To be a person is to have a story to tell.
>
> —Isaak Dinesen

So, just what is our story? Our stories are our story. Adulthood, in one way or another, makes storytellers of us all. Obviously, having children will induce the condition. ("When I was a kid, my mother made me eat Brussels sprouts, so be thankful I'm just pushing broccoli on you, young man.")

But just the act of living produces daily experiences that force us into becoming storytellers. Revisiting our stories is a way to evaluate the direction our life stories are taking us. And to be a family historian is to be a story-collector. The stories we find, stretched from end to end, all tied together, are the overall goal, whether we know it or not. In our own lives and in the lives of our ancestors, we will be looking for plot and we hope to find it through our stories.

What, then, you may ask, is the difference between plot and story? English author E.M. Forster had a wonderful way of explaining the difference between the two. "Plot," he said, "is the king died and the queen died." A story, however, "is the king died and the queen died of a broken heart."

The Queen's Broken Heart

Plot is the beginning, the middle, and the end, the fully told tale, the bare facts. Story is the heart, the meaning behind the bare facts, the reason for the tale, the life, the effort. Note the difference between my wordy, literal definition and Forster's succinct king/queen metaphor. It shows the difference between the two words with a picture. Without the help of the illustration, wouldn't my explanation of the king and queen be much more boring and unclear? Allusions, allegories, metaphors, even similes are all just tiny stories we use every day to understand and explain our world.

Forster's clever explanation is perfect for our needs. I could have listed pages of dictionary definitions to explain the difference between "plot" and "story," but Forster told a tiny story and got the point across in a single sentence. (And to underscore the power of even a hint of a good yarn, don't you suddenly want to hear the brokenhearted queen's story?)

History, Her-Story, Our-Story

You, the family history writer, will soon begin accumulating seemingly disjointed story after disjointed story. You might ponder your ancestors' lives as a whole and get a sense of the "plot of their lives," but you'll notice that any clear sense of the "plot" of a life must wait until the life is over. Life's theater never ends. Daily life can't be reduced to a plot until the days' end, yet its stories can be told along the way.

'Riting Reminder

Plot: the king died and queen died.

Story: the king died and the queen died of a broken heart.

—E.M. Forster

Deep Thought

Your Fairy Godmother Knows Best

Even fairy tales were not just for entertainment, but originally full of meaning about life for the listener. Think about our favorite fairy tales and their valuable moral lessons. Hansel and Gretel learned that they shouldn't talk to strangers. Jack and the Beanstalk's Jack learned that there's money in beans. Snow White learned not to trust the mirror.

And during this collecting process, the most interesting thing happens. From a family history perspective, the stories of our lives and of the lives gone before us create a *belief* in the "plot" of our lives as we go. How can we not feel we are part of on going tale, full of whatever invisible meaning we pull from each episode? We belong—to a family his-story, a family her-story, a family our-story.

Your Fairy Godmother Knows Best

So what is a story?

As happens all too often with our "living" language, the word "story" has had many meanings over the years. At this moment in popular culture, we think of the word "story" as meaning some sort of diversion or entertainment—a fairy tale or a sitcom.

But remember, even fairy tales have substance. Goldilocks reaped the consequences of making wrong choices, Hansel and Gretel learned quickly not to talk to strangers, and Cinderella learned the value of beautiful shoes. (What? That wasn't the lesson you learned?)

Wandering storytellers were once welcomed into a farmer's home, exchanging food and lodging for a good night of tales that spoke of heroes and villains, of morality lessons, and mythic insights. He was a valued, honored guest for the way his tales enriched a family weary of daily survival, yearning for meaning in their days.

The majority of the stories of today that we find in our movies and fiction are idle escapes more than meaningful allegory. And that's too bad.

Stories 'R' Us

Deep down, though, don't we all know better than to think that movies and television offer the only modern stories available? Every day we hear dozens of stories. Each encounter with another person is an invitation to their story: "How are you? What's going on? Wait until I tell you what happened today!"

And every story we hear becomes a part of us in invisible, unexplainable ways. Stories, fact or fiction, are not only based on experience, they are an experience in and of themselves. A memorable story stays in our memories because it means something to us, and so becomes an experience in itself.

Tell me the story of *Huckleberry Finn*. Now tell me where you were when Kennedy was shot, or the Challenger space shuttle exploded, or when John Kennedy Jr.'s plane went down. We were "there" in a very real sense, even if we were nowhere near the incident itself. We live in stories, both our own and all those that we hear, and so a little part of us is changed with each one. That's why it rings true to say that our stories are our bits of immortality.

And every story begins as a memory.

The Write Word

A **memory** is a recollection, an incomplete story waiting to be formed.

Memories vs. Stories

Well then, what makes a *memory?* A memory can be just a moment in time, a kiss, a "feel-good" movie, a loved one's tears, a walk in the park when the leaves were turning. A memory is a scene, an incomplete story.

A memory that becomes a story is one that has a beginning, middle, and end, however brief. A personal story is a memory that has been thought through for its inherent meaning. A repeated family story is a memory that has, in its retellings, become imbued with meaning. Interestingly, as a family history writer, you may be the one that gives a family member's chosen memory its thought-out meaning, not the teller. That's part of your job.

For example, my mother has given me only the barest details of stories from her childhood, because her growing-up years were dirt-farm hard. She's in an assisted living home now, a huge transition in the life of any parent and family, and recently I tried again to engage her in some memories. I took her to a nearby cafeteria, fed her lemon pie and iced tea, then asked her some leading questions. My reward was her telling me a few memories that came into her mind. They were not stories, just remembrances, faded mental photos of a few young moments, some good, some sad.

Here's one: When my mother was a teenager, her father, who was home from his job as a traveling salesman, taught her how to drive his Studebaker on the back roads around Austin, Texas. For her this is a memory, but for me this is actually a tiny story—especially since it's the only story I have of my grandfather and his daughter spending a carefree, exciting moment together, perhaps one of

> **Deep Thought**
>
> *The opposite of memory, according to the dictionary, is "oblivion."*

the very few they shared. It speaks volumes to me, and in the context of my knowledge of our family, that memory has become a story with much meaning. The same will be true for you.

Since we are a part of history by the very act of our being alive, stories also bring the world to us, past and present.

Your Window to History

When I was 15, with my brand-new license burning a hole in my jeans, I talked my father into buying me a convertible—a black Corvair with a white top that had a mere 100,000 miles on it. (Did I mention it was a convertible?) I loved that top-down car, and after I left for college, two sisters after me loved it, too, far beyond Ralph Nader's warnings, until one day my father got into it to move it out of his truck's way, and the fumes were so bad the car went straight to Corvair heaven.

I could tell you stories .... Oh, I already have, haven't I?

I've told you a very short story about a car, the ownership of which puts me into historical context—not only through the year of the car, but the model and the activist who made his name as a consumer advocate by helping send all "unsafe-at-any-speed" Corvairs to Corvair heaven. But I didn't tell you a historical story about Ralph Nader, the pioneering activist recognizable in the same breath as "Corvair" by anyone who lived during that era; I told you a story about three sisters' devotion for a wonderful, troubled little car, much-loved at any speed. And the rest of it just came along for the ride.

That is history on a personal level. That is the magic your family's stories contain, the view from your window of the history happening around you. While my future relatives may or may not be interested in the birth of consumer activism, they just might get a kick out of my little story for what it says about me, about my father, about my sisters, about my small town upbringing, and interestingly, about themselves as they see themselves in it.

Stories 'R' Telling

Just a few stories about that car alone could tell a lot about my childhood's era, just as yours could. We tell stories, but our stories are also telling. Each story allows us a chance for a healthy, personal reflection of how, what, and most important, why. Each story you polish to add to your recorded family collection will be full of sociological, historical, and psychological significance, as well as personal significance. At their best, family stories are a blend of history, biography, psychology, sociology, and genealogy, as well as creative writing. Let me tell you one more Corvair story just to drive that point home.

I grew up in small-town Texas. It was one of those towns with a train track that ran down the middle, where white people lived on one side and black people lived on the other. It was a town that was about to learn the meaning of the word "integration."

The year was 1965, and we were living by segregated rules that had been laid down generations before. As I began to think for myself, I noticed that even my parents, good people who knew no other way of living except by those rules, always made their black housekeeper sit in the back of their Buick on rides to and from our house.

On the day of this story, I had just done some fast-talking to get my pokey, ragtop Corvair and was looking for any reason to drive it.

"Take Dorothy home then," said Mother, weary of my car fever. I jumped up, bounding out the front door toward my car, and found our housekeeper Dorothy waiting. She was standing on the passenger side of my Corvair, staring at the excuse for a back seat that Chevrolet had designed for the car. I looked at her, she looked at me, and then I said, "Please, get in," and pointed at the front passenger seat. She slid slowly and apprehensively into the tiny car, ending up with her knees forced to all but touch mine. Then I pushed the little button that made the top go down, and Dorothy and I had a grand time sailing across the train tracks, wind in our hair and big smiles on our very different faces.

I could have told you about civil rights and preju-
dice and even the historical impact of train tracks
on the development of small towns, but instead I
told you a story. That story somehow gave you a
nice snapshot of all of those without a long trea-
tise on the state of the world in the '60s. Isn't
that something?

A Relatively Good Idea

What story do you remember
from your childhood that would
place you in a moment of the
world's history?

As the years separate me from that era, my stories
will take on even more poignancy and revelation
for the family listener. Without my sharing those
stories, though, some relative may remember only
that I had a Corvair, but the rest of the memory
would be lost. It would be just an unrelated fact
instead of a revealing story about an ancestor's
first chance to love her vehicle of freedom, or cross racial barriers, or even simply to
defy authority—all three of which are universal experiences and universal connections across time.

Think for a moment. Can't you do the same?

Why Did I Remember That?

You are mowing the lawn or washing the dishes and suddenly you remember a moment from your childhood that is so vivid and unrelated to what you're doing ... you
are surprised it popped into your head.

Why do you think you remember some things all your life while you have forgotten
hundreds and thousands of others? There has to be a reason. The moment had to
mean something significant, whether you knew it at the time or not. When you do
understand why it was significant, the memory becomes a story worth retelling.
There's something there that made you remember it, something significant, something meaningful.

Stories Mean Something

Our greatest desire is that our lives have meaning. We tell stories because we hope to
find or create significant connections between events. We look for meaning in our experiences and in our lives, and our story-filled words are how we get there. Humans
have been doing it since they first discovered language.

That's how, on the one hand, a father can talk of his World War II experiences as
both the worst time of his life and the best, because he felt a part of something
meaningful, a part of an important story of the world. Big or small, it is important to

remember that our stories have meaning—somehow, someway—because our lives have it, too.

Each and every human being longs to have his or her say. That's why your genealogical search can be so rewarding. You'll never know where and when you might hear that "say."

Related Facts

Tombstones once hinted at epic tales about the deceased that would have otherwise vanished. The tradition began in Europe, but it was brought over to the United States in Colonial days, and lasted as a common practice until the end of the nineteenth century. Some of the best epitaphs tell stories about America itself and add to legend and folklore. Some are even antiepitaph in their message and show their disdain of any attempt to capture a life in stone, sometimes wittily. Books listing some favorite epitaphs have even been published through the years, such as Thomas Mann, and Janet Greene's *Over Their Dead Bodies.* Here's an example of one of their favorites:

Here lies the body of Lieut. Mehuman Hinsdell.

Died May 9, 1736 in the 63rd year of his age.

He was the first male child born in this place and was twice captivated by the Indian Salvages.

Time, Time, Time Is on Your Side

While our ancestors may not have had much time for writing down their memoirs—they may not have had much chance to write down anything during their lives—quite a few still found a way in death. Until recent history, many people had an interesting personal attitude about their gravestones.

Talk about having the last word. Many early New Englanders made a point of leaving their last words in plain view for all to see—on their epitaph chiseled into stone. Others had their life stories written for them there. Some recorded their lives' pivotal stories or a colorful death. All of them told stories that begged for the complete tale, but would never have been heard without the abbreviated version being etched in stone.

Epitaphs were once a popular way to tell a person's story—as well as to get in the last word—as you can see in the following examples:

➤ **Unknown.** He Called Bill Smith a Liar.

➤ **Doc Holliday.** 1852–1887: He died in bed.

➤ **Anonymous.** I was somebody. Who, is no business of yours.

Just remember, no matter how seductive those ancient epitaphs may seem, the stories you can hear from today's living family members are just as important—if not more so—than the echoed voices of ancestors past.

Your elders are alive and, yes, their stories may be as old as they are, but they are still here to tell them to the next generations. That is priceless. Your children are already accumulating their own stories that they will retell the rest of their lives. They're precious. And what about your own stories? They are aching to get on the page, too, aren't they?

Through it all, the magic glue of stories brings everyone together. Even though we may be separated through divorce, geography, sibling rivalry, tragedy, or death, we must remember that none of us live our stories alone. I felt closer to my mother than I have in years when she shared that Studebaker moment with me over lemon pie and iced tea. And you'll have your own lemon-pie-and-iced-tea moments that will strengthen your own family ties. Such shared stories are the stuff of bonding and understanding. And like pie, you want to get it while it's fresh.

Our Storyteller Knows Us

There's a wonderful tale, retold by Vera Rosenbluth in her book *Keeping Family Stories Alive,* about an anthropologist who was studying a tribe in Africa. One day, this anthropologist decided to place a television in the middle of the tribe's village in order to observe its effect on them. As you might imagine, everybody dropped whatever they were doing and gathered around the magic box—but the fascination only held for a few weeks. Gradually, they all drifted away, until no one was watching the television at all. This wasn't what the anthropologist expected the tribe to do—considering our own society's fixation with the television—so he asked one of the tribesmen what happened.

"We have our own storyteller," the tribesman said.

"Yes, but the TV knows many more stories than your storyteller," answered the anthropologist.

"Yes," agreed the tribesman. "But our storyteller knows us."

These people remembered something we've forgotten. You know your clan, and you're the only one who can tell the stories you all share in a way that matters to them. Not even a magic box can tell your tales like you can.

You, O Storyteller

Now seems the time to ask you a personal question. Why do you want to write your family's history?

I know, you've had this idea for years. After all, you've always loved a good story, and now you feel that you have a purpose, right? This is one of the vital dimensions of storytelling magic—the need to tell the story. Even if you don't ever get around to putting a single word on paper, you will continue to feel the need to tell your stories. But beyond this warm, fuzzy, literary need to tell, asking yourself "why" you are going to do it is important.

You are doing this for many reasons, aren't you? Here are a few of the specific people and reasons for which you may be writing. Are you doing it …

➤ For your growing (or grown) children?

➤ For your parents?

➤ To remember?

➤ To understand?

➤ For yourself (as well as everyone else)?

For Your Growing (or Grown) Children

Helping children create a strong bond to their family is one great reason to write a family history. You might think that your kids are already too busy discovering themselves, right? Don't forget that one of the biggest parts of discovering themselves is discovering who their family is and learning where they came from. To instill that sense of belonging early is to give them a strength and security that is unshakable.

Today, we are too often cut off from our older generations. In the not-too-distant past, however, it was a different story. Nobody moved off the farm, so conceivably, you could be born and then die in the same house, surrounded by more than one generation of your family. Today's mobile society, unfortunately, encourages us to leave the nest as soon as possible, and our working lives rarely even allow for going home to spend the holidays with the kinfolk. The way things seem to be moving, it's not likely that we will ever have the type of family connections that people once had again. With the passing of that type of family closeness, unfortunately, also goes the ritual passing-on of family stories.

But don't let our present "gotta-keep-movin'" society change it all. Our children still yearn for ritual storytelling today just as much as they did when the storyteller would stop by the farmhouse—full of the entire extended family—and trade epic stories for food. Let this inspire you!

Take bedtime stories, for instance. Not only do most children love them, they tend to love the same ones. Often, they have come to love them so much that they have memorized them; they know each and every word and want to hear them again and again.

My niece taught herself to read somewhere around the age of three. The way her parents discovered this fact began with the bedtime stories that they would read to her. Whenever her parents would read her one of her favorite stories she would correct them if they happened to leave out a word here or there out of boredom or lack of time and energy. Finally they noticed that she was sitting with the books herself, turning the pages and "reading" every word out loud—telling the story to herself, the right way, with each word right where it should be.

Children live for stories, and they love the cadence, comfort, and sense of belonging to the tale that comes with its repetition and its content. What better definition of a family story can there be?

Or perhaps you are writing for your grown children. What better time to preserve all the family stories and genealogy than during your senior years when you have the resources, the drive, and the time to give your grown children something they did not know they were missing. Your children are always your children whatever their age, and they will always gain from the special gift of understanding their "you-shaped" world.

A Relatively Good Idea

As you research and write, audience will become very important. "Audience" may seem obvious for a family history, but the fact is your audience is more specific. Thinking about this now will help develop your focus.

For Your Parents

Just as much as you are writing for your children and your children's children—or even for your grown children, you may also be writing for your parents and your great aunts and all the older people who mean so much to you. Each day these earlier generations get older. Particularly if you're in a "sandwich" generation, where you're caring for kids as well as for elderly relatives, you could end up looking up from one of those hectic days and notice that a whole generation is disappearing.

It would be a tribute without equal to record their memories, especially if you can get your children to show some interest in helping with the interviews. Recently, a friend's daughter had a special school assignment. She was to ask her grandfather a long list of questions and write his answer into an essay. An exercise like this could be the start of something "big"—your family history, of course.

To Remember

You may be doing it to remember a loved one gone—a brother lost in a car wreck, or a father lost to cancer. Capturing the stories about these people can be very healing to a grieving family, even years after the tragedy.

You may also be doing it because the glue that kept your family together has gone—perhaps a granny has died—and extended family members have gone their own ways. Cousins who meant the world to you may as well be a world away. "Home" suddenly becomes a concept that is not so concrete. The family house is sold, a remaining parent dies, jobs force a continent between loved ones, buildings burn down, hearts are broken. Whether we want it to or not, life moves on, it's up to us whether or not we want to let life move on without us and without our stories.

The feeling is disconcerting to say the least. Most of us couldn't wait to get out of our parents' house, but something still calls us back—and back and back again (besides your parents picking up the phone and asking you to visit). Even places—old neighborhoods, childhood houses, high school hang-outs—hold stories frozen in time. The house I grew up in was recently sold, and I will never go back to it. In many ways, I had left it long ago. Now, though, a new family is making memories there. But no matter whom it belongs to, and how different it may look, it is in my mind, and in my memories. It is the same with you and for everyone else who shared your childhood. So maybe part of your purpose is that you want to create a little bit of home for the homesick—even the ones who don't know they are until they read a copy of your work.

To Understand

Do you feel the need to understand yourself and your life? This is a good place to start. Nothing clarifies like writing. (Do you keep a journal? We'll talk more about this later.) We write to explain the world to ourselves, but while we're at it, we might as well write to explain our families, too.

Many stories will be heart-warming, but some of the stories are painful and others embarrassing. Will anyone want to read such stories? You'll find out that those stories are the ones that will reward you the deepest (and be read most by others). But also be aware from the start that family members will come at their own pace, and at their own time to the wealth of family lore you've saved, perhaps even when you are gone. The stories are waiting to be repeated, understood, set down on paper, and then preserved. And best of all, you will have fun in the learning.

For Yourself (and Everyone Else)

You might never say this out loud, but doesn't a part of you relish the thought of kudos for such an important feat? The reality is you may or may not reap the praise you deserve for your effort. Who ever receives the praise they deserve for the things most dear to them? So just remember this: The effort must become its own reward. (And it will.) If you can keep this in mind, then even if the response is not as you might have imagined, it doesn't mean that you will never be appreciated for your work.

This is a truth every writer must embrace. A first-time author friend wrote a serious book on an important topic, sprinkling personal stories throughout. It was his first book, and he was proud. He sent a copy to his father overnight delivery, and waited for the shower of praise. None came.

Finally, on his next visit, he realized his father had not read it. His father's reading tastes after a long day were more along the lines of Zane Grey or Louis L'Amour. His father's only response was that he was very impressed with his son's name on the cover … which, of course, was also his name.

To say my friend was disappointed was an understatement—until he realized that a book is forever, and his father wasn't the only reader it would have. He learned the big-hearted secret to the printed word. Creating any book is what I call a "selfish/ selfless" gesture. What you are doing is truly the gift that keeps on giving as long as the pages exist.

Is it all beginning to seem like a monumental task, so formidable that you can't get started because you think you'd never finish? The fact is that even a stack of typewritten papers full of semifinished family stories will be cherished sooner or later. You can bet the farm on it.

Now you should have what any beginning family history writer must have—a good grasp of the true nature of "stories" and why you want to write your family history. So, now we're ready to move into the search. Before we throw you into the genealogical waters to sink or swim (never fear—we are chartering you on a very big boat!), let's introduce you to some theories you will want to take on the trip to help you steer.

The Least You Need to Know

➤ A family historian must understand the magic of "story."

➤ We are our stories, so our stories need meaning in order to give meaning to ourselves.

➤ Personal history is a window to world history.

➤ Your fairy godmother really did know best.

What Kind of Family History Should You Write?

Very soon, you will be spending lots of time in the past with your family history. Once, before you go, let's take a trip to the future. It could be a year from now, or two, or many more. The date isn't important, but the moment is. It's the moment in which you have finally finished your family history.

Author! Author!

Can you picture the glorious volume? See it there in your hand? It has a binding and a cover and all the things a good book built to last should have. Feels good, doesn't it?

Now picture four of your friends standing around you, with their family histories in their proud hands. (It's your fault. You've been talking excitedly all over town about writing your family history, and everyone wants to share in that excitement.) All of you are admiring each other's results. Let's look closer at all these finished pieces of family history and creativity.

All four of your friends have done something different from yours, not just in the way each looks but in how it was written. Everyone "personalized" their family histories by choosing the perfect format for their specific families and the perfect emphasis for their personal enthusiasm. The results were wonderfully special to each of you, as a family history should be. Their choices of formats, along with yours, are a good foundation for any writer's brainstorming. Let's look at them:

Narrative Genealogy

Yours is a handsome volume. It fits in your hand nicely. It's the size of a fold-out genealogy chart. Why? Because that's how it's been designed. You see, you got so intrigued with every last one of your ancestors and found so much interesting material (oh, they were a colorful group) that you decided to make your family history a *narrative genealogy*.

You decided to tell your genealogical adventure in story form—in a narrative, from generation to generation. You had a great time moving through the years connecting all your colorful ancestors to you, here and now.

The Write Word

Narrative genealogy is a recounting of your ancestral information in story-narrative form.

Memoir (Personal Memories)

Friend #1 is holding hers almost under your nose. So you tear your eyes away from your own volume and gaze at your friend's work. It's a rather fat volume. She had a lot of information to work with, she tells you, because hers is a memoir, her own personal memories, a family history version of the autobiography. And she has told *all*.

Biography (One Very Interesting Relative)

Friend #2 is proudly waving his around. His is an actual biography of one ancestor based on a story he uncovered from a battle diary and historical newspaper clippings—a Civil War lieutenant who was left for dead at Gettysburg yet survived, and then seized life by having two wives with two different families in two different states until getting caught. "Fascinating reading," the friend assures you, adding that he has done lots of Civil War research to make everything authentic.

Current Family Stories

Friend #3 shyly shows you hers. It has a homemade binding and what looks like a child's cover design. "My daughter drew that and we scanned it on our computer," she says. What she's produced is a fun little book of current family stories, about her nuclear and extended family, along with any and every story that her relatives could remember about family members long gone, all printed with desktop publishing computer programs.

Literary Snapshots

Friend #4, a literary fellow, has self-published his work in an extremely nice, faux-leather backing. He has collected all the family stories he could find, some going back five generations; then he took scraps of information, such as deaths and births and newspaper clippings, and fleshed out other stories with his imagination and historical research. He has written and organized each of his short narratives like short-short stories. On each page is a story of a relative or ancestor, told in memories, interviews, and historical data written in dramatic form, bringing the past to life in a format that is like a series of "literary snapshots."

Inner Family History

Now that we've acknowledged you will have a finished product in the future, let's back up and ask an essential question: Which one of these basic format ideas appeals to you most? Which one appeals to you "second most"? Don't try to choose now which one you'll finally use; just choose the two that sound good to you at this moment. So, what are your answers?

> **Deep Thought**
>
> *How does it feel to imagine your family history finished? Who do you see reading it? What will be the first thing you want to do once you have it?*

➤ Narrative genealogy

➤ Memoir—personal memories

➤ Biography—one very interesting relative

➤ Current family stories

➤ Literary snapshots

➤ Your own invention

Whatever your answers are will be a good guide as you begin your genealogical trek, even if you change your mind later. You probably will change your mind several times, trying to find the right fit as you do your research. But bringing some ideas of the finished product to your genealogy work will help your organization skills and fuel your creative juices.

Remember the book *Inner Tennis* that came out years ago? The concept behind the unusual instruction book was to imagine the perfect game as you played. Think of this chapter as "Inner Family History," imagining the perfect-for-you family history format.

Are there right or wrong decisions in this imagining? Not at all. You can't choose incorrectly. Unlike tennis, everybody wins. This is your project, you cannot go wrong.

Your Own Family Shaped Invention

The five possibilities previously mentioned are just some of the more obvious ideas for a family history. You may invent another one, a creative "background format." Let's brainstorm some highly creative family history background formats. One of these ideas just might suit your family perfectly:

➤ Cookbook

➤ Video history

➤ Interviews

➤ Newspaper

➤ Photo album

➤ Scrapbook

➤ Time capsule

A Relatively Good Idea

Does your family consider food to be a manifestation of love? Are most of your warmest memories centered around meals? Why not make your volume a family history cookbook?

Cookbook Format

Recipes are kinds of heirlooms handed down through the family tree. Even if you don't cook much yourself, it's still quite possible that you have a granny recipe floating around somewhere.

For instance, my grandmother could make an incredible pecan pie. Most families think of pumpkin pie at Thanksgiving dinner, not our family. There we'd be, waiting expectantly, salivating like a bunch of southern Pavlov's dogs for Mama Lee's pecan pie. After she died, the recipe in her own handwriting came into my mother's possession, and later, into my youngest sister's hands. And if she hadn't wanted it, I certainly would have. That recipe card is an heirloom, and not just because it was the recipe for her prized pie. My grandmother, a country schoolteacher, had beautiful handwriting—the handwriting that had addressed my wedding invitations. The sample of that handwriting is as special as the pie.

That is the little family story of just one recipe card in a family that didn't really take to the kitchen. Food is life, and it happens everyday in our lives, in the same place with some or all of the same people, be it a banquet or a grilled cheese sandwich.

So, in a house where cooking is also a family passion, a cookbook would be an inspired idea for a family history. To members of a family historically known for their culinary touch, adding family stories to family recipes is a natural evolution. Each family dish probably has a story or two attached. ("Remember the time Uncle Albert laughed so hard his upper plate went flying into Mom's Jell-O salad? What was he laughing about?" Someone remembers and off you go into another family story.)

A big-hearted woman, with a big Italian family and an even bigger talent with fresh pasta, opened a restaurant in my Chicago suburb. She soon became a dear friend through her food and my writing about it. She was definitely a "culinary legacy." She was the daughter of an Italian immigrant and became not only a famous cook, but also a Chicago neighborhood treasure. Her little neighborhood bar and cafe was surrounded by a community of people who became loyal regulars, part of the "family," by eating her food all of their lives.

Hers is a family with family stories happily intertwined with food. Clara tells a much-loved, long-handed-down story of her Italian grandmother taking her mother's young hands in hers as she left for America and saying, "Someday these hands will feed the world." When Clara took her culinary genes to the suburbs, my town became her extended family. "Eating at Clara's,"

A Relatively Good Idea

1. Think of one recipe that evokes a family memory from the past. What does it stir up besides your appetite? Can you place a family story of any length—short-short or full-length—with it? Jot it down.

2. Name a dish your immediate family loves (or hates) and a family story that you could picture your children telling about it one day years from now.

wrote one satisfied customer, "is like coming home." Food is home for that family. Food is where their family truly exists. Their big family get-togethers (to which I was always invited) were centered around lots and lots of Clara's food—inspired by her mother and her mother's mother in the "old country." Think of how many family stories were told and retold over her calamari and her pasta al fresca. A cookbook family history would be perfect for them.

Everybody has a story or a dozen stories that include what was cooking in the family kitchen. "Foodies" are everywhere. Be it West Texas barbecues, Cape Cod clambakes or Wisconsin fishboils, food, family, and stories go together.

Video History Format

A video family history may not sound like a good long-term idea—after all, who knows if videotape will even exist in two generations? Does anybody still own an eight-track tape? Or even a reel-to-reel tape recorder? But if your vision is first and foremost for the value of your living family, it's not a bad idea as a companion to your writing (especially if you have a budding filmmaker in the family). Shooting your oral history interviews with your elderly relatives or visiting schools, apartment

A Relatively Good Idea

Do you like the idea of capturing images of memorable places from the past, and oral history interviews with older family members? Do you have a budding filmmaker in your family whom you could entice into the project with this idea? Why not a video family history?

buildings, tombstones, churches, businesses, and old houses—all the places of your family's history—would be part of the fun you could have. You might even discover old acquaintances on neighborhood travels.

There's also something called a "video *heirloom*" that you might want to consider as a possibility. You'd be videotaping scanned photographs and clippings, even adding music, captions, and a voice-over narration to tell your family tale. Companies exist that actually do this for you, but you can certainly do it yourself with the right computer or video equipment and have a lot more fun.

One caution: With the words "eight-track tape" and "Betamax" to inspire you, boxing up an old, working VHS tape player "heirloom" to go along with your video heirloom tape would be a truly nice gesture for future attic-hunting descendants.

Photo Album Format

Some families hang art on their walls. Our house had photographs—professional ones of all sizes, with new ones coming in every year. What were they of? They were photos of my siblings and me at every different stage of childhood, from adorable toddlers to pudgy pre-adolescents to gawky teenagers. We were everywhere. I suppose

The Write Word

An **heirloom** is something of special value handed down from one generation to another.

their five children were our parents' art. No doubt that's the way a poetic psychologist would explain it. At my father's funeral, my small town's photographer told me, "I'd get to the end of the year and not know how I was going to make ends meet, and here would come Harold Rutledge with another of his kids."

Of course, I thought all families took pictures every year. Not until years later did I consider it unusual. One day, I walked into our rambling old two-story house with one of my sisters. She looked around, shook her head, and said, with a sort of uncomfortable twitch, "Boy, coming in here is like walking into a Rutledge mausoleum."

Granted, it wasn't much fun to be reminded of how I looked during my baby fat years with each visit home, but it meant the world to my parents. For my family, it was a saga in pictures, a visual family history.

Many families have been recording their family histories visually for years, with pictures of not only the immediate family, but relatives long gone or living far away. As Kodak and Madison Avenue put it so perfectly, "These are the moments of our lives." And these are the people who share our lives. One genealogical writer has called her home gallery a "living memory wall," because the influence of each family member is alive in her.

That, of course, is the spirit of your family history project. So why not consider the use of your photos? In this "instamatic" time we live in, you no doubt have drawers of snapshots. And, as we'll discuss later in your search, many of them are little stories in themselves. But for now, if your family loves pictures and has taken them for generations, why not begin to brainstorm how you might either incorporate your family snapshots into your book or make them the center of your whole family history saga?

Interview Format

Oral histories are incredibly compelling all by themselves. Theatre companies stage plays of oral history tellings. The Delany sisters' book mentioned earlier, *Having Our Say,* was made into a Broadway play. There's a long, proud history of theatrical treatment of such stories. By their nature, they are dramatic monologues, evoking a time and a place and a life told.

Whether your oral history interviews will ever make it on Broadway remains to be seen, but they can certainly be the star of your family history book.

Would this format seem natural to you? If you have a family of big talkers, especially perhaps a handful of elderly relatives who are fine storytellers, and if some of your interviews are knock-outs, why not consider putting everyone's remembrances in interview form? This background format could be a mixture of Q&A (questions and answers) and a series

A Relatively Good Idea

Does your family take lots of pictures? Do you have boxes of photos from the past that the whole extended family finds meaningful? Why not consider a photo album–style history?

Deep Thought

Look around you. Are there photos displayed on your walls? What stories do your photos and portraits tell about your family?

A Relatively Good Idea

Do you have elderly relatives who are storytellers? Are your family talks with them dramatic and wonderful? Why not consider an interview format?

of family monologues, or the interviews could be written like a series of long magazine articles in one volume. Of course, you could also pepper your own narrative with their interviews. But for an interview format alone, your own commentary or interpretations would not be needed, except for filling in gaps for the reader in magazine article–style. Their own stories and their own interpretations of their life experiences will create the world and the world's meaning all on their own for the lucky reader.

A Relatively Good Idea

Do you have budding writers in the family? Cartoonists? Photographers? Do you have lots of people in your family with life stories that would make "human interest" stories? Why not consider a newspaper format?

'Riting Reminder

Including your child in parts of the writing as well as the research might not only start an interest in family history, but also encourage the child's writing. The newspaper format is a natural format for a child's efforts.

Newspaper Format

How many writers do you have in your family? How many heroines or heroes? How many black sheep? How many overachievers or eccentrics who would make perfect examples of what newspapers call "human interest" stories? Your family stories could be written in newspaper form. You could enlist your children to help edit and produce it, and even conduct interviews for it. You could learn terms such as "tabloid size" and "gutter." Your paper could be called *The National* (insert family name here) *Enquirer*.

You could add drawings, cartoons, and definitely photos. This could be one of the best family projects you've done since that time you conned the kids into helping paint the house. (Okay, much better. This time the dog won't turn a mottled shade of Desert Sienna.)

Scrapbook Format

A package came for me a month ago. Inside, I found four moldy old high school scrapbooks, one for each momentous high school year. My sister had found them in some of the overlooked items after cleaning out our childhood home after our mother moved out. As I thumbed through them, trying not to let the dead carnation leaves and yellowed pages disintegrate in my lap, my mind rushed back to the days I spent earnestly recording each date with ticket stubs and prom pictures.

Back then, I was sure that my older self would treasure each reminder of every bad movie and cheeseburger and sweaty-palmed date I experienced during my small-town teenage life. The concept was fine, of course. We've all kept such scrapbooks or reasonable facsimiles. Anyone who pockets matchbooks and then pitches them in a dresser drawer knows this human impulse to save little reminders of "been there; done that."

Why not take that impulse and make something creative and beautiful (and a bit more selective this time)? Something done so well and richly that it would be intact, as well as treasured, in the next generation? This, of course, would work best if you find yourself in the middle of your genealogy/family history quest with a box of mementos and photos and important documents that cry out for "scrapbooking." You might add family anecdotes done with calligraphy pens or any other creative treatment inspired by what you find.

A Relatively Good Idea

Does your family story and genealogical search dig up lots of fascinating paper memorabilia? Do you have a penchant for scrapbooks and calligraphy? Why not consider a scrapbook format?

Time Capsule

No, this is not a suggestion to put up a monument housing your personal time capsule to be opened by the whole town a century from now. But this could be almost as much fun.

Just think: What could you imagine a family time capsule to be? Some things cannot be put into a scrapbook or photo album or a bound book. Each and every life leaves many items of sentimental value and potential significance for future generations. What better way to preserve them than a container that won't be opened for years? Granted, since a time capsule, by definition, is something put away to be opened in another time, by another generation, this way of saving your family history is one that needs some good planning to keep it from getting lost by future generations or just lost in general in the chaos of modern life. But if done right, it can be wonderful for those who open it.

A Relatively Good Idea

Do you like the idea that future relatives will see your work? Do you have memorabilia that won't fit into a scrapbook? Do you like making plans for the future? Why not create a time capsule?

Picture your little group opening your treasure chest in the next generation. Out comes the rimless glasses your great-grandfather wore at the turn of the century, or a cap pistol you loved as a child, or a favorite Beatles or Frank Sinatra album. Of course, you could put in a newspaper, but why not pick one with significance for you—perhaps an edition that includes a story about you or another family member? Why not a handwritten letter to your great-grandchildren? Of course you'd add photographs, but why not have some fun by adding some piece of gadgetry that will surely be outdated in 20 or 30 years?

The basics for preserving a time capsule would include choosing someone in the family to be the "archivist" to be responsible for it, selecting a place to keep it, and leaving some official record of it in writing somewhere "stable," along with a date for retrieval.

Your Ancestor's Idea

An ancestor may also jump out and suggest an idea by what he or she has left you. There are as many ways to tell a life story as there are ancestors. (And you've already done the math on that.)

PBS, the country's Public Broadcasting Station, has a popular program called *Antiques Road Show,* which sends antique experts across the country, inviting Mr. and Ms. Average American to dig around in their attics and bring in items for appraisal. The idea is so simple that it doesn't seem like it would make for good television, but a few moments watching this "real" program pulls you in for the very reason you are reading this. Each item is a story. Even the person in control of the remote will probably wait until whatever item they are discussing is done before flipping, because this is history come alive, and it doesn't even matter that it's somebody else's history. (Of course, the vicarious possibility of treasures in your own attic is also a draw.)

One Granny's Watercolor Girlhood

The way the segments on *Antiques Road Show* are set up, the viewer hears the heirloom owner's story first as the camera focuses on the object—a faded painting inherited with the house, a gilded vase brought to America by an immigrant great-aunt, or even a grandfather's pocket watch. Then it's the antique appraiser's turn to tell a story, a much broader one, about where the item itself fits into the grand world of antiques.

Each segment ends with a happy or bittersweet shock for the antique owner. ("Your old doll is worth $500, but if you hadn't let Fido chew on the dress, it would have been worth $5,000!") Or, if it's a truly unique find, the segment can end with a thrill for the antique appraiser, too. Of course, I'm sure for every segment viewers see, there are dozens of disappointments. ("What is the worth of this souvenir Las Vegas ashtray your grandfather cherished to his dying day? About a plug nickel, sir.")

But one segment in which the owners' item had no real market value I remember vividly. A parent and two children were showing the expert a wonderful diary full of watercolor paintings of everyday happenings painted by a great-great-great-granny during her adolescence. For instance, one showed her fishing with a brother, another cavorting at a party with friends. Each little painting included a jotted text, where she wrote about the misadventures of her upper-class upbringing. Her descendants wanted to know if the artwork was worth anything.

The expert, who was positively glowing as he gazed at the watercolors, told the family that the watercolors were just average in technique and style, so, from an artistic point of view, no, they were not worth a fortune like an undiscovered Van Gogh painting would be. But, he quickly added, from a family history point of view, these couldn't be worth more. Any well-brought-up young lady at the end of last century, as he explained, was taught to fill her time with the arts, such as painting and music. What they had here was a unique chronicle of a precious part of their family's past and they should under no circumstances, ever, *ever* sell it.

Journal Your Journey

I have the last installment of your family history volume planned for you, by the way. You should write about writing the family history. And you should start now.

Did that get your attention? That's good, because this is important. As you begin to "experience" your family's stories and your family's ancestors' lives, you will be flooded with inspirations and insights. What should you do with them? Jot them on scratch paper? In the margins of your genealogical notes?

No. You should be jotting down these feelings and ideas in a place just for them. By the end of your work, you will be very glad you did. Right now, you should begin to take notes of yourself taking notes, and answer questions that come to you, such as …

> ➤ What compelled you to begin?
>
> ➤ How long did it take you?
>
> ➤ Why are you more interested in one part of the search over another?
>
> ➤ What touched you deeply about today's work?

> **Deep Thought**
>
> *Your child's life is happening before your eyes. Why not create a time capsule for your child? A very special angle to consider with a time capsule is to create one for a newborn that includes family history of parents and grandparents for the child to open on, say, his or her eighteenth birthday. Think what a lifetime keepsake that would be for your child, and a once-in-a-lifetime shared experience.*

Write down your thoughtful answers. Was there one special story or person that affected you? Write down the episode and state why. Essentially, what you will be doing is capturing your thoughts during the next few months and years as you create your own "history" moments. There will be happy moments, frustrated moments, "ah-ha!" moments, heartwarming moments, and once-in-a-lifetime moments. As a family historian, you should be recording your own experience of recording the family history.

The Write Word

A **journal** is a notebook "playground" for your ideas in which you document your thoughts and experiences.

I have the perfect way to help you record these moments. Computers are the invention of the century (okay, maybe airplanes, penicillin, automobiles, and dishwashers are right up there, too). But really, if it weren't for computers and the incredible ease of editing they afford, I may have decided I'd rather be a pilot or a doctor or a drag racer or a chief cook and bottle washer instead of a writer. But computers also have a blank, impersonal coldness about them. Even typewriters are warm compared to the computer screen and keyboard.

A family history, however, is a thing of warmth. So if such an idea has always appealed to you, why not give yourself a bit of a retro-treat and allow yourself, for this personal aspect of your adventure, to enjoy the reflective, tactile thrill of putting pen to paper. Choose a notebook, choose a pen, and keep them both handy for jotting down your own feelings and insights as you go about accumulating your family's stories.

Journal Jogged Memories

Are you already keeping a journal? Good. Don't stop, just start another one.

Some writers find journals to be no help at all, but most writers find them incredibly valuable, if for no other reason than scribbling down ideas for other works. Today, journals are truly loved as an end in themselves, a self-expression that has been embraced by writers and nonwriters of all experience levels. Like that little red diary with the lock (and the key you immediately lost), it is the one place where you are you and you are writing only to you.

If you have one started, keep writing. If you don't have one, start. Learning to write down your impressions and thoughts is a good idea for any family history writer. As you begin to dig deeper and deeper into the past and talk to more and more family members, you will, without a doubt, be reminded of stories you want to add. The last half of this book is going to be all about organizing, and then writing, your research into some form—be it a book, an album, or even a hole-punched folder. (Don't laugh; you'll be amazed at how wonderful such a folder can look with the proper materials.) And if you begin jotting notes to yourself and determining how you might tell the discovered stories, you'll thank yourself when you get to that point.

A Handful of Journals

On that note, here's a valuable suggestion to take to heart. One expert who conducts workshops on journaling tells her audiences that she keeps over half a dozen journals—at the same time? How does she do that? And why? She has one for dreams, one for spiritual journey, one for her thoughts, and one for story and article ideas. Some she writes in daily, others only now and then. It is freeing to have so many places to write certain things rather than one place for everything. Our thoughts aren't organized, so why not try to add some organization to the process by categorizing them for later use?

Have you ever bought one of those nice "nothing" books? Blank pages beautifully, perfectly bound waiting for your inspired words to be recorded for posterity. I don't know about you, but I have a handful of them—perfect, beautiful, and untouched, because I've never been able to write in them. One part of me loves the idea of it all—a gorgeous, bound volume of my thoughts (written, of course, with a very expensive fountain pen)—but another part of me is so much the messy artist that something so outwardly perfect stops me cold. Somehow, it seems to imply that anything that goes into it must be just as perfect. Therefore, I couldn't be my creative (translation: messy) self. How could I mess up such a perfect book with my usual scratch-outs and start-overs? And that's not even mentioning all those bright-white blank pages. A blank computer screen or even an empty yellow-ruled legal pad is bad enough. All the "nothing" of a nothing book creates in me an ob-ligation to fill it up, and obligation is not much of a muse.

But what if I had several blank books, all nicely categorized? And what if they weren't so "per-fect"? Well, then, this journaling thing just might work for my creative, messy self. And maybe it would work for other writers for the same reasons.

> ### Deep Thought
>
> *What keeps you from journaling?*
> - ➤ *Time?*
> - ➤ *Fear?*
> - ➤ *The blank page?*
> - ➤ *Perfection?*
> - ➤ *(insert other here)* _____
>   _____
>   _____
>
> *Now, ignore them and write!*

Related Facts

Diaries once were part of everyday life. We think today that keeping a diary is reserved either for adolescence or for adventure. Your ancestors, though, thought nothing of writing long letters to others and penning their own thoughts in special leather-bound volumes meant to be treasured during each season of life.

Neatness on the Trail

Is a journal a diary? And if it's like a diary, does that mean you are preserving something for the future? Answers: Yes, no, and maybe.

Diaries have always been wonderful aids to a life and ones that survive are gifts to future generations. Reading historic diaries is quite an education in many ways. (See Appendix A, "BookMarks—for Further Reference," for some published diaries worthy of a look.) Very often, a travel adventure or a long migration was the impetus for keeping a diary, but everyday life was also a reason to write in a diary of one's own. If you're lucky, you'll find one of those everyday diaries that some ancestor's descendent saved for you. If you're very lucky, you'll find one of the diaries written during a travel adventure. We can only imagine how many diaries were never read by anyone because their writers never made it back from their adventures or didn't think their writing was important during homesteading efforts.

A Relatively Good Idea

There's a difference between a diary and a journal, from a writer's point of view. When you can express the difference, then you'll know that the writer in you has discovered the importance of "journaling."

And yet, before ballpoints and back-up disks, some of these adventurers, even during death-defying pioneer journeys, were neat and perfect with their entries and their word choice, to the awe of historians. One such diary was penned by an 1846 bride named Susan Shelby Magoffin—one of the first white women to travel down the Santa Fe Trail—who accompanied her merchant-entrepreneur husband into sudden intrigue during the Mexican-American War. But even with everything that must have been going on around her, the diary's neatness warranted a mention by its historian editor on its publication almost a century later. The historian was so impressed she wrote in her preface of the 1926 Yale University publication of it, "Mrs. Magoffin kept her journal in a book eight and a half inches wide, ten inches long and one and a half inches thick. The pages are lined and the binding is three-quarters calf. The handwriting is round, well formed, and legible, written in ink, with scarcely a blot in the whole volume. The pages are likewise clean, bright, and free from stain."

Most of us would love to have the adventures of a Susan Shelby Magoffin, but few of us could be so tidy while fighting off hordes of mosquitoes, marauders, and wild animals. But the historian, and surely Susan's ancestors, would have loved any surviving record even if it had a splotch on each and every water-soaked page.

There are many things that stop writers from keeping diaries and journals. Some worry about perfection, some worry about others reading it, some worry about the time it takes, some even worry about such "play" writing depleting energy for "real" writing projects. Anything that stops a writer from finding a "place to think," is an obstacle to growth and to any finished writing project.

So let's redefine "diary" and "journal" to make them work for us here at the beginning of your important writing project.

A Journal by Any Other Name

Until recently, if you had asked me whether I "journaled," I would have said "no." But that's not true. It's just that what I use wouldn't be called a journal by today's journal gurus. My "journal" has always been a notebook, sometimes spiral, sometimes perfect-bound like the kind a grade-school child might use, but nothing impressive-looking by anyone's standards. The sporadic "entries" are mostly unreadable; my scribbles are my scribbles and the notes speak only to me. Hardly anything is complete, but it serves its purpose. It is meant as a jumpstart for other writing—a playground, in a way, for my thoughts.

Whether you are the type who finds the perfect pen and the perfect blank book deeply inspiring and can produce a glorious journal that fuels you for years and years, or whether you are the type who thrives with a handful of journals, or whether you need just one big, messy notebook to feel creative and quasi-organized, the essential idea is a good one. And you should go for it and make it your own.

Journals 1, 2, 3

Sometimes the idea of starting a journal can be an impediment to ever beginning—too much to say to cram it all into one perfectly bound blank book. As mentioned earlier, journaling "experts" often suggest that a writer have many journals, each for special topics, freeing you, at the same time helping you to begin the journal life-habit naturally.

Let's say you follow the journal expert's example and have several journals. What would that be like? For your family history writing purposes, three could be the perfect number:

1. **Journal #1:** For Your Eyes Only
2. **Journal #2:** Family History Search Experiences
3. **Journal #3:** For Future Eyes

Journal #1: For Your Eyes Only

Remember the little red diary with the lock you began in junior high? Remember how you truly believed that nobody would be able to read your innermost, secret, adolescent thoughts? The moment I found my older sister's diary and pried open the lock, the "secret" part was out the window. (And so was I when she found out.)

There's nothing wrong with the concept, just the quality of your lock. Of course, anything written has a chance of being read (just ask my sister), but the value of being able to sort out thoughts on paper is positively therapeutic and bolstering. It is also the kind of writing that is usually burned before the diarist leaves this corporeal plane.

Seriously, though, this sort of journal is where a grief can be worked through, a betrayal or a spiritual doubt expressed, or a fear faced. (This can also be where you try out your life-long passion for writing bad limericks.) The trick is to not feel obligated to write. This is a book that you never pick up unless you feel you must. (And if you want to keep it under lock and key to create a secure feeling, then make sure not to leave it out for your nosy, pipsqueak of a sister to find.) How does this help you write a family history? The same way that any growth or insight can deepen a writer's craft. The better the thinker you are, the better the writer you are. The more you practice, the quicker you get to Carnegie Hall.

Journal #2: Family History Search Experiences

As previously suggested, this journal is the one you should carry with you as you work on your family history, jotting observations throughout your journey. It should be a place to record reminders and asides that you may or may not use later, but that strengthen your own memories of the "trip" through your ancestral "home."

For instance, this is where you'd keep a fun account of that road trip to Salt Lake City to study in their world-renowned archives. This is where you'd record the serendipity of stumbling across a will left by your great-uncle, a rich landowner in turn-of-the-century West Virginia, and finding out that the clerk who helped you is a descendent of a man with whom your uncle had a blood feud which continues to this day among your cousins still living there.

This journal is where you'd write about how you slowly became a whiz at genealogy on the Internet, when you didn't know a mouse from a rat when you began. This is where you analyze the sudden familial jolt of finding out you have a whole new set of relatives from a grandfather's first marriage, as you began to dig around in the records.

Beyond the invaluable focus it will add to your family history research and writing, these entries are an "adventure" story in themselves, worthy of their own little volume … which is exactly what it is.

Journal #3: For Future Eyes

This journal is the place where you begin to take notes and even jot down your beginning rough-draft attempts of your own stories. On these pages, you will first do your own personal family history work, write down the chosen memories you want to record for posterity, and practice perfecting the way you want them told before committing them to the reality of a computer disk. You may call this your "memoir" journal.

Whatever you call it, this is the journal in which you will jot down that jogged memory before it's lost. In a way, this is your autobiography-in-the-making, captured in the style of real life—in fits and starts, in insightful bursts, and in full documentation of crazy stories. The ideas would be recorded like notes to yourself, with the freedom to make perfect elsewhere. This will probably be the one your artistic granddaughter or grandnephew will uncover and find irresistible beyond their wildest ancestral dreams.

A Journal Guarantee

I can only guarantee you one thing: As you begin your genealogical quest and unearth family histories here, there, and everywhere, you *will* be inspired, and those inspirations need to be re-

> **Deep Thought**
>
> The better thinker you are, the better writer you are.

membered for future use. Finding the right "journal program" as you begin your family history project will add to every area of the experience. Try out several variations until you find the one that works *for* you, instead of feeling like "work" *to* you.

Journal Down the Genealogical Trail

Which chronicle formats best fit your family? Write down your favorites in your family history journal. Then, jot down the pros and cons of each to help jumpstart your thinking as you begin your research.

> **The Least You Need to Know**
>
> ➤ Every family history should have a well-thought-out format.
>
> ➤ Every family history writer should keep a journal of the experience.
>
> ➤ Keeping several different types of journals can be a boost to a writer's productivity and creativity.
>
> ➤ Picking a favorite format while researching will augment your efforts.
>
> ➤ Imagining your finished family history will energize your work.

Chapter 4

How Big Is Your Appetite?

In This Chapter

➤ How to find focus in family history research

➤ George Washington is not your ancestor and why it doesn't matter

➤ Giving your grannies their due

➤ How to decide on your focus road map and why

Now you are the biggest expert on the magic of the "story" on your block, and you have stored away some great, creative ideas for your family history format. But before you sail into your genealogical waters, there's one more "writer's skill stop" to make first. It's time to deal with the three most important words in any genealogical/family history writing: Focus.

Focus, Focus, Focus

When you take that first dip into your genealogical tidal pool, you shouldn't be focusing on anything but plunging in. But soon you will need to ask yourself a very important question: What are you truly interested in? What is it about this topic that gets your adrenaline pumping? Are you interested in finding out whether you really are related to the Duke of Windsor like Aunt Fanny keeps saying? Are you interested in your family's American saga? Are you mostly interested in historical background for your personal family stories? Or are you interested in every ancestor you can find, as far as you can go? Just remember that the answers are not as important right now as the questions themselves. Pondering these questions will be very helpful to you as you wade through all the available material that's out there—enough to overwhelm anyone. Focus will be the key, so let's plant some seeds for thought.

How's Your Ancestral Math?

How many ancestors do you have? That may sound like a silly question, but even a partial answer may surprise you. Your ancestral group may seem small as you move into the past, only two parents by two parents at a time. The wonder of multiplication will change that idea quickly.

The Write Word

An **ancestor** is a person from whom you are directly descended, i.e., parent, grandparent, great–great grandparent.

An *ancestor* is a person from whom you are *directly* descended—that is, not aunts, uncles, or cousins, but parents, grandparents, and great-grandparents. Can you guess how many ancestors you have only four generations back? Let's test your math prowess. Your parents are the first generation (two people); and your grandparents are the second generation (four people). Your great-grandparents are the third generation (eight people); and your great-great-grandparents are the fourth generation (16 people). The "great-greats" is the generation that tends to get lost, since everyone has passed on from those generations who could remember names and stories. It's also the generation that goes back approximately 100 years. So let's stop there for the moment, since it's where most genealogy searches truly become treasure hunts.

Are you calculating? (You can use your fingers, nobody's looking.) How many ancestors does that make for your first century of genealogy? If you calculated 30, you are correct. Does that number of newly discovered relatives sound manageable? Consider it in the light of, say, a family get-together. That's like having 30 people over for dinner when you thought it was going to be just a few family members, but you can handle it. (Maybe you'll set up some folding tables in the back yard.)

Now take that back another century. If you think of 25 years as a generation, hold on to your hat and your calculator. Double the 30 grandparents by their number of parents. In the same amount of years (100), you will be having to keep up with about 460 of your direct "greats" times 10 grandparents who are all direct "blood" relatives. And that's not counting even one "indirect" blood relative—such as an aunt, uncle, cousin, nephew, or niece—all of whom multiply that number exponentially into the *thousands*. Take a look at the following chart to help you do your ancestral math.

One generation = 25 years

Each generation doubles your grandparent quotient.

How many do you have?

Mini Pedigree Chart

			your great-grandfather's father
		your grandfather's father	
	grandfather		your great-grandfather's mother
			your great-grandmother's father
		your grandfather's mother	
mother			your great-grandmother's mother
			your great-grandfather's father
		your grandmother's father	
	grandmother		your great-grandfather's mother
			your great-grandmother's father
		your grandmother's mother	
you			your great-grandmother's mother
			your great-grandfather's father
		your grandfather's father	
	grandfather		your great-grandfather's mother
			your great-grandmother's father
father		your grandfather's mother	
			your great-grandmother's mother
			your great-grandfather's father
		your grandmother's father	
	grandmother		your great-grandfather's mother
			your great-grandmother's father
		your grandmother's mother	
			your great-grandmother's mother

Your four-generation TOTAL _____

More and More Mores

The PBS series *Ancestors* tells the interesting genealogical story of John and Betty More. In 1772, just a few years ahead of the birth of the nation, John and Betty, a young couple with two children, came to New York from Scotland. They found their way to the Catskills where John built his family a cabin, moved them in, and had six more children to bring the grand total of offspring to eight.

When John died at 94, he had forever become the first American ancestor for 89 grandchildren. A great-grandson thought that was pretty impressive, and felt the memory of his pioneer ancestors should be lauded for future generations. So in 1890, he somehow called together as many "More" cousins as he could from 14 states to hold the very first family reunion. They had such a good time that they formed the More Family Association, dedicated a monument to John and Betty, and vowed to hold a family reunion every five years.

The story gets better. In 1893, one of the cousins wrote a history of the family that has remained the touchstone for the members of the association. Since 1914, each reunion has been filmed. One cousin published a book called *John and Betty Stories,* a collection of stories passed down about their pioneer ancestors' adventures, aimed at children. Think how many young descendants of John and Betty heard them as bedtime stories. The association even publishes a family journal and a directory.

Recently, the association has begun to keep track by computer of all the descendants from the family's "original Americans," over the 200+ years. Can you guess how many More ancestors there are? Their computer files show over 10,000 ancestors from John and Betty.

Great-Grandparent Tally

Just because your cousins haven't shared potato salad for a century, don't think your family reunion wouldn't be just as big. Things were different in the past. Yes, people lived shorter lives, but they had big, big families and often several marriages. Who's to say your family hasn't been as prodigious?

Deciding to focus your genealogical search after realizing how potentially big your "historical family" truly is, may sound like a survival tactic, at least until you have another lifetime or two to devote to genealogy. (Be forewarned. Many, many people happily go hunting the rest of their lives.)

Just as we discovered in Chapter 3, "What Kind of Family History Should You Write?" the many ways to focus are as plentiful as your imagination, but let's look at a few of the most common and most productive for our writing purposes.

In Search of Your Lost Royal Relatives

If you happen to be one of the descendants of Anastasia or perhaps the Duke of Earl, then you probably won't be interested in this focus for your genealogical/family history search. Odds are you'd already be very aware of your genealogy and have your family stories ready for writing. If you happen to be a member of a family with only an unsubstantiated rumor/whisper/tall tale of lost royal lineage, then you have a harder question to ask yourself: Do you care about whether the rumor is true? If the answer is yes, then you have your focus, or at least part of your focus. Be prepared, though. Such a quest may mean disappointment and more than a few false leads.

For instance, if your family rumor is that you are a direct descendant of George Washington, sadly, it's a false one, since George Washington, the father of our country, was never a father. On the other hand, more than 100,000 people on both sides of the "pond" are known descendants of England's Edward III (and that doesn't account for all the unknown ones). And to be kinfolk with Ed III is to be linked to many of the royal lines of the Middle Ages. So, you never know who sits on the branches of your family tree.

Of course, the United States doesn't have royalty, so our next best thing is fame. Historical fame is usually the stuff of legend. Some genealogist somewhere has probably plotted the family trees of most of the United States' historical figures and famous people. So, if you find this is your abiding interest, and that pesky rumor includes someone like Clark Gable or Calamity Jane, you could always work backward from established, well-researched genealogies.

> ### *Deep Thought*
>
> When was the last family reunion you attended? Think back. How many people were there? Consider how many branches of your family tree they represent. That's how big your family tree is, and how many other family trees in your "family grove" you personally touch.

Remember the story of Pocahontas, Powhatan princess and early American history icon? Many people may claim to be descendants, but her genealogy is well known. When she turned 18, she married John Rolfe, an Englishman and Virginia colonist in April, 1614. Her new husband took her to England where she hobnobbed with all sorts of royalty, and gave birth to a son, Thomas, two years before she died.

So, simply put, if you can trace your genealogy to Thomas Rolfe of Virginia, you're in as a descendant of Pocahontas; otherwise, you're out. And Thomas Rolfe's genealogy can be summarized simply: He fathered one child, a daughter named Jane Rolfe. She married Col. Robert Bolling and produced one child, a son named John Bolling. Then John and his wife, Mary Kennon, had six children. And that fourth generation is what old-style genealogists call a "gateway" to the Pocahontas ancestry, because so many branches sprout out in so many directions. All of them, though, have been easily traced.

The same is usually true of the more historically famous figures. But if your name is Lincoln, it's still fun to check the forks on Abraham's tree. You never know what might shake loose.

Related Facts

Many famous people connected with public office or with exploration are true descendants of Pocahontas, including Richard Byrd, the discoverer of the South Pole; Harry Flood Byrd, a Virginia Governor; Robert E. Lee's wife, Mary Ann Randolph Curtis; New York City Mayor John Lindsay's wife, Mary Ann Harrison; and Woodrow Wilson's second wife, Edith Bolling Gait.

In Search of Your American Saga

John and Betty More's pioneer saga couldn't be more representative of the American saga.

The American saga intrigues us because it is our saga, our life, our destiny. For a vast number of Americans today, our family saga started with the first ancestor who found his or her way to the new world. Only Native Americans can lay claim to North American stories that don't begin with an immigrant story. Yet many of us don't even know who that ancestor was, as if our American life has always been ours and has always existed. Most of us have not been taught a sense of personal family history because, frankly, coming to America was most often about starting over, creating the American dream for the next generation and forgetting the past.

But we can't help being curious: When did our families came to this country and what happened to them after they arrived? Often, the only connections to the "old world" past are the oral history tales still told. A grandmother from the "old country" nostalgic for her old life, tells a grandchild stories of a fabled past long gone. A grandfather escaped over the Berlin Wall and made it to America. Finally, at the end of his life, he begins to talk about his past, and for the first time his children hear the names of their great-grandparents.

Most of us cannot name one, much less all eight, of our great-grandparents. This may have been a strange occurrence in the "old country" where generations of families never strayed from their ancestral villages, but not here. The whole American idea was to assimilate, become Americans, make the melting pot work.

Of course, even in our day of growing ethnic pride, the best aspect of the "melting pot" is laudable—we are Americans first. Tell an old Revolutionary War patriot that you might be descended from a king and he might run you through with his rusty bayonet. This was "paradise" to the immigrant, the dream come true, and the oppressive old country—be the oppression religious, classist, or ethnic—was the personification of what they were escaping.

So, except for the occasional dream of long-lost royalty in your blood, you may find it only natural that your family stories begin with the first American ancestor, the one who came by boat to these shores. Your genealogical trail may even hit a dead-end there, but your interest may not go further than these shores, either. If, after you have searched a while in your genealogical trek, you still seem more interested in what happened to your ancestors once they arrived in the "new world," then perhaps this is your focus.

In Search of Historical Background

Maybe you're interested in the past, but what you really want is to preserve the here and the now for those that are here and now. Maybe you'd like to create a historical context for the saga of your immediate family. Of course, don't be surprised if you get "hooked" on those interesting ancestors with just one piece of evidence about a horse thief or a Rough Rider veteran. Even so, you may still want to make these stories part of the background for telling your present family's story.

How might this affect your genealogical investigation? Perhaps this means you strive to find at least one good anecdote about each of the ancestors you decide to research, an anecdote that will educate and thrill your audience—both today's generations and tomorrow's. This type of family history structure might ultimately become a series of "profiles," and once you have a good profile of an ancestor, you move on. It would probably put an emphasis on oral histories of your living family.

Perhaps it also means that you include some historical context for each profile. This would mean that you would do some peripheral research about the different eras that involve your ancestors. That great-uncle who was a Rough Rider will surely have every reader of your family history wanting to know more about Teddy Roosevelt and the unusual war at the turn of the century.

In Search of Ancestors One and All

There are also the family historians who love everything! They just can't get enough of either the search or the find. To this historian, every ancestor seems to be worth as much time and energy as the investigator has. There's no end to how much or how long you can hunt or to the fascination the hunt offers.

If you find that you are this kind of writer/researcher, then your job will be to have a great time, but to keep your goal in mind as you go—the written family history to augment your detailed genealogy.

53

When you are ready to put pen to paper and include all the fascinating facts, figures, and stories you've unearthed into some sort of book form for others to read, you will thank yourself for having taken the time to put some forethought into how you might structure the piles of information for the enjoyment and education of others, too.

A Focus of Your Own

Learn of your genealogical tree as much as is needed for the practice of active love toward blood relatives.

—Mohammed

Remember, all of these thoughts are just to help you focus. You will probably find that you do none of these in a pure fashion. You'll probably cut and paste from each of the most interesting focus ideas to make your own creation.

There is one more focus, though, that you, the family researcher, should keep in mind as you jump into your genealogical search. Here's a hint: It's about all your grannies.

Related Facts

What's in a name?

➤ **Personal names.** In medieval ages, one name, a personal name that referred to some abstract quality such as "noble" or "friend," was all that anyone needed to differentiate one person from another in their small village.

➤ **Bynames.** Before there were family names, or surnames, there were "bynames," which later became many of our modern surnames. A community might add a word or two of description to defy confusion, which would be like a nickname. Of course, as is the nature of nicknames during any age, they aren't always flattering. For instance, Harold the Drunkard or Cuthbert the Clod would certainly help separate the reprobates from the other upstanding citizens also named Cuthbert and Harold.

➤ **Surnames.** While many bynames evolved into surnames, thankfully, most of the bynames' original meanings are no longer obvious in today's language. (Cuthbert the Clod's modern descendent, for instance, would now be Cuthbert "Clack," who probably lives down the street and is a very nice person.)

In Search of Missing Grannies

Question: What name will you first explore in your genealogy?

Answer: Your last name, of course.

That's only natural, isn't it? Odds are that your last, or your maiden, name is your father's *surname*. For most of recorded time, the world has been patriarchal. The majority of the world has lived by rules that were set down long, long, long ago by the males of the species. So you no doubt think of yourself as a "Smith" or a "Jones" or a "(insert your father's surname here)."

If you are male, you automatically think of your father's name as your name. If you are a married female who has taken your husband's name, you think of "your" name as your "maiden" name when the irony is, your "maiden" name is really your father's name. And the double irony is, of course, that even your mother's maiden name is her father's surname.

And the *triple* irony is that if you throw out all the names and all the hundreds of years of social conditioning, then the only clue to any ancestry at all would be who your mother is.

Genetically, though, you have two "last names." So what's in a name? Nothing much, really. The role of women in modern society has changed drastically, of course, and today, some couples are using the wife's names. Others are attempting equality by the use of hyphens, as in "Smith-Jones" (which will cause all sorts of confusion for future offspring and their future census-takers).

The Write Word

A **surname** is a second name held in common by members of a family.

Deep Thought

Until the twentieth century, women's names, beyond being the "Mrs." in "Mr. and Mrs. Joe Schmoe," were rarely mentioned in the paper trail of legal documents that genealogists must travel. Too often, grannies go missing several generations back. Are your great-grannies missing?

Yet the bald-face truth is this: Names are needed. Singular names were first given for identification, and second names (called family names or surnames), were first given for further identification as the village grew faster than the available names. So, if man hadn't invented surnames to delineate his group from other groups, something else would have been invented to do the same thing.

The Write Word

A **given name,** also called **personal name** or **Christian name,** is a person's first name.

The problem is that patriarchal control permeated most societies so deeply before the twentieth century that property was almost always in the man's name, and official records could easily mention Mr. and Mrs. Joe Schmoe without ever mentioning that the Mrs. had a name and a background herself.

After all, women in America didn't even have the right to vote until 1921, so their rights, especially when it came to matters that would entail listing their names on official documents, were few or nonexistent. You can imagine the trouble that practice has caused genealogists for the paper trail they must follow. It often means the loss of some wonderful great-great-grannies to the sands of time, who may not even have their *given names* on their family trees because no official documents exist that mention them.

Giving All Grannies Their Due

Of course, not all cultures were patriarchal when it came to names. The women of the Iroquois nation never take their husband's name nor give his name to their children. Her name was the name handed down. Like the English names, such as "Johnson," which obviously derived from surnames created to describe "John's son" in medieval villages, Norway and Iceland have names such as "Lavransdatter" and "Kristinsdatter," which would be "Lavran's daughter" and "Kristin's daughter." Until this century, many Dutch women kept their names after marriage, as their obituaries and tombstones testify. And other such ethnic traditions once honored the women in a family in different lasting ways, such as the old Scottish custom of preserving the maternal grandmother's name by naming the first daughter with it.

Of course, there was one thing more powerful than being male in European medieval days—that was to own land. The aristocracy were landowners, and their surnames came from the names of their estates. So if an "unlanded" youth happened to marry an heiress of such an estate, the fortunate young man would take her name.

From a genetic standpoint, there is no favoritism at all. We are our genes much more than we are our names. Your genes are tattooed with both "names," so don't make the mistake of not going down your mother's genealogical road back to the past, and *her* mother's road before her. With effort, hopefully, some wonderful family stories may surface because of your diligence. After all, wouldn't you hate to miss the story about how one of your great-grandmothers was a suffragette and another was a teacher in a one-room schoolhouse on the Oklahoma plains?

One male genealogist named Robert Marlin put it well and objectively in the pages of his own published "family history" search, *My Sixteen*. He says, "We all carry the surname as a supreme tribute to the male ego. In reality, we could carry the surname of any of our other forebears with equal dignity and historical accuracy."

Feminine Focus

Tracking your female ancestors may be harder than tracking your male ones, but the effort could be worth it if you reclaim even one of your great-grannies' or great-aunties' places in your family annals. (Tips on how to better track your "invisible" ancestral women will be offered in Chapter 15, "Kissing Kin, Black Sheep, and Granny Gaps.")

For now, this focus will alert you to the dynamic, but it may also intrigue you. Who knows? Maybe you'll come up with a focus of your own with this information. For instance, is your family a matriarchal one? Well, then, why not honor all these grand women and focus just on the female side of your ancestral line? Who knows what wild and wonderful women you may find and have the joy of giving their due.

A Relatively Good Idea

Every family history writer should have: a respect and understanding for stories, an open mind to the many forms a history can take, a strong focus in her search, and a journal to keep track of her trek.

Ready, Set, Go Genealogy

You now know the basics any family history writer should carry into his/her foundation work of genealogy:

➤ You have a healthy respect for oral history.

➤ You have an understanding of why stories are much-told testaments to life.

➤ You have a creative grasp of the many shapes a family history can take.

➤ You have a concept of the value of focus at the beginning of any genealogical treasure hunt.

You're ready now to turn yourself into the family investigative journalist. Ready, set, go genealogy!

The Least You Need to Know

➤ The three writer's skill steps at the beginning of your family history are: understanding the magic of the story, looking at a group of possible formats, and finding a focus for your specific interest.

➤ Focus is essential to wrestling your research into submission.

➤ Your family tree is a lot bigger than you probably think.

➤ The family name is basically paternal in almost all cultures.

➤ Extra effort may be needed to reclaim your missing great-grannies, but they're worth it.

➤ Feeling overwhelmed at the beginning of your genealogical work is natural, but you'll feel like a pro in no time.

Part 2

Becoming Your Family's Investigative Journalist

Get ready for a roller-coaster ride through the dips, curves, and thrills of genealogical research. In this part, you'll learn how to track down your family history, what things to look for, where things are hiding, how to find them, and who to interview. In other words, it teaches you to search like a detective, think like an historian, and report like a reporter.

Chapter 5

Climbing Your Family Tree

In This Chapter

➤ An overview of the genealogy research world

➤ All the tools you truly need to begin

➤ The important difference between primary and secondary sources

There's a world of information out there waiting. It's waiting in cemeteries, in dusty attics, in discarded boxes, in National Archive branches, on census record microfilm, on county courthouse record shelves, in yellowing newsprint of hometown newspapers, on elderly relatives' walls, between mouthfuls of pound cake at family reunions, in the pages of a forgotten family Bible, in the abstract on a great-grandfather's homestead, among a ship's manifest, and in the nether-regions of the Internet.

But how do you get there from here?

Genealogy is a topic worth a library of books in itself (and is a library, literally, in a growing number of places). My desire is to give you the basics that a family history writer needs. So, this chapter will breeze through the whole kit and caboodle and end with suggestions for your first baby steps into genealogy. The rest of the chapters in this section will explain the details, pointing you to the resources that can take you as far as you want to go for your family history needs and, in case you catch the genealogy bug, even further.

The Paper Trail Overview

All you really need to get started is a pencil, a notebook, and a cat-sized curiosity. Soon, you'll have to have a system of organizing and evaluating the flood of details, and a corner of your house to store it all in.

A Relatively Good Idea

All you need to start is:

➤ Pencil

➤ Paper

➤ Cat-sized curiosity

Your Family Connection

Your very first step is to obtain as much primary source information as you can from your family. That means you need to immediately talk to every relative you know about the facts of every family member in their memories. It also means asking to have a look-see at all the important and sentimental family documents they'll allow you to ogle. And what about their family stories? The anecdotes they remember are secondary at this point, and although you should certainly record them, the facts of their lives—names, dates, places—are what you are after at this point.

What the Paper Is

So just what is this paper trail that I keep talking about? Here's a list of the more obvious places to look for that "paper from the past":

➤ Vital records—birth, death, marriage certificates

➤ Census records

➤ Military records

➤ Immigration records

➤ Cemetery information

➤ Family Bibles

➤ Newspaper accounts

➤ Deeds

➤ Wills

➤ Probate records

➤ County court records (divorces, civil suits)

➤ Church and synagogue records

➤ Letters

➤ Diaries

➤ Old county platbooks, gazetteers, maps

Where the Paper Is

Each of these pieces of paper is waiting to be discovered and finding them is more than half the effort. Where can all these pieces of very important paper be found? Here's a list of places to start your search:

➤ Cemeteries

➤ Dusty attics

➤ Forgotten boxes

➤ Your local library

➤ National Archive folders

➤ Census record microfilm

➤ County and state courthouse record shelves

➤ Hometown newspapers

➤ Hometown church records

➤ Elderly relatives' walls

➤ Oral history obtained through living relatives

➤ Family Bibles

➤ The abstract of a great-grandfather's homestead

➤ A ship's manifest

➤ The nether regions of the Internet

First Rule of Genealogy: Prove It!

All those relatives are going to besiege you with lots of information and you are going to jot down everything. Here, though, is where you have to begin to put the first rule of genealogy into quick-and-steady practice: Everything has to be documented.

What does that mean? While you may not have any way to document that wonderful family story about your grandfather having once carried President Woodrow Wilson's bags while working as a hotel porter in Chicago, you could find some sort of documentation about his job as a porter which would give the whole story more credence and your desire to include this nice tidbit more authenticity and detail. Does it sound impossible? Not at all. That's the kind of search that makes genealogy so popular. It's like working on a mystery.

'Riting Reminder

The first rule of genealogy: Document it!

Verifying Is Vital for Vitals

So, while a family story may be beguiling, it needs verifying before you write it down as fact. Recording such an unverified story in your family history book will still be entertaining and not harmful to your family record (if you make a point to state that you couldn't verify it). But that's not true for vital records—births, deaths, and marriage information. Those written-in-stone facts are your foundation and are a verifying "must" for correct genealogical work.

Aunt Cissy's Memory

Let's say you are visiting your first elderly relative, your sweet little Great-Aunt Cissy, and upon asking her the name of her great-grandmother, she says, "Well, now, I remember that ol' Granddad once told me his mother's name was Clara Belle. No, Clara Delle. Yes, that's it. Clara ... uhm. What did I say? Oh, it's one of those, dear."

What do you do? First, you will smile, of course. Then you jot down both names ... in pencil. Then, you will sweetly explain to Cissy that what you're doing has to be absolutely correct. Otherwise, your research will hit a dead end, or you might wind up researching someone who isn't even your relative. So you lean near to Dear Old Aunt Cissy and you casually inquire whether she might remember an old family Bible or family papers that could have Clara Belle/Delle's name in it. If not, then perhaps Aunt Cissy can give you a clue to where Clara Belle/Delle might have married her ol' Granddad, so you can find their marriage certificate. (Yes, you can actually do this. You'll find out how very soon.)

"Why, yes," Cissy says after pondering your nicely phrased query. "I think I do remember where they lived. And I may have some of Granddad's old papers we can look at, now that I think about it. Let's see if I can find 'em for you, dear."

That sort of search is front-line genealogy. All genealogy research comes from two sources—primary sources and secondary sources.

Primary Sources

Primary sources are not hearsay but "straight from the horse's mouth." In effect, it's getting as close to the horse as possible. That means seeing with your own eyes and handling with your own hands as much of your ancestors' paper trail as possible.

Marriage certificates, death certificates, birth certificates, census records, old city directories, cemetery records, courthouse records—vital records, divorce records, suits; county recorder records—deeds, military discharge records; probate court—wills, deeds; church records—confirmations, baptisms, bar/bat mitzvahs;

The Write Word

A **primary source** is information received from firsthand knowledge.

letters, diaries, old county atlases and platbooks—landowners' names as well as property boundaries—all of these pieces of paper, here, there, and everywhere, are full of the facts you need for documenting the basics.

Vital Records

The granddaddy of all primary sources, and the best kickoff for any genealogy beginner, is to find those *vital records*. Vital records by definition are birth, death, marriage certificates, required by law to be kept by the prevailing local government. You'll find gaps, but it's often possible to trace three or four generations back almost exclusively from vital records. It's a great start.

As early as the sixteenth century in England and the seventeenth in the America colonies, each parish was ordered to report to the courts any births, marriages, and deaths in the local congregations. This was probably for tax purposes, but while being documented might not have been a great thing for your ancestor—especially if it meant paying more taxes—such record-keeping is wonderful for your search.

So, we've given you an idea of the types of records to look for, but what information does each one actually give you?

➤ **Birth certificates** are proof of the person's existence, and full of information beyond the literal fact of a new life—full name, exact date, full name of mother and father (if known; blanks also tell tales), attending doctor and location, and even witnesses.

➤ **Marriage certificates** can offer place and date of marriage, bride's maiden name, presiding minister or justice; names of witnesses, ages, birthplaces, current residences of bride and groom, and parents of both.

➤ **Death certificates** are full of good information, too, in a sort of reverse of the birth certificate—the deceased's name and age, date, place and cause of death, doctor's name, birthdate, names of deceased's father and mother.

The Write Word

Vital records are birth, death, and marriage certificates, required by law to be kept by the prevailing local government.

A Relatively Good Idea

Finding vital records is a great start. It's possible to trace three or four generations back almost exclusively from vital records. Before the twentieth century, birth, marriage, and death records were found in the county courthouse. At the beginning of the twentieth century, states took over registration of vital statistics (but the starting date of this takeover varies for each state). You can research to see if your state or county ancestral vital records are microfilmed and available for your convenience.

To Err (and Fib) Is Human

Of course, even vital records are still open to error. For instance, the death certificate's data is only as good as the person giving the information. Before copying machines, and even carbon paper, each "copy" of anything was handwritten. And to err is human; to be human is to err … and occasionally stretch the truth.

We've all heard stories of soldiers lying about their age to get into the army. Some brides may do the same to hasten a good marriage and secure their future. You should be suspicious of incomplete vital records but always record what you've found—in pencil.

Related Facts

Before the concepts of fencing and surveying, how did your early ancestors delineate where their land ended and their neighbors' began? They used the **"metes and bounds system,"** an early land deeds system using landmarks such as trees, rivers, and creeks as boundary descriptions (e.g., "… down the edge of said creek to the Lone Pine on the southeast corner of Church's Landing …")

Hometown Bonanza

In the city, limits of your hometown and your ancestors' hometowns, lie many other bits of primary source wealth. The town libraries and historical societies, the cemeteries, the courthouses with their different departments holding records of divorces, civil suits, deeds, and wills; the local churches with their confirmations, baptisms, and bar/bat mitzvah records all will be wonderful places for research. As you dig back into these original records, you will learn another language—the language of the past. For instance, the older a land deed is, the more likely it will include unusual terms such as *"metes and bounds."* A will, superb documents for relationship primary sources, abound with words such as "bequeaths," "legatees" (friends who inherit something), *"executors"* and *"executrixes"* (female executors), and "property partitions," to name a few.

But never fear. The more you read the language of the past, the quicker you'll be speaking fluent genealogical-ese.

Oral Histories

Aunt Cissy's memory for facts and figures is essential for your genealogical efforts. Her oral history memories are pivotal for your family history writing efforts.

Never forget, though, that oral histories are both primary sources and secondary sources. How can that be? Family stories, as mentioned, might be told, true or not, without much problem for your genealogical work. Facts that come through oral history (remember Aunt Cissy's uncertain memory of Clara Belle or Clara Delle?) have to be treated as secondary sources. But what if Aunt Cissy is positive her great-granny was named Clara Belle? Her memory, however "dead-sure" Cissy may be, is still a secondary source that must be verified. Why? Because it's "hearsay." A fact about herself or a story that happened to Cissy is a primary source, because it is straight from the horse's mouth, but a fact about someone else, even the name of her great-grandparent, is a secondary source that needs verification.

What if Cissy finds a family Bible that has her great-granny's name in it? That would be considered, by most genealogists, a primary source (although a true dyed-in-the-wool genealogist would still want you to hunt down her county courthouse vital records for your family history foundation). This sort of source distinction is why you need to develop your genealogical muscles.

> ### *Deep Thought*
>
> *Oral history can be both a primary source and a secondary source.*

Military Service Records

If your ancestors were soldiers—and considering the number of wars we've had in our short history, they probably were—their military service records will offer surprising information. The records will include discharge records, enlistments, company musters, pension records, and affidavits from family members or doctors, all full of information. Indexes will help you figure out where to look. (What's an index, you ask? Keep reading.)

The National Archives in Washington, D.C. stores the original military records. Its 13 branches have them indexed on microfilm. There's also the National Personnel Records Center in St. Louis. The National Archives also stores census records and immigration arrivals, not to mention other rather interesting documents such as the Declaration of Independence. (More on the National Archives, every genealogists' major pit stop, in Chapter 11, "Looking in All the Right Places—Library and Beyond.")

A Relatively Good Idea

Do you have copies of your birth certificate? Do you have copies of birth certificates for every member of your family? If not, it's a good idea to get them. They can be ordered from the appropriate state agency in the state where you and your family members were born.

The Daughters of the American Revolution is also a good source of original military information, for a small fee, and some of it is online. They have a large collection of family histories and cemetery records gathered from local chapters. Each state has one designated library that receives yearly bound copies of DAR records, and volunteers are transcribing new information all the time.

Immigration Records

At some point in your genealogical search, you'll want to experience a first American's entry into the country by exploring these fascinating documents. There will be wonderful fodder for your family history here. The National Archives has microfilm of almost all the ships' passenger lists after 1820. Finding an ancestor immigrating before 1820 is much like a treasure hunt—difficult, but not impossible.

Indexes will help you here, too. Several publications such as the book *They Came in Ships, A Guide to Finding Your Immigrant Ancestor's Arrival Record* are excellent places to begin. Chapter 11 will also go into further detail about this starting point for all American stories.

Other Primary Hiding Places

Other primary sources, as mentioned above, include cemetery information, family Bibles, old newspaper accounts, deeds, wills, probate records, county court records such as divorce proceedings and suits, church records such as confirmations, baptisms, bar/bat mitzvahs, and, of course, letters and diaries. These are hiding in old trunks and resting in courthouse files, along with other surprises you will only find once you begin to search.

So, let's review. Any document that is firsthand—something your ancestor either filled out personally or something official that contained information about the ancestor—is a primary source. You'll want to find as many of these as you can. They are your family history's backbone.

Secondary Sources

Secondary sources are compiled sources which have been interpreted or transcribed by historians or genealogists. Along with your vital records, secondary sources will be the vehicle that takes you down the paper trail to those primary sources, once you've explored all family connections.

The people who help compile these secondary sources, from county histories to the wealth of indexes available, have already done a huge amount of general work for you. You will be looking for your specific family needle in their haystack, but their work has made the haystack less formidable and more accessible—with friendly signposts that point the way.

Indexes

Indexes are big books that don't have the specific information you seek, but offer places for you to find it. They are those important-looking volumes that line reference shelves of libraries, and the tapes that fill microfilm drawers. Many of them will contain genealogical information you want. For example, the International Genealogical Index is a computer database that contains millions of names with citations to sources. They will be one of the first stops in your first library research visit.

County, Town, and Family Histories

Every town and county has a history, just like every family. My guess is there are very few counties in this country that do not have a compiled history waiting for the seeker in their city libraries. Many of our country's rural histories were recorded as part of the Great Depression's Works Project Administration. One genealogist in my family has copies of six different county histories and five family histories that he bought along his trek, some of which have never had more than two dozen in printed form.

Town and county histories are at best seen as secondary sources, especially considering that most of the entries have been contributed by a family member of the town's historical figures. But as secondary sources they are excellent, and offer a wealth of information and lessons for the beginner as we'll see in Chapter 7, "Getting It Right from the Get-Go."

The same thing goes for family histories. The Family History Library in Salt Lake City, Utah, for instance, specializes in having more than 80,000 compiled family histories to flip through.

A Relatively Good Idea

Might you have a relative who has a copy or two of town, county, or family histories? Take a look.

The Family History Library, by the way, has 3,400 branches (and counting) in the U.S. and in 62 countries. They are called Family History Centers. You never know what you might find through its catalogs and indexes to the Family History Library. While it is run by The Church of Jesus Christ of Latter-day Saints as part of their mission, its holdings are universal and open to the public.

The Cyberspace Signpost

"Be forewarned," stated a recent *Time* magazine cover story on the Internet and genealogy, "much of what is on the Web now is akin to signposts—lists of documents, but rarely the documents themselves." But what a great signpost it is.

The Internet could be called the biggest index of all. It has transformed genealogy in a way nothing has before. We'll talk more about what a revolution it is for genealogy later, but for now, realize it is another excellent place to begin.

The National Archives offers a description of its material, but considering it has four billion records, only a fraction of them are being digitized each year. Still, the Web sites improve daily and continue to be the threshold for beginning genealogists every day. And the same thing can be said for almost all the growing number of Web sites dedicated to genealogy. (More on the Internet and genealogy in Chapter 11.)

Scoping Out Your Paper Trail

Feeling overwhelmed yet? If so, then we should try an old writer's trick. Put yourself in the place of the people you are researching. What would a person find if they began to research you, looking for clues at the scene of your life? What would people say about you?

Imagining Your Life on Paper

Think of your own life as a paper trail. Can you prove you exist? Can you find your birth certificate? Your social security card? A diary? A baby book? Here's a short list of evidence that could prove you are you and have been all these years:

➤ Birth certificate

➤ Girl Scout/Boy Scout badges

➤ Yearbooks

➤ Diplomas

➤ Photos

➤ Diaries

➤ Objects with your name on them (class rings, trophies)

➤ Articles you've written or that have been written about you

➤ Marriage certificates

Can you think of other sources of concrete proof that you exist? List them in your family history writing journal.

You're Everywhere, Everywhere

Peruse your documented proof. Couldn't you write a short biography just from this evidence? Perhaps including a few good anecdotes gleaned from diaries, letters, newspaper clippings, and family anecdotes? Of course you could (and will). Your paper trail is immense. Doesn't it make you wonder how an ancestor of yours could have so little evidence left of *their* lives? Where did it all go?

Let's put you back in time several generations and see what happens when we try to find out about you.

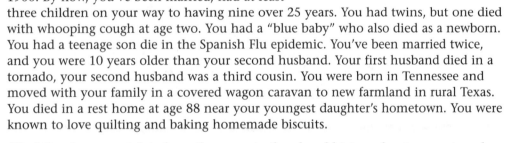

'Riting Reminder

How many "proofs of you" can you locate today? Place what you can find in a safe place for future reference, but first, why not write a paragraph about yourself that these things describe? What might a stranger deduce from them?

You as Your Great-Granny

Imagine yourself as your great-grandmother, circa 1900. By now, you've been married, had at least three children on your way to having nine over 25 years. You had twins, but one died with whooping cough at age two. You had a "blue baby" who also died as a newborn. You had a teenage son die in the Spanish Flu epidemic. You've been married twice, and you were 10 years older than your second husband. Your first husband died in a tornado, your second husband was a third cousin. You were born in Tennessee and moved with your family in a covered wagon caravan to new farmland in rural Texas. You died in a rest home at age 88 near your youngest daughter's hometown. You were known to love quilting and baking homemade biscuits.

All of the above was taken from the paper trail and oral history about my maternal grandmother. The only sources are vital records and snippets of oral history, yet you can still see the "outline" of her as a real person from that paragraph. With each generation back in time, though, more paper vanishes. For instance, what do I know about her mother, my great-grandmother? Only a list of seven children's birthdates, and not one scrap of oral history. Not one. Compare that to the current depth of my paper trail above.

Time's Eraser

Time is not kind to paper. That is why you are writing your family history, isn't it? To stave off time's eraser. Yet the paper trail is still out there, even as it slowly disappears, and next comes the fun of finding all of it you can while it still exists.

Now, you have a very, very brief overview of the world of genealogy. Learning anything requires small steps, baby steps, if you will. So, let's look at genealogical research in baby-step form, using what you already know from this chapter and a little of what you will soon know from the chapters to come.

Researching Baby Steps

Here is your simple plan to accomplish your family history research goal, in semi-chronological order:

1. **Think you.** Find out what you already know and write it down.

2. **Think family.** Ask family members all they know.

3. **Think vital records.** Verify as many as you can from primary sources (birth, marriage, death certificates).

4. **Think specifics.** Decide one thing you want to hunt for. Research one thing at a time. For your very first attempt, research something familiar for practice (e.g., your grandmother's maiden name and birth date, something you already have but want to verify by seeing a primary source).

5. **Think library.** Go to a library, preferably one that has a good genealogical section.

6. **Think help.** Ask for guidance. Ask your librarian if the library has a genealogical collection. Ask for names of local genealogical groups.

7. **Think signposts and indexes.** Secondary sources keep your trail warm.

8. **Think genealogical magazines.** Thumb through a few. For a beginner, especially a writer, doing so is an eye-opener.

9. **Think Internet.** Go online, find one Web site (e.g., National Archives), and look around.

10. **Think overview.** Familiarize yourself with everything before trying anything big.

11. **Think good note-taking.** Learn not to take short cuts now.

12. **Think logs, charts, records.** Decide on a system for your organization. The next chapter will cover your organizational tools. You can devise your own system, if you're sure no one else is going to ever attempt to use the information. You can use the time-honored system honed by genealogists already in place or you can adopt a computer software program's organization.

13. **Think sturdy.** Buy a decent filing cabinet. It's a safe bet you could fill up a filing cabinet within a year, but whatever you choose, start off with something solid, and that means no shoe box.

14. **Think copy machine.** Copy everything that can be copied.

15. **Think travelling shoes.** Sooner or later, you will be making plans to visit the hometowns of several of your chosen ancestors, including your parents and grandparents. Facts gained through cyberspace or in libraries will always feel less than the real thing. One quiet walk through an old cemetery will prove this to you. To truly grasp an ancestor's reality, you need to breathe the same air, stand on the same soil. You'll love it and your writing will show it.

16. **Think family-history-writing-journey journal.** There will be many moments, questions, and thoughts that defy your genealogical charts. You'll want to document them somewhere, and this is it. It obviously is also the place for all those pre-writing jottings.

The Forest for the Trees

There's an easy way and a hard way to turn these baby steps into giant steps without falling by the wayside. The next few chapters are designed to ease you into the vast world of the past by seeing it all from a writer's viewpoint as well as a researcher's assignment. After all, you're telling a story, leaving a legacy far beyond the ancestral facts and figures (however interesting) you will uncover. All the storytelling elements are there. You just have to learn how not to miss the family history forest while inspecting closely each of those genealogical trees. So while we are learning basics, we'll be sneaking in a little creative thinking.

Related Facts

Statistics suggest that we know more people than our ancestors did, but we also play pivotal parts in fewer lives. Of all the people who you know, only a handful would include you in their own oral history interview. Who are they? What might they say about you?

The Least You Need to Know

➤ Time is an eraser and your job as a family history writer is to rescue all you can before it disappears.

➤ Every genealogical trail begins with yourself.

➤ The paper trail you have already left through your own life is a good example of what you should hope to find in your ancestral search.

➤ Vital records, indexes, certificates, family histories, and immigration records are your genealogical touchstones for those pivotal moments.

➤ The first rule of genealogy is documentation.

Tools for the Task

Ready to get down to the nitty-gritty of being a bonafide genealogist? Then here we go. Besides your pad and pencil and cat-sized curiosity, you need to have along a few tools of the trade. Before you make the first call or visit the first Internet site, or even sleuth your first quote, you'll need more than scribbled notes to keep everything straight.

Genealogists learned this long ago, of course, but you're new, so we'll help you along. You will definitely need specific places to put all the bits and pieces of information you'll be gathering, and those places need to be designed to help you input those bits correctly and logically. Otherwise, months from now, you might want to seriously bop yourself on the head when you begin to write your family history and cannot, for the life of you, find that very, very important piece of information.

Now's the time to introduce yourself to the organizational aids that any genealogical research demands—charts and records that are destined to be part of the paper trail you hand down with your family history.

These are …

➤ Pedigree Chart

➤ Family Group Chart

➤ Research Log

➤ Individual Ancestor Record

➤ Descendent Charts/Drop Charts

➤ Historical Research Datelines

➤ Correspondence Log

Pedigree Chart

We talked about pedigree charts in Chapter 4, but now it's time to get serious. To begin with, you'll need a blank *pedigree chart.* You can use the family tree diagram in the back of this book (check Appendix B, "Sample Forms") for practice, or you can use it as a serious tool. Have you heard of any of the computer software that's out there for organizing family tree information? (See Appendix A, "BookMarks—for Further Reference," for a listing of some of the options that are out there.) If you've already bought one of these computer programs, then print out the pedigree chart template it offers and start filling in all those blanks with all the information you already know.

The Write Word

A **pedigree chart** is a family tree worksheet that starts with you, then moves backward through time showing your ancestors.

A Relatively Good Idea

Always enter information on your charts with pencil until you have verified with a primary source. Then, whip out your pen.

Once you have your pedigree chart ready for action, you'll start working with four generations. The normal pedigree chart page holds space for that amount. (Four generations is about the maximum that you will be able to fill in with primary sources or easily acquired documentation.) Begin with yourself and move backward. Above the appropriate line, fill in the ancestor's full name. Under the line, list the date and place of birth and then the date and place of death. Whenever you can, fill in as much geographical information as possible, too—town, county, state.

Never forget that the pedigree chart is just a tool. While your ancestors might read it some day, it isn't meant to stand alone as documentation. Think of all your charts as notes—guides to what you still need to know. You are going to write the definitive, stand-alone volume for your family.

First Genealogical Writing Lesson

You've probably noticed by now that genealogy has its own writing style. It's a tried-and-true genealogical way of recording information. Now is the time to learn it right even though it seems wrong at first glance. But never fear. There's method in this genealogical madness—a genealogical writing style that will soon become second nature.

First, notice all the people mentioned, and there is nary an abbreviation in sight. Your father-in-law isn't Joe Schmoe or even Joe J. Schmoe, he's Joseph John (Joe) Schmoe IV and Joseph Jonathan Schmoe IV and your mother-in-law isn't Mrs. Susan Schmoe (and definitely not Mrs. Joe Schmoe), she's Susan Sara (Smith) Schmoe.

Next, notice the dates. This is an important habit to begin now. There are so many ways to misinterpret dates that in genealogical work, this style is the choice for clarity. For instance, European dates usually begin with the day, then the month and the year, and so 2/8/99 would be in some parts of the world August 2, 1999, not February 8, 1999. In our genealogical world, it also might be August 8, 1899, for that matter. So genealogical dates are always listed as day, month, year, written out fully.

Pedigree Chart Tips

Sound complicated? It really isn't. Here are a half-dozen points to remember while getting up-close-and-personal with your pedigree chart:

1. Print instead of write.
2. List women under their maiden names since their husbands' names will be obvious.
3. List any nicknames in quotations.
4. Write all dates in genealogical form.
5. Use pencil instead of pen until you have verified your documentation with primary sources.
6. Adopt a coding system to help cross-referencing. All your other charts and logs will refer back to the code numbers you create for your pedigree charts. Genealogical practice assigns each ancestor a number. For instance, information on Joe Schmoe II will always have his number by it. You are number 1, your father is number 2, your mother is number 3, and on and on. Men are even numbers, women odd numbers. Believe it or not, you'll soon find this sort of organization very helpful and easy to read.

'Riting Reminder

You are not just a genealogist who researches records information. You are a writer who will compile all this information into written form. Nevertheless, you need to research with the best of them in order to write your best.

Family Group Record

Before your father was your father, he used to be a son. Your mother was the apple of her own mother's eye. They were parts of other family groups. This may not be something you've ever thought about in just this way, but as a genealogist you'll begin to think of it quite a bit. We are all, at different times of our lives, part of different family groups.

Pedigree charts and family trees don't offer much space for each family, and no space for recording sources. So family group records were invented to give you space to fill in complete vital records on one couple and their children in one place. It is the equivalent of a pedigree chart for one individual family.

As in the pedigree chart, put proper names, middle names, maiden names, and nicknames and fill in dates in the genealogical style (day, month, year—11 June 1939). Don't have the dates exactly? Then, you need to approximate the date with parenthesis around it so you can zero in on a certain time period to research. This is, again, why these charts are considered worksheets. And, again, unless you are a virtuoso with correction fluid, remember to use a pencil until the facts have been verified using a primary source.

So, the two biggest differences between family group record and your pedigree chart are that you'll be adding "your collateral ancestors," brothers and sisters, aunts and uncles and cousins galore, as well as have extra space to add extra information.

Individual Ancestor Record

For the sake of your family history writing, I suggest that you go a step further with your chart. When you begin to choose which ancestor you want to follow back down that ancestral path into the past for family stories, you should begin a page for each one. The accepted form has lots of space for interesting information you uncover, such as occupation, siblings, accomplishments, religious affiliations, oral history tidbits, and dramatically juicy anecdotes. (By the way, whatever you find, remember to always put in parentheses the source of each of the pieces of information.)

Of course, whatever you find, don't forget to cross-reference what you can to your family group record and your pedigree chart.

A Fine Example

Let's try it. Let's say your pedigree chart notes that your ancestor Joe Schmoe III was married on 12 July 1911.

You've immediately cross-referenced the information onto the Joe Schmoe III family group record chart and Joe Schmoe III's own personal individual ancestor record sheet. (On the latter, and on your research log, in parentheses, you also remember to jot down on the family record and individual record that this information was found on a marriage certificate in your granny's trunk.)

You smile, because the individual record sheet has lots of space to enter all the details you have dug up on Joe III, all of which is terrific material for your family history writing.

Here's an example of an Individual Ancestor Record Sheet entry for Ancestor Schmoe. Notice the genealogical style in which it's presented, and especially the source of each in parentheses:

A Relatively Good Idea

Choose a relative you know well and fill in an individual record entry using the example I've provided as a guide.

Joe Schmoe III

Graduated 1920, Kaufman County High School (diploma/granny's trunk)

12 July 1921, married Andrea Escondido (marriage certificate/courthouse)

1 January 1925, bought house, 501 First Street (deed/courthouse)

8 May, 1926, first child born: Mary Diane (family Bible)

15 October 1927, opened business, Schmoe Drug Store, Joe Schmoe III, Owner (*Terrell Tribune*, 20 October 1925)

20 October 1927, business has five aisles of merchandise, two pharmacists, and a bright marble soda counter with table area offering lunch daily. (hometown newspaper article)

18 February 1927, elected deacon, First Baptist Church (church record)

30 May, 1939, house burned down (*Terrell Tribune*)

30 May 1939, died of heart attack (death certificate)

Notice that all this information is from primary sources and offers proof worthy of using a pen instead of a pencil. They also offer a tidy little story for the family history writer, don't you think?

Activate Your Antennae

Look at Joe Schmoe III's list of facts again. Did you notice anything that piques your curiosity about this listing of individual information for Ancestor Joe? Did your family history writer's antennae go up? If not, look again. With practice, it soon will. Seeing all the information listed on each person in one place will help your story-telling tremendously. Without such focus, some very good leads to dramatic family stories can be lost in the shuffle of information.

Descendant Charts/Drop Charts

Serious genealogists also use something called a Descendant Chart or a Drop Chart that lists all the descendants of one ancestor at a time. Of course, first, you have to do full research all the way back to that ancestor and then double back, listing his or her offspring through the years to you. If you're interested, remember, your ancestors had big families and often several marriages, so this really becomes detective work to get it right. That's why it's used only by serious genealogists, people deeply bitten by the bug or for those attempting to prove lineage to a particular important person.

On the other hand, say you have a favorite ancestor that you'd like to see charted to show direct lineage all the way to your birth. This is the chart that will do it.

Research Log

Every time you go to the library, or log on to the Internet, or drive to a cemetery, or visit a courthouse, or have tea in a great-aunt's sitting room, you'll be gaining new information. Your research log is where you'll record new information each time you research a lead and list what you found.

"Every piece of information?" I hear you mumble. Yes, every one. You may not think knowing where you got each little piece of information is important at the time, but you will later. With each research effort, you should ask and answer the question, "Where did I do the research and what did I find or not find?"

What's that you're thinking? "Do I really need another chart for this? Isn't there some room on all the charts already discussed for such small notations?" You have a little box or two on the family record chart to fill in sources, but you'll be surprised how, once you are on the trail, you'll want to keep up with every little bit of sleuthing you do—where you did it and what happened. And you'll want it in one place, again for focus.

I cannot stress enough the importance of keeping the research clear and annotated, and I'll be repeating this genealogical mantra several more times. For the family history writer, meticulously recording your research's whens, wheres, and whats will become more important the closer you get to writing. If you don't do this religiously, you'll hate yourself in the morning.

A Relatively Good Idea

With each research effort, you should ask and answer the question, "Where did I do the research and what did I find or not find?"

Correspondence Log

Soon, if not already, you are going to be writing letters like a postal whirlwind— letters to long-lost kin and extended family members, letters to genealogical societies, county courthouses, and on and on. What to say and how to say it will be the topic for discussion later.

For now, though, remember that, like your research log, you'll want to keep a record of all your postal forays, too. Again, you'll have only yourself to hate if you don't keep on top of this. Besides, how else are you going to know that it has been three months since you wrote Cousin Bernie and he hasn't responded? And you don't want to forget Cousin Bernie. He knows lots of stuff, and is usually hard to shut up. Yet now that you are ready to hear it all, you haven't heard a peep. Something happened. Recording your letter to him will remind you to follow up.

Historical Research Timelines

Do you enjoy history? Before your genealogy adventure is over, I bet you will be fascinated by it. As we've pointed out earlier, your personal history shines a spotlight on the world's history. But the reverse can be just as true.

Creating a historical research timeline of the world's events to correspond with what you are uncovering about your ancestors' lives during those eras will not only be fun, but it will also give you a much-needed context. Such a dateline is also very useful in family history writing, too, when you begin to put everything on paper. In fact, don't be surprised if you tack it up at eye-level and use it as a visual aid.

> ### *Deep Thought*
>
> *There are the makings of a dramatic story waiting in the dates and facts of your ancestor's life to be uncovered by you. Check the dates—do you see a potentially interesting family history tale? How might you find out more details that might uncover a forgotten drama potentially worthy of your family history?*

To be honest, you will naturally find yourself in historical timelines anyway as you trek into the past. Creating a dateline will only help create context for your search and will come in very handy when you finally sit down to write.

Computer, Typewriter, Pencil

Got a computer? You might want to consider one of the popular genealogical programs that I mentioned earlier (see Appendix A for a sample list) to manage all your information. They were developed to help you keep track of all your research, offering all these logs and records and charts on-screen. The programs range from ones which do only the basics to programs that can produce customized reports, offer extensive footnoting and bibliographies, create programs which connect you to the Internet, show you the way through cyberspace, and even set up your own Web site.

One of the best things that any computer program does is to generate all the charts/logs/records we've been discussing. Doing all these charts by hand is very tedious. It can also keep up with all your information better than you can, cross-referencing every contact or ancestor for information in Georgia for instance, as well as any other fact that might escape your memory. Once you start accumulating over a hundred ancestors, your memory, as well as your pile of handwritten charts, just might not do the trick anymore, or at least do it as well. These programs are designed to do it for you.

Is your computer a laptop? You'll find out just how handy it is when you take it along on your research trips to the local library or around the world.

In Praise of the Printed Page

My only computer-age warning? Here it is: Your computer systems will go out of date, along with their software, often, it seems, at the speed of light. And computer advances will be happening faster and faster each year. My own computer history is a good example. I've had five systems in 12 years. And guess what—I cannot use any information I stored on those old, large floppy disks used with the first three systems, because the first three systems are not operational anymore. The information might as well have vanished. Instead, they sit in their file box and taunt me.

What is the answer? Print out frequently, certainly before you switch computer systems. Always have hard copy; never trust your computer to be your sole warehouse for everything.

'Riting Reminder

Computer users warning: Always keep a hard copy of your work, updated periodically with new additions (and keep it somewhere safe).

No Computer Access

Picture 20 years in the future. Think how sad it would be that your ancestor had your currently fancy CD-ROM in her futuristic hand filled to its brim with all your work, but no way to access it because not even a museum has one of those old desktop computers it was made on.

On the other hand, your family history *book* (underline "book") with its universal appeal and accessibility, is a another story (so to speak). Why, there are copies of that bestseller everywhere—hardbound, always-readable copies.

Just remember, when it comes to computers, change is the only constant. Those who forget that a computer is just another tool, albeit an incredible one, are the ones doomed to eternal shrieking in ten years when even the most pampered computers will probably not be functioning enough to access those backup discs. (This may be a good time to give this reminder: Have you backed up your computer files lately? You're welcome.)

Your Byte Is Worse Than Your Bark

Don't have a computer? Try a typewriter.

The recent *Time* magazine cover story mentioned earlier concerning genealogy tells a wonderful story about 70-year-old Ida Quintana, a woman who, armed with nothing more than an old portable Smith/Corona typewriter (and obviously a tiger-sized curiosity) created a 22-volume family history, a one-of-a-kind history of the Spanish in the Southwest dating back to the appearance of conquistador Don Juan Onate in 1598. Ms. Quintana discovered a French-speaking Pawnee grandmother and ancestors from New Mexico to Spain, delving into archdiocesan records, statistical abstracts and old Spanish histories—all while spending most of her research time at one library, the Denver Pubic Library.

Don't have a typewriter? Or even know how to type? As mentioned from the beginning, if you have a pen and a pad of paper and enough curiosity, you can still be in the genealogy business.

Let's Talk Note-Taking

How you take notes of all those deeds, newspaper clippings, family histories, primary sources, and secondary sources galore, is almost as important as what they say, where you record it, and where they lead you. Three ways to do genealogical note-taking are abstracting, excerpting, and transcribing.

➤ **Abstracting** is summarizing. Be careful, though. Summary doesn't mean sloppy. Try outlining important points and bulleting them.

➤ **Excerpting** is writing down the exact wording of certain parts of a document. (Extracting falls into this category. Extracting is taking a part of the information you need, but not necessarily quoting it verbatim.)

➤ **Transcribing** is writing everything exactly as you find it. Misspellings? Use [sic]. This is very important for family history writing.

The Write Word

Circa means approximately. Use its abbreviation "ca." for approximate dates when you are not certain, but still want to show a date on your charts.

The best bet for the best note-taking method of all? Make copies of all originals. In its own way, the copy machine is as revolutionary a piece of equipment for modern research purposes as the computer.

One last thing—be sure to write down information exactly as you find it. Don't alter it in any way. You could actually change the meaning of something, since customs change through the years. (Also remember to go ahead and write down everything you find, even if you don't think you are interested in it. You may be later.)

Now What?

Now you have the proper tools, you have an overview of where you're going, and you have some ancestors' names and dates. What's next? Believe it or not, the next thing is a choice. You'll have to choose which way to go. And how do you do that?

Which Way to Go?

How do you choose which surname, much less which ancestor, to chase? That may not seem a daunting question until you begin to work backward into your many ancestral lines. After you have filled your charts/logs/records with all your living relatives' vital statistics, that's the time you'll stop and ask yourself: Which name do I want to follow first?

The answer will depend on why you are searching. Some people are doing genealogy for documentation only, to link up to a famous ancestor or to gain qualification into a genealogical society made up of descendents of certain historical events, such as the Sons of the Republic of Texas or the Daughters of the American Revolution or the Jamestowne Society. Some people are just interested in the names, dates, places, and the thrill of the hunt. But the family historian is more interested in the stories connected to the names and will want to follow them wherever they lead. A black sheep scoundrel of a scalawag in the family tree will excite a family history writer/researcher as much (if not more) than a hero.

So, what to do? Which way to go? The path of least resistance is always the best way to start, and so is the path of affinity—the line for which you feel the deepest bond. Once you get started with your genealogical dig, and you watch those "new" ancestors' names pop into your line of vision, you'll know which way tugs you and why, be it a mystery to solve, a sentimental journey to take, or just plain cat-killing curiosity.

For instance, on the Kendrick side of my family tree, my great-great-great-great-grandmother was named

A Relatively Good Idea

Which way to go? How do you choose which surname to research?

➤ Choose the path of least resistance

➤ Choose the path of affinity

Thankful Wilkens, born 1765. With a name like Thankful on a pedigree chart, doesn't that just beg to know more about her? I'd like to find that story, if I can. And so off I go. You'll do the same.

Related Facts

Ever doubt how much naming customs and the meanings of names change with the times? The Puritans favored "message" names such as Hopestill, Yetmercy, Thankful, Mindwell, Submit, and Freelove. The latter names' messages would have been just as popular with a hippie in the 1960s and made the poor Puritans twirl in the grave.

Journaling Down the Genealogical Trail

Which will it be? The path of least resistance or the path of affinity? Write down which and why for your journal entry to help you better understand this first choice you'll be making.

The Least You Need to Know

➤ Genealogical charts are cornerstones to good research.

➤ Genealogy has its own "writing style."

➤ Make photocopies of all information to back up your written records.

➤ Write down all researched information even if you aren't terribly interested at the time. You may find it more interesting later.

➤ Be sure to take notes superbly or hate yourself in the morning.

Chapter 7

Uncle Shirley

Getting It Right from the Get-Go

In This Chapter

➤ Avoiding wild goose ancestor chases

➤ Discerning the good, the bad, and the sloppy of genealogy research

➤ Why you can't believe everything in print

Now you have the tools of the trade, and you have a basic grasp of the territory. Before you jump headlong into your genealogical research, let's look at a few more aspects of this brand-new world that you, as a smart writer/researcher, will want to know. Bland facts and figures are easy enough to handle, but as with any new world, the traveler who is forewarned is also forearmed, and able to enjoy the trip much more quickly.

Get your special family history journal, a pen and—if you already have acquired one—a family, town, or county history. We're about to enter the land of your ancestors for a look around.

The Name Game

"The name's the same" is one of the greatest potholes in beginning genealogy. Since names are the basic of the basics for your first research project, let's talk about the name game first. Even the simplest thing to research has to begin with a name, and believe it or not, names can be tricky.

The Write Word

Onomastic evidence is genealogical evidence based on the similarity of names.

A Relatively Good Idea

Try this eye-opener. Choose an ancestor's name, living or dead. Now look it up in a current telephone directory. What did you find? Now look up your own name. Is "The Name the Same"?

You may think the name you are searching for is unique, but the odds are that someone else also has that name, and could easily have lived in the same area as your ancestors. People didn't move around much in the past and names, being the cultural creations they are, were usually taken from a small list of choices.

Even in this mobile society of ours, the name game is a problem, much less back when people stayed put. In the decade I lived in Chicago, I tripped over several Linda Stephensons, only one other Lynda Stephenson, and no Lynda Rutledge Stephensons but me. The same will be true for any ancestor you are seeking. The more information you have, the more specific you can be, and the shorter the wild goose chase.

A Tree Full of Elroys

Scrutinize the ancestral names you've collected already. From our earlier exercises, you should have a nice long list, and hopefully some vital records to build on. But there are those blanks staring at you. Sadly, your maternal great-grandmother's maiden name seems to be lost in time, although you have her husband's name—Elroy Phillip Blankenship. This is your first granny gap.

But wait. You notice that his father's name was also Elroy and so was his father's father. It's bad enough that you have granny gaps with no name at all. Now you seem to have granddads that all have the same name. Why did they like the name Elroy so much?

How Many Elroys Are There?

All sorts of clues can be found in names of other ancestors, especially the Elroy kind. Like these Elroys, you may notice as you go back in your own lineage, that the same names keep popping up over and over. After you get past the irrational feeling that your ancestors are just trying to confuse you, you might just realize that this is actually a good thing. The purpose of the duplicate naming, no doubt, was to honor an earlier ancestor. Many families use surnames as given names no matter what gender. If you can get past the confusion, this helps reduce your paper trail. (It certainly underscores the need for cross-referencing ancestor's names.)

For example, in my father's surname line, beginning with our original American in the 1600s, there was a William and a Joseph in each generation. There were no middle names. You could only tell which William Rutledge was which by what century you were discussing and what state he was in, since with each generation, another William moved to another nearby state—Pennsylvania, Virginia, Kentucky, South Carolina, and Alabama. There were so many duplicate names that escalating numerals had to be used to keep them genealogically straight (William Rutledge III/IV/V).

Related Facts

If you found a Joseph Jones Jr. and a Joseph Jones Sr. living in the same colonial town, would you think they were father and son? Of course you would. But they may not be. In colonial villages, the "Jr." and "Sr." were often used to delineate between two people with the same name living in the same town, somewhat like, in a large group of friends and family, we might keep two guys named Bob separate by calling one Robert the Older (or Big Bob) and the other, Robert the younger (or Little Bob).

Writer's Reflection Time

After finding the duplicate names, I noticed something interesting. They suddenly stopped. In one generation, the use of William and Joseph as names in my Rutledge line disappeared. There hasn't been a William or a Joseph for over a hundred years—in my line. Why?

A Relatively Good Idea

Check your lists of ancestors' names. See any repeats? Make a note to watch these as your research begins.

Throughout your research, especially as you get more and more adept at thinking like a historian (see Chapter 10, "The Family Investigator on the Case"), your detective juices will stir up conclusions, theories, and thoughts you'll want to ponder since soon you will be writing pages of family history that will require some connecting of the family dots.

A little of this kind of reflection helped me theorize that the naming of offspring after dads and granddads of the past seems to stop the moment my Rutledge ancestor moved from being one of the older brothers to one of the youngest brothers of these perennially large families. The larger the amount of siblings, the less left for the youngest ones, of course. So many younger brothers left home, usually "going-west-young-man," to make their own way. When the first of "my" younger brothers went west all the way to Texas, cutting all his family ties much more severely than any of his ancestors had done since the one who had come to America from England, the "family names" seem to have been cut off, too.

But why do I have this feeling that there are Williams and Josephs still accumulating roman numerals down the ancestral lines of my distant Rutledge relatives?

Spelling-Challenged

We wouldn't think about changing the spelling of our last names on a whim, would we? So why did people in the past? One of the first strange things you'll notice about your trip into your ancestors' past is that the same name seems to be spelled all sorts of ways.

Until the nineteenth century, there was a lackadaisical attitude toward spelling in the Western world, and little standardized usage. (After all, so few people could read and write, why have rules?) That attitude seems to seep over to surnames. And it is a genealogical fact of life that can turn a researcher gray.

But this free-for-all spelling is really quite common before a certain point in history. Only three generations into the new world, a Rutledge ancestor dropped the "o" of his grandfather's Routledge, never to be seen again. One of my original American ancestors was a Rutherford, from Scotland. The name Rutherford through the decades and centuries has been spelled Routerford, Rutherfurd, and Rodyrforde. And we haven't even mentioned the Ellis Island "Americanization" of arriving immigrant names (discussed in Chapter 11, "Looking in All the Right Places—Library and Beyond")—which was, in reality, misspelling by government decree.

All of this might seem frustrating for you, the beginning researcher, except for the colorful information you might find, and what it might add to your family history writing. For all their seeming silence now, our ancestors led full, historically rich lives. Who knows what you'll find as you dig? For instance, nineteenth-century New England writer Nathaniel Hawthorne began life as a "Hathorne." One of his direct relatives, though, was a central legal figure in the Salem Witch Trials of the seventeenth century. To disassociate himself from his ancestor, the aspiring writer added a "w" to his name.

Related Facts

Anglo-Saxons honored their famous by not using their names for descendents. They retired the name—like today's sports teams might retire certain players' numbers.

A Boy Named Shirley

Your ancestor's name is Beverly Johnson. Without doubt, the ancestor has to be a woman, right? Make that *with* doubt.

Not too long ago, Beverly was a man's name as well as a women's, such as today's Tracy or Stacy. What about the name "Glenn"? Is it a male or female name? In my case, not only is it a female name, but also my stepgreat-aunt's name. I once knew a small town postal clerk whose name was Shirley. His explanation? It's a family name—his father's, actually, and his father's before him. So he could never understand what all the fuss was about. Always check for male/female information to go with every name.

Changing Names

And then there are the people who change their own names. A friend's grandfather hated his given name because he was named after a famous preacher of the time by his religious mother. So, he not only reversed the names, he also began going only by his initials on every document the rest of his life, which turned out to be very confusing for genealogical work—until someone remembered the family story.

If he'd lived today, he'd have probably gone to court to change it and there would have been a document produced that a genealogical search would uncover. But the past, remember, is a different land. He just decided to do it, and it was done.

Got the Right Ancestor?

The Cardinal Sin of genealogy, as you know by now, is not keeping your eye on documentation. And not keeping your eye on your ancestors' correct names may have you on the opposite side of the world researching a very nice person who isn't related to you at all.

> ### *Deep Thought*
>
> *The genealogist states facts and figures and writes about research. The family history writer is called upon to make connections to it all and offer it up in engaging narrative as any good biographer would.*

> ### A Relatively Good Idea
>
> How do you know if you have the right ancestor?
>
> Full Exact Name + Geographical Location + Date

Woe is you if you try to use the Internet to find an ancestor with only a name. You'll find out quickly how big the world really is.

So, as you understand the "Name Game" with all its potential changes and varieties, you can see why you have to continue to ask during every step of your research, one main question: *"Do I have the right ancestor?"*

A Relatively Good Idea

Let's say that there's a gap in your generations, and it feels like a dead end since you have only the slightest amount of information for the ancestor you know. Is there a way to leap into the next generation anyway? Yes, if that slight amount of information includes the ancestor's hometown.

Geographical Check

How do you know you have the right ancestor? By checking your ancestor's geographical location, that's how. Exact name plus birth date plus place are your no-fail guides. There may be two people who lived in the 1890s with your ancestor's exact name, there may even be two in the same state, but according to the size of your city, there will rarely be two in the same town. And even if there were two people with the same name in the same place, what could you do? You can always whip out your ancestor's vital records to nail down the right one.

Let's try this:

➤ Take the last name you have pre-gap (e.g., Edna Louise Humperdink from Dupage County, Illinois).

➤ Write the county courthouse for a copy of her birth certificate.

There on the document should be her father's name. Voilà. You have jumped into another generation.

Learning from the County

When I began my own genealogical research, my brother-in-law, a longtime genealogist, handed me a history of my home county. It was a slim volume, obviously more a labor of love than a professional publication, as are most histories of small towns and counties—a compilation of profiles of "VIPCs" (Very Important Persons of the County) contributed by family members and published over 20 years ago.

The Rutledges of my rural Texas county were an interesting bunch who more or less stayed put for over a century and five generations, and they happened to be the only Rutledges in the area during that time. So, checking a copy of the county history was a smart move to begin my detective work.

What did I find? I found a glorious trail of over a dozen leads, felt a newcomer's exhilaration at seeing my surname's lineage rolling back so many years, and then stumbled upon a big, fat red flag of a glaring error that brought me back down to earth.

In other words, that first search was a definitive eye-opener, errors included, a wonderful teacher for the beginner.

The Good, the Bad, and the Sloppy

As you know by now, there's a good way and a sloppy way to record genealogical information. And there will be a good way and a sloppy way to write your family history.

The proud family members who donated a nice profile piece for their town's history may or may not claim to be writers or genealogists. And they may or may not have meant their profile to stand up to such scrutiny. In fact, they may have been working with all that they had, many of the gaps lying in the passage of time and the ephemeral nature of the paper trail. But you, the genealogist, must take responsibility for verification of all of the information you find. And you, the family history writer, must have your writer's antennae always up, always finding a way to tell your stories, since someone will soon be reading your writing and believing it as gospel.

Let's see how the dozen or so leads from my first county history volume stack up—good, bad, or sloppy—for ease of genealogy use and for lessons in good family history writing. Inside the county history book's pages, I found three Rutledge entries.

➤ A short, general "family history" of this certain Rutledge line in America

➤ A profile of the first Rutledge to move to the state and county

➤ A profile of the Rutledge who was county sheriff for 20 years

History Lesson #1

Do you have a copy of a town or county history that includes your ancestors? Open it and compare as we go to see how many of the same sorts of leads you can find.

First Lead

Each of the three short compilations noted the source of the information. First was a profile taken from a published Alabama county history. The second was a summary from personal records of a Kentucky Rutledge cousin, and the third was written by my own great-uncle.

Why are the sources of these profiles important information for me, the genealogist? Remember any county history is a secondary source, so I should attempt to verify what I find here. Do I want to know more about my family pre-Texas? The first compilation was taken from another county history, Walker County, Alabama. I could write for a copy of the county history or I could even travel there, now that I know where "there" is. As for the second profile, the writer may be deceased, since the volume was published in 1978 by a Kentucky cousin. But if I decided to find him or his descendents, I now have a place to start. And the third source leads to my own grandfather's brother who lived across town from me during my childhood. I could easily find his descendents, but much of what he wrote I can check against my own knowledge (as we'll see).

History Lesson #2

Who is listed as writing the profiles of your family in your family, town, or county history? How might you contact him?

My Baker's Dozen (Plus a Few)

The profiles themselves, which covered several pages, offered the leads that I, the beginning genealogist, had to evaluate before I was able to use them for further research. I jotted down my questions and responses in my research log and journal.

Let's see how I did and what you can learn from my experience for your writing.

1. My "gateway" Rutledge, a 19-year-old named John, came from England. However, he spelled his name "Routledge." This is very important information if I decide to search back in England. *(good genealogy)*

2. He came over on the good ship *Merchants of Hope* in 1635. *(very good genealogy)*

3. Court records of Maryland mentioned him during 1642 to 1643, and 1644 to 1645. Did your research writer's antennae go up? Why were the dates written like that? Where in Maryland are these court records? And why was he in the court records in the first place? I sense something wonderfully juicy missing here. *(sloppy genealogy)*

4. His son, William Routledge, was born in 1653, as listed in the tax list of 1693, Philadelphia, Pennsylvania. *(good genealogy)*

5. He died March 30, 1728, in Abington, Pennsylvania and left a legacy for building a school, "for the people called Quakers." Notice it does not say where this information came from. Perhaps a will? *(sloppy genealogy)*

6. The next generation, John II, "died May 23, 1725, in Neshaminy, Buck's County, Pennsylvania." *(good genealogy)*

7. John II married Margaret Dalton. They were married by William Penn. "I have a copy of the marriage certificate," wrote the compiler. Wow. A genealogical hurrah. If my deeply distant cousin does actually have that certificate, that's impressive. But where might that document be now? Such is the mystery of genealogy, and the allure. *(good genealogy for 1978; sloppy for now)*

8. First granny gap. John II's son, the rebel who dropped the "o" from Routledge, married a woman named Eleanor, but no last name is given to my missing granny, my first granny gap. *(sad genealogy)*

9. His son Joseph, born in North Carolina and died in Kentucky, was a Revolutionary War soldier, since he is mentioned as an enlisted man in Gwathmey's *Some Virginians in the Revolution*. Good lead on the source, but strange, considering that, from the information given, we aren't told he was ever a Virginian. *(sloppy genealogy)*

10. His grandson William married Nancy Lawson and moved to Walker County, Alabama where, around 1835, he was "killed by a bushwhacker by a blow between the shoulder blades with brass knucks." William and Nancy had gone on horseback to the general store where this drunk bushwhacker got mad at William for not drinking with him. Quote: "This was before any kind of law and order, and the Walker County records indicate that the Rutledge kinsmen took care of the bushwhacker." What a family story! I wanted to know the rest of the story. The profile says this anecdote was documented in the "Walker County records." But how could there be records if there wasn't law and order? I wonder how much of this story is actually oral history. *(sloppy but fascinating genealogy; superb family story)*

11. John Joslin Rutledge, my original Texan, moved in 1883 to my hometown where Rutledges lived until 1997—and it even gave street addresses. *(good genealogy)*

12. His son Virge was the sheriff of my Texas county. He was married twice, his first wife having died of a flu epidemic called "Le Grippe." A year later, he married my great-grandmother and produced my whole line. So, in essence, a flu is the reason I am here to write this. *(writer's deep thought)* He's buried in College Mound Cemetery where most of my Rutledge line is interred. *(good genealogy)*

13. Virge was sheriff for 20 years. Wasn't there a tale or two that could have been told of his adventures? *(lost oral history)*

14. Virge's grandchildren are listed by first name and second initial, e.g., my father, Harold K. Abbreviations are a genealogical no-no. It should have read Harold Kendrick, especially since Kendrick was Virge's wife's maiden name, always a good genealogical lead. *(sloppy genealogy)*

15. His second wife and my great-grandmother, a Kendrick, was from Bremond, Texas. So off I could go on one of my granny lines. *(good genealogy)*

History Lesson #3

What if there were a mention of a famous eighteenth-century historical figure having signed one of your ancestor's primary sources? And what if you knew where the record was only 20 years ago? What steps would you take to find out where that paper is now so you can tell its whole story in your family history?

Big, Fat, Red Flag

For my first genealogical foray, this was all exciting stuff. Then there was the error I found, a glaring one, which sat there like a big, fat, red flag.

The first time you find a glaring error in something in print about your family, you'll have the sinking feeling I had. You may have been told about possible errors in genealogy, you may have been warned not to believe everything you read in print, and you may understand the nature of labor-of-love publishing. But until you catch such an error yourself, you don't feel it personally. There's something beyond the feeling of personal irritation—a sinking feeling that throws all the other published "facts" you've ever found into question, whether they deserve your suspicion or not. The only response is to see it as a learning experience, a burning reminder that secondary sources must only be signposts to primary sources, but you never forget that first strange moment.

So, what was my big, fat, red flag?

Annie Lee, Annie Lee

I would never have noticed the error if it weren't about my grandparents, at least not as a novice genealogist. The third compilation, done by my great-uncle, lists all of Sheriff Virge's seven offspring and all their spouses. There, alongside my grandfather's name is his wife's name, my grandmother, "Annie Lee." The problem is that my grandmother's name was Lee Anne.

'Riting Reminder

Coincidences should always be a family history writer's red flag.

What happened? I kept reading, and there in the line below the errant listing is a mention of an Annie Lee who was the sheriff's deceased daughter. The goof was made either by a volunteer who typeset the book, or by the brother of the deceased daughter who wrote the profile of my great-uncle.

What if both names had been Lee Anne? I might have investigated by checking my primary sources for their names, but I probably would have done nothing, chalking it up to coincidence. Coincidences, however, should always be a family history writer's big, red flag. Yes, they can happen, but no, they shouldn't be ignored.

The Moral of the Story

What's the moral? This illustrates the importance of primary source documentation and the fallibility of print. So, let's add:

16. "Eldest son of Virge Rutledge was Broaddus John Rutledge. Wife: Annie Lee Blankenship …" (*genealogical and family history mistake*)

History Lesson #4

Look closely. Do you see any possible errors in your own family's profiles in your town or county history information? What other documents might you use to double-check the questionable entry?

Don't Believe Everything You Read

The printed word is a powerful thing, perhaps too powerful considering the "to-err-is-human" factor. The small but serious mistake made with my grandmother's name in my county's history points to the problem. But, as mentioned, the vast majority of such county histories are projects done out of love and that usually means volunteer work, publishing on a shoestring, and few resources for double-checks.

Yet a printed page is forever, and it is so naturally authoritative, that there is incredible danger in listing unverified information. Because when they hit print, some readers—make that most readers—are bound to believe whatever they read. So the burden is on you, the researcher with your own charts and logs to catch any error along the way and to study any secondary source with a skeptic's eye. The burden for you, the family history writer, will be to get it right the first time (or be hearing about it from Crazy Aunt Edna or Cousin Bernie for the rest of your life).

A True Confession

Want to know the printed page's spell, even for an experienced writer? True confession: I am embarrassed to admit that, as I stared at my grandmother's name printed as Annie Lee, for a second—just a second—I questioned my own memory of her name being Lee Anne. Shaking the printed word's spell away, I couldn't quite rid myself of it all, because I actually jotted a note to myself to seek verification of something I already knew.

That's the power of the printed word. And there will always be people who can't get past that power.

If it's in print, it has to be true. I'll never forget the first article I wrote for *The Chicago Tribune*. I ached to use a perfect quote from a past news story. My editor shook her head, and said, in a voice too full of experience with the vagaries of print, "Never trust another article." And she was right. Until you get to the primary source yourself, you can't know whether a fact is true or not. And if truth isn't a good enough reason to document all you find, then potential embarrassment, especially as a writer, should be.

History Lesson #5

Stick with your blood line. This is a classic place where beginning genealogists get lost. Remember, your ancestors died younger and married more often. Multiple marriages may force you to skip to the wife instead of following the husband's surname in some generations. As Johnny Cash would do, if he were a genealogist, check and recheck where you are as you walk the line.

Proof and More Proof

So, verify—double-verify—even what seems to be obvious, not just for your sake, but your family's, because your family history will be an "infallible" printed page soon enough.

The problem is a big one. The Latter-day Saints' Family History Library, for example, attempts to handle seemingly contradictory information between different sources. They choose the one found most by their volunteers. The Mayflower Society, where membership lives or dies on verification, has a rule that one primary source is enough for documentation, but two sources are needed if the sources are secondary. Of course, no attempt is foolproof. Even a primary source can be mistaken. Babies can be accidentally switched at birth and the revelation not hit the headlines until years later. But while certainty will always be ephemeral, these institutions attempt to double-check their information, and unless it's your own grandmother, so should you. (And maybe then, too.)

Sloppy Genealogy

How can you avoid sloppy genealogy that might produce just as many questions as answers for some future "you"? After the facts are gathered and verified, it's all in the way a thing's written, as you now know. For example, you've found an ancestor's will that has helped with some essential names you've been looking for, and you want to write a notation to yourself about it on your charts. There's an amateur writer's way of listing this information and a pro's way.

An amateur family history writer's log entry would be something like example number one:

1. The names of John Schmoe's sons are proven by his will.

But your entry, as a budding professional family history writer, would proudly look like example number two:

2. The names are proven by a will, housed in the Kaufman County Courthouse, left by John Jacob Schmoe dated 28 Feb. 1844 in which he leaves his estate "to his three sons, Larry, Moe, and Curly Schmoe."

Pat yourself on the back, pro writer. Note that you, not that amateur writer, have given details in the correct style and have added a direct quote of the pivotal part of the will. That's an impressive notation. You've let the primary source speak for itself by quoting it. And you've given enough information to be a correct signpost for anyone else doing research from your work. You've also verified a nice, little gate opened for your own trek when you choose to walk through it. You'll thank yourself in the morning. And those future "yous" will thank you for decades to come.

Do You Have Standards?

"Oh, c'mon. Is sloppy genealogy that bad? After all, this is just for the family."

Did that thought cross your mind? I don't blame you. You have a point. Yes, for your family history writing purposes, your genealogical work is to be used more as background than important documents preserved for the future (unlike your family history volume), but even the background has to be done right, or the family history might be wrong.

Still, I suppose you could put a disclaimer at the beginning of your work to the effect that, "The contents of this volume are not verified in full." But really, that won't work very well, either. If you decide to let some unverified work go and think no one will notice, believe this—the moment your family history is in print, someone will take it as fact, error or not, because of the authority of print, unless they are fortunate enough to have firsthand information as I did with my granny. And don't think for a minute that someone won't find all your genealogical work and believe everything you researched, too, whether it was done in pencil or pen.

> **Deep Thought**
>
> *Our ancestors led full, historically rich lives.*

But What About a Great Story?

Of course, there will be stories you cannot verify that are too good not to mention, but there are ways to make sure the reader knows the legendary nature of the stories which we'll talk about later. There are ways to handle the stories you cannot throw back and yet cannot, in all good conscience, state as fact. We'll discuss such strategy in our writing section later in the book. For now, as you learn the genealogical ropes, concentrate on technique and form. Within a matter of weeks, you'll be glad you took the time to learn the groundwork right.

Journaling Along the Genealogical Trail

Still have that family/county/town history open? Open your journal and do your own evaluation of a profile of which you have some personal knowledge, as I did. Make the "good/bad/sloppy genealogy" judgments as you learned in this chapter for each fact and figure. Also, make a list of good leads you find.

The Least You Need to Know

➤ Your ancestors' names are not unique and constant double-checking is needed to keep you on the right ancestral track.

➤ Not everything in print is correct.

➤ Sloppy genealogy will be noticed and can ruin your family history.

➤ Practicing high standards as a beginning genealogist will pay off in spades later.

Chapter 8

Where to Begin

In This Chapter

➤ Where you need to begin and how

➤ Why you should cherish Crazy Aunt Edna

➤ How to start planning those interviews

A sea of sources stretches out before you—primary, secondary, oral, written, hidden, lost, stored away, and out in the open. Ready to find out if you'll sink or swim? Well, let's go ahead and take the plunge, but let's make your first big splash into the research sea easy and fun—as well as educational—by practicing with a person you know very, very well. Where do you begin your step back into your ancestry? You begin with yourself. Most genealogy how-to books will agree that this is where everyone should begin, but since we're all writers here, we're going to take that advice and go one step further.

To help you along I've included four tips within the chapter to keep your feet on the ground, called "Steps Back." These will prove invaluable as you search! Grab your family history journal and let's go.

First Step Back

Interview yourself. Begin with all you know.

All About You

What do you see in the mirror? That person looking back at you is the culmination of centuries of ancestry. Every generation you are going to be researching leads to you.

Looking at it that way, doesn't it make sense to start with yourself? Besides, this is one genealogical entry that shouldn't have any gaps. After all, you know everything there is to know about yourself.

So, pull out an empty Individual Ancestor Record and open your journal. List the facts first—birth date, whether you are married or divorced, full names of spouses, parents, siblings, children, and all their "vital" dates and places.

Then, around these vital records, fill in the "who" (that's you), "what," "when," and "where" of your life—the good stuff you want to share, the kind of things you'd love to uncover about the people from the past who made you. Keep these vital records in front of you, while we try an exercise for a creative writing jump-start.

The Late, Great You

Imagine that you find your own obituary in a genealogical newspaper. Be proud. You have been a very prominent person, a famed genealogist and family history expert known throughout the land. Someone who has known you all your life has decided to put all your information down for posterity, and to put it down in a style all genealogists will recognize. If your name happened to be Josephine Jean Jones and you married a man named Joseph Jonathan (Joe) Schmoe V, then the article would look a little like this:

> Josephine Jean (Jones) Schmoe, second child and first daughter of Jerrell Jacob and Julia Jane (Quattlebaum) Jones was born 8 June 1949 in Tupelo, Mississippi, confirmed 10 November 1949 at the Trinity Episcopal Church of Tupelo; married 22 January 1970 by Harold Higgins Hightower, Justice of the Peace, Chicago, Illinois, to Joseph Jonathan (Joe) Schmoe V, born 26 September 1970 in Waco, Texas, the youngest child and second son of Joseph John (Joe) Schmoe IV and Susan Sara (Smith) Schmoe.

Notice the unusual way that the obituary was written? It's not a normal obituary style, but it certainly does match the genealogical style you learned in Chapter 6, "Tools for the Task."

What else might an obituary offer you? Imagine the rest of the article running something like this:

> Josephine, an orphan at age 6, was raised by her uncle, a travelling salesman, and overcame a lack of normal education to receive a college scholarship, obtaining a Ph.D. in Nuclear Physics. She met her future husband on submarine duty. After a career-ending accident, she and her husband returned to Texas and ran a feed store in China Fay's, Texas, and lived off the land and became an institution in the area's first Yoga training center. She is survived by one daughter, Amy Lou.

Your Turn

Okay, now it's your turn. Use your journal to take a stab at writing your own obituary. Picture yourself as your own closest, dearest buddy. You are writing the first paragraph of your (The Late, Great You) genealogical obituary. Don't forget the form:

'Riting Reminder

Don't forget genealogical style—day, month, year (15 September 1919).

➤ Use full name, no abbreviations

➤ If female and married, list maiden name in parentheses

➤ Be specific about birth order and gender

➤ List parents' names in the full genealogical way

➤ List birthplace and date, as well as marriage place and date

➤ List full name of spouse and spouse's parents

➤ List home of your parents and your spouse's parents

➤ List offspring in genealogical way

➤ Use no abbreviations, no initials

Proving Your Existence

How'd it go? If you did nothing else but leave that little paragraph behind for future generations, it would be a gift in itself. You'll see how true this is once you start looking for this very kind of information on each of your ancestors. With this exercise, you've essentially started a Family Group Record. But did you use pencil? Because now you have to prove all this information.

"What?" I hear you say. "Pencil? I know when I was born." True enough. And the "writer" of your obituary no doubt knew all those facts, too, since he or she knew you all your life. But from a genealogical research perspective, that's still hearsay. You're a genealogist now. And you have to show documentation.

So get out your birth certificate and let's take a good look. When you have it in your hands, note

A Relatively Good Idea

1. Don't have a copy of your birth certificate?

   ➤ Write the courthouse of the county where you were born (or the responsible state agency), giving all the needed information, including your full name and date of birth.

   ➤ Ask for a notarized copy of your birth certificate.

2. Do you have birth certificates for members of your family? Are they stored somewhere safe?

that other handy information is also on it for any ancestral fact search. See a hospital name? See a doctor's name? See what I mean?

This Is Your Life!

After such a fine, full opening paragraph (now documented with your own personal paper trail), adding highlights and memorable moments of your life should come easily and quickly.

Write a sentence or two adding one moment of your life, then let it simmer. (Use that journal.) Then jot a note about another. The ideas will come. Try it.

Remember, you're just writing a nice article about this person (which happens to be you) to go with the rest of the opening paragraph's information. You've read a million of these types of articles—short but entertaining and often poignant, obituary. Begin with the usual life highlights—graduations, birth, death, accomplishments, but then stretch your memory and jot down what comes to you.

Write down the ordinary things, the memories that make good stories. Think of the audience for your extended "obit" and do some "editorial commentary." The connections you'll make will be fun to write and to read, a great tune-up to all the writing to come.

Let's say that your great-great-great-grandfather was a circuit rider for the Methodist church, riding between churches in a Missouri county. He left behind some sermons, a well-worn Bible with a family tree in it, and a notation in a family history volume about being an upstanding citizen in his frontier town. What he didn't leave behind is an account of his young orphan years during which he rode with the Pony Express before he was converted by a missionary of sorts on his route. The awful part about this dramatic segment of his saga is that it is lost. You'll never know about it, nor will anyone in your family, because once he was a preacher, he didn't think it was important to share that tough part of his life story ever again.

It's time to take out that journal again. What would you like your descendents not to miss knowing about you? Choose three pieces of hard data about yourself, accomplishments or experiences, and put them into your journal, both for yourself and for those future relatives.

Now, add three pieces of "soft data" about yourself, such as personal philosophies, defining characteristics, lifelong hobbies, and personal challenges.

Writer's Block?

Got a little bit of writer's block after this first salvo? No problem. Look through your papers, letters, diaries, the things on your walls, the books on your shelves, the trophies in places of honor. These may conjure up personal anecdotes.

Aim for a page or so, then keep writing as the stories come for as long as they come. Then, think about connections. As a writer, this is the magic. What reflection pops into your mind? Listen to your inner voice as the memories come to you. That little voice will help you make some connections a little more solid.

One friend of mine says he can tell his life story around wheels. He mapped out his whole life through anecdotes about his vehicles—tricycle, bicycle, motorcycle, high school hot rod, sensible station wagon, suburban minivan, then back to the reconditioned classic hot rod—every set of wheels inspiring a revealing personal glimpse of the seasons of his life.

You and I can do the same. Once, in talking to my grandmother while we sat on her front porch, she walked me through the twentieth century through her eyes with only a few sentences. As a jet went overhead, she said it was as if she had sat on her front porch and seen it all. Indoor plumbing? Come on in! Electricity, radios, washing machines, iceboxes, refrigerators, come on in! Television! Please! Come right in! In one lifetime, she had watched the world leave the farm and go to the moon.

Yourself in History's Parade

Seeing yourself in the parade of history is a terrific way to segue your "genealogical obituary" into a personal oral history. Think of your first kiss. Or the vacation you spent squeezed in the back seat with your sister. Or the family get-together you'll never forget.

> **Deep Thought**
>
> *Think of a memory right now in connection with an event or development in world history. What is it? What made you think of it? Record it in your family history writing journal.*

(Hey, didn't that remind you of the Thanksgiving when your brother and brother-in-law got into a chest-bumping argument over the outcome of the turkey day football game?) What other memories just popped into your mind? Pull out that journal and capture those stories while they're fresh on your mind.

See how this works? One memory will remind you of another. Chapter 17, "Evoking Your Memories," will keep this motor revving, but for now, just take it around the block.

Picking Your Own Brain

Well, there's your quick writing sample of genealogical style and family history storytelling using yourself. When you've depleted yourself of all the facts and figures that you know now—as well as a nice starting chunk of oral history—then it's time to think about what you know about all your relatives.

What hard data do you know about your parents, grandparents, aunts, and uncles—your whole extended family? I'm talking dates, places, and things like occupations and affinities. You have to start the research sometime concerning everyone else in your family. It might as well be from picking your own brain before you jump into documenting the paper trail.

Where did your maternal grandmother live? What was her full name? Where was your mother born? Pick your brain and jot down the pickings you find, first in your journal and then in your "tools for the task."

Filling In/Filling Out

Pull out your pedigree chart and fill in, in pencil, as described in Chapter 6, every bit of information you can come up with, for as far back as you can, from your own memory. If you have a computer genealogy program, now might be a good time to print out a few of the charts and records that it offers so that you can jot down your information as you think of it.

How far back can you go without any help, just penciling in information from memory? One generation? Two? Do you already have gaps? Don't be surprised. Gaps are there to be filled. By the time you've finished picking your brain about your family's vital records, you should have a good start on your pedigree chart as well as several of your family group records and individual ancestor records. Now it's time to begin contacting your relatives to see how much of what you think you know is true, and to find out what you didn't know about them that will fascinate you. Start with your parents.

Second Step Back

Look backward to your parents.

Look Backward

Mom and dad are, of course, the first relatives you should interview. Let them know you're coming (figuratively or literally), and your need for "proof," i.e., vital records. That will give them a chance to do some searching. (We'll dig around in their attic and closets in the next chapter.)

If their parents—your grandparents—are no longer living, then your mom and dad are probably the ones who have many of the handed-down important documents you need to get started. Granny's or Great Uncle Homer's personal papers might include funeral records, newspaper clippings, birth, death, baptism, bar mitzvah, property deeds, and letters. And if mom or dad can't remember all their grand-parents' or great-grandparents' names and dates, you can probably find them in these records.

After your first foray down memory lane with your folks, circle in pencil the blanks on your first pedigree chart/family tree you still need to fill in, then pull out the family address book.

Third Step Back

Look to both sides. Look to your siblings, aunts, uncles, great-aunts and -uncles, your granddads, and your grandmas.

Look to Both Sides

Now it's time to call all your siblings, aunts, uncles, every last living relative you know. Right now you are searching for information—mainly for vital record information, the foundation of your future genealogical search of your living relatives and of every last one of your deceased ancestors.

Considering how much time you have and the convenience or inconvenience of another visit, try separating the visits into those for an oral history interview and others for the searching of documents. (We discuss that in the next chapter.) Make the first trip focus on the primary sources concerning your long-gone ancestors your family may have in their possession. Make the second trip an interview, including a tape recorder, to allow you relative time to think (and dig deeper into old boxes).

Prime the Pump

Go ahead and prime the pump, of course, for your stories. When you speak to those relatives on the phone about their pieces of the paper trail, tell them that you'll be talking to them very soon about family stories, so they should be thinking about their favorites. Ask them if they would mind digging around in their closets and attics for old documents.

Considering that the average American extended family is scattered all over the country, you may be doing mostly long-distance talking, so there may only be a chance for one visit, and perhaps only one or two contacts by phone, so patience and persistence are as vital as the vital records you desire.

And even if you are able to set up two visits with certain pivotal relatives, making a later date for their oral history interviews, be sure and take your tape recorder to both. No way will you want to stop a belly-laughing Aunt Cissy from telling you the great anecdote about Grandpa Fred she just remembered when she pulled a certain old postcard from his personal papers.

Another Good Reason to Bug Relatives

A major reason for reaching out to everyone still living in your family goes beyond the obvious accumulating of stories and mining of Aunt Cissy's memory. Governmental agencies, by law, refuse to release records earlier than 72 years after their creation, so your extended family may be the only way you can acquire the vital records needed to get past this generation to the next.

So, go ahead and call. Your Crazy Aunt Edna will be glad to hear from you.

The Homesteaders

Any relative that has lived in the same place most of his/her life can be a treasure trove. If Crazy Aunt Edna still lives in the bungalow on Fourth Street she moved into in 1946, it's a safe bet that she has thrown very little, if anything, away.

I have vivid memories of my own "Crazy Aunt Edna" who was my favorite aunt as a kid just because she *was* crazy. No one ever visited without being subjected to the pile of scrapbooks that she stored next to her old electric organ in the corner. We had no choice. We were going to look at her scrapbooks. We all loved it the first time and hated it the dozens of times afterwards, especially as young adults. Now, of course, those scrapbooks would be a perfect example of a family story treasure trove and perhaps even some documentation.

A Relatively Good Idea

Things to say to Crazy Aunt Edna:

➤ You're writing a family history and wonder if she has any documents or personal papers that show names, dates, and places of births, deaths, and marriages.

➤ You'd like to know more about her side of the family, especially if she knows family stories to tell and has heirlooms to show.

➤ You truly would like to see her scrapbooks.

➤ Yes, you'd like some more iced tea and Jell-O salad.

Travelling (Too?) Light

I keep thinking about the retired couple I met recently while walking my dog. They told me they had moved to California to get out of the Chicago winters, just as I had, and before I knew it, I was listening to their life stories standing there on the sidewalk. What struck me most, however, was the big step they took when they retired and moved. They sold everything to save the thousands of dollars for moving expenses. They now lived in a condo with rented furniture.

While that must have been incredibly freeing for them, I couldn't help wondering what happened to all those years of memorabilia. Did they save any of it? Will the next generation of their family wonder the same thing in a few years? Our society is so mobile and our retired parents are so lively that the "homesteaders" of the family are becoming an endangered species—all the more reason to cherish them from a family historian's point of view.

Cherishing Crazy Aunt Edna

If your Crazy Aunt Edna and Uncle Leroy are like mine, they'll need help in staying on the trail for these vital records. Rambling can be good for oral history interviews, so don't stop them; just remember to turn on the tape recorder you brought just in case the stories began to flow.

But you should do some "guiding" on this first "paper trail" visit. Ask for exact names, dates, places, old forms or keepsake documents, books, letters, even old receipts—anything from any relative about any (and I mean, any) other relative. The stories will naturally come as your relatives go through old documents. Each piece leads to other pieces, each source leads to other sources, but the basics have to come first—names, dates, places.

Plan to take good notes and ask for copying privileges. Don't be surprised if Aunt Cissy states emphatically, "Grandma Frudigger's family Bible is not leaving this house!" No one's going to let you take any important documents, but maybe they'll go with you to copy them or, at the very least, allow you to transcribe them under their watchful eyes.

Reticent Relatives

Granddad may act like he doesn't want to tell you a few things. You asked about a brother you didn't know he had, and the man clammed up. What might that mean? He could be tired, he could not be much of a storyteller. Maybe his memory may not be as good as it used to be, and he's frustrated. Maybe you're coming on too strong, your enthusiasm getting the best of you. Or maybe there's an embarrassing event or some episode in his life that caused him pain. He and members of his family could have had a falling-out. Or maybe, just maybe, there is a family secret he is hiding.

A Relatively Good Idea

Your homesteader may appreciate some search suggestions: Review lists given in Chapter 5, "Climbing Your Family Tree," called "Where the Paper Is" and "What the Paper Is" to guide your initial phone contact with elderly relatives.

A Relatively Good Idea

Plan ahead to ...

➤ Take good notes and/or ask for copying privileges.

➤ See your elderly relatives first.

➤ Take a tape recorder.

➤ Take your journal and your charts and logs.

➤ Take some familiar memento or photos to break the ice.

Family Secrets

What might constitute a family secret? Before you get your hopes up, imagining a dramatically tragic tale or two, remember what we've said all along: The past is a different land. Often, another generation's family scandal is much less scandalous than you, citizen of the modern world, would think. A family scandal a century ago might be nothing more than an alcoholic—a "drunk"—in a strict, religious family.

'Riting Reminder

The past is a different land.

Remember the term "divorcee"? Haven't heard that one lately, especially since the divorce rate went sky high. Only a generation or two ago, though, a failed marriage was not just the heartache it is today, it was a black mark on the family. And the same can be said for an unwanted pregnancy, which not too long ago was called "having a child out of wedlock," and not long before that caused the wearing of scarlet letters and ousting from villages and church membership.

My point? The operative word in talking to someone with stories from another generation is sensitivity. Also a grasp of the past, and an expertise in how to ask questions will come in mighty handy. We'll be discussing both of these at length in the next two chapters. For now, let's move out into your community, an encouraging step you'll want to take while you are wooing those family story gems from your relatives near and far.

Fourth Step Back

Look locally for support, encouragement, and education.

Looking Around Town

The next step is to broaden out to experience the resources your own city can offer the beginning family history writer/genealogist. As you glean all you can from your family, a little hands-on encouragement can always help. Near you, there are probably good community resources, such as historical societies and genealogical groups. There also may be a surprising variety of libraries to visit, public and private. Chapter 11, "Looking in All the Right Places—Library and Beyond," will offer more detail into the universe to be explored through your local resources, but here are a few things to help you take this step confidently now.

Join a Genealogical Society

Wherever you live, you might want to consider joining a genealogical group. In your town, or a nearby city, there are enthusiastic and experienced genealogists who get a kick out of helping others. Networking becomes more and more important as you proceed further into your project. Often, there are local groups based on ethnic histories or nationalities. Take advantage of the CIGs (computer interest groups) of these genealogical societies. Again, there's nothing like a guiding hand when you're just starting.

Become a Library Regular

After you've exhausted all the family and local avenues, it will be time to go to the biggest local resource—your library. You've been there before, many times, but you're about to experience this special place in a whole new light. With journals, charts and unbridled enthusiasm, enter the doors of the repository of public information for your first genealogical research visit.

➤ **Library Beginner Tip #1:** Ask whether the library has a genealogical section or room and a librarian who specializes in genealogy.

➤ **Library Beginner Tip #2:** Ask whether there are special libraries nearby that might be geared specifically for genealogical research.

➤ **Library Beginner Tip #3:** Answer all the basic "vital record" questions possible before you visit the library. Have a specific task for each visit. Start small. Focus on finding one piece of the puzzle at a time.

➤ **Library Beginner Tip #4:** Check out your family's counties of residence at your local library. This will be basic the information needed throughout your genealogical treasure hunt—which county your ancestors' towns are located in. That's where lots and lots of those primary sources are waiting for you.

➤ **Library Beginner Tip #5:** Think city, county, state, national—in that order.

➤ **Library Beginner Tip #6:** Ask your librarian anything.

➤ **Library Beginner Tip #7:** Thank your librarian—often.

Looking "Home"

Any genealogical beginning will include "home"-work. Your home as a starting place is obvious, as the next chapter will show. But there will be a moment when you have to start looking toward your ancestors' hometowns. You will be polishing the travelling shoes mentioned in Chapter 5's overview. This is why geographical information is as important as vital records—for correspondence, for Internet searches, and also for real road trips. As you go further and further back in your genealogical timeline, you'll know what I mean.

For instance, your very first genealogical correspondence will probably be to write your county courthouse records for data and any historical society in the hometown. And when you finally make the trip to the most primary of sources, you'll be experiencing the real thing in the real place. You may talk to people who know your long-lost relatives. You may meet those long-lost relatives. You may touch documents filled out by your ancestors a century ago. You may even touch the old tombstone of an ancestor you didn't know existed. You can't get much more real than that. Chapter 12, "Looking in All the Right Places—in Hometowns," is all about the interesting things that can happen when you go "home" to your ancestors' hometowns.

Guess What?

Now you've seen a good sampling of ways to begin your own research. You've mined your memory and learned some more tricks of the genealogical trade. But best of all, you'll notice something as you read back through this chapter, something very important about your new family history research adventure ... You've begun.

Journaling Down the Genealogical Trail

Choose one of your grandparents. Take an empty Individual Ancestor Record and turn to a blank page of your journal. Try writing a genealogical obituary article for one of your grandparents as you did for the "The Late, Great You" exercise in this chapter.

The Least You Need to Know

➤ Every family history begins with you.

➤ Your elderly relatives should be interviewed first and soon.

➤ Successful library research requires a few basic, easy-to-remember steps.

➤ The past is a very different place from the present.

➤ Local genealogical groups will be glad to help you begin your research.

Looking in All the Right Places—at Home

Home. Of all the definitions you and I have heard for that word, there is also one you can create from your family history perspective. Home is where the memorabilia of your life is being created and stored as we speak. And remember that your stories surround you no matter how many homes you live in. You are creating a trail of your life, both on paper and otherwise—and that's how it is with everyone, your family members included, until the day you die when someone creates your death certificate, the end of the paper trail for you.

Beginning your family history research starts with looking in all the right places. So, the first "right" place is obviously home—your home and the homes of your family members—looking for stories through interviews, memories, memorabilia, heirlooms, and meaningful "junk."

In Your Memories

Right now, at this very minute, you are accumulating stories by the things you decide to keep. Photographs, school yearbooks, insurance documents, employment records, love letters, souvenirs—all of them tell a tale, however small, about your life. That Quantas airline ticket stub you saved has a story and your finding the stub reminds you of it. That snapshot of your new puppy will, years from now, make you laugh heartily while memories come flooding back. The Christmas cards you keep tell a silent story, each time you rediscover them, about friends and family and Christmases past.

Related Facts

We often save things for reasons of which we aren't consciously aware. Don't disregard the power of a little piece of paper to jog a memory. Those little ticket stubs and scraps with random names and notes scribbled down may just be the precursor to a story you did not want to forget. Open a drawer and choose a memory.

Jogging That Memory

In Chapter 8, "Where to Begin," you began your family history research by taking a firm family history fact and a firm family history action. Fact: The first place to start is with yourself. Action: Find your own vital records.

You've already scoured through your papers to find the proof of your own existence—such as your birth and marriage certificates. As you recorded your vital records, you found yourself thumbing through the other important papers of your life, and your memory no doubt was jogged as well. Memorable family moments came dancing through your mind. You told yourself you should be jotting these memories down, and you made a vow to keep your journal handy for that purpose. In fact, you got right up and went to find your journal. Pat yourself on the back. You are on your way.

Educated Eyes

Did you notice what happened as you moved through the house with your family history project on your mind? Your eyes are becoming family history oriented. As you walked down your hall, you suddenly looked around your home with educated eyes, wondering such things as, "What's in that box over there? And that drawer over here?" You make a mental note to check them all. You grab your journal and start back through the house.

Like a Whirling Dervish

So, as you walk through your house to retrieve your family history writing journal, you make more mental notes and you come to realize that your mental note file is getting a little full, don't you?

With excitement, you yank open a drawer to see what your newly educated eyes will find. What do you see? A postcard dated 1969 from your globe-trotting, hippie sister (now a CPA for a Fortune 500 company), a birthday card your father sent you last year, and a letter your favorite uncle wrote you when you graduated from college. You are suddenly happy to have kept them all because you realize that even the living pass through stages of their lives that stand alone, and those stages are full of moments that in and of themselves are worthy of recording.

Now you are inspired, and you hit your closets and storage files like a whirling dervish to see what you can find that tells a family tale. And when you finish, you will soon be doing the same at your parents' house.

A Relatively Good Idea

After you've told everyone that you are doing family history research, maybe it's time to call Cousin Bernie and see what he's already found. He may just be interested in the genealogy, not family stories, so each of your efforts may complement the other.

Heirlooms Tell Tales

Don't think for a moment that inanimate objects can't talk. It's just that they need us to interpret their message. Got your dust rag? It's time to go through your attic (or your storage equivalent). Let's see what you might find and what it might inspire.

Every Picture Tells a Story

Remember the day your dad brought over that old secretary that had once belonged to a maiden great aunt? Well, he left some old photographs in it, and you were smart enough to keep them. Such photographs are priceless for your efforts. Check them for details. Look for a date on the back. If they were professionally done, a photographer's name and studio might be printed on them. The older ones may even be old-time daguerreotypes, since maiden aunts have been known to keep many things from generations before theirs.

Photo Icebreakers

As Rod Stewart sang, every picture tells a story. Be they Kodak snapshots you've taken through the years or hand-me-down photos from another generation, each image is a moment frozen in time.

A Relatively Good Idea

Photographs are great additions to your research and your history writing, but they are also prone to being irreplaceable, so keep these tips in mind: Make copies of all of them, and write the names and dates on the back of your future heirloom personal photos with a felt-tip pen (*never* use pencil or ballpoint).

Do you have similar old photographs inherited from here, there, or everywhere? The ones you can't identify will be wonderful icebreakers for interviews with your older relatives. But even the ones you can identify can also do the same, as you and your relative laugh over Uncle Elroy having hair and Aunt Cissy having a waistline.

Odds are, if you continue to show these mystery pictures, some family member will sooner or later be able to identify "who" and "where" for you.

In fact, if your genealogical search takes you to meet a whole new branch of the family, perhaps left back in Virginia when your ancestor took your branch of the tree to California, they just might have some even earlier pictures of your shared ancestor to show you. You never know, and such shared moments are what make the effort worthwhile.

Lurking Pieces of the Past

What else have you found? Quilts? Needlepoint from an artistic ancestor? Jewelry? Pieces of the past can be anywhere.

One great example of a memory storehouse is a jewelry box. Think about it. What do you keep in the bottom drawer of yours? My longtime jewelry box was a mother-of-pearl beauty that my husband bought in the Holy Lands and gave to me before we became engaged. It became the one place in our house, beyond a locked, fireproof, metal box we used for our records, that remained the same no matter how many times we moved. A look in that bottom drawer was always a nostalgic glance at every fad necklace, mismatched earring, and cherished silver dollar I saved.

Everybody's Jewelry Box

What did I find in my jewelry box when I looked with my educated eyes? I found the pocket-sized picture of the bridal photo I handed out at my wedding. To look at it now made me smile at my pride and my naiveté, but it's certainly a piece of my past. Underneath it, I found a pocket watch I gave my husband when they were a short-lived fad. It has an inscription on it. I'd forgotten I'd given it to him on our fifth wedding anniversary.

Go on, take a peek in yours. And while you're at it, certainly don't forget to take a peek in your mom's or grandma's. That silver pin might hold a story of young love, that pearl necklace a story that might rival "The Gift of the Magi," and those love beads may echo back a whole decade of 1960s' memories.

Such are the stories of the objects of your life that you are going to bid speak for your family history book.

Old Junk Tells Tales, Too

One person's junk is another person's treasure. That's the motto of every garage sale. But let's amend that to read, "One person's junk is another person's memories."

As we all know, memorabilia doesn't have to be qualified as heirlooms or antiques in order to be important keepsakes. "Junk" can be just as important for family history purposes. Sure, these may be things that other people would consider trash and toss sooner or later, but that's only because they don't feel the personal connection you do. Letters, recipes, teenage diaries, news clippings, trophies, baby books ... the list of the "junk" memorabilia that you might find is endless. But just remember this: Everything you turn up has the power of turning from trash into gold through your educated eyes.

'Riting Reminder

Nothing is junk for you. Keep repeating that to yourself as you start down the research trail, otherwise you might regret tossing aside that ugly piece of kitsch once you discover it was the first present from your grandfather to your grandmother!

My sister graduated from high school during an autograph-book fad. Some enterprising company designed an autograph book for high school seniors complete with places for snapshots, autographs, and written sentiments from your best buddies and your old sweethearts (as if we didn't write all there is to say in our yearbooks). If one of her autograph-book-signing classmates turned out to be a Hollywood superstar, of course this autographbook would be worth much more than memories. But for my sister, the sight and sound of the note from her last high school boyfriend is reason enough to hold on to the little book. And no doubt it can remind her of an anecdote or two.

What Comes Around Goes Around

What is extremely fascinating, however, to take note of as you begin your search through old and new family memorabilia is the nature of fads—they come and they go and they come again.

In this case, when you begin to dig back through the generations, you could actually find an autograph book from the nineteenth century, owned by a young ancestor who used the book in the same way my sister did in the 1970s. And the comparison you might make about what it says about the eternal aspects of youth from any century is great material for a family history writer.

You never know what effect the objects of our lives have had on us until you explore them. One day my brother-in-law picked up the baby books collecting dust in his den, turned to the family tree pages and, for fun, began to fill in all he could with what he already knew. And when he couldn't fill in a few of the gaps, he began to ask his relatives for the remaining answers. Before he knew it, he had become a genealogist—all because of his children's baby books. Think about what a good story that would make for his family history volume.

Mom and Dad's Attic

Of course, some of your own childhood's important stuff may still be in your parents' attic. So, while it's true that you'll be visiting their attic for the stuff of their stories, also remember to walk down your own memory lane while you're there. You may be surprised what's still there and what it will evoke.

Marbles, watches, old coin purses, Superman comic books—don't overlook anything. You just might find a lot of your old heirlooms waiting for you (unless your mom got hooked on garage sales after you left the house), like that Barbie doll and your starter coin collection. (Surely that Mercury head dime is worth a fortune by now.)

A Relatively Good Idea

When you visit your parents' attic with your mom or your dad, remember to take your time and to take notes. Everything will inspire a memory. Take a small tape recorder and leave it running as you open boxes, wipe off the dust, sneeze, laugh, and share.

I'll never forget the moment I realized the potential monetary value of all those Superman comic books I saved throughout my childhood. I had all of them, including all those ancillary ones such as "Action Comics" and "Supergirl." (My father owned a drugstore that had a comic rack. Enough said.)

So, I called Mom about those comics, and what did she say? "Oh, those. I sold them at last spring's garage sale for a nickel apiece to Harvey Ledbetter who seemed delighted. He took every one."

Saved from Garage Sale

Never leave anything at the "old house" that you even vaguely think you might ever want to see again. You may think you don't have the room to carry around that Little League trophy or that old wooden tennis racket you bought with your own money, but if it's important to you, then do not pass go and do not collect $200. Go get it now.

But what if it's too late, you ask? Well, take out that journal and jot down any anecdotes inspired by the memory of those nostalgic objects before the memories are gone, too because that's all you have left of them.

With Your Parents into the Past

Be prepared for a revelation once you get your parents rummaging in their attics and closets and drawers. Anything can happen when you start tromping around in the past.

Let's say that your mom picks up an old frame holding a picture of her parents that she inherited from your grandmother. She decides to open the back to see if there is a date on it and what does she find but another photo behind it—and neither of you recognize the people in it. Obviously your frugal grandmother had slipped the picture in front of this other photo to save the cost of a new frame. So now you and your mom have a shared mystery to unravel. Then one of you notices an old painting leaning against a stack of boxes, and both of you head right over to open the back of it, too.

> **Deep Thought**
>
> What is one piece of wonderful "junk" from your past? Why does it mean so much to you?

"Großmama's" Glass

A glass, a chipped gravy boat, an ugly statuette—all of these things can give you a perfect family history story. Don't miss any chance to point at objects throughout a relative's house and ask for their significance. You never know what you'll hear.

> **A Relatively Good Idea**
>
> Don't forget to check the kitchen and the china cabinets. Old recipe books, recipe cards, and even china, crystal, and silver can evoke strong family memories.

My husband's great-great-grandmother (they called her Großmama, pronounced *grossmama*) came to America from Germany as a teenager. She brought with her, among other things, a set of chunky, hand-painted glasses. After her long life, only these few things remained of her "Old World" belongings. My husband-to-be, the all-American teenage boy, along with his cousins, also all-American teenage boys, didn't hear about these glasses until after his great-great-grandmother's funeral when his father and his three aunts and uncles were discussing the future of these glasses. There were four of them and five of the glasses.

The discussion over the future home of the extra glass was getting more and more intense, such were the deep feelings for "Großmama's" heirloom. Finally, one of my husband's cousins had had enough of all this fuss over a glass, and decided to take a look himself. He walked over, picked up the glass, and immediately dropped it on the hardwood floor—which brought a crashing solution to the problem without another word.

There's a nice hand-me-down end of the story, by the way. Last year, after my father-in-law's funeral, my husband brought home his father's German Großmama's glass and it is now in our china cabinet, story attached.

At Weddings and Funerals

Family get-togethers happen yearly. Were you planning to go to the one this year? No? Change your mind. That cousin's daughter's wedding coming up may be quite a long drive, but now the time will be worth it, because it is the perfect place to spread the word of your research to your extended family. (In fact, it's not a bad idea to bring some cards with your phone number and e-mail address, if you have one, to pass out in case you find someone who is eager to tell tales.)

Weddings are happy events and naturally create some vivid family history stories to immortalize in your family history book, but funerals, strangely enough, may be even more fruitful for your effort.

'Riting Reminder

Keep a hand-held tape recorder with you for all family gatherings. You'll never be able to write everything down as people begin to reminisce, and you'd hate to lose those great stories to a lapse of memory!

While funerals may seem to be the last place to swap family stories, in reality, it's one of the best. Why? Because when we lose a family member, the survivors want to share, bond, and remember the moments that they will forever keep of their loved ones, and they'll want to hear the others' memories so they can cherish those, too.

You'll notice this "dynamic" in the members of the community who drop by to pay their respects, too. Old neighbors, business associates, and church and synagogue friends will come out of the woodwork to tell you stories about the deceased. As if they are handing you offerings, they give you all they can give without knowing it's the best thing they can give— their memories of your relative. And those are the kinds of treasures no money can buy and no research can top.

Cleaning Out Mama Lee's House

Funerals also become times when the effects of the deceased need to be gone through, handed down, and cleared out. These moments can be painful, especially for the family members closest to the deceased.

After my grandmother's funeral, we realized that since we were all together, we should go to her house and help with this difficult task. My grandmother, whom we all called Mama Lee, was a woman of extremely modest means. Nice things, things we'd call essentials, came late to her life. But any life lived as long as hers is full of meaningful objects, and we all knew this was a moment that would never come again, however awkward it might feel invading a place still so full of her spirit.

One of my sisters, who had felt close to Mama Lee in ways the rest of us didn't, could not bring herself to go. One of the nephews took an old rocker. I found a tarnished locket given to my grandmother on her seventh birthday by her father, my great-grandfather whom I'd never met. The other cousins and sisters who were all leaving the next day for homes spread all across the country did the same, finding at least one thing of Mama Lee's to take with them. As we turned to go, one of us picked up a white pitcher to take to the sister who couldn't bring herself to come.

Seeing the objects so full of our grandmother in that little house suddenly made it unthinkable that the sister who could not make herself come would miss being a part of the experience—an experience which became for all of us that sad day, a wordless sharing celebration of the woman's long, loved life. We all wished for her, because of the shared closeness we felt.

A Relatively Good Idea

Think back to the last funeral of a family member. Do you remember a friend of the family telling you a cherished memory while offering condolences? What was it?

Deep Thought

Have you had a family member die recently? Pause and think of one moment you had with him or her and why you remember that one most of all.

That afternoon's experience itself is a family story, as is each object we took into our own lives. Each item will become a part of the life of another branch of the family tree, which one day, with any luck, will find its way to the next branch as well—in celebration of Mama Lee.

Too Many Funerals

There is a time when such moments seem to come fast and furious. The American way of death, contrary to some of the world's wiser cultures, seems to mute the celebration of a life lived.

A Relatively Good Idea

Name one hand-me-down object that is a celebration of a loved one's life gone by. What would be the story it could tell?

So, our unnamed way of celebration seems to be in the objects that are lovingly passed along, not so much the expensive pieces (which we all know can cause unfortunate tug-o-wars, even in the happiest of families), but in the objects possibly worthless, yet personally priceless.

Crazy Aunt Edna's Stories and Why You Hated Them

Of course, your Crazy Aunt Edna will be at every wedding and funeral. You used to groan when you saw her. She would inevitably leave a big, red, lipstick smear on your cheek, give you a bosom-busting hug, and tell everyone within earshot how she once powdered your little bottom.

You hated Edna's stories for all the right adolescent reasons. She was always telling stories about your family that embarrassed you—even the ones that weren't about you embarrassed you. Why did your family have to be so … colorful?

But now, colorful is exactly what you want. And if you're lucky, Crazy Aunt Edna is still around to retell her colorful stories. It's time you paid her a visit, with tape recorder and notebook in hand.

Interviewing (Crazy Aunt Edna Has Her Day)

The day has come. Your first interview with your elderly relative. How will this turn out? That probably depends on how prepared you are and how much of a storyteller your interviewee is. It may also depend on how interested the relative is in seeing his or her stories in print.

As a family history researcher, you will experience all sorts of responses to visits with their extended family members, especially the elderly ones, who, of course, happen to be the most valuable for your purposes. You'll experience the reluctant interviewee, the family member who believes she is too boring to be the subject of an interview, and the questionable interviewee, the one who tells tales you aren't quite sure are believable. How do you handle these?

The Reluctant Interviewee

Granny Schmoe is very, very reluctant to talk to you after hearing about your project. You can't understand why. She has always been so full of life, such a role model for you, but she dodged you at least a half-dozen times at Great-Aunt Joyce's funeral.

Finally, Uncle John explains to you what is wrong. Granny has just lost her sister Joyce and isn't feeling very well herself lately. Granny Schmoe thinks you believe she's going to die soon and so you want to get her talking before she goes. All she can hear in your words is her own mortality, and she doesn't like it.

This sort of situation takes a lot of sensitivity. How do you handle Granny Schmoe? All things now considered, her sister's funeral was probably not the place to bring it up.

> **Deep Thought**
>
> *The prime component for good interviewing: sensitivity.*

On the other hand, the moment Great-Great-Aunt Bebe, who just turned 92, hears about your project, she corners you. "When are you going to tape me? I got lots to tell before I go." Your eyebrows rise and your jaw drops. Great-Great-Aunt Bebe lived through the Holocaust, joined the family through marriage after finding her way to the United States, and was famous for refusing to talk about the horrid past. You look from your granny to your great-great-aunt, and then back again, totally confused. You would never have guessed this situation would arise.

You've learned the most valuable skill in acquiring interviews with your family members—sensitivity. What do you do? You set up your interview with Great-Great-Aunt Bebe and you give Granny Schmoe a hug, deciding to give her a little time.

The "Boring Life" Interviewee

Some of your potential interviewees will only shrug when you suggest an interview. "Oh, I don't have anything interesting to tell you," they might say. "I just got married, raised four kids, and led a quiet life." What do you say in response?

You assure them that their memories will be deeply interesting, that you also want to hear their memories of other family members whom they might think more exciting. You can also suggest that they'll only have to respond to some questions, if that will make them feel more at ease.

The wonderful side effect of your research is that during the course of these interviews and later in your family history writing, everyone—even those who believe they've led boring lives—can begin to see that their impact on the family has been invaluable, however quiet or subtle or seemingly boring it may seem.

The Believable Interviewee

Can you believe what you will hear in these interviews? Yes and no. You'll need to attempt verification even on oral histories. Why? Obviously, when Aunt Edna and Cousin Beula remember the same story different ways, that's a tip-off that someone's memory is a bit faulty. Or they might both be right—from their viewpoints. We'd probably be surprised how different our memories are of the same realities experienced with other people, if we had a chance to compare them.

Some experts even believe that no memory is exactly the way the real event happened. While it is happening, we are already reworking the experience through our own filters. There could be truth in that. No one really knows why we remember some things and forget others, or how we can experience an event differently from the person sitting right by us, but it happens.

Do we forget more as we get older? Someone older once quipped, "Sure we do, because we have more to forget and more that we want to forget." We don't know exactly what triggers memory. While writing this, I thought of an old theater in Ft. Worth, Texas, 20 years ago. I can see it clearly. What brought that up from my memory files? A smell? A word? A sound? After a look around, I still have no idea.

You know what I mean. Almost any baby boomer can hear a Beatles song, for instance, and instantly be able to sing along, knowing every lyric by heart decades after first learning them through sheer repetition. And with each song, some teenage memory is surely stuck like glue. Then, there are the times we even recreate scenes to help us cope with an experience and then forget we've done it, believing the stories we recreate and forgetting what is fact. (Confess—you've done it.)

So, can we believe what we hear in these interviews? Yes, no, and maybe.

'Riting Reminder

Here is a "Fact-Check List" to begin an interview:

1. What's your full name?
2. Where were you born and when?
3. What were your parents' names?
4. Who's the oldest living person you can remember in your family?
5. From what countries did your ancestors immigrate?

It will be your prerogative as the writer to decide whether to use a story that can't be proven (and we'll deal with that in a later chapter), but first let's get the stories recorded. And that calls for a tape recorder and an afternoon with your Aunt Edna.

Top Ten Interviewing Tips

Here are a few valuable interviewing tips. Remember them as you begin this important part of your family history work.

1. **Decide between videotaping and audiotaping.** This may actually be decided for you. A close friend's nephew is a professional cameraman. One Thanksgiving, he decided to videotape the family altogether. For a while it was fun, even for the grandfather of the group. Finally, Granddad walked over to him, gave him his legendary scowl, and said, "That's enough, Marcus. Turn that danged thing off!" "Of course," said my friend, "that's the prized moment on the videotape. I duped it and sent a copy to everybody." Such a granddad wouldn't allow a videotape interview. On the other hand, Crazy Aunt Edna no doubt would consider it her very own CNN interview, love every minute of it, and get dressed to the nines for the occasion. A videotape of a relative can become an heirloom in itself. Sometimes, for interviewing purposes, however, the camera can seem like an intruder while a cassette recorder can go almost unnoticed. Remember the prime interviewing skill—sensitivity. If you do decide to videotape, bring another family member to be in charge of the equipment.

2. **Jot down leading questions before you arrive.**

3. **Ask your interviewee to gather old documents and pictures that you can look at together.** These help evoke vivid memories and wonderful taped moments.

4. **Select a quiet place.** Or ask for the interviewee's favorite place and set up there. Good choices include the dining table or a sofa.

5. **Check the equipment. Take extra batteries and tapes.** If you want to be very sure, bring two tape recorders. Ask a trial question ("What is your full name, Aunt Edna?"), then play it back to be sure that your equipment is functioning.

6. **Always take a notepad, too, and take notes as you go.**

7. **Listen well.** Cultivate the art of listening. Ask questions about what you hear. Watch the interviewee's body language. Make eye contact, show your interest in nods, laughs, frowns—whatever is appropriate. It's a small thing, but it really helps.

8. **Don't overwhelm.** Don't worry about getting everything in one visit. A series of short interviews is the best way, if geographically possible. You can always come back.

9. **Before you go, write on the tape the details of the interview—who, what, and where.** Then, begin each tape by repeating the same information onto the tape, plus the order of the tape, e.g., Aunt Edna, Freestone, Idaho, Family History Interview, Tape 1, Side 2.

10. **Bring a few photos or other mementos along to help start the dialogue.**

Top Ten Interviewing Goofs

Of course, every interview is ripe for missteps. Let's look at a few and decide what would be the biggest mistakes you could make.

1. **Being a family member more than a family history interviewer.** Every family has a dynamic. There is love, but there are also mixed emotions about a lifetime of interaction. Can you interview a parent and see them as an individual? Can you see their lives as a whole, unattached from their role as your parent? Your interaction will set the tone, be it your parent or your uncle or your elderly cousin. Be the interviewer first; be the family member second. You'll see the difference immediately.

2. **Not having a specific agenda.** Try to have some research done before you go— basic pedigree chart work, dates, names, places—so you'll have a common frame of reference.

3. **Asking only general questions.**

4. **Jumping in at every sign of a pause.** Don't be afraid of silences. Let your relative think, contemplate, and muse. Good things may come from connections made over a long life.

5. **Not listening well.** Forgetting who is the interviewee and why you are there is a very big mistake.

6. **Not respecting the interviewee's right to refuse to answer.** Remember this is an interview, not an interrogation. Perhaps you should put your interviewees at ease by beginning each visit by stating that you are going to ask questions to stir memories and to inspire good conversation, but she does not have to answer any of them if she doesn't want to.

7. **Not bringing along someone to "man" the camera if you are videotaping.** You need to be focusing on guiding your interviewee into your family history tales.

8. **Not checking the tape occasionally to make sure it hasn't ended before you have. Not bringing along extra tapes. Not bringing along extra batteries or an AC converter plug.**

9. **Staying too long.**

10. **Not eating the sweet treat your elderly relative has made for your visit.**

How to Ask Interview Questions

Your questioning tone and style is a very big part of whether your interview is a success or a complete failure. Let's consider the difference between a good interview question and a bad one. The difference is in whether it is a leading question or not, for example:

1. Don't ask: "What was it like in the Depression?"

   Be more specific; ask: "What was the one thing you remember missing the most growing up in the Depression?" "Did you ever go without shoes?" "What would a nickel buy?"

2. Don't ask: "What was it like to have a daddy who was county sheriff?"

   Instead, ask: "Do you remember any times that your daddy was in danger as a sheriff?" "Or when he was in the newspaper?" "Did he wear a big cowboy hat?"

3. Not: "Was your mom a good cook?"

   Instead, ask: "What was one dish your mom made that you hated?"

If you make your queries leading questions, you may be surprised with a "You know, that reminds me of …" And you're off and running. Such specific questions leading from one to the other can't help but bring back memories.

Getting Children Involved

Granny Schmoe may still be somewhat reluctant to talk to you. But then you mention that your daughter wants to help so she can write a paper about it for school.

Granny lights up. "She's interested in the family?" Granny asks.

"Seems so," you say.

Granny suddenly agrees to be interviewed—by both of you.

Granny Schmoe is not unusual. Do you have a child, preteen, or teenager, who might be interested in tagging along on your interview? If so, and you feel comfortable with the idea, then definitely include your child. Often a feeling of "handing down" memories can be strong for an elderly family member if the child is interested in hearing family remembrances.

The dynamic will be different, of course, if a child is interviewing the adult, as for a school project like Granny Schmoe's granddaughter. You need to make the decision on how to handle this. Perhaps there need to be separate times and separate interviews. (If you aren't invited along, definitely ask your teenager to tape the interview so you can hear it later.) Or perhaps you can both interview the family member in a sort of conversation. Some great things may come from questions a child would get away with asking that you'd never have the nerve to broach. Then, with the door open, perhaps you can ask that one question you've always wanted answered.

Of course, this living family history interaction is good for your daughter or son, too. They remember everything, whether it seems like it or not, and they are hungry for stories, whether *you* still notice that or not. Most important, they are also hungry for "roots," whether *they* know it or not. Think what a positive impact it would be for your children to hear how the older people in their family lived through hardships as well as triumphs during another time in history very different from theirs.

Here are some thoughtful questions to begin an interview:

➤ Who were you named after and why?

➤ What's your earliest memory?

➤ What was the most exciting day you can remember growing up?

➤ Did your family tell stories when they got together?

➤ Did you have big family holidays? Who would come?

➤ What was your most favorite Christmas present?

Your Own Memories, Revisited

So, it bears repeating that you should be writing down your experiences with every interview and with every attic search.

Few are the family bonds that are not strengthened through these visits, discussing family memories in the quest of recording them for family posterity. You should attempt to capture your thoughts and how this is making you feel. Also, your own memories will continue to be jogged throughout your family history researching experience. Don't be surprised if you find yourself looking around Aunt Edna's house for something on which to write down your thoughts before you forget them. (The journal you brought along, perhaps?) Such memories and thoughts are the stuff you'll need, very soon, to bind all your separate genealogical anecdotes together.

Journaling Down the Genealogical Trail

You are about to visit an elderly relative with an interesting past. Perhaps she was an author. Perhaps he was a trial lawyer. Perhaps she married a war hero. Perhaps he was a preacher. What is the one question you'd like to ask? How might you ask it well? Jot down several ideas in your journal and rework them several times, adding and editing before your visit. After your visit, write another entry about what happened.

The Least You Need to Know

➤ Your own paper trail can evoke memories and teach research lessons.

➤ Your relatives' weddings and funerals are perfect settings for hearing family oral histories.

➤ Aunt Edna's scrapbooks are now priceless.

➤ Every object holds a family story.

➤ The skill of interviewing is much-needed and easily mastered.

Chapter 10

The Family Investigator on the Case

In This Chapter

➤ Why researching like a sleuth is a skill you'll need

➤ Why thinking like a historian is a skill you'll love

➤ Why compiling and reporting like a reporter is a skill you'll want

➤ How to learn these skills and when to use them

Think how helpful it would be if you could hire a detective, an historian, and a reporter to help you investigate your family history.

Well, believe it or not, that's exactly what you're going to do. How are you going to employ such professionals, you ask? (No, you don't have to get out your checkbook.) You're going to become all three yourself.

Uncovering clues like a detective, thinking like an historian, and checking facts like a reporter are easily acquired skills that will create an incredible difference in the quality of the work you, the writer, will be doing.

How to Research Like a Sleuth

Think of all the detective images that come to mind. Okay, now, throw away the tough talk, the fedora, the dark alleys, and the mysterious clients (maybe not the mysterious clients—some of your ancestors are certainly mysterious, especially

the long-lost ones). What you have left is the art of sleuthing, the gathering of facts. That's you, the family history sleuth, uncovering facts on the paper trail, using your sources.

Attacking your genealogical research with an image of yourself as a detective ferreting out clues to a mystery is a good tack to take, especially as you begin. You're already being quite sleuth-like. Think about it. Your first steps have been to identify what you already know, to decide what you want to find out, to choose one record you want to search for, to hunt down the record (asking for help when needed), and to write down every move in your research log and charts. Joe Friday and Sam Spade would both be proud of you.

Just the Facts, Ma'am

Sleuths use some of the same terminology as genealogists. You have primary sources that provide "straight from the horse's mouth" information—eyewitness stories that have happened to the person telling the story. And you seek out secondary sources that provide clues, hints of facts once removed (like cousins) that are hearsay.

Also, the detective hones in on one fact at a time and hopes others fall in his or her lap. By now, you know that's your first move, too. You choose a fact to hone in on, then the sleuth in you will turn that white-hot light of detective scrutiny on it. Why? Because good detectives always double-check their findings.

What sort of questions would a sleuth ask during a double-check? Here are some sleuth questions to ask about any piece of information:

➤ Is it from a primary source or a secondary source?

➤ If secondary, can it be traced to a primary source?

➤ Does it make common sense? Use your head. For instance, these items don't make sense: A birth date long before the person's parents were married perhaps. A mother who had 12 children in 10 years. A second wife married to a man before his first wife's death or their divorce. (Not unless he was a bigamist … which, come to think of it, would make a great family history black sheep tale.)

➤ Does the evidence point to the right person?

The Detective Double-Check

Got the answers to your sleuth questions for your selected fact? Good. Now you need to begin practicing the detective double-check by cross-referencing your facts with other facts. Reference books as indexes point the way for the sleuth to find records, such as probate files, obituaries, or naturalization papers as soon as the exact people are identified and identified well.

There are many ways to double-check your facts beyond your vital government records research, from family Bibles to Social Security indexes to Aunt Cissy's clear-as-a-bell memory. The only rule to double-checking is that you can't do it enough.

Digging Up Kin

"Missing persons" is certainly detective work. And in effect, that's what the distant relatives out on the far branches of your great, spreading family tree are—missing, at least from your world.

Here's an example: After talking to everyone in your family, you realize that your grandfather had another set of half-brothers and -sisters. His father had two wives, and his first wife died young. How do you find them?

The first sleuthing thing to do would be to ask your grandfather or any of his full siblings. But what if they are all gone? Or what if the ones remaining do little more than shrug in response to your question, either because of some old family grudge or the fact that they just lost touch. Do you give up? Not if that area of the family is one that intrigues you. Besides, a self-respecting detective wouldn't give up so easily.

'Riting Reminder

Why don't you take a second right now to make a little cheat sheet for yourself about sources? Whether it's on the front of your journal or stuck to your computer, put it somewhere you'll always see it so you always remember to double-check those sources.

A Relatively Good Idea

Always check primary sources against other primary sources, and check secondary sources against primary sources.

Private Eye Telecommuting

So, you decide to rely on a little oral history. There's a family hint that these half-siblings moved back to St. Louis where their mother was born two generations ago. Can you find them? Yes, you can, just like a private eye would. First, you'd try to locate the living relatives, especially if you have a name or two. Let's look at some of your sleuthing options:

➤ **Telephone directories.** Most public libraries have telephone books for most of the country's large cities. What if you find a few familiar names in the St. Louis one? Calling is not a good idea for your initial contact, but why not a letter? Zip codes are obtained easily enough, through the post office zip code lists or on the Internet.

A Relatively Good Idea

Resist the temptation to pick up the phone and call for initial contact. How would you feel if a stranger called you in the middle of a meal or your favorite television program claiming to be related to you?

➤ **City directories.** City directories were the precursors of telephone directories. They often listed cross-referenced street addresses, which would give names of neighbors who might have known your relatives. Some of the earliest ones also gave occupations as well as each adult living in the household. You can write to the library of the town where the family still live or have lived once and ask for help or use your local library resources.

➤ **Social Security Death Index.** The Social Security Death Index can also pinpoint branches of your family tree when family members have applied for death benefits—which means there had to be living relatives to gain such benefits.

➤ **Internet forums.** There are places on the Internet where you can post notices. As always with the Internet, doing so can either be an incredible waste of time or an incredible resource that connects you at the speed of cyberspace with the people you are looking for, and maybe much more. The sleuth in you must ferret through the rubble to find the gem.

The trick is to be as specific as possible or you may be doing a lot of chatting to people whose only relation to you is through Adam. Don't just say that you're interested in gaining information on the Schmoe family who once lived in Scranton. Is it Scranton, Pennsylvania, or Scranton, Ohio? Is it the Joseph Jacob Schmoe, or the Joseph Jonathan Schmoe? To be precise, it's Joseph Jacob Schmoe and his family lived in Peoria, Illinois, during the 1950s and what's more, they owned a drugstore. Add all that, and it can clear out pounds of rubble.

By the way, remember never to give any personal information on the Internet. That's what forums are for—a safe place to exchange information.

Here are some more tips for you:

➤ **Open letter.** Even an "open letter" in a hometown paper can help dig up kin or at least dig up someone who knew your kin. In small towns, until the last elderly person of a generation has died, someone will remember something about the Wilsons who owned the hardware store or the red-headed Treadways who went to the Methodist Church.

➤ **Alumni records.** Have any family knowledge about college graduates in those back branches of your family tree? Even if that ancestor only went off to college for a year, he may still be on some college mailing list somewhere. If he's still living, and even after his death, if any of his immediate family also attended, they may be on a mailing list, too. Alumni records are always a good place to look for information, and the alumni director is always on the job. Their job is to stay connected to all those thousands of alumni from now until eternity.

➤ **Wild goose chases.** Of course, again, wild goose chases are waiting everywhere. That's why those small facts, such as your great-grandfather's full name, are essential. This may seem obvious in a big city search, but it's also true in your ancestor's hometown, no matter what the size. The vital records you've accumulated—full names, deaths, marriages, places, and dates—will save you.

My father's family was divided into country people and town people. And until we sold my childhood home, there had been "town" Rutledges living in my small Texas hometown for over a century. That's why I found it more than a little disconcerting the last time I visited to see, with a glance through the new phone book, that there were "new" Rutledges in town who were not kin to me. It was almost as if they were interlopers. I knew the "new" Rutledges were from some other family tree, but had I not grown up in that town, I would not have known.

'Riting Reminder

Never give any personal information on the Internet. Forums were created as a safe place to exchange information.

Hitting the Road

Like it is for any good gumshoe, there will be a moment when you need to hit the road. Place is very important to both the genealogist and the detective. You can write for information from city directories, old school ties, church records, vital records, and newspaper morgues. You can contact county courthouses for vital records and church records for baptisms and bar mitzvah records, but going there is what every genealogical sleuth needs to do, sooner or later.

What's "There"?

What's "there"? The courthouse, of course, but much, much more. Visiting cemeteries, old homes, local historic societies collections, and libraries—and especially attending family reunions—will open up an amazing amount of information for you, as well as inspire insights to your heritage. You, the hometown private eye, will be looking for clues at these scenes of the past:

➤ Newspaper morgues

➤ Church records

135

➤ County courthouse records

➤ Local historical societies

➤ Cemeteries

Chapter 12, "Looking in All the Right Places—in Hometowns," will focus on all aspects of hometown sleuthing, but let's take a quick visit to one of the best hometown treasures for a writer/detective—cemeteries.

Cemetery Sleuth Philosopher

There is information galore in old cemeteries. You may not get much new information from your trip, but a cemetery gives you a reality check like nothing else can.

Your cemetery visit should get your creative writing juices churning on many levels beyond facts. The sleuth is checking facts, recording the reality of the body buried there. But the sleuth can turn instantly into a philosopher with the quiet wind rustling through the trees and the silence of stone speaking of mortality and ancestry and yet also of a life once lived—a life that begat your life.

Related Facts

What clues can you find just walking through a cemetery? Names, dates, and perhaps a telling inscription or two are pay-offs from an hour spent finding an ancestor's grave. But what does your writer's eye see and writer's heart feel in this place?

➤ Is there a monument nearby with inscriptions?

➤ Is the lot well-tended or overgrown and forgotten?

➤ Is the gravestone ornate or plain?

➤ Is the stone new, implying living descendents who care?

➤ Who are the extended family members buried near your relative, and what might you infer from their graves and markers?

How to Think Like an Historian

As the sleuth in you is tracking down all those facts and dates, the historian in you will be reconstructing them into anecdotal accounts, whether you're aware of it or not. To view all these facts from an historian's view is not only expedient for your genealogical work, but also fascinating from a family history writer's point of view.

If history is written by the survivors, as the saying goes, here's your chance to write history. That is what you are doing, of course, writing personal history. You should never lose sight of that. It's the reason that so much emphasis is put on documentation of everything before you commit it to the family history page. You only have one chance to get it right.

Those Family Legends

But how about a family story that seems to defy verification? If you cannot resist, say, that old family legend about the early pioneer ancestor who was rumored to have lived with a peaceful Indian tribe in 1840s Missouri, you should at least try to verify it before adding it to your lore. (We'll discuss myth-versus-fact much more in depth when we move into the next section.)

Yes, some digging may pop the legend's bubble, but you may find something just as fascinating in its stead. For instance, that westward-traveling brother may have fought against Indians for his homestead instead of fighting with them. Or maybe the rumor of his "living" with an Indian tribe came from the fact he married a woman from one of the Midwest's tribes. You'll have the excitement of exploring your Native American heritage.

You won't know until you try. And to try, you must think like an historian.

The Larger Picture

How do you begin thinking like an historian? The best way to do that, beyond making verification your passion instead of writing, is to think about the "larger picture" and to look for the unusual historic-laden ways that the picture might have been created.

Telephone Generations

Remember that old childhood game called "telephone"? Sitting in a circle with your friends, you whisper some message into your neighbor's ear ("I really like Freddy") and that person passes the message to the next ear and on and on, around the circle, until it gets back to you. And what do you hear? Something like, "I want to go steady with Teddy." Think what that message would sound like after a few generations of telephone instead of a few minutes. That sort of time-filtering is what you are working against. The answer for you as a family history writer is to learn all you can about the life and times of the centuries that your ancestors called home. And that can start as early as one generation back.

Each life holds its share of poignant stories, and your role is to find them to share with family members who care. The family stories are your interest, wherever you may find them, so don't make the mistake of not hearing the voices correctly from every part of your family tree.

Respect Context

Understand the importance of the "when" in your search and in your findings. Begin to work on that historic time line mentioned in the previous chapter. The more you know about context, the more you'll be able to understand puzzling information you'll find.

The Name's Not the Same

As we discussed in Chapter 7, "Getting It Right from the Get-Go," getting the name right is one of the greatest challenges in genealogy. It is also the first line of detective work. Nothing would be more embarrassing for a sleuth than to follow a trail, hazarding those dark alleys and back streets to only find he's been tailing the wrong guy. But what do you do when the right person seems to keep popping up with wrong given names?

Nicknames Can Nick

A common problem for beginning genealogists is that an ancestor might be found in official records under more than one given name, making the researcher question whether he or she has the right person. How can that happen? Nicknames. Each different given name is usually some derivation or nickname of the official given name.

Do you think nicknames wouldn't be a problem for a super-sleuth? Think again. We are familiar with many of the common nicknames still in use, but would you know that Bob was short for Robert if it wasn't still common? How about Betsy for Elizabeth? Did you know that Sukey was a nickname once used for Susannah? And that a Nancy or a Hannah might really be officially named Ann? The historian, though, takes it all in stride, finding each nickname fascinating material for later family history writing.

The Professor and the Illiterate

To think like an historian is to remember the realities of the times in which your ancestors lived. An English professor, after searching for her great-great-grandfather, found his will. There, on the signature line, she saw an "X." He was illiterate. She was surprised and strangely touched. Suddenly, she wanted to know all the forces that would make an ancestor of hers unable to learn the basics of the written language that gave such meaning to her world.

The Monument on the Square

And how about those monuments that seem to be in every little town across the land? Memorial plaques in city parks, cannons, and statues in courthouse squares, attempt to immortalize hometown soldiers who fought for their town's cherished way of life. As you go about finding the official story of your great-uncle's addition to one of those monuments, if you attempt to see such events through the eyes of the proud town members who wanted to preserve that pride for future moments like this one, you will give your family history writing a dimension that will surprise you.

Genealogy Is in the Details

Thinking like an historian deals with learning details of the past in order to decipher clues from the past. What may seem like tiny, insignificant historical details can open up whole worlds of new meanings for the facts you find. Let's take a look at four examples of such historical detail:

➤ Language of the past

➤ Old handwriting

➤ Occupations

➤ Name Americanization

Language of the Past

"Good day, brother." So might a man have greeted another man in colonial America, stranger or friend, and so might we today. But we would never do so in the text of official documents, while our colonial ancestors might have. "Brother" in an old document could mean a brother-in-law, fellow church member, lodge member, or even a buddy.

Our language is a living thing, always changing. Not understanding unfamiliar words is one thing, but discovering that familiar words may have meant something quite different a century ago is not only surprising, but confusing as well. Just knowing such an old meaning for a word can unlock the answer to a mystery. Keeping your antennae up for the potential "archaic definitions," as Mr. Webster would call them, will save you time and even embarrassment.

More examples? Until the late nineteenth century, the word "cousin" could mean any blood relative except sibling or parent. Recall how Chapter 7 pointed out that in colonial villages, a Jr. and a Sr. weren't necessarily related. The historian's lesson for the researcher is not to take such titles in letters or even wills as a primary source without a detective double-check when you're researching before the twentieth century.

Stories Within Words

Archaic words can tell a tale in themselves. Out-of-use words can easily capture your writer's imagination all by themselves. What if you came upon a document that called an ancestor a "bound child"? The sound of that term alone begs for the story behind it to be told, doesn't it? What is a "bound child"? That was a child who lived in an orphanage, "bound" out by his/her mother, because the father was killed in the Civil War and there was no way to care for the child without the father.

Related Facts

What's "bounty land"? From 1776 to 1855, the federal government began offering land, called "bounty land," from the frontier states as an inducement for military service or reenlistment. The amount of land was granted according to rank, i.e., a colonel was given 500 acres, a private only 100. Mention of bounty lands gained by your ancestors and their use or disuse by the ancestor and his immediate descendents can be found in many family and county histories.

Occupations

Occupations also come and go with the ages. Barbers no longer do surgery. Blacksmiths' and tinkers' skills are pretty much lost arts. The buggy whip factory is long gone—unless, of course, it diversified into baby buggies.

To uncover an occupation that no longer exists will be fun for you as the family history writer because it forces you to play the historian in order to explain it to your family history's readers. The connections of heredity and talents also will be fun to chart as you go. Is your family musical? Odds are you will find ancestors with the same musical genes. Are you good with your hands? Odds are you'll find craftsmen in every generation. Showing such a family thread of talents and skills will be a wonderful addition to any family history book, don't you think?

Two out of three of my sisters own horses and love them so much that they have somehow continued to have them to ride and train and breed no matter how many times they have moved across Texas and across the country. Through genealogical research, I found out that my father's grandfather, the county sheriff, was famous in town for "loving, training, and breeding horses" during the turn of the century. That may seem a small notation to a family record, but to the descendent recognizing him or herself in the passion and the skills of an ancestor, it will feel like a large, very personal connection.

Old Handwriting

To whome it may concern, an answer followeth of behalfe of ye ....

Handwriting has a long history, and an evolution all its own. And as for old handwriting, it can grow on you. Experts swear that the more you practice transcribing or rewriting in the handwriting you find as you research, the better you'll be able to decipher what you're writing and what the next signature, document or letter is saying.

A famous example of early handwriting customs is the first few lines of the Declaration of Independence using the "long 's.'" A first glance at the original cursive "s"s that came from Thomas Jefferson's quill pen on that glorious document—done in several different ways—will have you stopping and starting several times as you attempt to read the familiar words you know by heart.

Extra "s" maneuvers is just one strange usage. A colon was often used to signify omission of letters from a word. An equal sign was often used to divide a word at the end of a line instead of a hyphen. The capital letters "U" and "V" sometimes are hardly distinguishable. You'll also notice favorite phrases used in old documents. For instance, the phrase "To All To Whom These Presents Shall Come, Greeting" was a popular beginning to many old documents.

Reading and rereading old documents is the answer—understanding by familiarization. Soon you'll actually be able to read the language of the past.

Names Again

The further you rewind time in genealogy, the more you'll notice that there was a sort of spelling free-for-all (see Chapter 7). Some historical context will definitely help even the most creative of spellers in your line.

But when it comes to reconstructing the family name, nothing compares to the "Americanization" of so many immigrants' names at Ellis Island. In the years that Ellis Island was the gateway for the world's "huddled masses yearning to be free," the wave was so overwhelming that little importance was placed on the preservation of ethnic spellings. The whole idea of immigrating to a new land was all about gaining a new start, so it didn't seem too strange to give people new, "Americanized" names. (Ellis Island, by the way, is only one port of American entry, albeit the most famous and synonymous with name Americanization. Angel Island, for instance, the port for the Asian immigration into San Francisco, is now a national landmark like Ellis Island.) So, first, generation American names should always be suspect and in need of an historian's eye.

With the Federal Census, the spellings of Americans' names became almost a free-for-all. So much so that one of the productions of the Depression's Works Project Administration (WPA) was to invent a soundex coding system for the census records. Soundex is an indexing tool for census records, and it's been quite an aid for researchers. Working backward, it distills a name down to its sound, completely ignoring the vowels, as an attempt to match up the enormous number of people whose names, for instance, had been "Americanized" when they arrived at Ellis Island or just plain misspelled in these important records. (Chapter 11, "Looking in All the Right Places—Library and Beyond," will go into it in more depth.) You'll thank the WPA for the boost when you try to find your way around the census material, especially since it is not in alphabetical order but by date.

Related Facts

The Quakers called the calendar's months and years by the numbers instead of by the "heathen deities," such as January named after the god Janus. Believing in plain talk, they'd say, for instance, "I was born on second day, tenth month."

Double-Dating Isn't a Foursome

Then there are the quirks of history, such as double-dating. There you are, zipping along in your genealogical fun when you see a very strange date: 16 March 1700/1701. This puzzles you—is it a typo? You move along until you find another one. That's when you find out the real story, as any good historian would.

In the 1500s, everyone began to notice that the calendar wasn't quite lining up with the seasons anymore. Chaos reigned for those who had calendars—which weren't many, of course. New Year's Day was happening in March as the buds were blooming. Pope Gregory XIII realized he had to change the obviously flawed calendar set up centuries before by Julius Caesar. So, in 1582 the switch was made from the Julian calendar to the Gregorian calendar. The English didn't get around to handling the matter until 1752 and all back-dating had to note the change.

The World and Its Times

A grasp of history can also guide you in pinpointing dates, backgrounds, even reasons for traveling to the New World—all concepts you'll need for your family history. For example, England supplied the United States of America with most of its new settlers into the first half of the nineteenth century but Irish and Germans were the newest Americans in the last half of the nineteenth century. Why? Because of upheavals in their homelands. But how does knowing such seemingly unimportant history trivia help your genealogical search?

Sometimes an immigrant ancestor's story needs a boost from historical context to make sense for your family history narrative. Germans were fleeing political oppression during that time, and Irish were fleeing famine. Say you have both in your family tree. You need to fill a granny gap, but all you have about your great-great-great-grandmother was the family belief that she was Irish. Chances are, if she came to America sometime between 1845 and 1850, she came because of the potato famine. One million immigrants came from Ireland because of it. You may find her in the records.

History of the religious freedom that defines our country also can help, if you'd like to follow early freedom-lovers as they moved across the land. The *Mayflower*, after all, was populated with religious freedom-seekers. Is there a Quaker in your background? Check their treks from New England to Pennsylvania, Ohio, and Indiana. Is there a Mormon in your family? Check a cross-country trip to Utah in the mid-nineteenth century. Stories abound.

Cultural surprises await everywhere along with dramatic stories to tell. Chinese Americans have been surprised to uncover in immigration records that their first American ancestor was a "paper son." Laws were so restrictive from 1885 to 1965, that there were many who entered this country by identifying themselves as a citizen's son—with the permission of the citizen, of course.

A Relatively Good Idea

Did your ancestor come to America on, say, March 19, 1700? His record may show the date to be 19 March 1700/01. That's called "double-dating," and is due to a change in the calendar to correct a flaw in the world's time-keeping. Have you noticed any other discrepancy in your ancestors dates that might need your historian's eye? Jot it down and watch for signs of the solution to pop up as you go deeper into the customs of the past.

'Riting Reminder

Don't forget the basic tenet of family history research: validate, validate, validate! It's all rumor until you have concrete evidence to back it up.

The same can be said for ethnicity. African-American genealogy was, in a very real way, the catalyst that started our whole modern fascination with genealogy. Alex Haley made us all want to find our "roots." A good first historical stop for any African-American search would be the Kunte Kinte foundation—a clearing house for black genealogy.

A Relatively Good Idea

Is there a naturalized citizen in your ancestry? U.S. Immigration and Naturalization Service has all that information on file after 1906.

A Relatively Good Idea

Think you may ultimately research your ancestors in their native lands? A short course in naming customs of the past and the present is mandatory. For example, in many Spanish-speaking countries, a child takes both parents' surnames.

By the same token, knowledge of our country's history with Native Americans will point you to the right place to find your Native American ancestry. The first place to look would be the U.S. Government Bureau of Indian Affairs, which tells an historical tale in its own existence relevant to any family history with Native American heritage. (More on ethnic resources can be found in the next section.)

Natural/Cultural Obstacle Course

Documents are only as safe as the place in which they're stored. Most modern county courthouses have vaults where they store old documents, but it hasn't always been that way (and it isn't always the case even now). Many Southern courthouses were burned during the Civil War. The 1890 census was almost completely destroyed by a Washington D.C. fire. Tornadoes cut through the heartland, and hurricanes and earthquakes bedeviled important coastal cities throughout the country's short history.

Having trouble finding any information on your original American ancestor that leads back to the "Old Country"? Many of the very political and historical reasons people came to America would go hand-in-hand with records being destroyed.

Your grasp of history and what happened to those documents can add a lot of color to your family history, especially if your ancestor survived that hurricane or that religious or ethnic persecution and lived to write about it.

Expect the Unusual

A historian also wouldn't overlook the unusual. In fact, a historian would expect it, hunting the detours with as much relish as the wide highways because there is where treasure usually hides. And the surprises are always half the fun.

For example, soldiers' diaries and published letters exist in historical collections. Many are indexed in the National Archives and its branches, and they usually go into glorious detail. Say you have an ancestor who was a soldier in the Civil War. (In fact, let's say you have two from the same family and they fought on opposite sides. Do you sniff a good family story there? Sure you do. And so do I. It happened in my family and probably many others.) Odds are good that another soldier's diary exists that has entries about the same regiment and battles your family's Civil War soldiers might have been in.

At best, traveling this detour to check such diaries will give you a stirring account that includes his name. At worst, you can gain some exciting historical background. Check *American Diaries: An Annotated Bibliography of Published American Diaries and Journals, 1492–1980.* You might just decide to read a diary from a certain era for background on what it was like to live in that time. As a writer, that would be invaluable.

Surprising Pay-Offs

Aiming your fine-tuned historian's antennae to the unusual can offer many nice surprises. Some states had "Civil War Questionnaires" that were filled out by the surviving Confederate veterans and included questions about their ancestors. They were asked to fill in the questionnaire as fully as possible, even to the point of suggesting they attach sheets with exact records taken from such family sources as their family Bibles. Wouldn't it be wonderful to find a whole page of your lineage appended to an archived questionnaire filled out by your soldier ancestor? You'll never know unless you think like an historian and keep an eye focused and an ear tuned for such seemingly peripheral historical documents outside of the personal paper trail of your ancestors.

> **Deep Thought**
>
> *Genealogy and history are like heart and soul—attempting to understand one without the other is impossible.*

Heart and Soul

Obviously, thinking like an historian is a good thing for your efforts, but here's the wonderful side effect of the mindset: What you find, and how you reflect on what you find, will give a wonderful subtext and dimension to your writing that your family readers will deeply enjoy and you will love writing. Genealogy and history are like heart and soul—attempting to understand one without the other is impossible.

How to Report Like a Reporter

Even if you have followed the clues by working like a detective and have understood the information's place in time by thinking like an historian, you will still need to check facts of these potential family stories like a reporter. You will need to ask journalists' questions of everything to make sure all the elements for reporting are present—who, what, when, where, and why. You are, after all, going to be telling the whole story—just like a reporter—very soon. And, oh yes, since you are researching family history, occasionally, you need to add one more question to the list: "how."

The Five "W's" (Plus One)

Let's try it. Let's make up an ancestor and what you might have found about him through oral history, a death certificate, and a newspaper clipping you requested from the hometown newspaper.

A Relatively Good Idea

Checking a story's facts like a family history reporter, you should answer the five "W's" plus one:

➤ Who
➤ What
➤ When
➤ Where
➤ Why
➤ How

➤ **Who:** Alfonzo Cephus Kendrick *(pedigree chart)*

➤ **What:** Great-great-great-grandfather's father on his mother's side *(pedigree chart)*

➤ **When:** Born 1846 died 1927 *(death certificate)*

➤ **Where:** Born Alabama, died Texas *(death certificate)*

➤ **Why:** House fire *(newspaper obit)*

➤ **How:** *(Oral history/family Bible, Lila Smitha Jones, 1999)*

When you can go through your pedigree chart, your family group record, and your individual ancestor Record and answer these questions with some spirit, you'll be doing well. If you can't answer these questions, then it will be your choice to continue the specific search.

As for Alfonzo, I think you'll continue the search. Why? Because there's a story to uncover worthy of your family history efforts. Using your new sleuth skills, you noticed from your individual and family charts that you have another ancestor in the same town who died from a heart attack on the same day Alfonzo's house burned down—Joe Schmoe III, the owner of the town's drugstore, remember? Alfonso was Joe Schmoe III's maternal grandfather. So this information, cross-referenced to Joe's, begs a few questions: Were Joe III and Alfonzo's deaths related? Were both of them in the fire? Or … what?

Go ahead and admit it. You sniff a good family history story here like a good reporter should. Because even though we know that coincidences can happen, no self-respecting family history writer would not check one as big as this one.

Great Aunt Lilly Tells All (She Can Remember)

Another call to Great-Great-Aunt Lilly Smith Jones gains you an oral history memory of a tragic fire in her family, although she doesn't remember who died in it, since she was only a child on the "other side of the family," and living in another town. All she remembers was how everything was lost, including some valuable cows.

Well, that gets your attention, especially the cow part. And you remember, again, that the past was a different land, and cows were important. You decide to revisit the hometown paper's morgue. You may never get the full story, but with what you now know, you can answer some of the mystery's questions and tell a probable tale.

When and why you stop researching a specific ancestor or ancestral line will be up to you. How much of the story do you want to tell? How much can you tell? These are questions the family history reporter in you will help the family history writer in you answer. The trick is to get as close to answering all those questions as you can, at this point, and worry about how you will write the story later.

As you sail full speed ahead, looking in all the right places, these three mindsets will keep your writer's focus sharp. Practice them well and practice them often, until they become second nature—until they become you.

Journaling Down the Genealogical Trail

In the pages of your journal is where you can play with the questions that will pop into your mind as you work from the perspective of the historian, reporter, and sleuth. Here are three examples:

➤ **Search like a sleuth.** You might ask yourself, "Now that I've found out that my great-grandfather was a soldier in World War II, how might I find his service records?"

➤ **Think like an historian.** Reflect on how your ancestors could be illiterate only four generations back. What could it have been like for them?

➤ **Report like a reporter.** You've uncovered that a tragic fire may have taken two ancestors' lives. Might Lilly Smitha Jones remember more if you bring her some of her favorite chocolate? Would a city historian help find more on the tragedy? And what about those cows were so memorable?

Your turn. Try it, right now, in the pages of your journal.

The Least You Need to Know

➤ Learning the customs of the historical era of your ancestors will add color and depth to your family history writing.

➤ Using investigative skills will make the difference between a stalled search and a successful one.

➤ Viewing your uncovered facts like a reporter will give you a head-start on your family history storytelling.

➤ Using the detective's double-check is always a smart move.

Chapter 11

Looking in All the Right Places— Library and Beyond

You are now a sleuth, an historian, a reporter, a budding genealogist, and a family history writer. You have an overview of the genealogical world, you are getting to know the tools of the trade and the best ways to begin. Where will all this take you? Nowhere, if you don't look in the right places. So, let's review what the right places are.

➤ You

➤ Family

➤ Library

➤ Internet

➤ Hometown

You, the Genealogical Juggler

The experience of researching and writing a family history is really a lesson in juggling. By the time you have finished reading all the chapters in this entire section and are full-swing into genealogy research, you'll be doing a little of this and little of that—an Internet search one day and an interview with Aunt Edna the next—all at the same time.

So, what have you already begun to juggle? You've gleaned all the information from yourself you can remember, and you've begun contacting your family members, so now it's time to begin visiting libraries that can help you. From there, you can hop on the Internet and then hit the road for the real thing.

A Relatively Good Idea

Do you have the vital records on your family members going back as far as you can go? Is your pedigree chart as full as you can get it for at least four generations back? Yes? Then, it's time to go to the library.

But first things first. Do you have the vital records on your family members going back as far as you can go? Is your pedigree chart as full as you can get it for four generations back? If so, let's go to the library. (Resist the Internet for now until you've made a few trips to your chosen library. You'll see why.)

Library Research

After you have gotten as much of the basic family information out of your family members as you can for the moment, it's time to hit the library. There's a whole world of research out there waiting to be done, and the library can help you find it all. We've briefly covered what you will find in such a place, but it's time to go a little deeper.

First, choose the biggest library you can that has a genealogical collection, especially if you live in or near your hometown or any of your ancestors' hometowns. Thanks to the fact that there are so many people interested in genealogy today, the volunteers in your area may have indexed everything from cemetery records to obituaries to names in all the county's published local histories. How do you find out if that's true? By using the magic method—asking.

Inquire at your local library for the nearest genealogical society, and for the best library to do your first rung of work on your ancestor search. You may be pleasantly surprised. There may be a special library very near you, perhaps a Family History Library or even a National Archives branch, but a public library with a good genealogical collection will have all that you need to point you in the beginner directions, by indexes, records on microfilm, or Internet access.

A Library Is Not Just a Library

Do you know how many kinds of libraries there are? Almost as many as there are flavors of ice cream. Here are a few:

➤ Public branch lending libraries

➤ Main public lending libraries

➤ Private libraries

➤ Historical libraries

➤ Family history libraries

➤ College and university libraries

➤ Religious libraries

➤ Ethnic libraries

➤ Genealogical society libraries

Making Friends

After you've chosen a library, then choose a simple thing to research. Armed with as much information as you've already acquired, charts, logs, and records in hand (especially your Research Log ready for its first entry), it's now time to make that first contact with a genealogy-friendly librarian. Or perhaps you can make friends with another genealogist in one of the local genealogy interest group you've contacted—preferably someone who enjoys "breaking in" a newcomer. Usually, one librarian at any library will have a special interest in genealogy (or she becomes the designated genealogy librarian just because she's been asked the basic questions so much by people like you).

A Relatively Good Idea

Beginning is easy as 1, 2, 3. Birth. Death. Marriage. Collect certificates and sources for these three vital records concerning your:

1. Grandparents

2. Each of their children

3. Each of their parents

Go back as far as you can with this simple information first. Don't get sidetracked for the moment. (Later, half the fun is getting sidetracked.) For now, focus on just these foundation steps—1, 2, 3.

Now, even though you may be going into the library with all your charts and such, you should only have one specific fact in mind to research, not the whole of your genealogical work. (Trust me. This will also make the librarian much more willing to help you.) Also, never forget that *you* are doing *your* research. It's all yours, not the librarian's; she's just there to help you find your way.

It's All Yours

Let's say you choose a blank on your pedigree chart you'd like to fill in. The last remaining living relative on your mother's side of the family is Aunt Lila Smith Jones and she can't seem to remember the name of her grandfather's mother. This is your first granny gap and you decide to attempt to fill it today.

You show your work to the librarian, she notes the information you already have, and then she points the way to how the library can help. She will probably be able to tell you where to look outside the library, also, for what the library can't help you find—places to write or sites to check on the Internet.

She points you to their library computer catalog, or if you are in an older, small-town library, perhaps a card catalog. Then, she'll point you to the reference area where pertinent catalogs, periodicals, and indexes await.

This is a good time to embrace the wonderful world of indexes. Two good starter indexes are the International Genealogical Index Research, which contains the names of over 200 million deceased persons around the world, and the American Genealogical Index, a well-known, 48-volume index. Proceed to the reference section and settle in.

Reference Wonderland

Since you're there, look around. Wander. Check out the whole reference department. You might find an ancestor in a biography dictionary or the addresses of other libraries and history collections you may be writing to soon. Or you may need the help of the absolutely unabridged and big-as-a-house *Oxford English Dictionary* to figure out the meaning of a strange old word you find in an ancestor's will.

Genealogical Periodicals

The reference section will also subscribe to genealogical periodicals. There are hundreds of genealogy journals out now, from the scholarly to the popular. *The American Genealogist* is a good example for the beginner. Why should you read genealogical journals, you ask? After all, you've already got so much to read, right? Here's why:

➤ Education

➤ Information

➤ Book reviews

➤ Question/answer columns

➤ Writing market

➤ Future reference

But while you find the magazines fascinating, they may seem a little overwhelming. What if you just want to find out information pertinent to your own search?

Index to the Rescue

To the rescue come these indexes: PERSI (Periodical Source, Index), published by the Allen County Public Library in Fort Wayne, Indiana, a library deeply committed to genealogy, and GPAI (Genealogical Periodical Annual Index).

What do these do? They offer you a glance at what is in all these magazines—genealogies, lineage, Bible records, source records, and book reviews. As for your family, you'd look up your surname and the geographical area, and the indexes can tell you whether there has been an article written on your family, and where to find it. And if you can't find a copy of an obscure journal with just the right article, then the Allen County Public Library provides a copying service for a fee. PERSI even offers a CD-ROM version for you to keep at home.

(By the way, don't be surprised if you find yourself thinking about writing something for these journals one day.)

Hold Your Horses (the Basics First)

What else might the librarian suggest? She'll probably suggest general books that are in-depth guides to research. Then, she will probably point you to catalogs of family histories and an Internet connection or two. But hold off for now. You're not ready.

It's only after you've familiarized yourself with all that's available in your library of choice that you'll be ready to go on. Consider it a foundation. This is just as important as a writer learning the rules of grammar before rushing headlong into writing a book. Sure, you could do it without the basics, but it would be amateurish through and through, wouldn't it?

'Riting Reminder

Sure, you may feel overwhelmed already with all the reading that is involved with the research of your family in itself, but don't pass up those genealogical journals. Inside each of them is a wealth of tips, source ideas, and questions that other genealogists are asking. Odds are they're asking some of the questions *you've* been wondering about, too.

Family/Town/County History Surprise

Take a good, long look around your library's genealogical collection. Do you now feel you have a good grasp of a library's lay of the genealogical land? When you do, that's when you're ready to step into the world of family histories. You already know from our exercise in Chapter 8, "Where to Begin," how many leads, as well as lessons, can be learned from family, town, and county histories. Maybe by now you've been able to acquire one or two of your own.

You've got the tools now and the eye to make these volumes work for you. Remember these two tips as you begin:

➤ Remember that family histories will be chock-full of information, all fascinating, but only some of which is personally connected to your strain of the family name. Treat most of what you find as background work.

➤ Remember that town/county histories can get you out of the blocks with specific leads more quickly, since they winnow out your ancestor from all the others in the family history book. How? By that secret clue called geographical location. The sleuth in you would consider town/county histories a good detective double-check for your family histories.

A Relatively Good Idea

What are you looking for? If you're looking for birthplace, birth date, age, death, maiden names, wedding or divorce dates, check vital records followed by civil court records, military records, obituaries, newspaper indexes, and church records. If you're looking for homes and land once owned, check census records, land and property records, county histories, and maps.

Good Detective Double-Check

Be it family, town, or county history, however, you'll be incredibly surprised at how much research seems to have already been done by countless people about your ancestors. (Why? Because your ancestors are their ancestors, too.) It's a strange feeling. All those unknown distant cousins of yours having done all that work in the past, about the past, and there it is waiting for you.

Be sure, however, to never forget your lessons in sloppy genealogy learned in Chapter 8 and why you need to do the detective double-check on everything (unless you like the chasing of wild geese).

Census Research

In 1790, the new United States Government decided that it wanted to account for every individual in the United States of America on one designated day, and it's been happening every 10 years since. The original reason was to find out the number of congressional members each state was entitled to. For the budding genealogist, the records trail leading past those *vital* records usually begins with a stop at the U.S. Census. What's great about it?

➤ It's widely available.

➤ It places your designated ancestor in a specific time and place, which can lead you to more information. If your ancestor was in the United States on that day, you should be able to find him or her somewhere. Granted, people were missed, but since the census was taken every 10 years, the odds are good you can find your designated ancestor there sometime during his or her life.

Those Vital Questions

Census research can begin simply enough. So, what information can you glean from the census? Although the questions that are posed by the census takers have varied through the years, you can find out information on military service, citizenship, marital status, births, deaths, addresses, places of origin, and people living in one place. You will probably uncover an ancestor's siblings you didn't know existed, for instance.

Be prepared for discrepancies to sort out, as you take your first baby steps in census research. Some genealogists suggest that you should have your own copy of the census records that mention your ancestors whenever possible. In lieu of that, your individual record charts will fill up fast. Think about it. You can follow an ancestor as he moved every 10 years by the census record.

Want to know the questions census takers asked? The Census Bureau's "Twenty Censuses, Population and Housing Questions 1790 to 1980" will give you a list of all the queries.

County Factor

As with other ways of trekking down your ancestral paper trail, your ancestors' counties of residence come into play quickly with census research. Why? The town of residence you may find listed may not even exist anymore, as often happens with agrarian cultures as the country moved west. So, all you may be able to find is the county it was in. Don't have the county? Try a state *gazetteer* of the time period that shows the long-gone town or community.

The Write Word

A **gazetteer** is an index of homes, farms, and businesses in a specific township, county, or state during a certain time period.

Details, Details

Remember, privacy laws will keep you from looking at census records after 1920 until 2002, when the 1930 census is to be opened. So, plan on starting with the 1920 and move backward.

The 1890 census, by the way, was almost completely destroyed by fire. Some records survived of a few states and an index to them exists on just two microfilm rolls. (That one fire tells a story of the fragility of history, doesn't it? And it tells why this can be so much fun for the amateur detective who enjoys a good historical mystery.)

The 1920 census asked for the "mother tongue" and birthplaces of each person's parents. Add that to the existing information on each person's education, literacy, and occupation found there, too, and you can see why this census is very popular with genealogists.

Soundex Sounding

You'd think that being able to find a name in a census index would be a no-brainer. Surely they would be listed in alphabetical order, right? But with the mass of American population, including the influx of huge throngs of immigrants, all spelling their names for census takers standing in America's doorways, confusion reigned supreme. Federal indexes for the 1880–1920 censuses are, thankfully, indexed using a phonetic system mentioned earlier called a soundex system, and in some places, another form of soundex called "miracode."

Spelled, Misspelled, and Respelled

The soundex system was created to help arrange names by the way they sound because of the plethora of ways immigrant surnames were spelled, misspelled, and respelled. But be forewarned—learning the soundex of a name you're searching for is the best way to satisfy your needs.

Take heart, at first glance you are going to be confused by the soundex system, but keep trying. The system's rules of use may seem complicated at the beginning, but are worth the effort. When you do need to use it, you'll probably realize that it's not that hard to grasp, and soon you'll be humming along at the speed of sound. Archives with the indexes that use the system will have instructions for you to tackle one at the time.

Related Facts

Census search basic contents:

1890–1920—"Mother tongue"/birthplaces of each person's parents/full counts of whole households/birthplaces, years of each person's education/literacy/occupation.

1850–1870—Alphabetical order/full counts of whole households/birthplaces, ages, occupation, and property value.

1790–1840—Only households are mentioned by name. Head of household was oldest male or main property holder.

Microfilm and CD-ROM

Computers are glorious things to simplify research. And the census records are being put on CD-ROM, more each year, for our viewing pleasure. Ask for CD-ROM if you have a system that can use it, and remember to get directions for the soundex system used.

Microfilm copies, though, especially of a particular area, are widely available in local libraries. And there always the whole shebang waiting for you on microfilm—from

1790 to 1920—at your National Archives Branch. Is there a National Archives Branch nearby? There are 13 across the country. See Appendix A, "BookMarks—for Further Reference," for the one near you. Take the specific information you are searching for, and leave lots of time for learning the soundex system, at least on the first trip. These wonderful places are always full of fellow genealogists.

Other libraries also have the complete collection on microfilm. The Family History Library and the Allen County Public Library are examples of libraries that have the complete collection. The Allen County Public Library in Fort Wayne, Indiana, may have the largest genealogical collection in the country. Some libraries will even rent their collections to you, such as the National Archives and the American Genealogical Lending Library.

A Relatively Good Idea

Taking the census to granny: As an ice-breaker and even an inspiration, why not take copies of census information to your oral history interviews with elderly relatives?

National Archives

This is a good time to talk about the National Archives, where the original census records, along with the originals of many other documents, reside. Sooner or later, like most Americans, you'll probably visit the National Archives in Washington, D.C. (and the new facility in Maryland). And "sooner" seems to be the word for today's genealogy researchers. According to the latest NARA (National Archives and Records Administration) statistics, its major clientele is made up of genealogists.

Maybe you've already visited as a citizen tourist. On one side of the building are our documents of democracy, such as the Declaration of Independence and the U.S. Constitution. On the other side are the records of the almost 300 million people who have made up our democracy. They live on in such pieces of paper as census records, military records from the Revolutionary War to World War I, passport applications dating back to 1795, Bureau of Indian Affairs documents, ships' passengers lists—a nation's common documents that tell uncommonly personal, dramatic tales.

Holding the Papers in Your Hand

The grand thing about doing research in the National Archives is that every piece of paper you ask to see can be the real thing. You'll be holding history in your hands with each brown folder you are given to research, full of old ancestral documents. The feeling is overwhelming, the minutiae of life mind-boggling, but with each piece of paper pulled from those brown folders, you may be in for a wonderful surprise, all your patience rewarded. If nothing else, the heavy feeling of history in the air as you handle old documents is worth a family history writer's notice.

You'll need to get your plan of attack ready so that you don't waste any time. Why? The records were written by and for bureaucrats. Enough said.

Studying *A Guide to the National Archives* is a good idea before planning any trip there. Go online for information or call or write for a guide. (See Appendix A for the contact information you'll need.)

Related Facts

Your most-wanted FBI list: Does the FBI have a file on one of your ancestors? Why not see it yourself? A great story could be waiting. Files for deceased persons are considered to be in the "public domain." You can actually write for copies of FBI records on a family member if you can demonstrate that person is reasonably deceased. What is "reasonably deceased"? It means being able to show formal notification of death, through death certificates, obituaries, and gravestone photos. And, if all else fails, you can present a birth certificate that shows the person would have to be over 100 years old—that seems reasonable to the FBI. More information on perusing an ancestor's records can be obtained from the National Archives, "Guide to Federal Records in the National Archives, Record Group 65," also available online at www.nara.gov.

Special Federal Census Schedules

Here are the special federal census records you might also be interested in studying:

➤ **Slave schedules.** Lists slave owners and the number of slaves for years 1850 to 1860 in southern states, as well as former slaves freed in that period of time. Only the owners were listed by name as a rule.

➤ **Mortality schedules.** Lists the residents of a region who died during the 12 months prior to the census—not to be confused with actual death records.

➤ **Agriculture and manufacturing schedules.** Lists information on land your family may have owned and how it was used, and what was manufactured, the profits, and number of employees at your ancestor's company.

➤ **1890 special census of Union Civil War Veterans and Their Widows.**

Can You Trust the Census?

Are the census records primary sources? Here's the same waffling answer again: yes and no.

Think about the guy filling out the census forms after knocking on your door, while the baby's screaming and the dog's barking. Now, picture him at the turn of the century. This was a short-term job and, in many places, an almost impossible job for pinpoint accuracy. The census taker could be drunk, sweltering, and fed up with this temporary "Fed" job. And even if he wasn't any of these things, he may have had excruciatingly bad penmanship, which will bedevil you, the researcher.

You should use the census as you use most material, as a signpost, a big, wonderful, accessible index to check and double-check information. Beyond a few vagaries, it's so good that you'll return to it again and again for basic leads on the latest branch of your family tree you're climbing. Even early censuses, which weren't as detailed, will put your ancestor in a certain place and time for you.

For the family history writer, there are mysteries galore here, some that may lead you to some great family stories. Others may lead to a dead end, but the experience of interacting with the U.S. Census itself is like being immersed in history, from the language used in the census to the images conjured as you picture that specific day in history that the census was taken. The United States Census record is a written snapshot of our land.

Here are some tips to help you navigate through the census maze:

➤ Usually only the head of the household was indexed, not each family member. Remember to search under the father's/husband's name unless your ancestor was a single woman (who was probably called a "spinster" or a "maiden aunt" in her area).

➤ The 1850 census was the first to require the name and age of everyone living at an address. Information included: Name, age, sex, race, occupation, value of real estate, birthplace, whether they had been married within that year, whether they went to school within that year, whether they were illiterate or not, and … whether they were "deaf mutes, blind, insane, convicts, or idiotic." (Who would answer yes to those questions?)

➤ State and local census records were also taken, usually in the middle of a decade. Some ask for more information than federal census, including religious belief in some states.

'Riting Reminder

You'll certainly take your notebook to the National Archives Branch. But do you have your notebook always waiting? You never know when you'll stumble over information too good not to jot down.

Military Research

Sadly, each generation seems to have had some sort of war, and that means that each generation had young men, your kin, fight them.

But gladly, because of this, there is information galore about your ancestral soldiers. I have at least two Revolutionary War ancestors, a War of 1812 veteran, several Civil War soldiers on both sides, one World War I and two World War II soldiers in my genealogy, for instance. And these war records can offer an incredible amount of information beyond names, dates, and places. As always, all you need to begin is some basic information.

A Package from the Past

What happens if you contact the National Archives about a look at your family's soldiers' government paper trail? You will be asked to complete a form asking for information on the soldier you've chosen to research—age and place of residence—then you sit back and wait to see what comes.

You may be very surprised when a package arrives at your door with copies of compiled service files, bounty land papers, hospital rolls, draft papers, documents with your ancestor's signature and maybe even affidavits telling stories you can use for your family history. But keep looking in that package. Company musters, rolls, rosters, enlistments, discharge records, records of burials, oaths of allegiance, and pension records should also be in your soldier's files.

First, though, why not check your local library? It may have *Military Service Records: A Select Catalog of National Archives Microfilm Publications*. Thousands of microfilm rolls will be listed. You can see what is available and ask for specific microfilm. (If you're online, check www. nara.gov.) It is helpful to know what is already there, whether you're writing for the information or going in person to view the records.

War Stories

Does your family's oral history include a war story or two? You may want to also check published military histories. Town and county histories are good places to check for stories involving hometown boys. Daughters of the American Revolution and the Newberry Library in Chicago also have notable collections of military histories. The Library of Congress is also a place where such books might be hiding.

And don't forget to look in soldier's diaries or published letters for a taste of the way life was back then. (See Chapter 10, "The Family Investigator on the Case," for more on this.) Even if your ancestor didn't do the actual writing, reading a few of the diaries and journals by other soldiers who may have fought alongside your ancestor can offer rich background. And you never know when your ancestor might jump out from the page.

If you're not sure whether or not your particular ancestor was in the military or if you are not sure which war he would have been involved in, then this list should help get you started:

➤ French and Indian War, 1754 to 1763

➤ Revolutionary War, 1775 to 1783

➤ War of 1812, 1812 to 1815

➤ Mexican-American War, 1846 to 1848

➤ Civil War (War Between the States), 1861 to 1865

➤ Spanish-American War, 1898

➤ World War I, 1914 to 1918

➤ World War II, 1941 to 1945

➤ Korean War, 1950 to 1953

➤ Vietnam War, 1954 to 1975

Immigration Research

They came in ships—your ancestors, that is. Almost all of them did, and nothing is more dramatic than a ship's passage, from old world to new, from old caste systems to wide-open opportunity. New lives, new land.

Ships were how the world traveled and traded before we invaded the air in the last few decades. Ships and their safe harbor ports sculpted our geography. Almost everybody who came to America landed here after a sea voyage, the largest group arriving between 1880 and 1914. From 1565 to 1954 (the year Ellis Island closed and most passenger lists information indexes end), Asians, Africans, and Europeans sailed to these shores across the Atlantic, Pacific, Great Lakes, and Gulf Coast.

And Ellis Island wasn't the only entry point for immigrants. The country had dozens and dozens of them. For instance, Angel Island was the leading West Coast port, Galveston and New Orleans were the leading ports of Gulf Coast, and Chicago, one of the leading Great Lakes ports, all with rich histories.

At some point in your genealogical research, you'll want to experience the first entry on American soil by exploring some fascinating documents.

The Write Word

A **bird of passage** was a young man during the age of steam ships who traveled to America for the labor season and then returned to Europe.

There is wonderful fodder for family history writing here. You need to know three pieces of information to study passenger lists:

1. Full original name
2. Approximate age at arrival
3. Approximate date of arrival

Where do you find this information?

1. **Oral family tradition.** Ask granny.
2. **Family documents.** Check for passports, citizenship papers, ticket stubs, Ellis Island Inspection Cards, family photographs.
3. **Civil and church records.** Vital records, tombstone inscriptions, baptisms, census records.
4. **Published family histories and town/county histories.**

Passenger Lists

Ships' passenger lists are divided into two groups—before and after 1820. Original passenger lists between 1565 and 1819, if they still exist, could be in a museum, an attic, or an historical archive, but they are not in the National Archives. Indexes to published lists are one place to look for these early records. The National Archives has a microfilm copy of passenger lists for years between 1820 and 1954.

What will you find? Perhaps some dramatic information that will enliven your family history writing. You may be able to figure out many things about your immigrant ancestor's family, as well as home country, from what you discover. For instance:

➤ Was your ancestor a landowner?

➤ Was he coming to make his fortune?

➤ What family members came with him or her?

➤ Was your ancestor the trailblazer or was he the last to come?

➤ Did she come on a sailing ship or come later, during the age of steam?

➤ Some families went back and forth several times before settling in. Did any relatives go back? Even back and forth? Why?

Your "Original American's" Story

For any family history writer, this information is too rich with ideas for good storytelling not to investigate. Passenger lists will show family composition, where children were born and when, and the chronology of their travels. And if you're lucky, and intuitive, you may also be able to glean what immigrating meant to them.

The clues found for your "original American" ancestor's story will fit interestingly into your family's migration story, and then in the larger picture—the migration story of America. And, of course, if you decide to continue your search beyond the shores of the United States, this passenger list is where you'd start.

Two helpful publications to get you started are the Family History Library's pamphlet *Tracing Immigrant Origins* and the book *They Came in Ships, A Guide to Finding Your Immigrant Ancestor's Arrival Record.*

Land Records

A history of how the West—and for that matter the rest of the country—was won is really all about land. The majority of our ancestors who didn't have it probably dreamed of owning it, and may have spent their lives trying to get it. This is certainly true of the Western pioneers in our family trees.

So, following land ownership can be an exciting angle for a genealogical search, be it homesteading, a land rush, such as Oklahoma's, or bounty land warrants. You'll find stories there to re-create for your family history. Where do you begin looking? For most of the states, land records between 1800 to 1974 are in the National Archives. Some states chose to keep their land records in their state capitals, including the original 13 colonies/states along with Texas, Kentucky, Tennessee, West Virginia, Vermont, and Hawaii.

You'll find files holding private claims of individual settlers on land in public land states, bounty land warrants, land donation entries, and homestead applications. Each one holds a story.

An Internet Adventure

A wonder, that's what the Internet is, a wonder that opens up a whole new world for genealogy—but a virtual wonder. Still, virtual wonders can be incredible.

Log on to the Family History Library Web site, type in a few basic vital records, and stand back for the whoosh of all those front doors opening to you by thousands of volunteers attempting to compile data of everyone who ever lived. Check the Newberry Library site for resources to begin your Cherokee heritage research. Log on to the Shtetleseeker page of the JewishGen Web site, and you can be viewing maps of Eastern Europe from another time. (See Appendix A for addresses to these Web sites.)

Check out cyndilist.com—a Web site pioneered by a housewife genealogist—and find over 300 pages with links to an incredible number of genealogical sites around the world, including prison roles. From there, you can find yourself in a discussion group with others who are interested in Quaker ancestors (QUAKER-ROOTS). Or join a "mailing list" that shares information of everything from Mayflower descendents (MAYFLOWER) to Native American roots (INDIAN-ROOTS) to teenagers who are interested in genealogy (GENTEEN-L). Cyndi's list is a good start for beginners.

Hey, even old cousin Bernie might have his own family history Web site. And so could you. There are sites for every kind of ethnic group and every geographical location. One site in Newfoundland offers from 300 cemeteries headstones to view, for instance. It's a crazy quilt, the Internet genealogy world, and it's getting bigger and more varied by the day. Periodicals exist just to help you find your way around the sites on genealogy with reviews of the best sites as they come and go.

The Wonder of Internet Research

Where to go first? A good place to start would be the Family History Library, which is now online, a wonderful step forward for genealogists. Have you tried the site? Do you keep getting that busy signal? Now's the time for a friendly reminder that is the fastest-growing hobby in America and genealogy "surfing the Net" is probably second. It's also a good time to remind you that genealogy was around long before the Internet, so never give up your research because of a "traffic jam" on the communication superhighway. Genealogy has always been down the backroads and will always be there with or without the superhighway's help. That said, let's get back to the Internet's wonders.

Family History Library Online

Salt Lake City's Family History Library is a tremendous resource, whether you get there by communication superhighway, by "snail mail," or by automobile. The church has over 600 million names on record from all over the world. Their records draw from their mother lode of genealogical data, and their volunteers have spent three decades computerizing all the information. It's the world's largest genealogical repository and it's all free of charge.

'Riting Reminder

Don't forget to add each Internet visit to your Research Log.

The Web site offers a search engine that hunts for the specific name you input through the church's Ancestral File of 35 million names listed according to pedigree charts. And it also seeks out surnames among thousands of smaller, unrelated genealogical Web sites that have been evaluated by volunteers. It also has its own chat room/bulletin board feature called a "collaborative feature," which will allow users to share research with others searching similar lines, a nice feature for discovering more cousins and what they might know.

A Peek, Then a Point

Of course, just as we mentioned earlier, using the Internet is a great place to start, but if you don't watch it, you can get on the wrong track with the wrong ancestor and get lost. A recent *Time* magazine article put it well, "Like the Internet as a whole, online genealogy information is a chaotic hodgepodge." What it offers is a peek and then a point in the right direction. You should use it as a catalog, a wonderful resource for the detective double-check, and as a network for exchanging information with others who have your same research interests. Those are the formidable strengths of the Internet.

Related Facts

Internet addresses, or URLs, tell you what to expect: If an address ends in .gov, it's a government site; .com, it's commercial business site; .org, it's a nonprofit organization; and .edu, it's a university-connected site.

A Virtual Wonder Is Still Virtual

Believe it or not, some Internet sites will even do your ancestral search for you (for a nice fee). But where's the adventure in that? And how do you know it's real unless you've touched it yourself? Or if it's your authentic ancestral trail? Besides, no one's going to care like you do.

A virtual wonder, by definition, is based on the real thing, but is not the real thing. Virtual tennis may be fun, but it will never beat the feeling of the whap of the ball, the adrenaline surge of the match, or the cardiovascular benefits of getting out of your chair and getting into the game. And that brings us to hometown research.

Journaling Down the Genealogical Trail

What research area interests you the most right now? Why? Jot down the answer in your journal.

The Least You Need to Know

➤ The librarians are waiting to guide your work.

➤ The government's documents are a treasure trove.

➤ Your family probably included soldiers; their stories are waiting for you to discover at your local National Archives Branch.

➤ The Internet is an incredible genealogical search tool.

➤ Virtual genealogy is helpful but nothing beats "hands-on" genealogy, so make your Internet work a prelude to your genealogical trek, not the trek itself.

Looking in All the Right Places—in Hometowns

You're finally there. You've gotten in your car (or boat, plane, train) and you've decided to visit the hometown of a long line of your ancestors. You've already done all you can by mail. It's time to see the real stuff in hopes of finding some intriguing family stories.

Searching for Your Schmoes

You've chosen to research your grandmother's maternal line—the Schmoes who lived in this town, as did a long line of your ancestral Schmoes, circa 1870 to 1959. They owned farms and stores, attended church and social clubs, and experienced all the things of everyday life in their times. And you are sure that you'll find them in the leavings of this place's past.

Where do you start? (That is, after that rest stop to fill up the car and grab that grilled cheese sandwich.) Start at the same place you would at home—the public library.

The Hometown Library

Ask for the local history collection, and tell the librarian why you're there. You might be surprised when she says, "Oh, I remember that family! Mrs. Schmoe's bachelor uncle was a good friend of my grandfather's. He was quite a character!"

There are certain unique things a local library can offer about its town's past and the people who lived in it. Make sure to ask if the library has voting records, school records, church records, or old photographs for the time period you're researching.

Sometimes a hometown library will also go out of its way to keep a special section for its area's history and the people who made it. Here are a few unusual things a local library might have:

➤ **Necrology.** A collection of obituaries or a list of local people who have died during a certain decade or century.

➤ **Vertical files.** Letters from people just like you who have written for information. You might find more "cousins" who have asked and perhaps answered the same questions you're researching.

➤ **Mug books.** A volume in praise of their town's settlers and prominent citizens. If your ancestors owned a business or held an office, they will probably be in there.

➤ **Gazetteers, plats, and county atlases.** Indexes and map sketches of homes, farms, and townships during certain historical times. These may help you locate a family cemetery or the farm your ancestor once owned. They can also include pen drawings that capture the time period.

The Daily Hometown Tattler

You don't want to forget those hometown newspaper accounts. Granny Fanny Mae may have had her wedding mentioned, along with all the townspeople who attended, in the newspaper's weekly "Around the Town" column. If you're lucky, the town's newspapers will have some sort of index and the library will have a copy. Or you could visit the newspaper office, if it still exists, in person. That's not a bad idea, especially if you can find some old-timers there. If not, you always have your dates to check. Have a wedding date? Check the papers a week later. Have a death date? Look for an obituary following that date, too.

What else might you find in the city newspaper's files? Check public notices and appreciation notices. Birth, marriage, anniversary announcements, news stories, property sales notices, summons, advertisements, letters to the editor, church news, social club news, visiting family news—your ancestors, the Schmoes, could be listed in all of the above. The smaller the town, the more family news you'll find.

Around the Town with Tillie

Dateline: July 1, 1947

Angela Ann Shoemaker had the privilege of hosting her niece and nephew Joe Schmoe Shoemaker and Josephine Schmoe Shoemaker for a lovely weekend this June. The youngsters are here while their parents, Johnny Shoemaker and Jesselyn Sue Simmons Schoemaker, who are both 1936 graduates of our high school, are taking a short vacation down the coast from their home in Orangeville, Florida, where they now run a successful dry goods business. A good time was had by all.

The sort of information that would have bored you to tears as a child is genealogy heaven, as well as a lot of fun to find. The larger the city, the larger the paper, and the less detail you'll find, but it's always still worth a look through the local paper's index, especially at the town's library. You never know what news your ancestors might have made.

If nothing else, a glance through old newspapers can give you a great feeling of the times. It's not called the "first draft of history" for nothing.

Take another look at the example of the type of newspaper article you might find. How many leads can you find in Tillie's gossip column for your Schmoe family branch?

Open Letter

Remember the open letter idea that we mentioned in Chapter 10, "The Family Investigator on the Case," when you were learning your sleuth skills? This is the perfect time and place for trying this "missing persons" technique.

Consider taking out an ad, an "open letter," to the residents in the hometown paper about your search. In most small towns, someone will remember something about longtime residents like the Schmoes, if given a chance. If nothing else, an open letter might find you a new lead or two from the local townfolk, and that will be worth the small amount paid out.

Besides, you will have endeared yourself to the hometown newspaper's owner. And an endeared newspaper owner is a newspaper owner who might answer your questions, open his morgue files to you, and even take the time to suggest ideas for finding who and what you are looking for. You never know. Don't want to spend the money? A letter to the editor can also do the job.

What might a hometown open letter or a letter to the editor say? Try something like this—but you may want to make it shorter if you're paying by the word:

Dear Editor (or if an ad, "To Pleasantville residents):

I am researching my grandmother's branch of the family tree, the Schmoes, longtime residents of Pleasantville, for our family history. Angela Schmoe Shoemaker was married to Joshua Jacob Schmoe, who owned the corner drugstore, from 1889 to 1939. Her brother, Joe Schmoe V, is buried here. I am interested in contacting anyone who knew them or know how I might contact Joe Schmoe's descendents.

Please contact me through this newspaper office, or at the address below, and thanks for your help.

Sincerely,

(Your name and address)

Get Me to the Church on Time

Don't underestimate the power of church records in your ancestors' lives. Religion so ruled our ancestors' lives that you may find more documentation on church records than you'd ever expect (if you can find the church records). It's worth a stop by the local church the ancestral Schmoes attended. The Yearbook of American and Canadian Churches offers a history of all denominations and a listing of addresses for each church's national headquarters and church history archives. The Official Catholic Directory is another resource that has been published since 1820. Many denominations have historical collections.

Be they Catholic, Baptist, Jewish, or Puritan, their religious activities are quite telling and worthy of your family history research. These records might even fill in a granny gap or such in unusual ways. Some records are kept in central locations, some in historical collections, some were considered personal property of the minister.

Episcopal parish registers are extremely helpful and many of the ones created during colonial times still exist in some published form. The Quakers and Mormons both kept excellent records. Catholic records are also excellent, but be warned that they can be a bit harder to gain access to. But others, especially the

A Relatively Good Idea

Don't forget to check newspapers within your ancestors' social, ethnic, or religious circles. There used to be a newspaper for everything and everyone. Was your ancestor a member of a fraternal organization? Was he/she an upstanding Methodist, Presbyterian, or Catholic? Genealogical libraries will know about these sorts of newspapers that might offer information on your ancestor's life, full of details you'd find nowhere else.

Protestant churches that grew up with the frontier expansion, have less formal records. Early record-keeping was scant and yet some still exist in church and town historical associations' archives. Later record-keeping though, centering on hometown churches can be very helpful and worth a stop on your hometown trip. But stories your great-granny may tell could be your best clues.

Also, don't underestimate old customs. Inquiring about your ancestor's religious past may help you find answers as well as history. For instance, do you know what a "bann" is? It was a spoken or public announcement of an intention to wed that was made on three successive Sundays in a community's church. If you uncover that trail, you may find information on the certificates filled out before any wedding you haven't been able to find elsewhere, including a dispensation for the bann—a document that allowed a couple to dispense with the public announcement—which includes all birth dates, places, and comments.

Of course, since one of basic freedoms in this country is religious freedom, don't forget that your ancestor could easily have been born an Episcopal, converted to the Methodist church, and died a Baptist. Oral history can help corral such wandering pilgrims.

Is the hometown church not there anymore? If you can pinpoint the name of it, you may be able to find its records in the historical society or library where they have probably been transferred.

> **Deep Thought**
>
> *Don't underestimate the role the church played in your ancestors' lives. And don't forget that our country was founded on religious freedom, so your ancestor could easily have been born a Catholic, marry as a Lutheran, then die a Baptist.*

Just Enjoy

Beyond your research contacts, make sure to take an afternoon to just enjoy the town. Be a tourist. Look around. Drive to the old farmland or to the house the last Schmoe lived in. Picture your ancestors in certain places. It's no stretch to think that your ancestors may have walked where you're walking. Look down at the steps as you go in to the old library or the courthouse and picture it happening. That will place you in the right frame of mind.

Courthouse Research

The courthouse looms ahead of you. It's a quaint-looking place (except for the brick institutional-looking extension in the back), and just the high ceilings and creaky wooden floors give you a feeling of walking back in time.

Which office do you visit first? County Clerk's office? Circuit Court Clerk's Office? County Recorder Office? So many places, so little time.

Touching Granny's Birth Certificate

Touching granny's birth certificate is a good feeling. When you uncover any original document, you will be holding a paper your ancestor held, too. All that separates you is time. So, even if you have these facts and figures, even if you have a copy at home of this sort of vital records of your ancestors, don't pass up a chance to see the real thing.

If you've contacted the courthouse records clerk previously for the vital records, perhaps you can meet the person who fulfilled your requests and thank him personally. Who knows? Small towns are small places, remember. Odds are you can make this natural connection now that you are finally here.

Courthouse Wish List

Walk up the courthouse steps, go through the big doors, stroll down the musty hall, and choose an office for your morning's work—one specific mission at a time. Where to go? After the obvious vital records search, you should include an ancestor's will, deed to once-owned land or probate of an estate. Your courthouse wish list should include:

➤ Vital records

➤ Wills/probate records

➤ Land deeds

➤ Civil/common court records

Wills and Probate Records

Did your ancestor own property and die in the county with a will? The ancestor was known then to die in *testate*. In the probate office, look for court minutes, court order books, inventory books, bond books, account books, settlement books, and estate packets.

If the ancestor died without a will, that is known as being *intestate* estate-wise. Of course, if he or she didn't have any property, there won't be a record at all. But sometimes, finding no records can give you important information, too.

Wills and probate records can help re-create a family tree. They can …

➤ Explain the disposition of an estate after an owner's death—who got what.

➤ Show family relationships as well as pivotal social connections to follow.

➤ Give addresses of next of kin.

➤ Offer clues to land owned in other places.

➤ Mention religious affiliation.

➤ Give names of executors and witnesses.

The Write Word

To die **testate** is to die with a will. To die **intestate** is to die without a will.

Finding witnesses is a good lead, even though by custom, such people are not family members. One woman learned about a devoted friendship between her grandfather and a famous state politician of the time by noticing the witness signature. That's a story worth pursuing for your family history.

Local Land Records

Did the ancestor own land? Then he or she had to have a deed. Deeds are land records ranging from private land claims to homesteader's applications. State archives and tax records are a good source for these (see Chapter 11, "Looking in All the Right Places—Library and Beyond"), but the courthouse is probably the place to begin this search.

If you haven't found such a deed in the ancestor's personal papers through your house-to-house relative search, they just might pop up here in the county courthouse. In the deed offices, look for survey books, plat books, mortgages, oil leases, power of attorney books, and tax books. In fact, you never know—you might also find the original deed. Sometimes people did not come back to get the original deeds. The courthouse might still have them.

By the way, indexes to such records have a style format all their own. Be sure to ask for help with understanding any you find in the county courthouse. If the clerk has had three genealogists in the office that day asking the same thing, you may be on your own, but a simple explanation should be included inside the front cover of each index, and once you get the hang of it, you'll start all your county courthouse searches with an index—with no help at all, thank you very much.

Civil (Common) Court Records

Was your ancestor in the courts for any reason? Was he or she a rebel, divorced, subject to suits, or any other reason we all go to court through our lives? Was he a country lawyer? Such accounts are stories in and of themselves, if you can just uncover them. In the civil records office, look for papers of small and large claims, debts, levies, summons, notices required by law to be published in the local newspaper, depositions, and divorces. Other interesting civil records you might find are orphan guardianships.

D-I-V-O-R-C-E

What can divorce records offer the researcher? Divorce records yield names and ages of children, state or county of their births, when and where the marriage began and where it ended and often on what grounds. While divorce is not a pleasant topic to explore for any family, much less family history, its reality deeply affects a family's ancestral lines and must be included in all genealogical chartings.

'Riting Reminder

Remember to be careful taking notes. Abstract meticulously and look for clues incessantly.

All Kinds of Documents

Our society and our lives are replete with documents. You never know what you'll find. For instance, somewhere in my sister's home, as well as mine, is a legal document that lists our possible guardianship of our underage children in the case of their death, including signatures all around. When the children all passed 21, we received another legal document absolving us of that responsibility. A copy of that document may survive us all to be found by some ancestor of ours. Such are the odd genealogical primary sources that might pop up in your digging; they may or may not add facts, but will always add humanity.

Cemetery Research

Where is your ancestor buried? Is it a public cemetery, a private cemetery, a family cemetery, a church cemetery, or even a fraternal lodge's cemetery?

Or could it even be an abandoned cemetery? The farther you go back in your search, the more of these you will find yourself searching for. But, as macabre as it may sound, this can be a fascinating experience.

Graveyard Philosopher

If there were ever a place to feel philosophical about life and death and all things mortal, visiting a cemetery, especially an ancestor's old cemetery, has to be it. To stand at your ancestor's place of rest is to experience a place of wonder and sudden belonging, roots in the truest genealogical meaning of the word. And it doesn't take too long in any cemetery to be amazed—beyond genealogical interest—at the effort the generations gave to not being forgotten. Of course, every time a genealogist finds an ancestor's tombstone, that's exactly what has happened.

But you have to find the right cemetery first. So, the big question must be, where is it? And is it still where it's supposed to be? Laugh as you may, considering the usual lack of mobility after death, but this is very real problem for a genealogical search past a certain point. If the cemetery stood in the way of urban sprawl, it could have been dug up "en toto" and placed elsewhere.

Maybe the town is gone and there's no one to keep the cemetery up. Maybe a family cemetery is forgotten because every family member who knew of its existence has died or moved. Or maybe the land changed hands and the new owner had no clue what to do with it. As "forever" as tombstones and cemeteries may feel, there's nothing forever when it comes to time's eraser, as we've discussed.

But serendipity awaits those who go searching. One of my family's genealogists recounts the exciting trip he took in search of two of his Revolutionary War ancestors' graves in two very out-of-the-way places in the South. One grave, that of a major, he found in a completely overgrown corner of a place called "Picken's Chapel," a site that took some genealogical sleuthing and historical map-studying to find. The other grave, that of a colonel in the Continental line, was an even more interesting site—it was a heap of native stones in a private cemetery where the owner kept the grounds immaculate and placed dozens of red, white, and blue birdhouses nearby. Time may keep trying to erase these places, but graves tend to be very persistent in not going away, thankfully so for us as we search for this unique family history experience.

Cemeteries Galore

The first step in planning any cemetery visit should be finding the type of cemetery you're looking for. What kind of cemetery is your ancestor buried in?

> ➤ **Public cemeteries.** Cemeteries maintained by a city or county. The records, open to the public, may be available at the courthouse, city hall, or on the grounds.

> ➤ **Private cemeteries.** Also called memorial parks are run as a business, and are a more modern development. Many of these are the kind that don't have standing tombstones, only in-ground markers (better for mowing if not for ambiance). Their records are private, but don't hesitate to ask.

175

➤ **Family cemeteries.** Private cemeteries, which can take all shapes in all kinds of places; you may find these under an old shade tree in the back pasture of family land or at the edge of a small town, full of extended family members' graves. Records, if there are any, will probably be at the local historical society or library, or in the hands of remaining family members. Check deeds of the property, especially if it has been sold out of the family; such deeds usually mention preserving the cemetery. Local gazetteers, plats and maps of land, found at the local library or historical society, might show old cemeteries' locations when all else fails.

➤ **Church cemeteries.** Cemeteries that usually surround the church. More often than not, the church will be a country church. Sometimes all that's left of an old settlement is its country church and its cemetery. My father's family has five generations buried in a country cemetery out in the middle of nowhere, yet it's attached to a thriving little white clapboard Methodist Church that people from neighboring towns attend. The cemetery is so well-loved, well-known, and well-maintained that many people from our small hometown, with no ties to the church or the long-gone community, chose this place for their family plot. The city public cemetery seems cold in comparison.

Every year, a "Decoration Day" is held at cemeteries on Memorial Day. This happens at many cemeteries, especially private and church ones. If your cemetery search can coincide with such a day, it's a great time to go, because the families of those buried there make this a time to decorate and to honor their generations. Family tales will be in the air.

Records for church cemeteries may be harder to find, but are usually accessible once found. Cemetery records should show the names of those buried without tombstones, too, which may be more than you think. Ask a local funeral director if you find no one available to ask at the cemetery you're visiting.

Family gravestones are waiting to deliver their messages to the person who wants to receive them. What can you do to "hear" them?

1. Study the inscriptions, such as "Beloved Wife" or "Taken Too Young." Some of the inscriptions are stories in and of themselves, and will certainly add to whatever family story you uncover attached to this ancestor.

2. Listen to what monuments are saying. Usually, the stone structures are in memory of someone, but that someone may not be buried there. Why would your ancestor be honored with a monument?

3. What else is the tombstone whispering? Is there a Bible passage quoted? Is there a fraternal order's symbol? Is a military service mentioned? Why were these the defining phrases and information chosen for this specific ancestor?

4. What does this information say about who the ancestor was?

Cemetery Cleanings

Finding private and family cemeteries, in some rural areas, can be a detective adventure as well as a family history lesson. I found myself living in a back-road town right after college for a short time. My small Texas hometown was cosmopolitan in comparison. This tiny place was an old dried-up cowtown that came into existence as a stop along the Chisholm Trail, and hadn't seen much traffic since.

Living there for that short time was a strange experience, almost like entering the Twilight Zone, since I was so young and the town of less than 1,000 was almost all elderly. It was as if time had stopped inside its city limits, and that must have also been true for the people's customs, many unusual to me, but normal to them. For instance, in the short time I was there, I was invited to half a dozen cemetery cleanings.

A drive down any of the country roads forking out every which way from the quiet town square would be a drive by some little metal archway with a faded family name hanging from it and a smattering of tombstones beyond. There was no perpetual care, no cemetery association. There were only these yearly gatherings of the many branches of each family in their work clothes with their hoes and rakes and their lawnmowers and picnic lunches, prepared for their all-day celebration of respect for their family's past.

> ### Deep Thought
>
> *Gravestones can speak to the visitors, especially those with ears to hear. Considering you are a writer and a family historian, that should be you and your listening ears. What might you try to hear?*

Of course, the significance of this was lost on me at that age, but not the care and concern these people took in remembering their long-gone own. Today, though, I cannot help but wonder, "Are they still being maintained as well as they were twenty years ago?" One day, descendants from these families will trek back to their hometown to find their country cemetery and will enjoy the search to find the one person still alive, or the one document still existing, that will lead them to the rusting arch and the overgrown cemetery.

Grave Expectations

You should remember a few things about any cemetery visit. Being prepared beforehand is a good idea. What do I mean by prepared?

Be prepared to get dirty. Except in private cemeteries, weeds, as well as overgrown rose bushes, thorns and all can obscure graves.

Be prepared to have bittersweet feelings, especially in older cemeteries. Not so much because of the setting or even the fragility and temporal nature of life (okay, those, too), but because of the loss of these precious places' markers. Age, weather, and vandalism are all conspiring to ruin these solid pieces of the past.

'Riting Reminder

When you go to a cemetery, be prepared to ...

➤ Get dirty.

➤ Have bittersweet thoughts.

➤ Take pictures of the head-stones.

➤ Be a detective.

➤ Take notes.

Be prepared to take pictures of the headstones. While this may sound morbid, there is so much detail on older tombstones, you'll consider a snapshot easier than relying on voluminous notes. (Of course, go ahead and take notes, too.) A photo image, in this instance, is truly better documentation. And there is no way to know when your picture may become the only evidence remaining of that tombstone. Cemetery rubbings are also popular with genealogists, although they are now discouraged because of the possible damage to these wonderful historic, delicate pieces of stone.

By the way, be prepared to play detective. Did you notice that this branch of your family has quite a few children buried here around the same time? Could there be a reason? What about the entire family in the corner of the family plot who died within weeks of each other in 1918? Could they all have died of the Spanish flu epidemic or perhaps a house fire or some other catastrophe? Is a young mother buried near her child with similar death dates? Stories are everywhere. And you can find them.

Family Reunions

Another "don't-miss" reason to go home for the family history–writing private eye is a family reunion. An oral history bonanza is waiting there. Between mouthfuls of potato salad, you will have the chance to hear about your roots in ways you've never heard before. (Those cousins have never looked so good to you.)

And don't forget to take your kids. You may be surprised. The time has to be right, but, when it is, any child can thrill to the sense of belonging that comes from being around family, experiencing firsthand the concept of family roots. This can be especially true for families that have moved a long way from that ancestral home.

My high school tennis doubles partner and I have stayed in touch over the years and remained close friends even though both of us left our small Texas town far behind. She had married a talented drummer during college and immediately moved to Los Angeles with him and has lived there ever since. Her daughter grew up a California girl, through and through. Texas was very far away. She'd visited her granny in our small Texas hometown, but she'd never gone to the family reunions in West Texas that her grandmother had always talked about.

One day, my high school friend decided it was time for her whole family to go to the family reunion. Her mother was getting older, and her children had never met that side of the family. To my friend's surprise, her California daughter listened, mesmerized, at the stories about her grandmother's grandmothers—one pristine and sweet, remembered for the way she sat at the head of the table every morning and poured bowls of Post Toasties for each of her children, the other who worked out in the field alongside her farmer husband and all the other men picking cotton.

As her cousins laughed warmly about these long-gone matriarchs of the family, my friend's daughter, the California girl, was suddenly seeing the pioneer West Texans from whom she came. She was meeting women who were hers without her knowing it, and feeling the inexplicable feeling of belonging to a family, not only living, but dead. It was all happening through the magic of family stories. And my high school friend noticed that her daughter's eyes were suddenly brimming with tears.

Such is the magic of "place" to make oral history and family bonding real. Don't miss the opportunities hometowns offer for you and your immediate family. You'll notice many such opportunities as you go further down your genealogical trail. Choose one and enjoy yourself. And keep your journal always near.

Following the Literal Trail

Now that you're on the road, this would be a good time to picture your ancestors on the road. They may not have had interstates and truck stops and Golden Arches along the way, but they traveled down many of the same roads you took to get to this hometown of theirs. Why not research their leaving of—or arriving at—this place as well as the years of living there?

Each ancestral line will have branches that stay put for generations at a time. But more than not, since America's history is one of mobility, their stories follow the trails that lead to new lives down the pioneer road. So, at the same time you may be researching those ancestors who stayed put, you can also be researching the ones who had the American wanderlust and moved on.

The roads may not have been called Interstate 5 or Route 66, but they had great historic names even two centuries ago, such as "The Old Northwestern Turnpike" and the "Chisholm Trail," trod by thousands of American dreamers. Maps exist of each one of these routes taken. *The Handy Book for Genealogists* offers maps showing approximately a hundred migration trails along with state and county descriptions of each dusty route.

A Relatively Good Idea

Why not track your ancestors' trails to your very own doorstep as a family history writing angle? Think how much fun you and your family can have plotting your family's trek to your driveway. You can even add maps to your family history.

So, since you've planned this road trip, why not really make it a genealogical one by planning to drive as close to your ancestors route as you can? Just compare what you already know about your ancestors' travels and then use common sense to trace the logical route taken.

Journaling Down the Genealogical Trail

Are you going beyond genealogy? Are you getting excited as you find a will or a deed, searching for a narrative strain? Are you beginning to see the stories in the genealogical facts and figures you find? Jot down in your journal one story you see hiding behind the facts you've already uncovered.

The Least You Need to Know

➤ Your family history becomes real when you experience the actual place where it all happened.

➤ Local historical societies and libraries are the first places to visit.

➤ Talking to old-timers can uncover stories of powerful hometown connections.

➤ Cemetery visits are especially moving for the family history writer.

Part 3

Getting Organized

Have you noticed the mound of paper growing in your home office/spare room? That's what happens when you begin your family history research trail. This section will keep you from going crazy as you add to your research pile. You'll learn creative ways to organize your work, how to correspond in writing during your research, what to do about unusual information you may uncover, and how to know when enough is enough.

Chapter 13

Writing All the Right People Right

In This Chapter

➤ The importance of your "other" ancestors

➤ How to contact the right people

➤ How to write the right people right

Often, half the battle of getting a family history research project going in earnest is to know who to contact, where to contact, and how to contact. You now know where, and you've begun to understand who. Now let's discuss how—writing all those letters and what they should say.

Your Collateral Ancestors' Value

Genealogy talks a lot about direct descendants and ancestors. Most genealogists would suggest tracking only one or two siblings of an ancestor, but you definitely want to practice whole family genealogy by including the stories of your ancestors' siblings, your *collateral relatives*.

Can you pass up a story to add to your family history about Great-Aunt Lula, the flapper, when you unearth a photo of her doing the Charleston along with a letter that tells a Roaring Twenties tale of speak-easies and bathtub gin? Or that amazing story about the Civil War hero who happens to be your second cousin on your mother's side? I don't think so.

The Write Word

A **collateral relative** is a relative with whom a person shares a common ancestor, but not the same ancestral line, i.e., your ancestral aunts, uncles, cousins.

Pause your headlong rush to visit your dead ancestors and look around at the long-gone uncles and aunts, your collateral ancestors, along the way. As we've already established, your goal is different than a pure genealogist's. Since your emphasis is more on family history and not ancestral genealogy in the strictest sense, that great-great-uncle, aunt, or cousin thrice removed may have an amazing story to tell that sheds a grand spotlight on deserving relatives with no one else to tell their tale. And they've been waiting for you to tell it.

You, the family history writer, wouldn't think of not tracking down and adding colorful stories of your whole family just because the person isn't a direct ancestor. And you certainly wouldn't ignore those collateral stories that may have seemed risqué at one time, or even criminal. As one family history writer put it, "pray for a few sinners in your family." (See Chapter 15, "Kissing Kin, Black Sheep, and Granny Gaps," about "black sheep" in your family and their value.)

But beyond telling ancestral "cousins'" stories, there's a living cousin factor you cannot ignore, either. Your living cousins just might be able to tell parts of your own story better than you know. Your cousins may know information you don't about your own direct descendants.

Cousin Connection

My husband's father spent four hard years in Europe during World War II as an Army officer. He never talked about it to his family. As teenager, my husband asked his father the usual questions, but he would never answer them. Older than most of the Army troops he led, when he returned, he wanted to waste no time on the past.

A Relatively Good Idea

Make a list of your collateral ancestors, living and dead, for three generations back.

He was also a Texas Aggie, having graduated from what is now Texas A&M University that, then as now, has a legendarily strong tradition. In his day, to be an Aggie was to be in the "corps," one of many campus military groups, all of which were connected to the real armed forces.

His two sons, however, didn't follow him to A&M. So, after my father-in-law's death, one of my husband's cousins who did become an Aggie, wrote a dramatic obituary for the university magazine's "Silver Taps" section. My husband was incredibly moved when he read it, moved and surprised, because the article mentioned information about his father's war experiences he'd never heard. His own cousin knew more about his father than he did. While his father had never talked about it with his children, he had obviously shared his experiences with his sisters and brothers, and through the years, they had shared the stories with their own offspring.

Think this is uncommon? Not at all. Your cousins may know more than you can imagine about your own parents and grandparents, as well as the story of your long-ago ancestors, but you'll never know unless you ask.

A Relatively Good Idea

Make a list of your first cousins. What might you ask them about your own parents?

Saving Your Ancestors

Your cousins may even come to the rescue by giving names and places to the things you've inherited through the years, the photos and memorabilia that came to you with no explanation at all.

One beginning genealogist had just moved across the country, and as most of us do, she had given away many things she thought she didn't want in order to travel lighter. In fact, before she left her old home, she had taken half a dozen boxes of old things to her church's thrift store. One box was full of things from an aunt who loved garage sales, and was always buying odds and ends, especially ugly, old frames with unidentified photos in them, none of which were the budding genealogist's taste. At the same time, just before she left, she sent out an introductory letter to some distant cousins she had uncovered through a family history volume, with her new address on the enclosed SASEs.

One day, after settling in at her new hometown, she received a package from one of those distant cousins, and inside was a long, chatty letter, and some photos of the ancestors they had in common. And there, in those photos, was an old photo she recognized. The very same picture was in one of the old frames she'd given away. As you might imagine, aghast that she'd given away great-great-granny, she called the thrift store and asked if they still had her boxes. They did, and soon, granny was saved. All because of her cousin connection. She came away with a valuable genealogy lesson as well as a doggone good cousin story to tell.

Reaching Out

After you decide that communicating with these relatives is a good idea, what's the best way to do so? Let's explore several ways you can reach out and touch them.

Announcing Your Search

You know Cousin Bernie who showed up on your doorstep announcing his genealogy search? Bernie's example is probably not the best way to announce your family history project. What might you do? You can compose a letter, one you can adapt to each situation, as you uncover more and more branches of your family tree.

> Dear Cuz,
>
> I'm working on a family history and just found out that we may be third cousins. Our great-great-grandparents were John Joslin Rutledge and Annie Lou Perkins of Elmo, Texas. As everyone, but my family line, moved away the siblings lost touch until even your names were lost. My family history work led to your door, though. And my letter is to just announce my project in hopes that you may have some original documents that would help make these great-grandparents or any of our common "greats" come alive for us.
>
> Might you have such documents or photographs or know who does? I would truly enjoy hearing from you and hopefully exchange facts and family stories about our different branches of the same family tree.
>
> I'm enclosing an SASE, in hopes you will take the time to help me in my family quest.
>
> Relatively yours,
>
> your name

You can write this sort of letter and use your own common sense about how much charm or decorum to use. (I'd suggest erring on the side of decorum, considering you are writing to complete strangers, whether they have your name or not.) For the relatives you know, of course, you can personalize the letter any way you see fit.

The Write Word

An **SASE** is a self-addressed stamped envelope included in all your correspondence out of courtesy and expedience.

The Eternal SASE

Always enclose an *SASE,* though. Because of this one forgotten item, you may never hear a peep from anyone. An SASE—a self-addressed, stamped envelope—shows you to be courteous and thoughtful, and it also is a compelling impetus, believe it or not, for the relative to respond in some fashion. That letter with your postage is almost like an obligation. Use it lavishly.

Open Letter

As mentioned in the sleuthing section of Chapter 10, "The Family Investigator on the Case," an open letter in a hometown paper can help uncover new contacts and new leads. What would you do if you opened your hometown paper and found a big ad or a letter to the editor that seemed to be written to you? My guess is you'd tentatively respond after a few well-chosen inquiries. Think of what you'd respond to in such an open letter and try to write your letter that way.

Progressive Letters

Ever been to a progressive dinner? You have cocktails at one house, then salad at another, then soup at the next and the entree at the next, and on and on to the final cup of coffee. That's the idea with a progressive letter. It's a generic letter that you send like a happy chain letter through your nearest relatives. Why not use it with rela-

'Riting Reminder

Don't forget these open letter content basics:

1. Details of the family for reader identification.
2. Help in finding relatives.
3. Mention of your family history writing project.

tives you know, either well, or at least marginally? Why? Because the ones who know you will probably be less likely to ignore you and not send it on its way. You will only be disappointed if you choose even one relative who might let it sit on a desk and never find its way back to you. So, choose your mailing list well.

How might it work? You would have to include a big manila envelope already addressed and stamped for the next person in the chain, and you'd have to ask specific questions for each to answer—a questionnaire of sorts. The design would not be that complex. Just leave a page for each question and mention they can either fill in information on that page or clip their own page to the information before it is sent on to Cousin Hubert in Boise.

Postal Family Reunion

The fun thing about a progressive letter is that each new relative who receives the letter will get to read the entries added by all the prior relatives who've received it and sent it on. It's like a postal family reunion. Your relatives' quotes, stories and comments are the reason for the postal effort, as well as the facts and figures they can offer. Tell them so.

Compile your list of questions, then make out your list of lucky relatives to get the letter, adding stamped envelopes for each new place it's to be sent to, being clear about the path you want it to follow, i.e., telling each relative who they specifically should send it to next. (And don't forget to add an envelope with your name and address attached.) Also suggest a time frame, a week or two for each relative, then add the weeks and the number of lucky recipients to give yourself an approximate time to get it back in return mail. (Think about adding your calculations to the package for the guilt factor. That may help it on its way, too.)

What might be your questions to ask at this postal family reunion? Why not use the same questions you would for a face-to-face interview? This is, in a way, a postal interview, isn't it? The main idea is to help get your relatives' juices flowing, their memories returning, and the results coming your way. Here are a few good questions you might add to the interview questions suggested earlier:

➤ What is your strongest memory of (insert certain relative's name)?

➤ Do you have any memory of stories being told about any of our ancestors?

➤ What is your earliest memory of meeting second or third cousins for the first time? Was it at a funeral or wedding? A family reunion? Who do you remember most and why?

➤ What is your strongest funeral memory? Wedding memory?

➤ Did you ever hear your parents tell stories about their parents or grandparents?

➤ Do you have in your possession any historic family documents, newspaper clippings, or heirlooms that may tell something interesting about our family?

Always remember to add a nice space at the bottom of your letter with words introducing it to the effect of:

➤ Did these questions make you think of any other moments you could share? Please note them here:

You get the idea. See Chapter 9, "Looking in All the Right Places—at Home," for interview questions that might stir up more specific family questions you could ask this select group of your relations.

Even a Personal Ad?

What if the hometown happens to be a large one as is the local newspaper? Then an ad in the "Personals" section might be an adventure. Whatever you write, though— be it open letter, personal letter, or genealogical magazine query section entry— remember to give a few details so the reader can easily identify the family, ask for help in finding relatives, and mention your family history writing project. And also remember, in this day and age, giving out your phone and email may not be a good idea—consider using the services of your newspaper where applicable.

Genealogical Periodical Personals

There are literally thousands of genealogical periodicals, as we've already discussed. Flip through the pages of a few and you'll see that in most of them you'll find a sort of "open letter" section for family queries much like the one you'd like to write. Contact these periodicals for the cost involved in placing your query in their magazine.

Related Facts

Here are more relative letter questions you might add:

1. What cousin did you like the most?

2. Did you live near lots of family, and did you socialize?

3. Was your mother a good cook?

4. What was your favorite toy?

5. Can you remember any stories your parents told about their parents?

6. What one memory do you have of your father's job?

Many national journals are connected to genealogical societies and come as part of membership, such as *The National Genealogical Society's Newsletter,* and *The New England Historical and Genealogical Society's Register.* Other national periodicals *not* affiliated with societies are by subscription only. *Reunions Magazine, Heritage Quest,* and *Everton's Genealogical Helper* are three periodicals that have query sections.

Personalizing the Style

Studying a few query sections in your library's collection of such magazines will remind you that writing for the genealogical world has its own style. Here's what your ad might look like in such a query section:

Seeking descendents of Angela Schmoe Shoemaker.

B. 10 June 1878, Pleasantville, Georgia, m. 1 May 1896 there to J. Schoemaker. Had 6 children—George Jay, b. 1900, Jimmy Joe, b. 1901, Ann Lila, b. 1903 (who m. Virgil Cane, 1920, moved to California), Robert Poe, b. 1904, Patrick Lee, b. 1906, Lyman William, b. 1910. Wish to contact descendents.

Letters, We Get Letters

Of course, your major correspondence will be with your genealogical search in county records departments, historical societies, and state agencies. The first step is to learn how to ask the right questions. The more questions you ask, the better you'll get at asking them. The more letters you write, the better you'll get at wording them correctly. Letters are the first link to finding those great family history stories. There are a few tips to use in your first few letters that can help you find success faster. Let's look at them.

Becoming a Superb Correspondent

The credo of genealogical letter communication is "Don't overwhelm." Keep the letter to one page and try to ask only one specific question or request. You can always ask more once you've established a relationship.

'Riting Reminder

Always type letters to professional agencies. The more professional you appear, the more preferential treatment you'll receive.

Tell what you already know, so you won't waste the clerk's or librarian's time (or yours). Write as you talk. Make the tone conversational, not stilted. Everyone, even a hassled clerk responds to a warm voice if not overdone and not long-winded. You're only trying to find out what they know. Save your best style for your family history. Get in and get out, with a thank you. Show appreciation. Show a *lot* of appreciation.

And always, always, always, include an SASE. If you are asking for photocopying to be done for your work, including a check or money order for a small amount will also gain results. Otherwise, you may be ignored. (They have budgets, too, you know.) How much to add? Calculate at about ten cents a page.

You can be a superb correspondent with just a little practice. When you write a letter asking for genealogical information, remember these tips:

➤ Don't overwhelm.

➤ Keep the letter to one page and try to ask only one specific question or request.

➤ Tell what you already know succinctly.

➤ Write as you talk.

➤ Get in and get out quickly.

➤ Show appreciation.

➤ Show a lot of appreciation.

➤ Include an SASE and a pittance for requested photocopying.

What a Good Letter Can Do

Contrary to how your relatives might treat your missives, a professionally written query to a professional office, even a bureaucratic one, will be handled professionally.

The better you write your query, the quicker and more efficient your response from the agencies and offices you write to will be. As with every search, focusing on one fact or document you want is the best way to get a good response.

Remember the bushwhacker story from my ancestor's profiles in Chapter 8, "Where to Begin"? If you recall, William Rutledge, in the early 1800s, was killed by a bush-whacker. This was "before any kind of law and order," the county history profile stated, and the Walker County records indicated that the Rutledge kinsmen "took care" of the bushwhacker.

Do you also remember my common sense question about that information? (That's part of the genealogical test of any piece of information.) If there was no law and order, what kind of records could there be? It's too good a family story not to research for a family history, so the lead is a good one.

How might a letter help me on my way to learning the whole story? Let's take it step by step. What would be your best guess on how to proceed? Would I try finding my long-lost relative who wrote the profile? Well, no. I actually have a trail that might get me to the original account faster—the mention of a published Walker County history.

A letter might start the ball rolling to my bushwhacker. I'd look up the address or per-haps make a call first for specifics to Walker County historical societies or the like. Perhaps the local librarian will know a local genealogical society that I might write to. (Maybe there's even an Internet genealogical forum group on that area.) My local library or Internet access can help get the addresses of the local library or a Walker County historical society, or the county clerk, or even phone numbers. By the way, if I'm lucky to find a historical society with the first phone call, should I ask my bush-whacker question over the phone? No. While I find my family history fascinating, the poor clerk or librarian has lots of other people asking the same sort of questions, perhaps even daily.

Finally, when I know where to write and to whom, I would write a letter, probably asking for a photocopy of any mention of my family in the county history. I'd men-tion that I'd like to verify a story found in information reportedly gained from Walker County history (and are there copies for sale?), a story that is credited to "Walker County records," supposedly before there was, in the words of the county history, "law and order." With help, I'd like to begin a search for that citation in such records. What records might have existed in that year before "law and order?"

Simplify, Simplify

Of course, that's a complicated request. I'd try to take great pains to make the letter as simple as possible and my request even simpler. This is where you begin to acquire correspondence expertise.

But most of your successful letters should and will be simple and very much to the point. And they should definitely be to the right place. Unless you never want to see your request again, be specific, even in its destination, i.e. the right department (see Chapter 12, "Looking in all the Right Places—in Hometowns"). Are you requesting a will? Try the probate department. A divorce document? Try the civil court records department. A vital record? Ask for birth, death, or marriage records departments. Unless, as mentioned, the state was already taking care of registration. Want to know who to ask and where for what? And you only have one record you're searching for? You can always pick up the phone, use the hometown's information (or use the telephone directories at your local library), call the county department yourself, and ask a *general* question such as "I'm looking for a death record in 1901 in your county. To whom do I write?" You'll usually get a very quick, very correct answer, all for the price of a phone call.

Let's try a letter asking for something very simple. Let's say you want to find out if one of your Civil War era grannies left a will. How might your letter take shape?

> Your name
> Your address
>
> The date
>
> Probate Office
> [insert name] County
> Its address
>
> Dear Probate Office Clerk:
>
> I would like to obtain a photocopy of the will for:
>
> <u>Janice Jane Jolyn Schmoe, died 26 May 1864</u>
>
> If she did not leave a will, might I obtain a photocopy of the petition for *administration?* Enclosed is an SASE along with a check for $2.00 to cover photocopying.
>
> Thank you so much for your help.
>
> Sincerely,
>
> Your name

The Write Word

An **administration** is an estate that *is* intestate—with no will. A petition of administration might have been called for that sets out the name of heirs and their addresses, even without a will.

You can't get much more simple than that, can you? The trail can start from there. When you receive a copy of that will in the mail, it may show she had land. That information will lead to a search for deeds and geographical location and all sorts of fun stuff.

Do Your Homework

We've talked a lot about county courthouses, and yet you should never take for granted that writing a letter and shipping it off to a county courthouse will do the trick without a little homework. Our nation is original in every meaning of the word, so there are always exceptions to every rule. For instance, some cities keep their own records. All states after the beginning of the twentieth century took over the registration of vital statistics. (For that matter, the starting dates of counties being the repositories of vital records also vary a century or more earlier.) In some states, county courthouses are called town halls, in others, a county might have more than one courthouse, and in at least one state, counties are called parishes.

In other words, you may be wasting postage and your precious time if you don't do the research on the place to which you are writing, to find out the terminology, the customary place certain documents are stored in that area, and the exact addresses. Besides the obvious places that offer guidance, such as the local libraries and genealogical groups, resource books such as *The Genealogist's Address Book,* and *The Source: A Guidebook to American Genealogy,* which offers a good appendix called "Where to Write for Vital Records," can help alleviate lots of waiting for nothing to return in the mail. (Also helpful is a booklet published by the United States Department of Health and Human Services called *Where to Write for Vital Records.*)

An hour spent making sure you are writing to all the right places right could be the difference between spinning those wheels or speeding on down that family history trail of yours.

Thank-You Letters

What other correspondence might you find yourself in need of writing? Thank-you letters are a must, even if you haven't written one since you took three years to finish all your wedding thank-yous.

Beyond common courtesy, nothing gets repeat performances from the busy people who work with the paper trail you are on better than appreciation. You never know when you'll pass their way again.

Journaling Down the Genealogical Trail

Okay, now it's your turn. Good writing is rewriting, so why not practice writing your version of the preceding letters in your journal. Choose one specific cousin, for instance, to write a letter to and one specific hometown library for a specific research question.

The Least You Need to Know

➤ Your cousins may know important stories about your own parents and grandparents that you don't.

➤ The kind and quality of your correspondence can make the difference between failure and success.

➤ As in most things in life, doing your homework matters.

Chapter 14

Your Do's and Don'ts Checklist

In This Chapter

➤ Remembering certain "do's and don'ts" can make a big difference

➤ Why ethnic resources are plentiful, interesting, and helpful

➤ Why letters are very important in family history research

➤ How to handle your "unusual" relatives and why

➤ Grasping the dangers of generic genealogy and relative "short-cuts"

Take a big, deep breath. You've learned quite a bit by now, enough to call yourself a family genealogist. You'll be reviewing the preceding chapters' information many times as you research, so let me give you a few do's and don'ts to help you remember some important things *outside* the genealogical focus. Keep these do's and don'ts in mind, as you go, and that way you won't miss some of the most interesting aspects of your job as a family history writer.

Do Find Letters

Make a special point to uncover diaries and letters of your extended family and your ancestors. Start with yourself, pulling together your personal letters to help with your own "memoir" addition to your family history. (See Chapter 17, "Evoking Your Memories," for more on this.) Even the smallest amount of correspondence from or to a family member can be an incredible help in knowing your relatives.

Do you doubt how important these letters could be for grasping that coveted glimpse of your ancestors? Let's go back to you for a second. Choose one of your own letters at random. Now, what have you found? An old letter from a college roommate? A love

The Write Word

An **epistolary** story is one told through a collectin of letters.

letter from your spouse? A note from an old flame? A rare letter from a late grandparent? Read them with a writer's critical eye. Do you see the humanity peeking out from behind the words? Letters are so revealing that there is an actual literary term for using letters to tell a story. If an author were to use letters to tell a story, that novel is considered *epistolary*.

Once, letter writing was considered to be an art, and the letters left to us by the past are like diamonds found along the path. Sadly, for all of our technological progress, we have all but lost the passion other generations felt for expressing oneself on paper to others. It almost seems a luxury today to spend an hour composing one's thoughts and writing a long letter to someone, and the future will be the poorer for having lost this practice, if for no other reason than an historical one.

While collecting letters for a book project called *Letters of a Nation*—which tells the history of the U.S. through the letters of both famous and ordinary citizens—a letter lover named Andy Carroll was inspired by World War II letters that he included in his work. He began a new project of collecting and preserving wartime letters called "Operation Mail Call."

Soldiers, inspired by their circumstance, often expressed themselves in letters home. Those that returned home, though, usually tried to forget about the experience, and often the letters were forgotten, too. Carroll's goal was to preserve these little gems of history that would otherwise have been left in trunks, bottom drawers, and attics, and even perhaps lost out of neglect. People began to send their soldiers' old letters to him for posterity's sake. After being mentioned in a "Dear Abby" Veteran's Day column, he received thousands of letters from attics and trunks.

As with all letters, these war letters are tiny worlds in themselves, but because of their context, they are chapters in a larger drama. They are stories of courage, sacrifice, and homesickness. The most poignant are from the soldiers who didn't return.

One unusual letter tells a tale of personal history touching world history in a great family history detail: An army sergeant was part of the troops occupying Adolf Hitler's apartment in Munich after it was captured. He wrote his mother on letterhead he found there. The letterhead read "Adolf Hitler." On impulse, the U.S. Army sergeant that was using it to write home crossed out Hitler's name and wrote his own across the top instead. His mother saved that—as well as the rest of his war letters—even though he wasn't interested in ever seeing them again himself. But as so many of us do, he changed his mind as he grew older. Recently, he decided he needed to make copies of that letter and his other wartime letters for his grandchildren. When he heard of "Operational Mail Call," he also sent them to Carroll, to be preserved for history's sake.

In a large sense, such wartime letters tell the story of our national family just as much as they tell individual stories of the members of the individual families who made such a huge sacrifice. Such letters are treasures of family history, and yet they are not that different from the letters we can find in our own trunks and attics. The people who sent their pieces of personal history to be preserved by "Operation Mail Call" were inspired by the same sense of personal sharing that has inspired you to research and write your family history.

You'll probably find everyday letters from cousins and daughters. You'll find love letters and letters of condolence. You'll find postcards and celebratory cards. If you find enough letters, you can piece together a life, with chapters as dramatic as a wartime letter, and as playful as a postcard from Coney Island. That's how powerful such letters can be, from the humdrum of daily living to the moments of joy and tragedy that make up any life story. So, look hard for those letters. And when you find them, consider offering the best portions of them in your family history account.

Don't Let Time Slip-Slide Away

> *The closing years of life are like the end of a masquerade party, when the masks are dropped.*
>
> —Arthur Schopenhauer (1788–1860)

> **Deep Thought**
>
> *When was the last time you wrote a long letter worth keeping to someone? When was the last time you received a long letter from someone that you kept? Why did you keep it?*

Don't forget that each day that passes is one less day you will have to talk to your elderly relatives. As we mentioned in our discussion about oral history, once the storyteller is gone, so are the stories not shared. Before you know it, a whole generation can pass on, and so does all their stored memories you have not captured.

A friend called the other day to say she just realized that her mother's sister, her 80-year-old Aunt Gloria, was the only one left of her parents' generation. When she dies, my friend will be the eldest generation of her family. But she also realized something even more sobering than a passing of the generational torch. When my friend's Aunt Gloria is no longer living, there will be no one alive who will have any memories of her life as a little girl. My friend will be alone with her memories.

Is that what our elder generation is feeling? What elderly relative do you have that might feel alone with his or her memories? Now is the perfect time to allow this relative to pass on memories through oral history, the only way to keep them alive forever.

A Relatively Good Idea

Who might remember you as a child and share your memories? Talk to them soon. What memories do you have that no one else might know? Share them soon with others in your family.

Don't Ignore Your Crazy Aunt Ednas

My grandfather used to make home movies and edit out the joy.

—Richard Lewis

What about your other elderly relatives? Do you have a strange or cranky relative you'd rather not contact? My question to you is: Just how cranky are we talking about? Because as crazy or cranky as these relatives seem now, once they are gone, make no mistake— you'll wish you had interviewed them (if for no other reason than telling the story of trying to interview them).

Some "blacksheep" in your family may qualify for an interview, but for now, don't automatically cross these living—albeit less than pleasant—relatives off your contact list. There may be a very good family story explaining their life-long bad mood. Even if there isn't, this person's life, by decree of genes, has criss-crossed your life and the lives of those you are researching. Go visit such relatives armed with questions about other long-gone relatives. Most people, whoever they are, cannot resist telling stories, if not about themselves, then most certainly about others. Just remember to take more than a few "grains of salt" with you to apply to each family tale. And remember, every story tells a part of your family's world, even from a cranky point of view.

Do Make Copies of Everything

Great-Aunt Cissy finally lets you take the family Bible, but only as far as the nearest copy shop. You gaze at the embossed family tree design in the big, black, gilt-edged Bible, and you want it for your own work so bad you can taste it. Years ago, you would not have thought twice about evoking Great-Aunt Cissy's wrath by never returning the Bible. Cissy knows her way around (and you know her wrath is a formidable thing). But now, in this marvelous world of copies at pennies a page, and color copies for not much more, you can have Cissy's Bible and so can she. You decide to make a dozen color copies of it, as well as a few in black and white. Why? You just had a brainstorm. You're going to use it in your family history volume, as art. Maybe even on the cover.

Note-taking is essential, but so should be copy-making. As you blow full steam ahead into your family history writing work, you will find yourself in lots of similar situations. Make copies of everything—photos, letters, diaries, newspaper clippings, old souvenirs, old receipts. When it comes time to write and these things want to retell their stories to you, you'll be glad you have the exact copy on hand.

Do Collect All Those Old Photographs

You know all those photo albums your mother has kept forever? The ones you go through each time you're home and stuck in the spare bedroom with the big pile of them? Now is the time to talk Mom out of them. The same thing goes for any photos you uncover as you go with relatives interested in your project. Keep your eyes open for the important photos of your generation and your children's generation, too. Adding photos to your family history project will be, next to the actual words themselves, the heart of your book.

'Riting Reminder

Have you had any brainstorms about additions to your family history? Just like the family Bible brainstorm, you, too, will have brainstorms as you go. Jot them down in your journal.

Don't Let Your Organization Go

You have been so busy lately that you've hardly had time for your family history writing project. You've been lucky to even squeeze the interviews into your schedule, much less the library research. And when you do have time, you'd rather spend it on advancing the family history, rather than organizing all the things you've already accumulated.

Does that sound like your life right now? Warning! Warning! If you don't keep up with your filing, you may actually become so bogged down with sorting through the growing mountain of paper in your extra room's corner, that you just may stop work altogether.

Choose a system of organization at the beginning and stick with it, creating new spin-offs as you go. Do not let it stack up. Chapter 16, "How Much Is Enough?" will give you ideas on how to tackle this demon of genealogical work.

A Relatively Good Idea

Begin now to date and name photos you decide are worthy of keeping. Future generations will thank you.

Do Browse

When you are in the middle of research, you will find an amazing amount of interesting information about a plethora of things. If something takes your attention, don't feel guilty. *Browse.* Who knows what you might find.

The Write Word

To **browse** is to look through a collection of things casually in search of something interesting.

The historian in you will be fascinated by an uncovered tidbit that can shine understanding on what life was like in the past. The detective in you may just uncover the one fact you had given up trying to find. The reporter in you may find help in answering one of your "W's"—who, what, when, where, why, or how. And the family history writer in you will find the time well spent no matter what you find.

Do Use Common Sense

Document, document, document. This has been my refrain for so long now that you know its importance in genealogical work. That also goes for information given to you by other genealogists—family or otherwise. Resist becoming lazy about your family detective double-check. (See Chapter 10, "The Family Investigator on the Case.") If you get in the habit of using it, your common sense will kick in when you come across something that doesn't seem right. When Great-great-great Uncle Thaddeus seems to have been married to two different women during the same years; something has to give. Don't let it be your commitment to the truth.

Don't Be Afraid to Ask for Help

From Internet forums, to local genealogical groups, to genealogical historical societies, to local librarians, to hometown old-timers—people are out there with the answers, and are usually willing to help. You can never get back the wasted hours you spent blindly pushing ahead on the wrong track. A few minutes spent asking the right questions at the beginning of a search can keep you smiling throughout your journey.

'Riting Reminder

Don't forget the "right ancestor" formula:

Full Exact Name + Geographical Location + Date

Don't Take Help Without Question

Never forget, however, when you ask for help that you still need to apply your detective double-check and your common sense. What would be worse than wasting hours because you didn't ask for help? There's only one thing worse: Wasting hours because somebody casually told you a piece of information that was wrong. Keep your antennae up and your common sense working overtime. The detective double-check, especially matching names with dates and geographical information, will help you separate the "sheep from the goats," when it comes to help offered.

Don't Be Tempted by Relative Shortcuts

Also be leery of shortcuts offered by relatives. Cousin Bernie, for instance, may hand you all his work and suddenly you think that a whole branch of the family tree is done for you. Remember that you are writing a family history that will be in print and handed down for generations. Don't take anything for granted. Bernie could have been just as sloppy as anyone else, and just as lazy. For all you know, a family genealogist made a goof three decades ago and it's been handed down ever since by people like Bernie who didn't do the family detective double-check.

Saving time by taking Cousin Bernie's genealogy work without double-checking it may seem to be gaining an "instant" family branch without the sweat. However, if any of the information is wrong, you will be losing not gaining. The rightful family branch might as well have been sawed off, because a wrong one would have been transplanted in its place. It would be just as "gone with the wind" as the oral histories that don't get shared. And that would be a true family history shame.

Do Let Your Curiosity Be Your Guide

What is in that camelback trunk in your great-uncle's garage? Why does that 1850 cemetery marker seem so new? What was that old story you used to hear at family reunions about your great-great-granddad's traveling-salesman days? Why is everyone on your mother's side red-headed? What was it like for your father to grow up in the Great Depression? Why was it so important for Crazy Aunt Edna to keep those scrap-books all these years?

A good writer knows how to listen to the questions stirred by his or her natural curiosity. If yours is already in high gear, jot down the questions it conjures. If your curiosity isn't in good running order, give it a jumpstart and enjoy where it takes you. Often, just another question or two spurred by your writer's curiosity can get the details you desire for the family story you want to include in your book.

Curiosity and the Genealogist

An interesting historical term or topic can be the start of a fascinating search for your family history book. Using Chapter 10's three family history writer personas, the *family history reporter* wants to answer a few of the five "W's." The *family historian* is curious about what life must have been like to live in that century if selling oneself into serfdom seemed a viable option. The *family history detective* wonders how to find out more.

So let's say that there's some aspect or tidbit about one of your ancestors that piques your interest, but you don't have much background information on it, and you're not sure where to start. Let's try to attack it by looking at an example I faced regarding indentured servitude.

My family lore has always said that my original Rutledge American ancestor came over on a ship as an indentured servant. How might I trace this, since no mention of the term exists in print in any of my research? First off, we need to find out just what an indentured servant *is*, right?

Question: What Is an Indentured Servant?

Indentured servitude was an accepted way for a man or woman to gain access to the new world. Young men and women would contract to work without pay for a certain amount of time in exchange for passage to America. While the popular image of the indentured servant is a young man, some historians estimate that in the seventeenth century, ten to twenty-five percent of the country's women, for instance, were indentured servants. It was also a way to pay off large debts owed that could not be paid any other way.

Okay, so now we know what the term means, but how do we go about tracking down hard evidence to back up this interesting family history tidbit?

1. Why not try going backward? Since I know he came over on the ship *Merchants of Hope* in 1639 (see Chapter 7, "Getting It Right from the Get-Go"), I could think back and see if my ancestor's original American name was different—by checking one specific index (suggested to me by a genealogically savvy librarian). If he arrived before 1700 and was a man of property—meaning he wasn't an employee of other men of property—he'll be listed in *Persons of Quality Who Came from Great Britain to the American Plantations, 1600–1700.*

2. If he's not listed, then what do I do? I could do special research on the indentured servants in America's history and see what historical documentation trail might pop up. The National Archives, always a good place to start, would tell me that they do not have any immigration documentation for 1639. So I begin to find documentation on the ship itself in historical libraries, and focus on the immigrant himself.

3. And what if I still find nothing? I now have background information on the topic, "indentured servants" for my family history writing. I also have the choice to keep following the original American's trail as long as my curiosity is strong.

There may be no existing record that survived since that day in 1639 when my original Rutledge ancestor bound himself into servitude to start a new life in America. Yet the family history writer in me is deeply curious about the why's of all my "original Americans." So the trail is there and waiting for my family historian sleuth to decide the time is worth the journey.

Do Respond to Responses

Let's say that today's mail included several surprises for you. Cousin Leona in Pittsburgh—who lives in the same house she grew up in—was so intrigued with your letter announcing your family search that she stopped what she was doing and went browsing in some old papers left in the attic after her parents' death and came up with a nice bundle to send you. Also, two of your SASE's came back in the mail. One held only a single piece of notebook paper from another cousin, Jennifer. She's written back to tell you she does have a family Bible and other heirlooms she'd be happy to show you if you'd like to visit her. The other, from a newly discovered cousin named George in Kansas, explains in jerky, unsteady handwriting, that he cannot help you because he is in ill health, but offers you another cousin's name for you to contact.

What do you do? Before the hectic pace of your days makes you forget to acknowledge these long-distance relatives' courtesy, you should write each of these people a nice note of thanks, as well as a few words on how your quest is coming. Past common courtesy, such action only makes for good family relations, don't you think? Besides, you never know when you'll need to send another letter their way. And you never know what interesting relationships can form from these contacts.

Don't Treat Computers as Filing Cabinets

You will see many ads for computer programs about genealogy. You will also soon be overwhelmed with your accumulated research and wish for some high-tech help. Go ahead, if you are so inclined, and buy one of these. Resist, however, storing everything on your computer, even if you are doing this resisting from under your pile of research created by following your family's paper trail.

Never, ever forget that computers are changing, not only day to day, but minute to minute. This year's floppy disk technology may not even be in existence in 20 years. And 20 years is nothing in genealogical terms.

So, go ahead and enjoy the convenience of computer programs, but always print out your work periodically onto good ol' paper for your own nonvirtual backup. Its chances of surviving outside the computer world's planned obsolescence is much, much greater than any back-up floppy disk you might make of all your work. (If the paper burden gets too great, and you must choose an area of your research to keep solely on computer, then my suggestion is to choose your correspondence. Pick the ones you might want to survive your lifetime, though, and make hard copy of them.)

Do Treat the Internet as a Big Index

You finally have a computer and an Internet connection. You log on and glory be—what do you see but several search engines waiting for your click. There are so many!

How can you choose? You hit a key and find out that you are automatically on one already, and there are advertisements flashing at you, plus news to read, weather to check and on and on. You blink and focus, remembering why you're here, and you type in the word "genealogy" in the space provided.

What happens next depends on your experience, your search engine, and your computer. But it's a good guess that you have just been inundated with information, much of it useless. What your search engine has done is given you a listing of every last mention of the word "genealogy" in every listing it found.

You have just learned your first lesson about the Internet. The more specific you can be on your search entry the better. Type "Hispanic genealogy" and that narrows the field and lowers the flood. But still, it is all too much and too general.

If the Internet were published and bound, it would be in the reference section of your library and you'd be searching for information the old-fashioned way, ignoring irrelevant information as you go. You certainly wouldn't waste time going through every book on the shelf checking each mention of the word "genealogy," would you? Your search would be more refined than that. And "refined" is not a word used to define the Internet. It is all up to you to refine.

Here's the solution: The Web sites mentioned in this book and obtained through your own research are established sites that you can go to directly, without wasting time finding these places through a search engine. These sites will index other sites to choose. And you know that if you keep working with an index—if it's the right index—it will get you where you want to go, won't it?

So, do a little homework in the beginning for the right places to start, and you'll be okay. Instead of browsing the Internet, which will start up those search engines offering every listing of the word "genealogy" in the universe, go straight to the Internet address slot and type in the URL address you've researched. Doing your homework first will get you there quickly. It's true about any journey, and this is certainly a journey, isn't it? Remembering that the Internet is this kind of entity will keep your frustration level down and your productive, memorable "ah-ha" moments high.

Don't Believe in Generic Genealogy

Let our local experts find your ancestors for you!

We have written your family history! Get a bound copy of your family history for only $49.95 including actual names and addresses!

Once you begin your genealogical search, you'll notice big ads in genealogical journals and on the Internet (especially if you use a search engine instead of going straight to the Web site address).

Does this ad sound good to you? When you are tempted to have someone else do your research for you—when something looks too good to refuse—that's the time to remember P. T. Barnum's heart-warming philosophy about the human race, "There's a sucker born every minute." Publications abound that purport to offer you everything you want to know about your surname including your coat of arms (see the following section) and the names and addresses of everyone in America with your surname.

Run, do not walk away from such offers. Not only are they scams, they also put a large commercial pallor on your personal project inspired by the warmest, honorable impulses.

And That Goes Double for Heraldry

Ever buy anything with your surname's coat of arms? Most of us have. Recently, I received a whole catalog showing full color photos of all the nifty things I could buy with "my family's" coat of arms on it. (I was especially impressed with the toaster.)

Well, this may come as a shock, but no surname automatically has a coat of arms. Heraldry happened to specific individuals. Honored knights in twelfth century Europe were given their individual "coat of arms" to identify them in tournaments and in battle. Through the years, the coat of arms, which seems to connote your connection to some far-off land's nobility (or some such royal thought), was taken to be a coat of arms for a family. And the definition of family became everybody from Adam to your granny who happened to have that name.

Heraldry is a fascinating subject, but odds are extremely high that it has very little to do with your family. (I'll take that back if you trace your lineage to a brave nobleman granted a coat of arms for courageous duties to the crown.) So, if you like the looks of that sweatshirt or that toaster with your surname and nifty coat-of-arms design, buy it for fun, but don't be taken in by any genealogically related advertising concerning "heraldry for the masses."

Do Find and Use Ethnic Resources

Are you of ethnic descent on any branch of your family tree? Most of us are. The stories for each ethnic mix of our American melting pot are always illuminating, dramatic, and worthy. And there is a burgeoning amount of material to help you in your search. Each year new books are published and new Web sites are established to help anyone trace any ethnicity anywhere around the country and around the world.

Do you have Acadian heritage? Welsh? Spanish? South American? Nova Scotian? Lithuanian? Bavarian? Outer Mongolian? Chances are there is a forum group, an Internet mailing list or a book published to guide you in your special genealogical needs. Check your local library. They are bound to have the latest group of these wonderfully specific books. And the Internet is already deep into "ethnic specificity." You'll find your ancestral ethnicity there, somehow, someway.

For instance, a stop at the Cyndi's List Internet Web page at www.oz.net/~cyndihow/ sites.htm offers you a list that goes on and on with categories from Huguenot to Mennonite to South African to Hispanic (including lots of other interesting stops along the way). For instance, one Web site for Jewish genealogy is "JewishGen." Its URL (Internet address), www.jewishgen.org/, is a very popular one.

The National Archives is always a rich place to begin ethnic genealogy, especially for the harder problems. For example, Chinese lineage is understandably hard to trace due to the fake names many used to circumvent hard immigration laws during a long period of American history. But the National Archives comes to the rescue with some ideas on how to hop over these seeming dead-ends. A visit to www.nara.gov/regional/ findaids/chirip.html may offer surprises. You can actually peruse cemetery records that might hold your ancestors' real names.

National Archives microfilm catalogs are available through your library for such subjects as "American Indians" and "Black Studies" (also available, for instance, on the NARA Web site "American Indians: A Select Catalog of National Archives Microfilm Publications"; "Black Studies: A Select catalog of National Archives Microfilm Publications").

Does your heritage include Native American Cherokee? Chicago's Newberry Library specializes in Cherokee genealogy, holding one of the country's largest collections of the study of all American Indian tribes. The Newberry's Web site gives good advice on how and when to begin such specialized research. The Newberry also has a very large holding of Irish, Germanic, Jewish, Polish, Bohemian, English, and African-American genealogy resources. Its Web site is www.newberry.org/nl/genealogy.

Were your ancestors from Scotland? Do you have a clan connection? Scotland was the first nation to put all its records online. Try www.origins.net/GRO.

The Write Word

Manumission was the name given to the act of, and the document created, giving official freedom to a slave before the Civil War's Emancipation Proclamation.

Is your heritage African? Of special note is African-American genealogical research. The stories of your ancestors are heartbreaking, dramatic and soul-stirring, from Alex Haley's *Roots* to the Delany Sisters' *Having Our Say*. If possible, check out the recent PBS Series "Africans in America: America's Journey Through Slavery" at your library. Microsoft offers a CD-ROM encyclopedia called *Encarta Africana,* and it's a good place to begin this area of research.

The University of North Carolina is in the process of digitizing pages and pages of slave narratives, diaries, and other historical documents before they vanish. The Pennsylvania Historical Society has thousands of records of *manumission* granted pre–Civil War. Each one is a short document that tells a huge tale. One genealogy writer, while researching there, found a ripped and decaying 1747 manumission written by a man who declared he was giving "Abraham," after 10 years of service, his freedom "from the yoke of slavery for ever." If Abraham was your ancestor, wouldn't you be incredibly excited to find this document for your family history?

The National Archives gives special attention to the records they have offering any sort of trail for the African-American search, since the whole research process is different from any other. The Web site constantly offers new areas to search. Click onto the site today and you may find an eight page entry on "The Freedman's Savings and Trust Company and African-American Genealogical Research," which NARA's genealogy experts consider one of the most under-used bodies of federal records. The bank was charted by Congress in 1865 for the benefit of ex-slaves. For the protection of their depositors, the bank gathered a substantial amount of information on the families who deposited with it.

Other examples of special lists to check and bureaus to peruse are …

➤ Special List 34: Bureau of Refugees, Freedman, and Abandoned Lands Bankruptcy

➤ List of Free Black Heads of Families in the First Census of the Unites States 1790

➤ Special List 36: List of Black Servicemen Compiled from the War Department Collection of Revolutionary War Records

Related Facts

New to the National Archives Web site is a special area for women—genealogy research for all our granny gaps. Click on today and you might find a long article about the difficulties of searching for our female ancestors through naturalization records, called "Women and Naturalization, ca. 1802–1940." Click on tomorrow and find something else. The National Archives promises to add more helpful ways to give names and facts to the women the past denied their own easy-to-find paper trail.

Do Check Lesser-Known Resources

There are so many diverse records to research with so much information about your ancestors (and everyone else's) who built this country that you should keep your eyes open for any "less-trodden" places to take your research.

Homestead Records, for instance, are fascinating. The opportunity to own your own land was "The American Dream" and the reason that many left everything familiar to come to this new land. The word spread around the world that anyone willing to work hard could buy cheap land and know a kind of freedom not possible anywhere else.

Free land was available, and if you couldn't get that, you might pay as little as 33¢ an acre. "Donation land" was one midnineteenth-century program in which anyone who would go to the eastern parts of Florida or to the New Mexico, Oregon or Washington territories could acquire 160 to 649 acres of land. The idea was that these people, by their homesteading presence, would protect the government's interests in these far-off territories.

Later, the Homestead Act of 1862 allowed our ancestors who wanted to be settlers to apply for 160 free acres in the territories. All the settlers had to do was go live on wilderness land for five years, build a home on it, and cultivate it. If they did all this, the land was theirs, free and clear. Few American families during that time period didn't have a settler ancestor we can document. Think how exciting it would be to uncover this record. Who knows? You might even take a road trip to stand on the original homestead land.

Other records that are worth investigating are …

➤ Passport records

➤ Naturalization records and voters records

➤ Tax records

The Least You Need to Know

➤ Beware of relative "shortcuts," organization lapse, and Internet time-wasting.

➤ Your curiosity should guide you as a family history researcher.

➤ Family letters are wonderful glimpses into your ancestors' world as well as your own.

➤ Ethnic resources are plentiful for your family history research.

Cousin Ba·a·arnaby

Chapter 15

Kissing Kin, Black Sheep, and Granny Gaps

In This Chapter

➤ What to do with your family's "black sheep"

➤ Who are your cousins and why it matters

➤ Learning ways to fill your granny gaps

➤ How to handle conflicting versions of family stories and facts

Everyone who undertakes genealogical and oral history research will find themselves in for a few surprises, as well as disappointments. You will be no exception. Odds are you will be uncovering some very interesting tidbits about your family members. And you won't be sure what to think of them. There's a story that your granny doesn't want to tell. There seems to be some interesting duplicate names popping up on your family trees, and there are far too many female ancestors who are "missing in action." Let's take a look at these interesting layers of your research and what to do with them for your family history purposes.

Granny Scandal or Granny Romance?

Your granny is tight-lipped about your great-granny. Through the years, you've asked about her and gotten no response. Now, though, you are writing a family history, so you bring up the subject one more time, and suddenly you hear this amazing tale that sounds like something out of *The Scarlet Letter*.

The story unfolded this way. It was World War I. Your granny was a child, and your great-granny, who was much younger than your great-grandfather, but had been forced to marry him by her father because of his wealth, began a correspondence with an old childhood suitor who had joined the war effort. First, she wrote to this old friend out of sympathy, but then it became much more as she gave and received increasingly intimate missives from the front—at least according to great-granddad who discovered the letters.

Great-granddad, being a very pious, but not very forgiving man, hauled his young wife before their church for a little help in pulling her back onto the "straight and narrow." But then, in the midst of all this public emotion, great-granddad bursts a blood vessel in his forehead, the one that was always throbbing about something or other, and he died right there in front of the church altar. After a certain discreet amount of time (and the end of the war), your great-granny married that old suitor, only to watch him die from the effects of the nerve gas he was exposed to in the war.

Wow, you're thinking. You are struck by the drama and the romance and the twists of fate of this family tale. You are very excited, your writer's imagination bubbling, until you look at your granny's face. This is not romantic at all to her. In fact, it is a disgrace, and she has never forgiven her mother or accepted that "soldier" as her stepfather. She had been her father's favorite, so she blamed her mother for his death.

Talk about two different takes on the same drama. Is this a Granny Dark Scandal or a Granny High Romance? What do you make of this as a family history writer?

Once-Removed Factor

You have just come into personal contact with the "once-removed factor." The closer you are to a scandal in your own family, the less objective you can be about its story value. The further away you are, the more it becomes a wonderfully human tale that brings your ancestor to life.

Most family genealogists scramble to find any story at all beyond dry facts to tell about ancestors. That goes double for the kinds of stories that were perhaps so tragic and painful that no one in the family spoke of them until there was no one still alive to do so. But time really does heal, and a story so heartbreaking or scandalous it could not be talked about can actually become a wonderful addition to your family history saga after several generations have passed. If, that is, it didn't die with the last relative who knew the story, as oral history can do.

Take It All In

Whatever the fascinating story, be it a scandalous romance, a criminal tale, or a tragedy, you will soon have to cope with how you handle it, or if you handle it at all. We'll talk more about how to handle such stories in the following chapters on writing.

For now, what's your job? You should become the objective reporter—answering the who, what, where, when, why, and how questions as well as taking copious notes and interviewing everyone, including your granny. You need to grasp both sides of the story as fully as you can, be it on tape, transcription, journal responses, or notes. Take it all in—*all of it.* The question will probably not be *if* you will use it but *how.* Such is the power of forgiving years. Your future readers will be charmed and enlightened, as their ancestors become human before their eyes. You'll be doing your literary magic, telling the stories you are lucky enough to uncover, which, in the way you tell them, will honor your grannies' and granddads' life stories.

Your Personal Black Sheep

But what if you find something that embarrasses even you? Do you think that's possible? Maybe. You are going to be uncovering newspaper articles and court records. Even if your family members have shoved their *black sheep* under the sands of time (to mix a metaphor), your job is to dig. And those who dig, find.

Are you up for it? Are you up for a devil among your ancestral angels? A rascal among the decent folk? Look at it this way. No one should start a family history search without an open mind, able to accept anything found. Where once genealogy was about uncovering nobility or fame in one's blood line, it seems today, to a new generation of genealogists, about connections, roots, about your fascinating relatives scattered through history. And in that context, genealogy seems to be about what those people's lives offer for your own take on life.

The Write Word

A **black sheep** is a family member or ancestor with a questionable reputation.

Many genealogists revel in their "sinners." There's even an International Black Sheep Society of Genealogists with its own Web site and e-mail list, for those who have "a dastardly infamous individual of public knowledge and ill repute in their families."

As writers looking for good stories to tell, how can we not revel in our colorful ancestors? These wayward ancestors offer your family and your writing a feeling of truth that is hard to convey in most family histories. Unless we happen to be married to them, wronged by them, or have bad personal memories about them, like your granny in the preceding story, their rascality and scofflaw ways are what good stories are made of. From horse thieves to bigamists to bushwhackers, these are real people, and they are your relatives.

Always remember, however, that you should be offering a balanced account when you have the good fortune to have a granny around to talk about the personal side of it, too. Granny, interestingly, may find it therapeutic to talk about such memories.

How to Handle Family Secrets

But let's not underestimate the strong feelings evoked by hurtful memories our elderly family members may not want to share with you in an interview. The shame felt by a young girl whose father had a drinking problem or whose family business failed can be felt just as strong eighty years later when her earliest memories are evoked.

How do you handle these moments?

➤ In an interview setting, remember you are a family history interviewer, not an interrogator. If you know of "bad blood" between older members of the interviewer's family, and want to know more, you may broach the subject, but do so in an objective, nonconfrontational way.

➤ Let the interviewee decide how much he or she wants to talk about the "family rumor." You may be surprised. If you handle the moment with sympathy and with tact, you may give the elderly relative a chance to talk about something that should have been talked out long ago. You may be the one who hears some touching story about a tragedy or personal heartbreak that makes your elderly relative even more special to you. (Even Crazy Aunt Edna.)

➤ You may also see the relative explode. Time can heal, but it can also magnify the episode out of all proportion, "even unto the grave."

➤ Be ready to take no for an answer, as well. Often, a secret that evokes such strong feelings might not be one you want to add to your family history, anyway.

➤ If, however, you keep hearing the same unusual story from other relatives and in your research, and you decide it's worthy of your family history, then it will be your decision whether to continue your research as mentioned above, in order to tell the story in an even-handed fashion.

Remember that the prime rule is sensitivity. But also remember, you should make the decision of whether a story is included in the family history.

'Riting Reminder

Don't forget that the prime rule of interviewing is sensitivity. And that goes double for moments dealing with "family secrets."

Why They're Called "Kissin' Cousins"

There's another dynamic you will inevitably notice as you begin to go farther and farther back into a family history. It could be called a "double-back dynamic." It's also called, by professional genealogists, "pedigree collapse."

For example, here were 25 families who came over on the *Mayflower* and about 25 million Americans have descended from these people over that time period. That may sound impossible, but what's more incredible is how many ancestral lines that number of people supposedly created, a number that is truly impossible.

Let me explain. Ready for a little theory and logic? (Get out your calculator.) Remember the numbers we used earlier to calculate your number of ancestors in 10 generations, about 250 years back? We calculated that you'd have 1,024 in the tenth generation alone, and 2,046 when you added all the other generations to that. (The usual way to figure the total amount is to double the number of ancestors in a specific generation and take off 2—which is your presence in both lines.)

If that's true (and numbers, it is said, never lie), then 20 generations back, you'd have a million ancestors from the twentieth generation alone and a billion combined. What does that mean? Obviously, if everybody had a billion ancestors just 20 generations back, then 40 generations back would be a billion and a trillion combined. That number alone is incomprehensible. But going back another 40 generations, which would land us only about the time of Socrates, the same math would make the number of people who have ever lived about a trillion trillion—a septillion—which is not only unimaginable, but impossible, as even the experts agree.

Other Fish in the Pond

So what's the answer? Cousins. Lots of them marrying each other, and creating duplicate lines. That old maxim that says, "We're all related," is true. Your ancestors are my ancestors somehow, someway, sometime.

We smile at the idea of marrying cousins and consider it a bad idea for many reasons we don't need to go into here. There are laws that do the talking for us (when it comes to marriages between first cousins, anyway). But the reality is that we can choose not to be "kissin' cousins." We have lots of choices. We may say (and frequently do) about romance, "There are other fish in the sea." Using that analogy, most of our American ancestors, up to only the last couple of generations, weren't swimming in a sea at all. They were living in a lake at best, and more likely, depending on the wilderness being settled, a pond.

The longer a family stayed in one area, the greater chance for duplicate ancestors and "pedigree collapse." When you think about the astronomical changes the world has seen in the twentieth century—in every conceivable part of life—it is not outlandish to say that a person from 1850 actually had more in common with a person from 100 A.D. than with us. Until this century, not only did people not consider moving far from the place they were born, but they probably couldn't fathom it. So for millenniums, it's been socially acceptable to meet a mate at a family reunion. The marriage pool was so shallow in places, it was acceptable to marry your first cousin.

Actually, the same was even true for our pioneers. Our history being one of Western expansion, migration to the wilderness was a time-sensitive dynamic and a generational thing. Each generation pushed farther West, and usually in groups. In the wilderness, that group would be the only one from which to marry for many, many years, until civilization approached. So never fear, your family, my family, every family has several duplicate lines.

Related Facts

In 1620, 25 families came over on the *Mayflower*. Twenty-five million Americans have descended from these people.

Cousin Surprise

So, be prepared for cousin surprises in your research. The past was a small place, especially in America, and couples could have a dozen offspring. Our cousins are everywhere, even in our own family trees. In fact, you may be married to one.

My brother-in-law got hooked on genealogy when he stumbled onto the fact that his wife, my sister, was actually a cousin of his by way of a common ancestor, a War of 1812 veteran. An elderly great-aunt had sent him the genealogical work she had researched on our side of the family. As he was perusing the charts, he kept feeling he'd "been this way before." Grabbing his own charts, he saw the same names appearing on one particular branch of the family tree. His mind was blown away. As my brother-in-law put it so well in his family's newsletter, "Herein lies an aphorism: My wife and my children are also my cousins."

Sudden Double Cousins

These "small pond" situations go beyond "kissin' cousins." You may find other surprises. The numerous offspring from one family marrying the equally numerous offspring from the family living on the next farm down the road was also socially acceptable. Family branches from separate trees very often became intertwined when brothers and sisters married brothers and sisters from another family. Becoming sudden "double cousins" was the result.

A widow with five kids could marry the brother of her late husband (who could also be widowed and have his own mess of offspring he's raising alone). Survival, especially on the pioneer farms, was the rule of the day. Of course, that sort of situation would create an aphorism much closer to home—the uncle would become the step-father of all his nephews and nieces.

Is there a story for your family history writing in these revelations of your genealogical digging? Of course there is. When you find such double cousins and "kissin' cousins" situations in your research, you'll begin to grasp a kind of isolation our ancestors experienced that we cannot fathom in our modern lives.

Think what it was like to be born into a frontier community, to know everyone in your town, and to have only them to interact with, from the dry goods merchant to the blacksmith to the saloonkeeper, to the circuit-riding preacher. Once you put a face on such community members, they no longer seem like something from a movie writer's pen. Always keep your writer's antennae pointed toward these unusual twists and turns that make for good storytelling.

What Is a Cousin?

This seems a silly question, but what is a *cousin*, anyway? We know our first cousins are the children of our aunts and uncles. But what about second cousins and third cousins? And what in the world is a third cousin "once removed"?

Here's one way to look at it: Cousins share common grandparents, but different ancestral lines. That is, sisters and brothers share a parent, first cousins share a grandparent, second cousins share a great-grandparent, third cousins share a great-great-grandparent, and on and on.

> **The Write Word**
>
> A **cousin** is a child of one's uncle or aunt, or a relative descended from one's grandparent or other ancestor. However, cousin may also mean a kinsman or distant relative. In years past, the term was also used as a title by a sovereign in addressing a nobleman.

For example, remember my great-grandfather Virge, the Texas sheriff? He had lots of children besides my grandfather—my great-aunts and -uncles. All their children would be my second cousins because we share a common great-grandparent, the sheriff. Excluding my father, of course, my grandfather's children had lots of children, and all those children are my first cousins.

> ➤ First cousins share a common grandparent.
> ➤ Second cousins share a common great-grandparent.
> ➤ Third cousins share a common great-great-grandparent.

What's a Cousin Once or Twice Removed?

Fine, you say, but what's this "removed" concept? To be honest, the only way I've been able to grasp this is to remember that the "removes" are all about my first cousins' having children. My first cousins and all their offspring will always be first cousins to me. With each new generation, though, they are a generation "removed" from me. In other words, my first cousins' kids are my first cousins once removed. My first cousins' grandchildren are my first cousins twice removed. My second cousin's kids are my second cousins once removed. Get it?

So who are second cousins? The children of first cousins are second cousins to each other. To check it out, go back to the grandparent figure. Second cousins should also have a common great-grandparent.

> ➤ A first cousin once removed is the offspring of a first cousin.
>
> ➤ A second cousin once removed is the offspring of a second cousin.
>
> ➤ A second cousin twice removed is the offspring of a second cousin once removed.
>
> ➤ In the immortal words of *Seinfeld,* "Yada yada yada."

A Relatively Good Idea

In Chapter 13, "Writing All the Right People Right," you named all your first cousins in preparation of announcing your family history project. But can you name your "other" cousins? Make a list of all the cousins you have met, be they first, second, third, or removed several times. Now make a list of which grandparents or great-grandparents you have in common with each of those cousins. Why not use this detail in your contact with them?

Henry IV Got It Right

And now that we are dizzy attempting to understand all about cousins, maybe we should just follow the lead of King Henry IV. Since he was related to just about every earl in the kingdom, he grew tired of worrying about the consequences of hurting somebody's feelings, so he began addressing everyone as "Dear Cousin" and was done with it.

You'll find lots of cousins in your research, and they can tell stories you wouldn't want to miss. A lot of the confusion will be fun, as well as interesting to discover, as did my sister and brother-in-law.

You just never know, "dear cousin."

Alive vs. Dead

Is it possible to tell a family member's story, going past the facts, without knowing them? This is a question you must have asked yourself by now, considering that you are going to be trying to do exactly that with your family history book. There's actually a word for it—*psychobiography,* telling the story of an interior life. In an article that went across the country's wire services recently, a professor at Douglass College, interested in psychobiography, presented a challenge to her students. She had found the donated papers and letters and diaries from an alumnus who died young, donated by the woman's sister, and offered them to her class with this challenge: Could they reconstruct the woman from the papers?

What resulted was a heartwarming, yet heart-breaking story. They studied her college scrapbooks, the receipts for her tuition, her yearbook entries, followed her education trail to Columbia University where she got a Master's degree, read her thesis, then deduced from her letters that she had a breakdown, perhaps after a failed love affair.

A flurry of letters between the woman and her sister were studied, letters full of hope and aspiration, despair and depression, and especially frustration with being a talented woman during a time when opportunities were limited. And then, they visited the place where she took her own life, the fact that the professor had not told them about until the moment they were on the scene. And many found themselves moved to tears, because they had gotten to know Clara so well.

Even though there is nobody left to tell someone's story, if you have enough preserved material to use, you too can reconstruct your ancestors' lives, feel their humanity, and write about them glowingly for your family. There are Claras in everyone's family. I hope that you find a trunk full of papers that offers you a chance to know your ancestors and share your knowledge with the rest of your family.

The Write Word

A **psychobiography** is the attempt to capture a person's interior life without actually having known the individual.

Deep Thought

Which ancestor would be your Clara? About which one do you have enough information already accumulated that you might be able to reconstruct a touching, human profile of him or her? What one fact intrigues you the most and why?

Myth vs. Reality

Can you believe everything Crazy Aunt Edna tells you? That story about once being the girlfriend of Charles Lindbergh sounds a little suspicious. Nobody tells that story but Edna (and everybody knows that nobody tells Crazy Aunt Edna anything), so you don't know how to handle such tales, except with a grain or two of salt. But what do you do when you hear two different versions of the same family lore?

Conflicting Versions of the Same Family Tale

There's a story your second cousin keeps telling about your ancestor who came from Scotland through Nova Scotia, finally landing in Chicago where he was a federal agent during Prohibition. The problem is that Crazy Aunt Edna tells it differently. She says the ancestor was more of a gangster than an entrepreneur.

What's a family history writer to do? Conflicting versions will be heard, and this will be the challenge for obtaining the proof you can find during genealogical research. The primary sources that can be checked should be. One woman heard for years about an uncle who was on the *Titanic*. One cousin told the end of the story with the uncle surviving, the other told it with the man hitting the freezing water and drowning. You can verify the truthfulness of a story like that because there is data to check. And you should make the effort to check the truthfulness of a story before you add it to your family history book.

What about the conflicts you can't resolve? Try interviewing your relatives more, attempting to find other oral sources to check. But beyond that, it will be all in the telling. We'll discuss how to handle the problem in a later chapter on writing, but for now, one answer for you to think about is to consider the power of legend. You can feature both of your aunts (who are definitely players in your family drama) telling the story the way they heard it, even in interview style, giving your prose a feeling of oral history on the page. This way you get to use the story without raising the hackles on the back of your genealogist's neck.

Conflicting Versions of Genealogical Facts

What do you do, though, when you find a "fact" that comes in two versions according to your research ... something that facts aren't supposed to do?

What would a detective do? You, the family history detective, would check all your sources, then try to find new primary sources for new leads. What do I mean?

For example, you find a big discrepancy in an ancestor's birthday. The census says he was born in 1880, but the death certificate says he was born in 1878. What else might you check for other listings of his birth date? His birth certificate, his will, his baptismal record, his military records—you know the drill. The detective double-check forces you to get the correct information to avoid finding yourself in someone else's family tree, or worse, finding yourself at the end of the branch with nowhere to go.

Often, you'll notice, if you've taken good notes (and, of course, you have), that the discrepancy is from a secondary source. Perhaps you have several secondary sources and no primary ones. There's your problem. Keep tracking; you'll find the path again.

Should you write down the discrepancy? Yes. Make a note of it, because you can bet it will pop up again somewhere along your genealogical trail, and you don't want to lose valuable time backtracking.

Again, remember to use common sense, and take nothing for granted. In that sense, the detective, the historian, and the reporter in you will keep you on the path.

Bridging Your Granny Gaps

The forgotten women in your ancestry need you to rediscover them. Can you? As we've discussed, before the twentieth century, the women in our lineage did not leave much of a paper trail. Property was in husbands' names, and if the wives were mentioned, it was usually as a "Mrs." only.

Any attempt to fill your granny gaps won't be easy, but there are a few secret places to which you can go, if you decide to. The first steps, of course, will be the ones you've taken for all your ancestors. You should check for her vital records, working from what you have (which is probably her husband's vital records). You can move on to census records, which occasionally list women's given and/or maiden names. But more than likely you'll use the census as a secondary source pointing you to other places. Then, when oral history, family Bibles, deeds, wills, obituaries, cemetery records, and family histories don't offer much more, you accumulate what you have and reassess the situation.

Sometimes the best you can do is keep your antennae up for leads as you research all around your granny gap. Sometimes you may have a given name, but no maiden name that dead-ends any research for your female relative's family's ancestral line. And many times, you will have a maiden name but no given name. And there is something so jarring about seeing a female ancestor on your pedigree chart known only by her married name with a blank preceding it.

The Write Word

The phrase **et ex** after a man's name in a deed means "and wife." The phrase **et al.** after a man's name in a deed means "and others."

Our names humanize us in ways we never realize until we begin genealogical research. For that very reason, if your quest only surfaces a female ancestor's given name to fill one of your granny gaps, I guarantee you'll feel the effort was worth it.

So, where might you search for the barest of information on your missing grannies after the obvious places offer nothing? Here are a few possibilities:

➤ **Civil death certificates.** The death certificates for any family member, her husband or her children, may list her name as well as other information you'd want. They will give ages, dates and places of birth and death for the deceased and also the deceased's parents. Infant mortality was high, remember. Uncovering death certificates for all her children might also uncover information on the mother.

➤ **Land deeds records.** Did your missing female ancestor own land along with her husband? A woman, i.e., a wife of the land's owner, usually was only identified when the land was sold, not when it was bought. This was done to show her dower right to the land. (A "dower" is a widow's interest in her deceased husband's land given to her by law.) If you still have no luck, check the deeds for a listing of heirs, which usually will include both daughters and their husbands. Even after the land was passed to another generation after a widow's death, before it could be sold, her name would have to be given to prove inheritance of the land. Also, tax records of the time might list female land owners when they are the head of a household (as a widow might be), because that would make them taxpayers.

➤ **Could your female ancestor have been married to a soldier or even have been a soldier herself?** Check pensions data. The Revolutionary War, War of 1812, and the Civil War pension records, as noted earlier, are available for a small fee from the National Archives. But wouldn't it be wonderful if your female ancestor herself had played some role in, say, the Revolutionary War and is listed somewhere for her efforts? Believe it or not, this is not that incredible. Histories have been written about the female heroines of almost all our wars, and official records will show their efforts. Follow the information you have, and perhaps you'll not only find her whole name, but also an intriguing story about her. Two books on this topic are Eileen Conklin's *Women at Gettysburg, July 3, 1863* and Charles E. Claghorn's *Woman Patriots of the American Revolution: A Biographical Dictionary*.

➤ **Do you have a suspicion that she died young?** Perhaps in childbirth? If so, this might inspire a second look at her local cemetery. She might be buried in her family's plot instead of her husband's, for instance.

➤ **Could she have been a pioneer or frontier woman?** Does your family tree show your ancestors being part of the great westward expansion? If so, these women were working so hard to survive that there was little time for creating a paper trail for us to find. Too many granny gaps occur when these women married and moved West as partners with their pioneer husbands in a new life. Check the geographical information and the husband and child information you have against the town, county, and national historical accounts written about women's roles in the way West. For instance, if you can pinpoint, through oral history or research, that your missing granny traveled along the Overland Trail between 1840 and 1870, you'd want to check the book *Women's Diaries of the Westward Journey*, edited by Lillian Schlissel. Other books of note are Norma O. Ireland's *Index to Women*, Kenneth L. Holmes's 10 volumes of *Covered Wagon Women*, and Joanna L. Stratton's *Pioneer Women: Voices from the Kansas Frontier*.

➤ **Multiple marriage alert.** Don't forget that multiple marriages were not uncommon. People tended to die younger. A woman might disappear, it would seem, after one husband's death, and a granny gap deepens, all because she has married again, and no longer goes by either her maiden name nor her first husband's name. "Mrs. Joe Schmoe" can turn into "Mrs. Jack Spratt" without ever surfacing under her own name in the documentation of a century or more ago. Again, following the deeds, wills, children's vital records, and cemetery records may uncover the real granny for you.

Silence may await your efforts, but a frontier diary page or a mention of your missing granny in an account of early state settlers may also be waiting for you to uncover. And your female ancestors await, too. They await their names to be known.

The Least You Need to Know

➤ Your family secrets can turn into wonderful family history stories.

➤ There's a reason they call them "kissin' cousins."

➤ You'll come across conflicting versions of family stories and facts as you research your family history.

➤ Your missing female ancestors deserve to be known.

Chapter 16

How Much Is Enough?

In This Chapter

➤ Rethinking the scope of your project

➤ Understanding numbering systems and why you need one

➤ Brainstorming organizational strategies

➤ Knowing when to stop

I can see your future. For months, you have been a family history researching whiz. Your extra room is no longer "extra." Your guest room no longer has room for guests. You have been very, very busy and successful, and you have the paper piles to prove it. You have found out the dirty little secret about genealogy work: It produces an amazing amount of paper, and it does it very, very quickly. A family of rabbits could not multiply as quickly and prodigiously as genealogical research results.

This productivity is a good thing and a bad thing. First, as any writer knows, the more information you have, the better the writing effort. More is always better from a writer's viewpoint. But there comes a time when even the most ambitious writer must ask, "How much is enough?"

The answer to that question is also the answer to many of your organizational needs, such as the following:

1. What's the scope of my search?
2. What are my options at this point?

3. What do I do with all these pieces of paper?

4. How do I recognize a natural ending?

5. How do I safeguard all these papers?

6. Where do I put the in-laws since the spare room is full?

How Big Should You Go?

Question #1: *What's the scope of my search?* Earlier in this book I talked about possible formats and the importance of focus at the beginning of your research. What was important then is essential now. So, let's take another look, now much more educated, at how big your family history appetite is after you've been researching for a while.

'Riting Reminder

More is always better from a writer's point of view. The more rough material you have, the richer your storytelling can be when you begin to write your family history volume.

You could spend three lifetimes on your genealogy, and you'd still never be finished. There's a genealogy legend about a 90-something woman who had been working on her family history for 50 years, and on her ninety-fifth birthday, she finally took it to a printer. (She said she would have waited for her one-hundredth birthday, but she wasn't feeling too good.)

For most of us, we'd burn out much earlier, and nothing would ever be taken to a printer. There's only one way to avoid being overwhelmed. Focus on a certain area or format. Give yourself a break. Do a small book, or at least a specific one—find a format in Chapter 3, "What Kind of Family History Should You Write?" and write according to that format. Later, if you have more energy, you can always produce a second volume.

What if you still aren't ready to focus? If that's so, let's think through a few basic ideas. Since your interest is writing a family history and not do-or-die genealogy, then you will probably have as your first focus the two ancestral lines of most interest to your family—your spouse's and your own.

Ask yourself some basic questions, such as:

1. What ancestor/relative has the most colorful story to offer so far?

2. What story speaks to you most personally?

3. What research is most interesting to you right now?

4. What interview has been most helpful?

5. Who are you most interested in contacting next and why?

6. What aspect of your work thus far would most interest your family?

7. What natural stopping point might you see right now?

8. How might you find a focus in the answers to these questions?

When you can answer most of these questions, you will find that you are already focusing on the future content of your family history. What you find and how you feel about it will offer some very good parameters for your project.

What Were Those Formats Again?

Question #2: *What are my options at this point?* The wide world is your option, of course. Only your own imagination can fence you in. Following are the ideas I offered in Chapters 3 and 4, "How Big Is Your Appetite?" just to get you thinking. Now that you are farther along the genealogical trail, go back and review these chapters. Your educated eyes will see many things you didn't as a beginner, and you may be ready to find your focus:

➤ Narrative genealogy

➤ Memoirs—personal memories

➤ Biography—one very interesting relative

➤ Current family stories

➤ Literary snapshots

➤ Cookbook format

➤ Video family history format

➤ Photo album format

➤ Interview format

➤ Newspaper format

➤ Scrapbook format

➤ Searching for your lost royal relatives

➤ Searching for your American saga

➤ Searching for historical background

➤ Searching for ancestors one and all

➤ Your own unique idea

> **Deep Thought**
>
> *While more material is always better when it comes to writing, there must come a moment to stop. How much is enough? How might a chosen format help you recognize that moment when it arrives?*

Oh, No! Where Did That Paper Go?

Question #3: In the meantime, as you continue to research at full speed, *what do you do with all these pieces of paper?*

At first, you will have only a few files, maybe just one binder with all your charts and logs in it, and you will know where everything is. Then, you will outgrow your binder. There will be many interesting scraps of paper that don't necessarily fit in your binder, so you'll begin to fill up a storage box with these periphery pieces of paper that you just can't throw away. And from there it grows to new binders, new boxes, and even filing cabinets. One day, after the fifteenth time you've groaned, "Where did that paper go?" you'll decide that another layer of organization must be created. And the answer may be your very own index.

Creating an Index

"What?" I can hear you say. "Me, create an index? Isn't that something that librarians and academics do?" Never fear. Creating an index is as easy as creating an outline, if it's your stuff you're wanting to index. What is an index, anyway? It's just a paper signpost, right? It's a signpost pointing you to what you want to find. And that can begin as simply as a pad of paper and a pencil.

A Relatively Good Idea

Each time you decide to work on your research, save a half-hour for a little bit of filing. If you do this, your mountain of paper will stay manageable and your irritation level won't ruin your fun.

So how do you create an index, especially after you are deeply mired in stacks of paper? You back up and you begin again. The only true skill creating an index will tax is your skill at alphabetizing. I somehow think you can handle that without much ado. That is where you start. You spend an hour today systematically going through your piles and listing on your rough "index" pad—what you have and where it is. (Or, if you have a laptop computer, you might list everything onscreen as you go. This can save editing time later.)

Creating Your "Oriental Box"

Once you have a rough list of what you have, you begin to sort your entries by where you want them to be in the future, a simple system that can grow without too many pains. Need something that's more fun than a filing cabinet? Think of one of those oriental stacked boxes that always have yet another, smaller box inside each box you open. For each box inside a box (or file within a file), let's decide on some arbitrary headings. (You can always make up your own, as you go, but these will give you a start.)

You have letters, you have census records, wills and vital records copies, you have family histories, Cousin Bernie's genealogy charts, and transcribed interviews with

Crazy Aunt Edna and Great-Aunt Cissy, as well as all your other relatives you've talked into sitting still for your family history research. How best to organize it all? A simple way to start is to categorize by a series of the largest subject you have—family names—which has many simple subjects filed within it:

➤ Family name

➤ Geographical location—state

➤ Geographical location—town and county

➤ Topic

    ➤ Vital records

    ➤ Wills, deeds/land records

    ➤ Census records

    ➤ Military records

    ➤ Family/town/county history records

    ➤ Newspaper clippings/obituaries

    ➤ Miscellaneous records

    ➤ Oral history interviews

➤ Background historical research

    ➤ By timeline

    ➤ By ancestor

➤ Correspondence

    ➤ Ancestors' names—letters about ancestors

    ➤ Relatives' names—letters from "cousins"

    ➤ Simple alphabetical order: A–O, P–Z

Family Name File

Each file will begin with your father's and your mother's names. It will expand to your spouse's father's and mother's names. That will expand to their mother's and father's parental names. Generally, stash pieces of paper dealing with each ancestral line here until you decide what lines you are going to concentrate most of your energy on. Then, of course, you will need more specific organization within the family name.

Geographical Location—State Subfile

Inside the family name heading file, you should add a geographical filing system. Again, as you begin, you can make these files very general, lumping everything under states, but soon you'll want to have the town and county inside the state file. Your ancestors, being the all-American group they were, probably moved a lot. My Rutledge group, for instance, seemed to have moved to a new state with each new generation. This geographical filing will help you sort out who is who in your family name headings.

So, sooner or later, inside the "Geographical Location—State" file, you will divide the mounting information into another subhead, "Geographical Location—County." After that, why would you need more? If you find that you have lots of ancestors in the same county and town, you may have to create new files within this one to keep all those stay-put generations in the same place: "Geographical Location—Town," and even inside that, "Geographical Location—Ancestor."

When you find that much information in one place, you'll know you're really cooking.

Topic Subfile

This subfile inside your family name file can begin as a place to hold the literal paper trail you'll be accumulating piece by fascinating piece. You know these by heart at this point: vital records, wills, deeds, census records, military records, immigration records, family/town/county history profiles, newspaper clippings and obituaries, etc., etc., etc. As with the other headings, you can subdivide these into more specific files when you acquire so much paper that you find yourself and your file on overload.

Oral History Interview Subfile

Here is where you keep the transcribed interviews with Aunt Edna, Aunt Cissy, Uncle Jacob, Cousin Leroy, and all the living relatives who have offered their memories to you for the family histories. Perhaps, in a way, this file is the most important to take seriously in keeping current and correctly filed. Taking the time to transcribe each tape, or paying a service to do so, is a must, not only for your future writing efforts, but also for the historical value that the words of your elderly relatives, as well as any living relative, has for the future family.

Background Historical Research Subfile

One of the more fascinating parts of your research will be the historical education you'll be receiving as you go. As you think like a historian and plow through recorded history as a researcher, you will be grabbing any piece of information that will help illuminate your future writing. This is the place to put such information until you are ready to use it. The two headings inside this subject head would be "Timeline" and "Ancestor." File more general information in the "Timeline" subfile, things that go along with the timeline you have created to help you understand your place in history as you work your way back in time. File more specific background information that pertains to an individual ancestor's place or time in a file with the specific ancestor's name on it here.

Correspondence Subfile

All the letters you will write and all the letters you'll receive need their own special place. The most logical way to start would be to begin with two subfiles:

1. File by ancestor's name every correspondence about a particular ancestor in one subfile.

2. File by relatives' names all the correspondence between you and your cousins et al., far and wide.

Of course, you could just make it very easy for now and for the future by using a simple alphabetical order format, having two files to begin with—A–O and P–Z—and getting more specific when these are bursting at the seams.

Computer Filing Cabinet

Although I have suggested in Chapter 14, "Your Do's and Don'ts Checklist," not to use your computer as your sole filing cabinet, I know that once you are a computer person, the temptation will be far too great not to keep most of your correspondence on your hard drive. Go ahead and give in. It's okay. But wait until you feel you are being overwhelmed with paper to do it. Until then, keep printing out your first efforts for storage with the rest of your genealogical research files. It's like they say about grammar and style rules for any writer: Once you know the rules, you can break them (when you have a good reason, that is). You will be generating your letters on your computer and sending them by postal mail, so there will be a paper trail.

Just don't forget that if posterity is a goal in your research, as a "here's-the-proof" back-up for your family history volume, then remember that future generations will probably not be able to access your computer files. So, keep an eye toward the future when you look at your genealogical filing cabinet or binder-filled shelf. If you feel your work is well-represented by its paper trail, then you can break a few rules for expediency.

You can organize your "genealogical filing cabinet" as you did your oriental boxes (see the list given in the "Creating Your 'Oriental Box'" section, earlier in the chapter).

Related Facts

Interested in some of the commercial computer programs designed to help you do this filing? Research the advertisements online (you won't have to hunt; they'll find you once you begin to browse) or in genealogical journals. Better yet, visit regional or national genealogical seminars and peruse the vendor booths for demonstrations. A good computer program can be an enthusiasm-saver, as well as a space-saver.

What About Those Genealogical Numbers?

Are you a name or a number? No red-blooded American likes the idea of being a number. And yet what are all these strange numbers attached to every genealogical chart you see? Your confusion started the first time you opened a published genealogy in a library and saw some sort of complex numbering system under those "named" limbs of the family tree. Do you have to use a numbering system in your work? Do you need to be a code-breaker to figure out the system?

The answers are, "yes, probably" and "probably not," in that order. Whether we like the idea or not, in the genealogical world, we and all our kin may each need to be a number just to keep us all straight. And whether we like it or not, it's probably best to learn the numbering systems already widely used in genealogy. Remember that if you create your own code, you may someday not be around to explain your system. Each day you use your own code will make it harder to change it to a system that your family can interpret when you're gone.

Genealogy, not too long ago, had no accepted system, and to be honest, it caused quite a bit of hair-pulling for modern genealogists. So a few systems were created.

Having said that, what systems are we talking about? Several publications can help you understand and even embrace a system you and your kin-to-be can live with. Joan F. Curran's *Numbering Your Genealogy: Sound and Simple Systems* is a very good introduction to the most accepted systems used in today's genealogical world.

For your information right now, though, the two most well-known systems are the Register System and the Modified Register System, referred to as the "NGSQ System" because *The National Genealogical Society Quarterly* uses it.

Dueling Number Systems

So, what is the difference between these two hallowed methods? Basically, the difference is Roman and Arabic numerals.

Both are used with descending genealogies, which means that number one is your original American—your immigrant ancestor, usually. And that means you need to have trekked all the way back to that ancestor before beginning your numbering system. And that's okay. It will give you a chance to get used to all things genealogical. If you can't resist, or if you find a dead end in your attempts to find your number one immigrant ancestor, then numbering can begin with the earliest known ancestor, and you can always renumber, if you soon find your "original American."

Basically, the Register System will give your number one ancestor a superscript 1 by his/her first name. Following that would be a list of his offspring, using Roman numbers i, ii, iii, etc. Say you had Jefferson Schmoe as your number one. His firstborn son is George Schmoe, so he'd be listed as an "i." But you have more information on George, enough for a little paragraph to follow, so you also put a "2" in the margin by his "i." That will point the reader to the "2" paragraph below for more about George J. Schmoe.

The NGSQ System does the same thing, but instead of messing with Roman numerals for children, it gives the children Arabic numbers—i.e., instead of George having an "i," he is given a "2." That will be his number forever, right from the start. To indicate "more information to follow," the NGSQ System uses a "+" in the margin.

All of this formal listing is for published genealogy lists, which you may or may not add to your family history volume. You'll use a corresponding number only for your pedigree charts, so you can see why the NGSQ System works better for the family history writer who just wants to keep up and not chart genealogy as the end-all project.

Choose the numbering system easiest for your purposes, but you'll thank yourself in the morning if you'll begin using an accepted numbering system and stick with it. Study the different systems, choose one, and keep a copy of the system's explanation with your filed research, for future eyes.

Here is a comparison of the most common numbering systems: first, the Register System, and following it, the NGSQ System.

➤ The Register Numbering System

1. **Thomas Jefferson Schmoe**[1] **was born 1 June, 1699 (etc.)**

   Children: surname Schmoe

   i. George Washington Schmoe

   ii. John Adams Schmoe

   iii. Betsy Ross Schmoe

2. **George Washington Schmoe**[2] **was born 8 June, April 1719 (etc.)**

231

➤ The NGSQ Numbering System

1. Thomas Jefferson Schmoe[1] was born 1 June, 1699 (etc.)

Children: surname Schmoe

+ 2. George Washington Schmoe

3. John Adams Schmoe

4. Betsy Ross Schmoe

2. George Washington Schmoe[2] was born 8 June, 1719 (etc.)

Where Does It End?

Question #4: *How do I recognize a natural ending?* Peek even further into the future. You've done months and/or years of good, fun, family history research. One morning, you walk into your study, look around, and wonder, "When is the time to end all this work and begin writing?"

A Relatively Good Idea

Which folders do you choose for your organization? Legal or letter size? Legal-size folders may seem to be the smarter choice, since many of the old documents you will be photocopying and keeping are that size. But letter-size folders and filing space are much easier to handle. Otherwise, you'll be juggling both sizes to fit the same space, and it won't be pretty. Learn to fold those legal documents and use letter-size folders.

Or, perhaps the question is the one you ask with each ancestor search. Let's discuss this one first: When do you stop pursuing one ancestor and begin searching for another? Often, you will hit dead ends, and they will be your natural endings for each ancestor. Sometimes, you will be so fascinated with a specific ancestor that you won't let a seeming dead end stop you. You find a way around the obstacles and keep going. Other times, you find nothing for so long that you know the dead end is real—at least for the time being. (You'll find little surprises along the way, of course. Items will pop up that could start a whole new investigative push for this ancestor or that.)

How, though, can you recognize a natural end to all your research? We talk about that more at length when we discuss how and when to start writing, but perhaps choosing a format, as mentioned above, will help you feel the natural ending. And perhaps, you may just keep that 95-year-old genealogist in mind who spent half a century doing the research and still didn't want to quit. There is no end, really. Your "inner writer" will tell you it's time to begin writing. So don't worry about it now. You truly will know the natural end to your research when the time is right.

For Future "Trekkers"

Question #5: *How do I safeguard all these papers?* Preservation is a big part of your work. What can you do to keep time's eraser from ruining your files over the decades to come? You may not think this is important now, but future family history "trekkers" who uncover your work certainly will. There are a few simple things you can do and a few that are not so simple, depending on how much money you have to give to the cause. An easy first step is to make photocopies of all your newspaper clippings. Newspaper clippings will yellow and crumble within months and definitely over the years. Photocopies have a nice, long life span. You could use acid-free paper, and that certainly goes double for photo albums you may fill while doing this work. For photos, you shouldn't use adhesive tape, for instance. There are photo albums today that are designed for longevity. Interviews on audio- and videocassettes are extremely vulnerable. The best you can do is store such things in covered boxes away from sunlight, dust, and dampness. (And don't use metal boxes!)

If preserving these tapes is important to you (the sound of an ancestor's voice is one good reason), then there's another step you can take. Who knows if the machines they need to be played on will exist when a descendent of yours wants to hear or see these wonderful keepsakes? Remember eight-track tapes? Seen an eight-track tape player lately? Really, there's nothing much you can do to stop technological progress, but you could add to that storage box an old video or cassette and hope that plugs or batteries will still exist when they need to be fired up for your future "trekker."

About That Extra Room

Question #6: *Where do I put the in-laws since the spare room is now my genealogy room?* Sorry. I can't help you there. (Think about it this way. It could be a good excuse to suggest to your in-laws that a motel room down the road would be much more comfortable for their visit.)

The Least You Need to Know

➤ Organization is a must in family history research.

➤ Focusing on format and scope will help you know how much is enough.

➤ Steps can be taken to preserve your research for your descendents.

➤ Your "inner writer" will tell you when it's time to begin writing.

Part 4

Creative Jumpstarts

*Writing isn't easy. Getting started on writing a very big book project is even harder.
How do you get there from here? This section offers lots of exercises to help you make
the transition from researcher to writer. It gives you ideas to evoke your memories, lessons in telling your family stories well, and prepares you to focus on a chosen creative
format to structure your writing.*

*Exercises never sound like fun, but if you love to write, and you love your subject
(which you do), you'll have fun with these writing warm-ups geared toward your
family history work.*

Chapter 17

Evoking Your Memories

In This Chapter

➤ Mining the wealth of your own memories

➤ The power of your own oral history

➤ Learning how to wax philosophic

➤ Recognizing the magic in storytelling

Crazy Aunt Edna, Mom and Dad, Uncle Elroy, both your grandparents, and a dozen cousins have been telling you wonderful family memories. They've turned you into a recording and researching whirlwind. And as you've listened to their stories, your own memories have flooded back. Hopefully, you've been jotting down these memories in your family history journal, but even if you've been a jotting fool, you may have the sneaking suspicion that there is an incredible amount of other memories you still want to include—if you could only remember them.

Your Own Oral History

Is remembering your own stories all that important? After all, you're not writing a memoir or an autobiography, are you? Don't underestimate yourself. Your own memories are going to be the foundation of the current family history portion of your writing. You should begin now to coax the best of your own stories into your mind and then into your journal to frame your family's oral history. How do you do that? Easy enough. Your first step is to think of your memories as your own oral history. After that, well, the writer in you will take over, and you'll be very surprised. See for yourself with the following exercises designed to help you remember.

Exercises to Remember

Actually, in a way, you are writing a memoir—if not in the strictest sense of the term, then in a broader way. You are writing an autobiography, all right—the autobiography of a family.

A *memoir* is to a family history what a short story is to a novel. It can stand alone, but it can also be part of a larger work that illuminates a larger story, as in the case of a novel that's comprised of a series of short stories linked together by some common narrative thread. Your story is one part of a whole. It is a very important part that links to living relatives, as well as to your ancestors.

The easiest way to begin remembering your own oral history is by interviewing yourself. Impossible, you say? Not at all. The trick is to have an audience—a person to tape and listen to your stories just as you taped and listened to Crazy Aunt Edna's and the rest of your family's.

Corralling a Listener

I know what you're thinking: Who would want to sit still and listen to your memory ramblings with the same interest as you gave to Edna's, Cissy's, and Great-granddad Fred's? Well, for starters, how about Edna, Cissy, and Great-granddad Fred or someone else like them? Perhaps it's a sister or a brother or a high school buddy who might help trigger more of your own memories by sharing his own memories.

Make a list of people in your journal—of all ages—who might enjoy exchanging memories with you, and in doing so, help spur your own memories.

After each of their names, note their relationship to you and why they might be a good candidate for your audience.

Do you see the trick to capturing your own oral history? If you choose your audience well, picking someone from each stage of your life, you can cover your whole life in a few conversations—and have fun doing it.

The Power of Hearing Your Own Tales

Have you ever thought about or analyzed how you tell a story? Sharing anecdotes with friends probably comes so naturally to you that you've never given a second thought to how it's done. Think about it now. Remember the last time you told a story so well that everyone responded just the way you hoped? Somehow you chose exactly the right words, body language, mood, and context that conveyed exactly the emotions you felt about the telling. Everything worked. And a moment later, you had the overwhelming wish you could hear how you told it, so you could write it down and always tell it that way.

There isn't a writer alive who hasn't told a story more than once and gotten very different responses without having a clue why. The magic can disappear between oral and written storytelling. In a project such as a family history story compilation, you are going to be on the look-out for ways to keep that magic.

In her book, *Becoming a Writer,* Dorothea Brande, a writing teacher in the 1930s, states that a writer shouldn't make a habit of sharing his or her tales out loud. She claims that often the very act of using that creative energy all but ensures the energy will not be there for the writing of it.

You've probably noticed that problem in your family history sharing, but you also have a vested interest in telling your story again and again. Sharing family history stories out loud should gain strength by their retelling. Yet the energy for writing a story can be dissipated after you tell it orally. What can you do? Capture the oral version of the story on tape. Listening to your own storytelling can reenergize your memory of it and help you write it down. Comparing your own oral history on tape to the transcription can be as good as having a writing teacher stand over you. You will remember your own feelings as you told the tale and, thereby, see if that feeling was articulated vividly enough to transcend the leap away from oral history.

> **Deep Thought**
>
> *Choose your "memory partners" well. Each stage of your life is shared by other people. Identifying who those people are and including them in recovering your memories can help you see yourself as others saw you—a very good thing for any writer.*

Granted, you may cringe when you first hear yourself on tape. No one likes the sound of his own voice (unless you're a budding politician), but soon you will hear what works and what doesn't.

Besides the opportunity to study how your own brand of magic is made, this exercise will help your effort in several other ways:

➤ Taping your stories, then listening to them can spur other memories, from your first birthday to yesterday, especially if you've chosen your "memory partners" well.

➤ The transcriptions can be the outline from which you pick and choose for your writing.

➤ At the very least, if no ideas spring into mind on how to recapture the magic of your oral storytelling, hearing your own anecdotes will help you be your own audience. That can be a powerful writing aid in ways you may not be able to articulate.

Stirring Up the Memories

After your initial attempt of listening to your own oral history, you'll have the sound and the significance of your stories in your head. Now is the time to begin stirring up your past and writing the memories in your journal.

A Relatively Good Idea

Transcribe Crazy Aunt Edna's tape. Read and mark the places that seem strangely lifeless on paper compared to your memory of how it felt to hear her tell the anecdote. Listen to the interviewed anecdote again. What do you think is missing? Why?

No doubt you have remembered a few of your own memories already with your oral history taping exercise. It's time to build on those. The best way to do this is systematically, moving through the major events of life:

➤ Childhood

➤ Family vacations

➤ School

➤ Big family events

➤ Holidays

➤ Summer

➤ Church

➤ Animal companions

➤ Transportation

'Riting Reminder

Keep a pen handy, even when you can't keep your journal handy. Don't trust your memory. Write it down. Use napkins, toilet paper, matchbook covers, your palm—whatever. Many a good idea was lost due to a writer's laziness.

Your One and Only Childhood

What pops into your mind when you see the word "childhood"? When I think of that word, I see my backyard and the view of it from the upstairs bedroom I shared with my sister. When I asked a friend, he said "sandlot baseball." Another friend instantly said "Lassie—the TV show and my own dog." Yet another said "my Schwinn bicycle." Did a memory worth telling float into your consciousness, too?

What did you remember? You might have thought of your grandmother's house, Camp Kitchie Kootchie, chicken pox, Girl Scout cookies (four boxes of thin mints, thank you), the neighborhood bully, or your second grade teacher, mean ol' Miss Toddwaddle.

Whatever came to mind, one thing's for sure: It was something vivid, and there is much more where it came from.

Try this exercise: Name six things that the word "childhood" brings to mind for you, and write them in your journal.

Now, beside each one, in parentheses, write two new memories inspired by association. Here's an example:

➤ Your grandmother's house (her big front porch swing) (watching fireworks from it on July 4th)

➤ Camp Kitchie Kootchie (getting lost in the woods) (being found in the woods)

➤ Tonsillitis (having my tonsils out) (eating vanilla ice cream delivered to my hospital room from my father's drugstore)

Inside every last one of these memories is a story waiting to be told. Turn to a clean page in your family history journal and write "Childhood" at the top of the page. Since more is always better when it comes to raw material in writing, give each memory at least a paragraph. You'll thank yourself later.

Try this exercise with each heading as we go.

Family Vacations

The car was a red Chevy station wagon. The time was August, 1959, just before dawn. It was the launching of our one and only family vacation that included my whole family—Mom, Dad, and all five kids. We were going cross-country all the way from Texas to Jekyll Island, Georgia, seeing the sights, the all-American-family-vacation way. Of course, that meant sibling fights, whining, and begging for Dad to stop at each tourist trap along the way ("Look! Go-cart racing, Daddyyyy! PLEAAAASE!"). And, as these things go, it also meant seven different sets of memories about that trip. Whether the family vacation was one from your childhood or one from last year with your own family, the topic is perfect family history fodder.

List six vacation memories in your journal, and beside each, as you did earlier, write two new memories inspired by association.

School Daze

Quick! Name your grade-school teachers in order. Mine are Ms. Blankenship, Ms. McCraw, Ms. Burns, Ms. O'Neil, Ms. Deuschle, and Ms. Jackson.

A Relatively Good Idea

To give the topic of family vacations its full due, interview yourself first, then interview others who also went on the trip. The outcome should be fun and fruitful. Keep the transcripts handy for the moment you can bring everyone's memories together for inclusion in your family history.

241

Two of these small-town women taught my perfect older sister (who graduated high school valedictorian) and were openly disappointed over my own stubborn imperfection. One adored my older brother and made a point of telling me so each time I gave her trouble. Two more would teach my younger sisters and tell them tales of me. And one, especially unforgettable, made my fifth-grade year a holy hell, and the feeling was probably mutual. (I distinctly remember a certain Halloween trick—minus treat—involving Ms. Deuschle's house. I confess this only because the statute of limitations has expired.)

Considering all my siblings' involvement with these same hometown teachers, wouldn't this sort of saga be a good addition to a family history, especially including input from all my siblings? At the very least, it certainly gives me a dozen or more stories to explore from my childhood. And that's just talking about my teachers, the proverbial tip of my grade-school-memory iceberg. The same is true for you, too, isn't it?

The years from grade school through high school inspire an incredible amount of vivid, formative memories. Shall I tell you about my playground tether-ball prowess? Shall I tell you of losing the big election or the big district tournament? Shall I tell you about the cultural phenomenon called my prom? Or shall I attempt to capture what it was like to go to public school in a small town in Texas during that era, encapsulating as much colorful, time-specific detail as I can to make it interesting for my family history readers, whoever they are, now and in the future? When it comes to our school years' memories, the possibilities are seemingly endless.

What could you tell me about your school years? List six school-day memories in your journal, and beside each, write two new memories inspired by association.

Weddings and Funerals

The wildly popular British film called *Four Weddings and a Funeral* captured our imagination and hearts for a very obvious reason. The settings were universal and so were the feelings we all experience during these occasions. Weddings and funerals—we've all been there, done that.

You could probably write your own story and call it "A Dozen Weddings and Funerals." These are the moments in your life and your family's when memories are made, futures created, and lives ended. This is the stuff of life and of family histories.

Is your most vivid wedding memory …

➤ Your own wedding when you tripped walking down the aisle?

➤ Your cousin's wedding when she sang the solo herself and was so nervous, she could only squeak out a rendition of a very wilted "Evergreen"?

➤ Your brother's wedding when Uncle Elroy threw his back out trying to disco?

➤ Your Aunt Sally, who, on her third marriage, got married on a yacht?

➤ (Insert your memory here)

➤ (ditto)

Funerals are sad events, but when it comes to "family times," they are unparalleled. At their best, funerals are a celebration of a deeply loved person and his or her impact on each family member. What better time to sum up a life for your family history, which in effect, is what you will be doing many times over for ancestors you never knew? At their worst, funerals can also be incredibly painful times as well, with old family hurts surfacing. Either way, funerals are unforgettable. And to state a brutally honest fact of life, family gatherings after funerals are often the last chance many family members have to interact.

What are your most vivid funeral memories? What one funeral memory do you have that your family members might appreciate you incorporating into the family history? Why?

That Old-Time Religion

The role of religion in the average American's life is the great untold story in our country's story. Good or bad, crazy or touching, life-changing or repressive, the words to describe the experience of church attendance for those of us growing up under its influence are boundless. Whatever adjectives describe it, though, all of the experiences are unforgettable. We can often even laugh at the memories we wish we could forget, and sometimes find ourselves waxing philosophic about them.

Were you raised in a church or a synagogue? Were the members of that congregation the "village" who helped raise you? Was there a village "idiot"? Was there a village "saint"? Was the church part of your family's life? Did your sister sing soprano in the choir or did your mother break the stained-glass ceiling to become one of the church elders?

List six church memories in your journal and think about which of these might be wonderful additions, with a little added reflection, for your family history writing effort.

> **Deep Thought**
>
> *What distant relations did you only see at weddings and funerals? Were they "different" than your other family members? Or were they incredibly similar? What interesting observations do your answers create about your family tree?*

> **'Riting Reminder**
>
> Don't forget to consider how you might connect the influence of church or synagogue in your family life with the role religion played in an ancestor's life.

Holidays, Family Style

Christmas lights. Making ornaments. Mama kissing Santa Claus. The year your sister got a pony, a bicycle, and a puppy when you only got socks. Indigestion after eating Thanksgiving dinner. Cousin George and Cousin Betty getting into a fight over whose pumpkin pie was better. The year the oven blew up, and everybody had to eat bologna sandwiches with Jell-O salad and pumpkin pie. The year the television blew up and every male in the family went through football withdrawal.

Holidays are perfect family memory-makers, whatever the quality of those memories. Want to have your family smiling as they read your history? Add as many holiday stories as you can. Perhaps create a model holiday, incorporating all your holiday rituals everyone will remember, to serve as your introduction to specific holiday anecdotes.

What holidays could you include? Remember to include all of them, not just Christmas and Thanksgiving. Add any holiday during which your family would congregate, from backyard hot-dog grilling on the 4th of July to a Halloween costume party.

A Relatively Good Idea

What was your most unforgettable Christmas present? Why? Ask your relatives this question to spur their own holiday memories as well as your own.

Now (you guessed it), take out that journal and pick six holidays. Beside each, write two new memories evoked by association.

Animals in Your Life (Excluding Your Prom Date)

Eight dogs, four horses, a duck, a lamb, one cat, three birds, and a baby rhino. These are the accumulated animals that have played parts in my life and would be included in any autobiography I chose to write.

The eight dogs cover my childhood up to this very moment of my adulthood, and they define me perhaps more than my human friends. I'm one of those people for whom the bumper sticker "Love Me, Love My Dog" was created.

The four horses were the ones my sisters and I rode along the dirt streets of Texas behind our house, down the parade routes of our town, across the pasture of my dad's farmland, and straight into the doctor's office after I fell off one and broke my arm.

The duck was our father's idea; the lamb my sister's wish; and the cat my mother's 20-year pet.

The three birds were a parakeet of my youth and a pair of supposedly mated finches I owned as a newlywed for a very, very short period before they all but killed each other.

Like a tiny tank, the baby rhino rubbed up against me at the San Diego Wild Animal Park when I first met her. I was working on a year-long book project there, and I found myself watching her grow along with my work. As an endangered white rhino, she was the symbol of the unique, endangered species-focused park, and she became a symbol for that special time in my life.

Each is a story I would relish telling, and some are ones my family would enjoy as part of its saga, especially the parts that overlapped theirs.

Like the mention in a county history of my great-grandfather, the sheriff, being a trainer and breeder of horses, often there are animal connections you can find through your genealogical research. Following that thread through the writing of your ancestors, as well as extended family, can be wonderful.

Are you an animal person? Then your family probably is full of animal people. You have stories of your "animal" family members that illuminate the life of your family. Some families' daily lives center on animals so much that they could use the topic as their family history format. But even if you aren't one of these people, not being an animal person can also be a tale worth telling as well.

'Riting Reminder

Make a note about any connection you find between your ancestor's genealogical information and the stories you are gathering for your family. Every time you can refer back to your ancestors as you tell your own stories, your family history writing is given an extra dimension.

Mapping Your House and Town

Here's an exercise that never fails to stir up the memory dust. On a large pad or in the pages of your journal, draw three maps—one of the house you grew up in, another of a house that meant a lot to you as a young adult, and another of your current home. Focus on each of the rooms and visualize the memories that happened in each. Remember to add the backyard, especially for your childhood house.

My image of my childhood backyard from my second-story bedroom is one full of giant sycamore-tree branches. In all my travels, in all the different places I've lived since those small town days, I have yet to see a sycamore tree anywhere near its size. That tree was so big that a traveling postcard salesman took a picture of it (with my brother and me sitting like tiny dots under it to show its magnitude). The sycamore's long and glorious limbs seem now to be leafy arms enveloping my childhood. I see its shadow looming large over the back driveway as I sneak out of bed to watch my father come home late each night from work. I can hear its big leaves' distinct rustling in years of Texas wind and weather. The sycamore was a deep, abiding presence in my whole family's life. These are the surprises of memory evoking. Drawing a

A Relatively Good Idea

Do you have your own type of picture postcard from your past, an unusual picture or object that speaks volumes for you and about you? How might you make it a part of your family history?

map of my house and yard would remind me how important that tree was to my earliest recollections.

My best friend tells a similar tale about a tree from her childhood. It was a spreading oak with a big, inviting limb in front of her small town's library. She'd scramble up into it and stay there for hours reading her latest library choice. As a writer, she has made the same meaningful, layered connections with her oak and her childhood as I have with my backyard sycamore. Our houses, our neighborhoods, and our towns are all creative forces in our memories. All we need to do is reclaim them in order to share them.

Try sketching a map of your whole neighborhood or town. Draw scary ol' Mrs. Ramblow's house across the street. Draw the candy store down on the corner and Great-Aunt Gladys' three-story dilapidated mansion across town. Mark the spot of your own oak tree in front of the library. Then, open your mind and let the memories come.

Planes, Trains, and Automobiles

The covered wagon may be gone, but our ancestral wanderlust isn't. Like my friend who can eloquently explain his life through the cars he has owned, we often find important parts of our lives defined by our modes of transportation.

This reminds me of two train trips of my childhood. The first was a graduation trip for my older sister when I was nine. We bought compartments to ride in all the way to New Orleans. I got to go along only because I was going to visit an aunt. But that night spent in the train with the lights and the sounds and the motion may have been my first moments of my love affair with travel. And the rest of the story was a family travel story worth examining for our family history.

The second was a train trip I took as a 13-year-old with a friend whose father worked for the railroad. That adventure to visit her unusual relatives in Louisiana opened a whole other world to me as a very sheltered child. It is an important coming-of-age story I should not forget. Such are the memories evoked by experiences in travels.

Your first plane trip, your first car, your first accident, and your first feeling of the freedom, expectancy, and hope of the road are all natural memory-makers. So it was for our ancestors; so it is for us.

Consider your own transportation history. Can you come up with six "transportation memories"? Which of these memories might be wonderful additions to your family history, with a little added reflection?

Digging Out Your Sister's Diary

After you have remembered all you can of your own past, don't underestimate what others might have written about you. What am I suggesting? I'm suggesting you go take another peek into your sister's diary, your parents' letters, or any other place with the potential of "mentions" about you. Perhaps it's even time to interview that sibling and ask her to be honest about what a brat you were. Be sure to also discuss what family memories you share.

Learning to Wax Philosophical

I have purposefully not attempted to corral your memories. Right now, summoning as many as you can from wherever they are stored inside you is the important thing. Later, when you are ready to write, I will talk about respecting your audience and about choosing the memories that will have significance for your family members as well as for your own place in your family history. Such discernment is hard when you are accumulating autobiographical material. It's *all* interesting to you. How you choose your memories, how you tell them, and how you frame what you tell to engage your reader is a topic for another day. For now, think of the words "contemplative" and "philosophical." Get yourself into the mood, because that sort of insight into your memories will help you pick and choose which stories to share and which to keep for yourself.

Don't fret; just keep the need for such "transitional" thoughts about your memories in mind. Being philosophical is not that hard. It's a very natural extension of living. The passage of time automatically creates the mindset. You ruminate on a past memory and try to make sense of it. What results is the act of being philosophical, and this turns memories into stories.

Topics Galore

Other topics of memory are numerous. The list will always be incomplete, but here are a few more to stimulate those memories of yours:

➤ Summer jobs

➤ First romances

➤ Sibling rivalry

➤ Kitchen memories

➤ Those "talks" with Mom or Dad

➤ Bumps, scars, and stitches

➤ Sports

➤ Best/worst friends

➤ Favorite relatives

➤ Family births and deaths

Journaling Down the Genealogical Trail

Review all the memories conjured in this chapter. Choose one. What did you choose and why? When you can answer these questions, then you can probably turn the memory into a story.

Try it. Open your journal and write for a few minutes. Now go back through what you've written. Do you see what has turned from a memory into a story? What contemplative thoughts, judgments, or insights have you added that make the difference?

The Least You Need to Know

➤ Your memories hold essential family history.

➤ Remembering your experiences is more fun with a "memory partner."

➤ Reflection on your experiences will help you in your family history writing.

➤ The surprise memories you recall, such as those about your neighborhood or your pets, will sometimes hold the most insight.

Chapter 18

Telling Your Own Stories

In This Chapter

➤ Telling your anecdotes

➤ Compiling your stories into a list

➤ Learning narrative elements through exercises

All your great memories are rattling around your head. You've jotted them down and attempted to record some of what you remember to help you write your memories fully later. But you wonder how you'll ever capture them as vividly as you feel them.

How to tell an anecdote is any writer's first ambition. Yet the telling is as varied as your memory. A writer can tell a story a dozen different ways. So perhaps your real question should be, "Which way should I tell this one?"

The path to that answer can best be found through a little writer's exercise.

Cross-Training Is Good for You

Cross-training is good for your body. Different exercises make your muscles stronger. Different exercises make your writing stronger, too. Let's do some cross-training, trying out varied writing muscles that can inspire your own writing skills while honing them.

Remember, this is all practice. These exercises are writing warm-ups and stretching exercises that will get you ready for the real thing. Take these exercises seriously, but be sure to play, too. Use your journal or keep a notepad just for this purpose. Be bold, be creative, be open to trying new ways of telling things. The real writing is still ahead. For now, these exercises are stretching you. You are working to understand how to make these memories into stories and make them yours.

You're Just Warming Up

Okay. Ready to do your stretches? In a piece of narrative writing, which is the bulk of the kind of writing you will be doing, there are certain elements. The quality of each part will determine the quality of the whole. Strong legs and weak arms do not a healthy body make, if you catch my drift. You need everything to work, or you probably won't be at your best. So, what story-telling elements are we talking about? Description, characterization, dialogue, dramatic tension, tense, and tone are the elements I'll be exploring in this chapter.

Listing Your Memories

First, let's take an account of your collection of family *anecdotes* thus far. List the memories you have from the "memory reclamation" work you did in the last chapter.

The Write Word

An **anecdote** is a short account of a personal or family experience.

How many do you have? How many *should* you have? That depends. How many memories do you think you have? Your list will never end, really. After all, it took you your whole life to experience them. To remember all of them would take another lifetime, wouldn't it?

Write down all you can remember right now on one sheet, if you can. Use double or triple columns and abbreviated names. If your journal page is too small, use notebook paper.

This will be your master list for this chapter's cross-training writing exercises. Keep it handy. You will be picking and choosing from it for your warm-ups as you go. (And don't be surprised when you jot down new memories that come to you as you work.)

Listing all your memories on one page as they come to mind will help you think and plan. I've started you off with a "master list" of sorts to get those memory juices flowing. You might be surprised to see how much farther your memories go when you give them a little bit of a kick start.

➤ **Holidays.** We're not just talking Christmas morning here! Open your mind on this one.

- ➤ Christmas-pony jealousy
- ➤ Jell-O/Albert's teeth
- ➤ BBQs/dog ate steak
- ➤ Christmas traditions
- ➤ Cousins' pumpkin-pie fight

- ➤ Oven blew/bologna sandwiches
- ➤ No television/touch football tradition began
- ➤ Tackling Aunt Sally

➤ **Animals.** Okay, so it reads kind of like "The Twelve Days of Christmas," but there are a lot of stories in these lovable friends of ours.

- ➤ Eight dogs
- ➤ Four horses
- ➤ Duck
- ➤ Lamb
- ➤ Cat
- ➤ Birds
- ➤ Baby rhino

➤ **Weddings and funerals.** There's more than just the memories of the "guests of honor" for these occasions. Go ahead, laugh a little.

- ➤ Tripping
- ➤ Cousin's solo
- ➤ Elroy/disco
- ➤ Sally #3 yacht

➤ **Church.** Sure, we're supposed to be serious and mature at church, but there's more to those memories than just sitting on a hard pew on Sunday mornings. You know what I mean. Add the funny ones, too.

- ➤ Sister's soprano
- ➤ Mom/first female elder
- ➤ Sunday tradition
- ➤ Easter dress-up
- ➤ Giggle-squelching with your friends in the back row

➤ **Sports.** Whether it's memories from your own childhood or someone else's, those sports events are full of learning experiences, amazing moments of success, and plenty of bloopers!

- ➤ Summer baseball
- ➤ Tennis team
- ➤ The big game

➤ Twirling moments

➤ Tiddlywinks champ

➤ Breaking leg

➤ **Childhood.** Our childhoods are treasure troves for memories, our first impressions of our older relatives, big family gatherings—you name it. If you can remember how you saw some of your family as a kid during those experiences, you might realize that you remember more about those distant relatives than you realized.

➤ Granny's house/watching fireworks from swing

➤ Camp/getting lost and found

➤ Tonsillectomy/ice cream

➤ Best scars and stitches

➤ TV

➤ Best/worst friends

➤ Favorite relatives

➤ Summer jobs

➤ First romances

➤ Kitchen memories

➤ Sibling rivalry

A Relatively Good Idea

Glance down your list. Close your eyes. See with your mind's eye whatever comes. What *is* it? Why did you remember it?

Your Description Warm-Up: How Did They Look?

One of the first things that gets lost in a specific memory is what things looked like. Over the years, the tiny details seem to disappear as your senses continue to be bombarded with new stimuli. And yet, haven't you remembered something after sniffing a certain smell, hearing a certain tune, or seeing a certain object? Your mind may seem to have forgotten such details, but obviously your senses remain keyed into your past as well as your present. Isn't that incredible?

So, let's see if you can use *description* to your writing advantage. When the average person tells a story that includes a man, he or she might tell you that the man is a certain age. Unless it has something to do with the story, any more detail will probably not be offered.

You know what I mean. We've all listened to stories and found ourselves having to stop the storyteller and ask for details to help us get the mental picture we need to enjoy the story. ("Was he tall?" "Was he well-dressed?" "What kind of car was it?") If the same person *wrote* the story instead of telling it, the result would probably be bland and not very compelling.

A good writer knows how to capture detail without drowning the reader in it and without letting the detail get in the way of the telling. How much is too much? How little is too little? It's a balancing act you learn only through practice. But first you have to learn the fine art of observation, even in your memories. Your senses have captured everything—you just have to learn how to access them and then weed them out. Ready? Open that journal. Here we go.

Describing Your Grandmother's Face

Picture your grandmother's face. What do you see? List her features.

Zoom In

Now, beside each characteristic you've listed, go farther. Add one more detail. Close your eyes, picture your granny, and zoom in. What was the quality of her hair? Was it all gray? What's that holding back her hair? If you let yourself zoom in, you might rediscover images you never fully registered before—like that diamond hair clip she always wore. You didn't really know it was there until you really focused on how you remember her, right? What else might you "rediscover" with a little focus and concentration? Do the same with the rest of your descriptions of Granny.

Location, Location, Location

Place is a big part of any story, but it is fundamental to description. So, let's add a description of your grandmother's location. Picture your granny again. Where do you see her?

The Write Word

Description is an attempt to paint a word picture of a scene, a person, or an adventure.

A Relatively Good Idea

At your next family event—a family reunion, a holiday gathering, a wedding reception—attempt to capture a dozen sights and sounds. Such a list will indelibly mark your memory of the event. It will be the first step in making observation a part of your daily life.

Zoom Out

Here's where you pull it all together. Zoom out. Sit back, as if you were with your grandmother in whatever location you envision her. Put yourself into the memory. Now you are ready to describe your grandmother's face. In your journal, finish this sentence with three or four descriptive phrases:

My grandmother had a …

_____

_____

Stuck? Here's an example to get you going:

My grandmother had a square, proud jaw, a dainty nose, fine wrinkles, drug-store glasses, and a pair of false teeth she never let anyone see her without.

Ready, Set, Exercise: Adjectives Out

Are you finished with the paragraph on your grandmother? Good. Let's try another exercise to prove a point about your style and how to make it more effective. Take a red pen and cross out every adjective in your paragraph on your grandmother. My example paragraph would look something like this:

My grandmother had a jaw, a nose, wrinkles, glasses, and a pair of teeth she never let anyone see her without.

Wow. Adjectives make a difference, don't they? Some are factual ones needed for clarity, "false" teeth, for example. All the rest are chosen for descriptive clarity. The difference between a "dainty" nose and "big" nose is important. The difference between a "dainty" nose a "small" nose, though, is more about your ability as a writer to choose the perfect adjective for descriptive magic.

The word "small" can mean only one thing. The words "dainty," "wee," "tiny," "dwarf," and "miniature" all say her nose is small, but they add a lot more, don't they? That's why the thesaurus was invented.

But there can be too much of a good thing. A common writers' mistake is relying on adjectives to the detriment of powerful verbs and vivid writing. For instance, in my enthusiasm to describe my grandmother just right, I packed the previous example with a dozen more adjectives.

My grandmother had a big, square, proud, boxer-like jaw, with a dainty, pink, perfect nose, and deep, thick, layers of wrinkles, cheap, pointy, ugly glasses, and a pair of chalky, loose, ugly teeth she never let anyone see her without.

See what happens when you use too many adjectives? You can't see anything else. The whole thought is weighted down. Be very stingy with your adjectives. Use only one or two adjectives in most sentences. You'll learn what happens to your writing when you allow your verbs to shine.

Ready, Set, Exercise: Verbing Actively

Let's check out your verbs in your previous description warm-up paragraph. One of the best-kept secrets of vivid and powerful writing is the "health" of your verbs. Are they weak and skimpy? Passive and lifeless? Or are they big, bold, brawny, and powerful as a punch?

Take that red pen and circle your verbs. What's the diagnosis?

Do your verbs jump out at you? Are they overshadowed by your adjectives? What verbs might you choose if, under penalty of death, you couldn't use any adjectives at all? Suddenly your verbs would have to do double-duty, and all that extra effort will make them strong. The difference is amazing. "He walked quickly down the street" becomes a more powerful and vivid statement when you change it to "He charged down the street."

Add your own big-muscled verbs for the word "walked":

➤ Ambled

➤ Strolled

➤ Dashed

➤ _____

➤ _____

➤ _____

> **Deep Thought**
>
> *When we picture our relatives, we always picture them in a place, as in a mental snapshot. Think of your mother. Where is she? Why do you see her in that location? Your answer may tell you some interesting things about yourself, as well as your mother.*

The difference between powerful verbs and wimpy verbs is usually whether they are passive or active. List three of your own verbs along with their adjectives. Brainstorm at least one adjectiveless verb that could take the place of each and jot it beside it in parenthesis:

➤ _____

➤ _____

➤ _____

As Mark Twain once said, "The difference between the right word and the almost-right word is the difference between lightning and the lightning bug." The difference between the right adjective and the right verb in your descriptions—and the restraint with which you use them—will be the difference between poor writing and vivid writing. You'll see it yourself.

Here are a few examples to get you started. Which sentence is the most vivid in these pairs?

➤ My grandmother had a square jaw.

➤ My grandmother was square-jawed.

➤ She cooked rings around everyone else in town.

➤ She was the best cook in town.

Now read the following sentences. They're all descriptive, right? Which one is the most vivid? Which one puts an instant, clear picture in your head? Now think about what it is in that simple sentence that makes it pop out for you so much.

➤ My grandmother had a square jaw.

➤ My grandmother was square-jawed.

➤ She cooked rings around everyone else in town.

➤ She was the best cook in town.

➤ She embraced many aspects of life.

➤ There were many things she enjoyed about life.

➤ She was a loud piano-player.

➤ She pounded out tunes on the piano.

Your Characterization Warm-Up: How Did They Act?

Describing how a person acts—adding *characterization*—can be as obvious as the way your granny baked a pie or mowed the "back 40." You could say she was a good cook, or you could show she was a good cook by describing how she did it, how she acted as she did it, and how everyone lucky enough to eat the pie responded to her and how she responded back. That's showing, not telling, and it's much more fulfilling for the reader and the writer.

Characterization can also be created with an observation you make as your describe her. This observation can speak volumes in a few words by painting a word picture. You are showing *and* telling. For instance, let me add a paragraph to my description of my granny's face.

> My grandmother had a square, proud jaw, a dainty nose, fine wrinkles, drugstore glasses, and a pair of false teeth she never let anyone see her without.
>
> Her smile, though, she couldn't corral, no matter how she felt about her false teeth. It was ear-to-ear and nose-to-chin. By the time I knew her, she was hardly 5'2", already with a bit of a stoop in her walk. But the way her face could brighten with her cackle of a laugh, your first instinct was always to lean over and hug her hard and happy, waiting for her to return the same.

> **The Write Word**
>
> **Characterization** is the infusing of life into a character through action and description.

I have now added my observations of my granny, showing the kind of woman she was—a bit of characterization with only a few words—like a snapshot. Can you see which words did what? This now is my memory. Yours will become clear as well once you move into describing habitual actions and your response to them.

Your Dialogue Warm-Up: What Did They Say?

Dialogue in a family history is usually a part of an anecdote you're putting down on paper for posterity. Dialogue from interviews will be easy. It's already done for you in the context of the story you've been told. But what about the dialogue you will have to—go ahead and say it—"make up"?

I grew up reading the humor sections in my mother's copies of *Reader's Digest*. "Life in These United States," "Humor in Uniform," "All in a Day's Work"—I read them all. Odds are you've read them, too. For decades, people just like you have written 300-word anecdotes, usually humorous, but sometimes dramatically heartwarming and submitted them in the hope of seeing them in print. Each are short stories complete with beginning, middle, and end. They are good examples of how to tell an anecdote, although your kind of anecdotes don't necessarily need to have a clever ending.

If you have a copy of this popular monthly magazine, peruse one of these anecdotes. Notice how *dialogue* is used. As I'll discuss later, your use of dialogue in your family history, except for straight quotes from your interviews, will have to be created using a bit of artistic license. So, capturing how people sound, developing an "ear" for the way people talk, and then imagining what they might say is a pivotal skill. Why? Every writer loves to use dialogue, but few writers can make the reader hear the character—or, in this case, the ancestor—instead of the writer's sound and style.

The Write Word

Dialogue is the spoken words of persons in a story, as in a conversation, and is usually set off by quotations.

'Riting Reminder

If you haven't transcribed your interviews, don't wait. You will need to see hard copy of the interviews for your writing. Hire someone (maybe a teenager good with a keyboard and a tape recorder), or do it yourself. Transcribing your own interviews will allow you to relive the interview, capturing the essence of your relative's personality again.

How can you sound like someone else when you write dialogue? The answer is to begin to listen. Try to answer this question: In what ways do people sound different than you do? If you cannot capture the technique of other ways of speaking, the dialogue you write is forever doomed to sound like you, no matter who you have saying it.

Eavesdropping for a Good Cause

Immersing yourself in other people's chatter is a good idea as you focus on this dialogue-writing exercise. Pick a place in which you can overhear others' conversations without the talk being directed at you and without drawing attention to yourself as you scribble notes about what you're hearing in your journal. It can be in a restaurant, in a mall's food court, on a commuter train, on a plane, in a library, or in waiting rooms. Attempt to scribble down the way things are said that are completely different from the way you might say them.

What Crazy Aunt Edna Can Teach You

Want to know a good trick for learning how to really hear how other people sound? You have all the ingredients already. Use the interviews you've taped with your relatives. Everyone will have his or her own distinctive way of talking. You can stop and start these chatterboxes anytime you want to hear things again. Here's how to do it:

➤ Sit and listen to each tape—really listen.

➤ Read along with the transcriptions to see how each one of the "characters" (and Crazy Aunt Edna is certainly a "character") actually says what they say.

➤ Take notes on what makes them work as dialogue: "Sounds like her," "Word choice," etc. Analyze your comments to incorporate what you've learned into your own dialogue efforts.

Your Dramatic Tension Warm-Up: What Happens Next?

The story of an ancestor's life may seem to tell itself. You just have to relate every anecdote and fact you uncovered in chronological order, right? But even the most exciting life can seem boring in the way it's told if there is no sense of *dramatic tension*. A mystery would just be a recounting of a list of facts if it weren't for the way it was told. It would lack the page-turning suspense it offers the reader.

The Write Word

Dramatic tension is the suspense created to drive the story forward.

Ready, Set, Exercise: "And Then ..."

While I'll deal with the elements of dramatic tension and suspense in more detail later, let's try two exercises now to give you a taste of how it's done:

In your journal, write at least six "And then ..." phrases and spread them several lines apart. Now, using one of the anecdotes from your master list, and fill the happenings of the anecdote, step by step, one at a time, under the "And then." Phrases.

Here's an example:

And then ...

... the electricity went out on Thanksgiving Day.

And then ...

... Mom's turkey was ruined.

And then ...

... all the kids began to gripe and whine.

And then ...

... Mom began to cry.

And then ...

... Dad told us all to hush up, sit down at the table, and not make a sound.

A Relatively Good Idea

Do the "And then ..." exercise with a pencil so you can juggle each "And then ..." with the others to make the story's progression work best.

And then ...

... Mom and Dad went into the kitchen, and in a few minutes, they came out with Jell-O salad, bean salad, tossed salad, potato-chip salad, bologna sandwiches, and pumpkin pie. And that's the Thanksgiving we had bologna—and liked it.

What do you see about the progression of your story? If you left out an important part, would you notice it was missing? Charting the progression using the "And then" phrases can help you make sure you create a swell of suspense or drama, however small, to make the ending better.

Ready, Set, Exercise: Action/Reaction

Every action has an equal and opposite reaction, and so it is in writing—at least if you want dramatic tension. The "And then ..." exercise certainly shows a series of happenings that seem to be related in any story. Some of them will be like the Thanksgiving bologna story with lots of "And then ..." phrases. Most of your memories will be simple action/reactions—one of each. An anecdote has to have at least one reaction or it isn't an anecdote. It may be a sensory memory instead. I'll prove it to you: Choose another anecdote from your master list. Write down an action that happened in it.

Here's an example:

➤ You had a summer job as a lifeguard.

➤ You met your future spouse.

Now that's an action/reaction, and it's the beginning of a family history anecdote that begs to be told.

Start noticing how your stories—and everyone else's—flow. That's the first step to creating dramatic tension in your narratives.

Your Tense Warm-Up: When Did It Happen?

Have you ever noticed how people tell stories? It usually begins like this: "You should have been there! I couldn't believe it! Here I am minding my own business, when in walks this guy with a B-B gun ..."

When it comes to storytelling, the past isn't always in the past. As I mentioned earlier, William Faulkner once said "The past isn't gone. It isn't even past." In the case of *tense* in narration, especially with oral history, that idea takes on a whole new meaning when the present tense is used. We instinctively tell stories that obviously happened in the past as if they are happening in the present. We somehow know the power of present tense immediacy. Diaries and letters are all written in present tense unless their writers are recounting a story (and sometimes, even then). We are constantly attempting, however unconsciously, to capture that immediacy.

Believe it or not, you have a choice of what tense you use to tell parts of your family history. Try this exercise:

In your journal, turn to the paragraphs you wrote for Chapter 17, "Evoking Your Memories." Choose one. Write it again but this time in present tense, just to see if it works.

The Write Word

Tense is the "time" in which you create a story, as in present tense, past tense, or future tense.

If it doesn't work, peruse all your paragraphs and see if another is more likely to benefit from a feeling of immediacy, of conveying a feeling of happening right now. A good candidate would be a "story within a story," which in reality is what your whole family history is. Did you have an adventure during a trip? The trip is a *story,* and the adventure is a *story within the story.*

Here's an example:

> My cousin and I, during the 1960s, were driving across Arizona during spring break in our Volkswagon van and passed a lone roadside store out in the middle of nowhere. I was suffering after far too much liquid intake while cruising across the dry desert. I pulled off the road to use the store's facilities.
>
> Joe laughed. He said, "Yeah, well, get ready to buy yourself a $5 soda. I thought the same thing last year as I came through here. When I walked in the door, the first thing I saw were Christmas lights hung everywhere, an Indian in full war paint behind the register, and in the back ... there was no back. The building had three walls."
>
> "That's when the 'Indian' calls out to me, 'Hey, hippie college boy. You want to use my bathroom?'"
>
> "I say, 'Yes, I do.'"
>
> "'There you go.'" He points toward the back of the building, to the dust and the snakey brush beyond. "'You buy something, you use my outhouse. You don't, you can commune with nature. Got it?'"

Did you notice when the past tense turned to present tense? Can you see why? The answer can be anything from the writer forcing the reader to "come closer" or just the act of capturing dialogue a certain way. Try this for yourself with several anecdotes to see if it can work for you later.

Your Tone Warm-Up: What's Funny About Humor?

Tone is usually not something you naturally think of when you write. Somehow it seems to come with the story being told. If it's a sad story, the tone is sad; a happy story and the tone is happy; an exciting story, and the tone is upbeat and fast-paced. But you can manipulate tone, too, and you should.

Let's try humor to discuss tone, since it is often hardest to recapture the humor of a family anecdote, especially a much-loved one.

How would you tell about your Uncle Albert's false teeth falling into the Christmas Jell-O salad? Would you have to be there to think it was funny, or could you try to capture it on paper because everyone will remember it?

The Write Word

Tone is the attitude that the writer brings to a story.

'Riting Reminder

Humor can be broad or subtle, heavy or light, tasteful or tasteless. Subtle and light is always the safest choice in a family history project (with the possible exception of that insane story Cousin Herb III tells about his granddaddy, Herb Sr.).

Let's try it. Choose your own moment with your extended family. Got it? Okay. What elements do you need? Description. Dialogue. Dramatic tension. Characterization. Tone.

Here's a little outline for telling a funny anecdote for your family history:

➤ Summary introduction

➤ Body of story, told vividly

➤ Wrap-up or finishing statement

Start with a summary introduction, such as "No one will ever forget the Christmas that something extra went into Mom's traditional Jell-O salad. It was the year that Uncle Albert had just been fitted for his new teeth …" See the suspense setup? It's called foreshadowing.

Tell the funny body of the story, using the most vivid verbs you can think of for the situation. Verbs such as "plopped," "gasped," "gurgled," "squished," and "fished" come quickly to mind.

Last, think up a way to end that will say something about Uncle Albert and the way he, as well as his misadventure, affected the rest of the family, including the retelling throughout the years and the related facts too good to leave out—such as the fact that only Crazy Aunt Edna would eat the Jell-O that day. ("She loved Mom's Jell-O salad and would not be denied it at Christmas—no matter what had been in it.")

Using Reflective Humor

Using humor in your writing can often pay off well and surprise your reader. Using the technique with topics that don't seem to lend themselves to humor is also a good strategy if you can do it.

Remember the definition of "waxing philosophical" in the last chapter? You'll be doing that every few pages in your family history, creating connections across the years and between your family members. This is good place to use humor in your reflective musings.

For example, let's choose the topic of church and add it to a particular place—in my case, it was Texas. In an introduction, or punchline of a story about my church upbringing, using my own tone, my own philosophical rumination, as well as my own experience (which means my entire accumulation of wisdom over the years, even from country and western song lyrics), I might write this:

> Growing up in the Bible Belt usually meant going to church in some shape or fashion. It was a place to learn about love but also a place to learn how to act "right" as well. This manifested itself for me as a teenager as deeply mixed messages. As one country singer put it, church was where we learned that sex was a sin and we should save it for marriage, and that God loved us and was going to send us to hell ....

Think you can't do the same? Wrong. Try it. Take a serious topic. Wax philosophical. Then, using your own accumulation of wisdom over the years (i.e., your experience), clear your mind, think humorous, and see what pops up that might help describe the topic, lightening it as well as illuminating it.

When Funny Can Be Serious

Humor can also be used to lead into a serious topic and help you as the writer get into the subject. Humor can also help the reader prepare for the tragic event you may feel you need to add to your family account.

How could this type of personal memory be incorporated into a family history project? It could be part of an interview of a family member's memories, or a stand-alone remembrance of a family member about a painful part of the family history. Or it could be original material you write, a personal reflection on a tragic time in your life and your family's life softened with time. But whatever it is, notice that the humor is used as preface and is aimed in a completely opposite direction from the tragedy. Note the change in tone as you reached the end and the humor disappearing at the mention of the tragedy. Any other technique would be totally inappropriate.

Think of a sad occurrence in your family's lives that no family history could be written without its mention. What personal memory of it might you write that could touch all the family members who were affected by that pivotal event?

Journaling Down the Genealogical Trail

With all this work, your journal should be completely warmed up now, too. Using it should be second nature. Flip through all the work you've done in your journal for this chapter. Summarize the experience of this chapter's warm-up exercises, focusing on the one that taught you the most.

The Least You Need to Know

➤ Each family history anecdote has one best way to be told.

➤ Practicing narrative techniques will strengthen your real family history writing.

➤ Writing cross-training exercises can't make you sore.

Chapter 19

Telling Other People's Stories

In This Chapter

➤ What to do with Crazy Aunt Edna's (and everyone else's) memories

➤ The benefit of compiling all your accumulated stories into a list

➤ Practicing your new narrative skills through more exercise

Telling your own stories is challenge enough for any writer. Writing a family history, though, challenges you to write the stories of all your relatives—living and dead.

Did that statement momentarily take your breath away? Never fear. The last chapter helped you explore ways to tell your own stories. Now, let's try some exercises to help you think creatively about the most intriguing way to tell all the stories you have the privilege of putting on paper.

What to Do with Crazy Aunt Edna's Memories

Edna, Granny Lou, Cissy, and a dozen cousins—both the long-lost kind and those twice-removed—all have lined up to give you their best family memories.

You've transcribed all your interviews, you've compiled all the historical accounts you've uncovered from your research, you've bugged every relative with a photo album to give to the cause. And it is all piled before you, raw material waiting to be compiled. Just looking at your work fills you with a sense of achievement ... and anxiety. Want to know a secret? That feeling is normal.

There's a very real battle that goes on with a project of this magnitude. Like that old ABC *Wide World of Sports* opening that spoke of the "thrill of victory and the agony of defeat" (while showing some poor skier do a half-gainer off the side of a ski jump), you are probably feeling the thrill of having raw material and the agony of having raw material. What can you do about it?

The answer is in your bones. You gotta write. Writing—any writing—will have you feeling on top of it all. Some of these warm-up exercises you'll use in your family history writing. Most of these, though, are designed to just get your juices flowing, to give you experience for the moment when you finally, *finally* begin to write "for real."

Listing Your Memories

Your first step is to take inventory of your memories, just as in Chapter 18, "Telling Your Own Stories." Although you'll probably be adding to such a list until the moment you are taking your final manuscript to be printed, right now you need to see what you have to work with. Write down all the memories you have at this point, yours and everyone else's, and try to do it on one sheet for easy viewing, using double or triple columns and abbreviated names. If your journal page is too small, use a larger notebook.

Take a second to flip back to Chapter 18 and look at the Master List of Other People's Memories. Now, with journal in hand, fill in your own family stories just as you did for your own memories. Use your pedigree chart to help with dates and other information. Structure it any way you think best, by family name, by generation, by decade, or by individual ancestor.

The Write Word

Point of view is the position from which a story is told.

More Cross-Training Exercises

Remember, these are all practice, writing "warm-ups" that will get you ready for the real thing. Use your journal or have a notepad just for this. Take it all seriously, but make sure to play. Be open to trying new ways of telling things. The exercises are stretching your skill and imagination.

Okay. Ready to do your stretches? As with the exercises you did for your own memories, each of your relatives' and ancestors' stories use the same narrative elements: description, characterization, dialogue, dramatic tension, tense, and tone. To them, let's add *point of view* and beginnings.

A Whole New Point of View

In writing any sort of narrative, you have several choices about the angle it will be told from—what pair of eyes you create for the reader to use. In literary terms, the choices are first person ("John Jacob Schmoe was our ancestor who went to California for the gold rush. I uncovered this cousin in an old deed ..."); second person, which neither you nor anyone else, has much use for, past our daily conversation ("It's awful. You wait for the bus. It finally comes, you step on and what do you see? A rolling garbage truck, I tell ya.") and third person, the overall or omniscient, invisible narrator. ("John Jacob Schmoe fled the tobacco farm for the gold fields of California and never came back.")

Oral history encompasses very distinct point-of-view structure. Think about it. The person sharing the story is seen as the overall narrator with an overall point of view, while at the same time taking the part of all the characters in the anecdote and explaining things from their vantage points, as well as telling how they feel or what they think, which is their internal points of view. If that writer's information sounds confusing, you can make it very simple for now. You can use your own selection for your family history work. For our purposes here, let's just handle three of our own points of view.

➤ **First person, interview:**

Aunt Edna: "I remember the day I was born. It was a cold morning ..."

➤ **First person, personal experience:**

You: "As I drove through our ancestor's hometown ..."

➤ **Third person, invisible narrator:**

You, hiding: "Jason Jay Johnson Schmoe was a steel-driving man ..."

> **Deep Thought**
>
> *Admit it. For months now, you've felt the thrill of the project and the agony of the project. Is the agony of the project winning out? If so, that's when it's time to start writing.*

I predict that you will be using all these, choosing the point of view that best suits what you're trying to do in your family history at different moments. Here's a warm-up to challenge you.

Ready, Set, Exercise: Point-of-View Warm-Up

First things first: Choose one relative or ancestral anecdote to tell fully. Got one? Great! Now let's go!

➤ Choose which point of view would be best for this particular ancestor's account. Is it an interview? Then use quotes and first person: "I couldn't ever forget Uncle Ed. And Lord knows I tried ..."

➤ Is it a historical recounting of names, dates, occupations and adventures? Use third person, invisible narrator.

Choosing Where to Begin

With an anecdote gained from a taped interview, the question of where to begin is simple. You begin, usually, the way your interviewee did.

But how about the stories you've uncovered in your research about long-dead relatives with no one to tell their story but you? You've probably found your information in all sorts of places, and a few of them were narrative accounts. (Remember my bushwhacker story retold in a county history book? That was a short narrative.)

You can start your stories anyway you want, being as creative as you can be. Beginnings are so important that we will devote a significant portion of a chapter to it in the next section.

Ready, Set, Exercise: Beginning Warm-Up

Think of the ancestor or relative you chose for the previous point-of- view warm-up. What is the first thing that pops into your mind about that ancestor? Whatever it is, that's probably the most interesting thing about him. And beginning anything interestingly is very good. Was your ancestor a sea captain? That would be a good fact with which to start. Then you can fill in the rest of the account with all you've found out about your ancestral sea captain, adding background as you go to evoke the period, which fills up narrative holes very well for the reader.

'Riting Reminder

Your journal, by now, should be an indispensable part of your project. You don't want to lose it. Make sure to write your name and address inside its cover in case you misplace it.

What if the information you have on an ancestor is mostly a listing of facts and figures that only hint at his personality? Then you will be writing a paragraph about that ancestor from that information, and the "how to begin" question is even more important.

So, have you chosen your ancestor? Open your journal and—begin.

The Value of Writing Short

> "In every fat book, there's a thin one trying to get out."
>
> —Unknown

I'm going to make an outlandish suggestion: You can write "short." In a world which confuses quantity with quality, this may sound odd, but I subscribe to the preceding quote. No where is it written in stone that you have to write as long as possible with each section you create for your family history. Writing short is about editing. We'll discuss editing later. This is experiencing the result of writing "tightly." More words don't necessarily result in better writing, and quite often result in sloppy writing.

So, for this "writer's stretch," write long. Write whatever length the writing sample turns out to be. But remember from the get-go that you will be cutting some of it. The actual writer's term for this is "rewriting"—playing with your words to make them perfect. Someone once asked Ernest Hemingway why he rewrote the end of one of his short stories over 30 times. He answered, "To get the words right." The moment you begin to like the rewriting process as much or more than first-draft writing, you'll know you're really a writer.

How is this feat accomplished by beginning writers such as you? Have I got an exercise for you.

Ready, Set, Exercise: 2,500/500 Words Warm-Up

Here's a wonderful warm-up to show the power of condensing your work. It's a great editing exercise, but it also proves to you that you can write vividly with fewer words, and in some cases, write more compelling prose.

Choose your longest raw material anecdote from your master list. Write it as well as you can. Count the words. Let's say it is 2,500 words, which is about 10 pages long. Your mission is to cut it down to 500 words (about two pages).

Impossible? Not at all. Your favorite magazines do this all the time to conserve space. The first time I was told to do this with an article I wrote, I thought doing so would cut the heart out of it. Know what I found out? I discovered that it did the opposite. I could only save the most important parts, so out went the unneeded adjectives, in went the most powerful, vivid words, and the remaining sentences all but jumped off the page.

Does writing 2,500 words or 10 pages sound intimidating at this point? Then start with a shorter one. Take an anecdote that is 500 words long (two pages) and make it 250 to 300 words (one page).

How do you know when to stop? The time to stop is not when you've finally arrived under the designated number of words, although it could be (but you don't strike me as either the lazy or unmotivated type). After you've trimmed the words down to the designated number, that's when you have a chance to massage what's left. See if you can make your tight piece of writing sing with vivid language, an interesting opening, and fluid sentences.

So, how did you do?

'Riting Reminder

What happened when you edited your writing? Why did you cut what you cut? Analyze what happened to your writing and record your answers in your journal.

Your Description Warm-Up: How Did They Look?

A good writer knows how to capture detail without drowning the reader in it. How much is too much? How little is too little? It's a balancing act only learned through practice. But first you have to learn the fine art of observation, even in other people's stories.

How do you do that? You do that by doing your homework. All that historical context and historical background reading about your ancestor's historic time and place is about to pay off.

A Relatively Good Idea

Haven't done much background research? Do you have any town, county, or family histories on your shelf? Dip into the sections beyond those that mention your ancestor to get a flavor of the past where your ancestor lived. There is historical context and background galore to be had there.

Being Told Tales Fully

How about the stories of your *living* relatives? Well, let's say that the family story about Uncle Albert's new false teeth falling into the Thanksgiving Jell-O was your Aunt Edna's instead of yours. During your interview, you should have coached her to describe the surroundings, to tell the tale fully, asking pointed questions we discussed in the chapter on interviewing tips. If she did a good job of describing the setting and the main character of the unfortunate, yet memorable incident, you can evoke a wonderful image of family Thanksgiving gatherings during that period of your family's life.

If not, well, you still have Edna's phone number, don't you? I'm sure she wouldn't mind adding to your account of her story by going back over descriptive details for you.

Describing Your Ancestor's Face

You might have Aunt Edna's phone number, but you certainly can't call up your turn-of-the-century ancestor. What do you do? You imagine—with a little help from some photographs.

Fortunately, photography captured most of our ancestors who lived in the last four or five generations. Whether in a county or family history or framed and sitting on Aunt Edna's electric organ, you probably can find some image of many of your ancestors. You may be lucky to have accumulated a pile of them by now. Now's the time to pull them out and sift through them.

Ready, Set, Exercise: Description

Choose one of your relative's or ancestor's pictures. Choose a story from your inventory list about that relative or ancestor. Study the photo, taking in every detail. Then, read the raw story. Close your eyes. Think of the ancestor. What do you see? Describe him. Give any obvious physical characteristics gathered from the photo.

Zoom In

Now, try to add one more detail. Close your eyes again, and zoom in even further. What was the ancestor wearing? What might you imagine the ancestor wearing in other moments? And what does that evoke about the era?

Location, Location, Location

A sense of place is a big part of any story, but it is fundamental to description. Can you add a description of the ancestor's location? Study the photo you have again. Then use all the background information you've uncovered in your research to help evoke a mental picture. Where do you see the ancestor? Do you see him on his cotton farm? Do you see her in her parlor playing the upright piano? Do you see him behind the counter of his dry goods store? Or sailing the sea in a Civil War Navy battle? Describe in your journal six elements of the location.

Zoom Out

Here's where we pull it all together. Zoom out. Sit back, as if you were actually sitting with the relative, living or dead, in whatever location you see him or her. If it were my great-granddaddy, the sheriff, for instance, I would imagine myself in his office. Do the same with your ancestor. Pull yourself into the memory. Look around and try to create the scene for this exercise. What objects do you see? What clothing, hairstyles, furniture?

'Riting Reminder

How are your adjectives and verbs? In your description exercise, check your adjectives. If you have more than one or two per sentence, you have too many. Now check your verbs. Are they muscle or fat? Are they powerful without the help of an adjective?

Ready, Set, Exercise: More Description

Turn to a new page in your journal. Study a photograph of your chosen ancestor. Then close your eyes. Try seeing 10 things in your ancestor's life. Count them as you go with your eyes closed. Then open your eyes and write them down in sentence form.

Now is the time to go overboard. Overwrite. Each time you falter, glance at the photo, then close your eyes again. Don't stop until you have 10. If all else fails, re-read some of your historical background material.

Find the Description and Add Characterization

Below, I have given over a dozen details describing my sheriff ancestor's locations and his "look" from two photos. Circle 10 of these details in the following paragraphs:

➤ The first photo is a full-length image of my great-grandfather, the sheriff, sitting in his dark office in front of his rolltop desk in a swivel chair, as if it were taken for a newspaper story or posed for a movie scene. He is wearing a long, duster jacket and a Stetson cocked high on his head. He has a long, silver, handle-bar mustache and the way he has posed for the camera—confident, authoritative, impatient and yet obviously proud—you could see it was taken at the height of his 20-year career. Even though his face is barely visible, you can feel a steely eyed peace-officer gaze aimed your way.

➤ The picture inspired my cousin to say, "Now that's the kind of Texas ancestor you want." It made you almost imagine a horse tied outside for him even though you know that by his era he was probably driving a Model T. (You never know. This was Texas and he was known for his horses.)

➤ The second was a picture taken in his retirement in front of the county jail-house surrounded by all his family, including children, their spouses, and grandchildren. No one is smiling (except for Crazy Aunt Edna, age seven). Minus the Stetson and the long duster jacket, the sheriff looks older, and more tired, but he still has a square jaw, a handle-bar mustache, a shock of thick, white hair, and that steely eyed Texas, peace-officer look.

Do you detect any characterization among the description? Any details that make him come to life? Circle them.

See where we're going with this? Now it's your turn. Choose a photo from your ancestor pile.

Imagine.

Write.

Then, circle your details, checking and analyzing your blend of description and characterization.

Your Characterization Warm-Up: How Did They Act?

For the ancestors you didn't know personally, tiny bits of characterization will be all you can hope to evoke as you tell their stories. But a tiny bit of characterization may be enough. Oral history tidbits about long-gone ancestors are the best source for adding dimension. Remember my high school friend who took her California daughter to a West Texas family reunion? Her daughter heard two stories about the great-grandmothers she never knew—one granny was pristine and sweet, remembered for the way she sat at the head of the table every morning and poured bowls of Post Toasties for each of her children; the other granny worked out in the field alongside her farmer husband and all the other men picking cotton.

The people who knew them best remembered these two images above all others. This is why oral history is so good for characterization. Those memories create characterization by creating a context in which the people lived their lives. Ask people to tell you about someone they've known most of their lives and the first thing that pops out of their mouths is going to be vivid and important.

What characterizations, aspects of these women's characters, do you think are evoked by their respective snapshot memories mentioned above?

Ready, Set, Exercise: Characterization

Your turn. Choose five ancestors from your list. What one piece of information do you have about each ancestor or relative that evokes characterization—giving them a three-dimensional, flesh-and-blood feel? List them in your journal for future reference.

Your Dialogue Warm-Up: What Did They Say?

As mentioned in the last chapter, dialogue will be used with many of your anecdotes as you write your family history. Practicing now will give you courage, as well as give you pause about over-doing it. As with your own memories, the memories of those you've interviewed and taped will also command you to use familiar patterns of speech and usage in them because of their oral history tradition.

Capturing the sound of an ancestor's patterns of speech, however, will be incredibly hard without some context of history. (See Chapter 10, "The Family Investigator on the Case," for the discussion on how words' definitions change through the years.) But you'll find that your family history text will need such breaks in tone and readability. How do you handle it?

During your research, you probably came across older books, pamphlets, newspaper clippings, legal documents, and dusty published histories. Read through these again to get the "sound" of a certain era, your ancestor's era, in your mind.

Ready, Set, Exercise: Homework and Imagination

Go to your list. Choose an ancestral anecdote. After reading old books, documents, and newspaper clippings from your research to capture the sound of your ancestor's speech, attempt to use some imagined ancestral dialogue to add vitality to your narrative. Write three pieces of dialogue in your journal. Mark out two, and keep the best. (As with all imagined dialogue, don't forget that it's best when used sparingly.)

Dramatic Tension Warm-Up: What Happens Next?

As we learned in Chapter 18, every anecdote, no matter how short, needs pace and suspense to make it fun to read. Telling your ancestors' stories in chronological order, relating every anecdote and fact you uncovered, may work just fine most of the time. Sometimes, though, it won't work at all. The information and interesting tidbits just sit there, flat and uninteresting when you know very well they are not. What do you do? You try the "And then ..." exercise.

Ready, Set, Exercise: "And Then ..."

In your journal, write at least six "And then's ..." and spread them several inches apart. Now, just as you did for your own anecdotes in Chapter 18, apply this exercise to a relative's or ancestor's anecdote. Take one of your anecdotes from your master list and fill in the happenings of the anecdote, step by step under the "And then ..." exercises. Here's an example:

And then ...

... the electricity went out on Thanksgiving Day. Uncle Buster blew a fuse.

And then ...

... the big football game couldn't be watched on the TV, and Uncle Buster blew his own fuse. Uncle Buster almost busted.

And then ...

... everybody went outside to play touch football, including Uncle Buster.

And then ...

... my Aunt Sally wanted to play.

And then ...

... I threw her a pass, she caught it and headed for the goalposts (the driveway).

And then …

… in the heat of competition, Uncle Buster busted Aunt Sally. He not only touched her, he tackled her, breaking her collarbone.

See the progression in suspense followed by the payoff in my poor Aunt Sally's encounter with Uncle Buster's testosterone level? Without the feeling of some invisible "And then's …," you might naturally tell a story in such a "building to payoff" way, but you might also just tell the facts in a jumbled-up way that doesn't create such suspense. Take a look at this:

We played football one Thanksgiving. Aunt Sally played. Uncle Buster tackled her and broke her collarbone. The television wasn't working. Uncle Buster blew a fuse. And when he couldn't see the big football game he almost busted. Uncle Buster busted Aunt Sally when I threw a pass to Aunt Sally, and she caught it and headed to the goalposts (the driveway).

Feel the jumbled sense of that paragraph without a suspense-building order? Look at your own story. What do you see about its progression? Juggle its components until it fits well into your own "And then …" payoff.

> **Deep Thought**
>
> As you read old books, documents, dusty histories, and newspaper clippings to capture the way people "sounded" in the past, are you struck with a formality we are missing today? If so, how is that good and bad?

Ready, Set, Exercise: Action/Reaction

Every action has an equal and opposite reaction, we are told, and so it is in writing—at least if you want dramatic tension. "And then …" exercises certainly show a series of happenings that seem to be related. Some will be like the Thanksgiving tackle story, with lots of "And then's …" Most will be simple action/reactions. An anecdote has to have at least one reaction or it isn't an anecdote. It can be a sensory memory instead. I'll prove it to you. Choose another anecdote from your master list. Write down an action that happened in it.

1. Abraham Lincoln Schmoe, your ancestor, was born on the day that Abraham Lincoln was shot.
2. His parents named him after the slain president.

Now that's a definite action/reaction, and it's the beginning of an ancestral anecdote about your great-great-great-great-grandfather Abraham Lincoln Schmoe that begs to be told more fully. What about yours? Start noticing how the family history stories flow. That's the first step to creating dramatic tension in your narratives.

Getting Serious About Humor

Are many of the family stories people have shared with you funny anecdotes? Will they be as funny as they were when you first heard them? That's the trick, isn't it?

Most people wouldn't have had to know Uncle Albert to think his false teeth falling into the Christmas Jell-O was funny, but we all know it's funnier if you do know him and even funnier still if you were there. Sometimes you do just have to be there.

Let's face it. Much of what is funny in an oral telling may be lost in a written story. How do you capture the same tone and timing in your funny family story that always makes Cousin Leroy snort his eggnog out his nose?

In Chapter 18, I suggested that you listen to your interviews on tape, following along on your transcriptions to try to capture the "voice" of the teller in learning how to handle dialogue. Now I suggest you do the same thing with one or two of your funniest taped stories. Your mission is to capture as much of the story in its original form as you can. Write it almost exactly as it was told.

A Relatively Good Idea

Grab a few family members (the more, the better) and try out a funny family story you wrote that was taken from an oral story. Have them first read it silently, then listen to you read it out loud. Ask them if it sounds different on paper.

Journaling Down the Genealogical Trail

Which of these warm-ups helped you most? Why? Write a few sentences in your journal about what you learned in this section for your future family history writing. Remember to refer back to your comments when you begin your actual writing.

The Least You Need to Know

➤ Telling other people's stories takes skill and imagination.

➤ Compiling all your relatives' accumulated stories into a list is extremely helpful.

➤ Each family history anecdote has one way to be told best.

➤ Narrative technique exercises will strengthen your family history writing.

Chapter 20

Time to Structure

In This Chapter

➤ Test-driving your family history format choices

➤ Listening to what your work is telling you

➤ Understanding your audience

You've exercised your imagination, your memory, your creativity. You're almost ready to start actually writing your family history. You take a big gulp at the thought and wonder how you can ever take that first step.

I'll tell you how. You finally choose one of the family history formats we've been mentioning throughout the book. That will lay your foundation for the book you're building and give you a road map for the whole project (forgive the mixed metaphor).

Now seems the appropriate time, so let's take a close look at your choices to help you choose well for the material you have. I'll even offer some exercises to help you take a few for a test-drive around the writer's block.

Revisiting Formats and Focus

If you'll recall from Chapter 3, "What Kind of Family History Should You Write?" I discussed over a dozen formats or structures that your family history could be shaped into. There are as many formats, no doubt, as there are families to write about, but here are a dozen samples taken from Chapter 3, offered for your tasting (review Chapter 3 on your own for more):

➤ Narrative genealogy

➤ Ancestor's biography

➤ Family profiles

➤ Family stories

➤ Literary snapshots

➤ Cookbook family history

➤ Your own family documentary

➤ Family journalism

➤ Pictorial history

➤ Your ancestor's choice

➤ Your own invention

Which ones looked good to you when you first saw this list? Do they still look as inviting? If not, now that you've gone this far down the path, which one does?

Revisiting Your Pile of Research

After you've revisited that format list, it's time to re-visit all your raw material. Go stand in front of your piles of research. Think good thoughts. Then slowly go through every last piece of information to get a sense of all you have and the number and the types of things you've acquired. (If you're an organizational whiz and have been keeping a running tally of everything you've acquired, good for you. Get that list out. Now is the time you'll be glad you have it.)

Take both master lists you've created for Chapters 18, "Telling Your Own Stories," and 19, "Telling Other People's Stories," the lists of your own remembrances as well as your relatives' and ancestors' stories, and place them side by side. To those, add all the little bits of information—genealogical tidbits, facts, dates—everything you think you want to put into your family history, even if you don't know exactly how you'll use them.

Your Work Is Talking to You

Got this "master of master lists" in hand? Let's look at it together. How do you see it in your mind's eye?

➤ Do you have a wealth of great interviews? You might want to think about a family monologue book and call it "Having Our Family Say."

➤ Do you have lots of newspaper article–type stories and a child or two who's a budding writer or artist? Creating a family newspaper or magazine might be perfect.

➤ Did you uncover an incredible number of colorful characters, following them back over two centuries? Then you might relish writing a narrative genealogy all the way up through your present family.

➤ Do you have mounds of photos dating back a century or more? Then you have to think seriously about a pictorial history of your obviously photogenic ancestral group.

What you have in the way of research will tell you what format is best for you. Now's the time to sit down with it and listen very closely to what it's telling you.

Reassessing Your "Readership"

There's another factor you want to consider as you contemplate this important decision. That's your audience, or "readership." I'll be discussing this at length in the next section, but for now you should add your family—which is, of course, your readership—to the many angles to consider when thinking about your family history format.

➤ What format might suit everyone's interests?

➤ What format might involve those ancestors you want to involve?

➤ What format would offer the most important stories of your ancestors the best?

➤ What format might thrill your future family, your descendants?

➤ (Your own question here.)

When you can answer a few of these questions, you'll know you're almost ready to choose the format that is best for you.

Your Format Test-Drive

Want to take a spin around the block with a few of these formats before you make your big decision? It will give you a chance to kick the tires, fiddle with the radio and gun the engine. For each format, you'll be given a little summary of what it is, and a clear explanation of each one's specific focus for your interest and your research. Then, you can choose the exercise option and really give it a workout.

Narrative Genealogy

Focus: *Your genealogy findings*

Wow. You started digging around in your ancestors' lives and you hit a mother-lode. You've got saints and sinners, heroes and scoundrels, soldiers, pioneers, politicians, and priests.

You are intrigued with every last one of the ancestors you've discovered and you found so much interesting material (oh, they were a colorful group), that you think you might make your family history a "narrative genealogy."

279

The Write Word

A **narrative** work is writing that tells a story.

What does "*narrative* genealogy" mean, really? It means you are going to take all the genealogical work you've done, all the bits and pieces that speak volumes of lives that are connected to you and your children, and you are going to create a narration of it all. You will probably use chronological form, but you don't have to. You can punctuate each listing of births, marriages, and deaths of your line with a long profile of each generation's most interesting ancestor or two.

You will use a third-person point of view probably, but you don't have to. And you can use first-person point of view anytime you want, when it is appropriate. For instance, you can interject yourself into the narrative when the stories you are telling are your stories, but also, for example, when you feel it would be fun to give an account of the road trip you took to uncover a certain ancestor's story.

Why, you might even think adding a fold-out genealogy chart is a great idea. If you enjoyed the genealogical treasure hunt, this format is for you.

Ready, Set, Exercise: Narrative Genealogy

String out the information on your master of master lists and count the anecdotes and the ancestors. How many do you have in each generation? How far back? If your genealogical cupboard seems quite full, make an outline of each generation and its many ancestral characters. That will help you decide yea or nay on this format.

Ancestor's Biography

Focus: *One very interesting ancestor*

An offshoot of the narrative genealogy is an ancestor's biography. How is this still a family history? He's your ancestor, isn't he? And you can use him (or her) in context with the other stories you have to tell.

You might write a short narrative about your genealogy and how this ancestor fits into it and connects to your family. Or the section on your interesting ancestor could be in the middle of the rest of your family history narrative. Whatever you decide, don't be surprised how tempted you will be to create some sort of format like this if you uncover an ancestor's diary or letter stash—or even better, if you have a prominent ancestor who gained a lot of newspaper coverage and you are fortunate enough to have the clippings.

Like the fictional friend of yours in Chapter 3 who proudly shows you his ancestor biography book, you, too, might be tempted by a story you uncovered from a battle diary and historical newspaper clippings. Why, your friend's story almost sounded like a movie: A Civil War lieutenant who was left for dead at Gettysburg yet survived, then seized life by having two wives with two different families in two different states until getting caught. How could you resist? You might also become an expert on the Civil War through all the research you added to your schedule to make everything authentic.

Your own creativity is your only boundary when coming up with a format to showcase such an ancestor, while also offering the rest of your research and family anecdotes.

Ready, Set, Exercise: One Central Ancestral Figure

Make a list of all the facts you have on your colorful ancestor. Fill out details at length. How many pages of information do you really have on this ancestor? How much you have should tell you how big a portion of your family history work you can devote to this ancestor.

Family Profiles—Having Your Family Say

Focus: *First-person interviews and profiles of family members*

Is your brood a family of big talkers? Do you have elderly relatives who are fine storytellers who have given you fascinating, knock-out interviews?

You might consider an interview format for the majority of your book. This format could be a mixture of Q&A (questions and answers) and a series of family monologues, or the interviews could be written like a series of long magazine articles in one volume. You could add your own narrative and personal memories to their interviews.

The Write Word

A **profile** is a concise biographical sketch.

Do you have enough information on several ancestors generations ago that you could write profiles of them to go along with these strong first-person accounts from your living relatives? If so, that fact could make this format even more inviting, since you could write your genealogical research in a profile form to go along with these first-person family memories.

Or you could consider it your "background format," and you could write the rest of your family history, including your genealogical findings, intertwined with these monologue interviews. Your job as a writer would be to clean up the interviews for the page, making them more like magazine articles.

But for an interview format alone, your own commentary or interpretation would not be needed, except for transition and genealogical sections that you need to give voice to for your silent ancestors. Otherwise, capturing the oral history of your living family will speak for itself, to the enjoyment of your whole family.

Ready, Set, Exercise: Family Interviews and Profiles

Who are your big talkers and how much oral history have they offered for your work? Now's the time to transcribe all that you have and count pages of usable stories. Do you have a dozen, two dozen? More? Then this format might be for you.

Family Stories/Family Memoir

Focus: *Your immediate and extended family*

Your family interviews have gone very well. You have stories from cousins, uncles, great-aunts, and grandpas. And they've all told you stories about their grandparents and others who lived several generations back. You don't have enough for a full book of interviews, but interestingly, you do have enough for your immediate and extended family history with just interviews, anecdotes, and pictures. So, what you might produce is a fun little book of family stories about everyone's extended family—any and every story that everyone's relatives could remember about family members long gone. Such a format would emphasize the last several generations for the major portion of the book.

The Write Word

A **memoir** is a first-person narrative composed from personal experience.

Or this could be a cross between family interview format and a narrative genealogy, especially if you've done some good genealogical work but haven't found as much success as you'd hoped past a certain point in the past. This format may appeal to the most writers as well as the most readers, a nice collection of everything.

Another derivation of this is the family *memoir*, of course. After you've done your research, you realize that what you really want to do is add all the stories you know about your extended family to your own experiences and offer it to your family as a gift for the ages. Perhaps you've had an incredibly unusual life, traveling extensively or adventurously, or lived through a dramatic part of history that affected your whole family, relocating around the world or across the country. Perhaps your parents were the ones with the story you need to share with the rest of the family, and you will be offering the extended story from your point of view, adding genealogy around the narration. It's all up to you.

Ready, Set, Exercise: Family Stories/Family Memoir

List all your family stories, interview transcriptions, anecdotes, and pictures. How many pages do you have? How much effort would it take to connect these with a bit of narrative writing? Does your work cover most of the family and how would you fill in the gaps?

Literary Snapshots

Focus: *Each ancestor's "short" story*

Do you have a talent? Then you may see all these ancestor stories as short-stories in a very personal family novel. You might take all the family history stories you could find for as far back as you could dig, then take the tantalizing scraps of information—such as deaths and births, historical profiles, gossip, and newspaper clippings—and flesh out the "rest of the story" with your imagination and historical research.

A Relatively Good Idea

What relatives, using what you have now, would be left out of a family story format? How might you go about filling in these gaps? Each member should be mentioned somehow, some way. Giving everyone their due would be very important for this format.

This could be lots of fun if you have a gift for dialogue and for creating three-dimensional characters. Call this "fictional nonfiction." Of course, you'd have to be very careful to only make up things logically, based on information you have. And you'd have to be sure to state the "fictional nonfiction" nature of your work in the opening pages of the book. The more full anecdotes you have, the better for this one.

You could write and organize each of the short narratives like short-short stories. On each page is a story of a relative or ancestor, told in memories, interviews, and historical data written in dramatic form, bringing the past to life in a format that is like a series of "literary snapshots."

This format will work best once you have established its tone. Notice that I didn't call it "nonfiction fiction." I called it "fictional nonfiction." There's a big difference. The noun is the operative word, what the work truly is, not the adjective. So, in fictional nonfiction, the emphasis is on nonfiction, and the adjective "fiction" suggests that you've used literary license occasionally to create a narrative tone. So remember, with this format, you have to practice quite a bit to not overwork the profile. You are not aiming for a fully told story (unless of course you have one!). You are aiming at profiles which are more true to life, that give you glimpses in a literary format.

There's a reason I call this format "literary snapshots." A snapshot is a moment in time caught by your Instamatic—a moment in time that tells an instant story. If you think of your work in this format as single, stand-alone snapshots, which are part of a whole group of snapshots, you won't stray from your family history objective.

Ready, Set, Exercise: Literary Snapshots

Take your most interesting ancestor. Try writing his or her story using this "fictional nonfiction" angle, using literary license to create a narrative tone, and a smattering of dialogue using the knowledge acquired in Chapter 19. Keep it to a page to reduce the threat of over-writing. This should help you assess whether to use this idea sporadically or make it your major format.

Cookbook Family History

Focus: *Family's generational love affair with food*

Is your family one of those in which the most important room in the house is the kitchen? Where food is also family? Then a cookbook would be an inspired idea for a family history. Adding family stories to family recipes would be a natural choice.

'Riting Reminder

Don't feel that you have to mention the recipe in the anecdote. It can just be an inspiration for it.

Recipes are kinds of heirlooms that get handed down and down and down the family tree. Each family dish probably has a story or two attached. Can you name a dish your immediate family loves (or hates) and a family story that you could picture your children telling about it one day years from now? Have you handed down recipes through several generations? Then those recipes are the best kind of ancestral anecdotes, full of humanity and good family experiences. Why, after reading about granny, you could actually make the recipe and get a taste of your granny's cooking. Isn't that incredible? And just think: This can continue to happen for generation after generation, because you added the recipes into your family history.

This idea could be:

➤ A section in your family history book instead of the whole format.

➤ The way you begin each section of genealogical information and family branch descriptions (Aunt Sophie's recipe for "haggis" could be a good introduction to your Scottish family tree branch, for example).

➤ Or it could be your full-focus format, everything centered on stories about family and food, along with the included recipe.

Ready, Set, Exercise: Cookbook Stories

Think of one dish that evokes a family memory from the past. Place a family story of any length with it, and write it in full. Do the same for six more recipes. If you can add six more from your aunts and uncles and great-aunts and cousins, then you may have found your format.

Your Own Family Documentary

Focus: *Visual images and script with companion family history book*

Do you like the idea of capturing images of memorable places from the past and oral history interviews with older family members?

Do you have a budding filmmaker in your family you could entice into the project to help you?

This could be great fun if the answer to both of these questions is "Yes." If your vision is first and foremost for the recording of your living family, if you like the idea of creating a script as well as a book, and if you know someone who is very handy with a video camera, this could be an exceptionally exciting idea.

You can add visual images to oral history interviews with your elderly relatives. You could visit schools, apartment buildings, tombstones, churches, businesses, old residences, all the places of your family's history. You might interview a deceased relative's old acquaintances you stumble across on old neighborhood travels. You could even offer on- or off-screen narration yourself. You could take video shots of your old photographs to add material about ancestors, perhaps as you visit their old hometowns.

A video family history may not sound like a good long-term idea—after all, who knows if videotape will even exist in two generations?

So, since books can last centuries—literally—you will want to see this as a companion piece to your writing. Your writing could actually use the format of the family documentary, following its script as well. You would commit the action and the people and the words of the documentary to paper and then add your other genealogical work around it, including the still photography, offering more to the family member who wants to know more about the family beyond the video documentary.

> ### *Deep Thought*
>
> *A picture is worth a thousand words, they say. Why do you think that an image is so powerful? The most vivid writing comes from using words to describe what we as writers "see," be it an idea or an actual visual image. Do you do that? If not, how do you describe your personal style or process?*

Ready, Set, Exercise: Family Documentary

Do you have a video camera? Try writing a video script around one of your relatives and then taping a short segment about him or her. It could be Crazy Aunt Edna showing off her scrapbooks (she'd want to be the start of the movie anyway). It could be a deceased grandfather, while you shoot video of his old farm and describe his life. The former would test your interviewing skills, asking the right questions as you film; the latter would test your script-writing skills, since you'd be writing a monologue about granddad for you to add over the farm footage. Either experience will let you know if you like this very different family history format.

Family Journalism

Focus: *Family stories and profiles written in newspaper/magazine style*

For the record, let me ask you a few questions:

➤ Do you have budding writers in the family? Cartoonists? Photographers?

➤ Do you have lots of people in your family with life stories that would make "human interest" stories?

➤ How many heroines or heroes do you have in your family?

➤ How many black sheep?

➤ How many overachievers or eccentrics who would make perfect examples of what newspapers call "human interest" stories?

If the answers to most of these questions are positive, then you might have great fun writing your family history in newspaper style. Your family stories could all be written in newspaper form. You could enlist your children or your siblings to help edit and produce it, and even conduct interviews for it. "The National (*insert family name here*) Tattler" could be a bestseller, at least in your family circles. Think of all the "far-fetched" cousins who'd beg for a copy.

A newspaper/magazine format is a natural format for children. Including your children in parts of the writing as well as the research might inspire not only an interest in family history, but also a child's interest in writing. You could add drawings, cartoons, and photos. This could be a family project you'll never forget.

Printing it in newspaper form instead of bound-book form, however, requires a few cautions. You want to be sure to print on better paper than the average newspaper, which is called "newsprint." It would yellow within months as your daily paper does. If this concerns you, then study the magazine formats and paper quality. Some magazine-quality paper can last as long as a book, and a magazine is "perfect" bound, meaning it has a spine, which actually makes it almost a book in itself.

Ready, Set, Exercise: Newspaper/Magazine Format

Turn to the feature section of your daily newspaper and choose one of the articles. Attempt to emulate the style and length of the article using one of your ancestors or relatives as its focus. If you like the results, count how many family anecdotes could be told in this style. If this answer is also positive and plentiful, then check to see how many family members you might enlist. Their enthusiasm and your article-writing prowess should help you decide yea or nay on this format. This is not a format that most people would enjoy doing alone in comparison to a book-length project.

Your Pictorial History

Focus: *Your family photos as introduction to family stories*

Does your family take lots of pictures? Do you have pictures on the walls and in drawers? Do you have scrapbooks full of photos from the past that the whole extended family finds meaningful? Do your elderly relatives have lots of pictures of their generation as well as their parents' generation?

If the answer is yes to more than one of these questions, then you should answer one more question:

What stories do your photos and portraits tell about your family?

Many families have been recording their family histories visually for years. They just don't know that they do it. During every trip home to see my parents, I'd go to a certain place in the dining area where they kept the latest pictures of all my sisters and their families. I knew the pictures alone would offer a unique update for the whole extended family.

If your family loves pictures and has taken them for generations, you might make them the center of your whole family history saga. You could tell stories around the photos, and you could use the photos to introduce whole chapters on a family tree throughout your book.

But at the very least, you can incorporate your family snapshots into your book in some form or another. Your question will be, for this format possibility, whether it will be the dominant theme that explains all your family history writing or the complementary one that everyone enjoys first.

A Relatively Good Idea

Remember that an addition to any pictorial history can be a scrapbook component, including photos or scans taken of important documents or newspaper headlines, which vividly help tell your ancestors' stories as well.

Ready, Set, Exercise: Pictorial History

Go through all your photos. Have you begged, borrowed, or stolen every family picture you could get your hands on during your research? If not, now is the time to finish your pilfering. If you have, now is the time to spread all the pictures out on a large table and see if these photos can be the "guiding light" of your whole family history writing. Choose a dozen of your best photos, keeping your "master of master lists" in mind. Are the stories tied to the photos or can the photos inspire the stories?

Your Ancestor's Choice/Your Own Invention

Then there's the serendipity of a unique format that either comes to you through your research into an ancestor or two or is an invention purely of your own imagination. Don't be timid if you have a good idea that pops up from nowhere and gets you excited. The ideas I've offered to you are for brainstorming as well as actual choice. Maybe you'll take two or three of these ideas and meld them into your own unique format. You have the last say and just as you're listening to your work, you should also listen to yourself. So, what is that great idea that just popped into your mind? Consider it well.

Flexing Your New Writing Muscles

Through all these exercises, have you remembered all the writing "stretches" you did in Chapter 18 and 19? Here's your handy review guide:

➤ Description

➤ Characterization

➤ Dialogue

➤ Tense

➤ Tone

➤ Dramatic tension

➤ Point of view

Review the previous two chapters' work. Apply all these newly acquired writing skills to your exercises for the formats that most interest you. These will help you make each exercise as good as it can be. When you've done that, then it's a safe bet you're going to know which format to pull into your garage.

Journaling Down the Genealogical Trail

You've tried all the formats. You've pushed yourself to be creative and organized and analytical. Which format will you choose? Write the answer and the reason for your choice in your journal as a prelude to the real writing to come.

Ready, Set, Write

Are you ready? You may not feel that you are, but it's my job to inform you that you are ready to begin writing.

You've spent months filling that extra room with all your genealogical and family history research from across the country and into the past. You've written enough of your own memories that you could write an autobiography, and you have a journal full of insights and thoughts and ideas about just what to do and how to do it ... when this moment finally came.

Everything you need to know to finally begin writing is waiting for you with a turn of the page. When you're ready, I am.

On your mark. Get set ...

Turn the page.

The Least You Need to Know

➤ Choosing a format is the best way to begin writing.

➤ Your research results can help you choose a format.

➤ Blending formats may be your best solution to your family history.

➤ Sampling formats can help your decision.

Part 5

Finally, Finally Writing

It's time. You are going to finally start writing your family history. You're all warmed-up after the last section's focused exercises, you've "journaled" lots of ideas, and you're ready to jump right in.

Or are you?

This part is designed to get you revved up and headed down the writing track. It helps you "imagine the telling," offers ideas on creative beginnings, and then pushes you to finally write until you have a complete manuscript in front of you. It's a big job, but you know you're the one to do it. And with the help of the ideas contained in the following pages, you're going to love every minute of it.

Chapter 21

Making It Happen

In This Chapter

➤ Having your special writing time and place

➤ Discerning your style, voice, and audience

➤ Avoiding "purple prose"

➤ Learning the secret of outlining

You are sitting at your desk, waiting, fingers poised over your computer keyboard. Today is the day you are going to finally start writing your family history.

But those fingers aren't moving—no matter how much you will them to begin.

Writers have been talking about the terror of the blank page for centuries. Your feelings are very natural. It's called writer's block when it's at its worst. But trust me, you don't have it at its worst. Beginnings are always the hardest part of any piece of writing.

Getting Serious

I can hear you now. "Well, thanks loads for the encouragement but—how do I *start?*"

Getting serious about finally beginning to weave all your research into a literary work is the first step. Getting serious means you're ready to do what it takes to get something on paper, to make the commitments needed to make this whole, big, wonderful project finally happen. Getting serious means you're ready to hear the writers' passwords for productivity.

The Secret Passwords

The secret productivity passwords for any and every writer are "time" and "place."

I bet you thought I was going to give you the word "discipline." That's what most books on writing discuss at this point, isn't it?

For the entire decade I've been writing professionally, not a month goes by that someone, in effect, makes this comment about my writing life. "Boy, you must be disciplined." I never know quite what to say, because I know myself. Discipline is not one of the words I live by. Never has been; never will be. I'm one of the most undisciplined people I know. And yet my life revolves around deadlines. So what's my secret?

Here it is: It's easy to make yourself do something that you love. That's the opposite of "discipline."

And while implementing some amount of discipline at this point in your project is probably appropriate, I believe that to pound a writer over the head with the need for discipline is to reinforce a very negative idea into a wondrous, happy process. That alone may create writer's block. I'm one writer who will never tell you to "get disciplined."

On the other hand, I *will* ask you how much you love what you're doing and then ask you why you aren't doing it. Then I will mention the merits of having a sort of freeform schedule—a time set aside that is all your own, nobody else's, in a place that is all your own.

Your Writing Place

Virginia Woolf believed for a woman to write she must have *A Room of One's Own,* the title of her famous little essay about the subject. Flannery O'Connor set aside time every morning to sit in front of her typewriter because, as she put it, she wanted to "be there just in case something happened."

Some writers call that "something" a muse and spend their lives waiting for it to visit, while others tromp in like a storm trooper trying to make that muse sit down and behave on schedule.

And some people have to take the concept of "place" and make it over into their own image. These are the people for whom laptop computers are made. I have written books in coffee shops on latté refills. I have written articles standing up at my kitchen counter. I have written pool-side. I have written in bookstores and libraries. I also write in my office on occasion. I accept this as part of my process, what stokes my muse and revs my discipline into overdrive. Yes, I have a place at home. No, I can't always stay there. There's something so alive and energizing about the creative process that when it starts bubbling, so do I.

You may not have the wanderlust I have during the writing process. All you and Virginia Woolf may need is that one room with a "Knock and You're Dead" sign on the door. But whatever and wherever it is, you do need a place that feels comfortable, be it the kitchen table and your manual Underwood typewriter or the broken-down sofa downstairs with a pen and a yellow legal pad in your lap. And don't let anyone tell you different. It's an aspect of the creative process, and it is real.

Your Writing Time

After you've found the place, you need a natural time to write. It doesn't have to be a forced one (forgive me, Flannery). Go ahead and try it Flannery's way, but don't be upset if it doesn't work for you. I'm guessing she was a morning person. That was probably her natural time. I'm a night person. I would hate being told I should force myself to write in the mornings.

Choose your place and your time. Doing so is the first step in making your writing finally happen.

Now for the "D" Word (Discipline)

After you've created your time and place, that's when you can use the "d" word. A modicum of discipline will come in very handy at this point. If you are one of those people who has to answer a ringing phone, then try to be out of ear-shot for the time you set aside for your writing.

Setting aside a day once a week instead of an hour or two each day may be a more realistic plan for you. Hire a babysitter for an afternoon. Forego a committee membership. Give up your poker night. You will probably have to make such choices to take the step into finally writing, but if this is truly a project close to your heart, the sacrifice will soon seem a pittance compared to what you are receiving in return.

> **Deep Thought**
>
> *We all have a certain amount of time in our lives. What do we really want to spend it doing? Most people search externally for fulfilling things to fill their time. Writers feel deeply that they have something internal that makes them able to write. Only another writer will understand why you choose to spend a lovely afternoon inside with your computer.*

Being Realistic

Try to remember that your writing time is not a guilt trip or a torture exercise. Yes, it may be hard to begin, but it should always be a labor of love. Don't let yourself see this as work. Life is too full of things we *have* to do. This should be something you *want* to do. Being realistic will help keep that truth in your mind.

Spinning all your research into well-written, fun-to-read narrative prose is going to take a nice chunk of time—hopefully a pleasurable chunk—but a chunk nevertheless. Does that sound formidable? Then I have a cliché for you. There's a reason that clichés are clichés—some ideas are so true that we can't help but use them to death. But, begging your forgiveness, here's one of the truest for our purposes: "Every journey begins with a first step."

Can't take a big step today? Then take a little one. A step is a step is a step. Any forward movement has you closer to your finished written family history product.

Partners in Crime

Are you one of those writers who do really well through polite coercion, peer guilt, or just plain communal cheerleading? Maybe this is the time to make some writing friends, or corral a few you already have.

Keep in mind, though, why you are there. Try to stay focused on your project and not theirs. Sharing the cheerleading is a good thing, but never forget who's the home team.

Also, if you choose a bunch of writers to be that support group, remember one more thing: Don't believe every writer's process story you hear. When fishermen get together, they swap tales about the size of "the one that got away." When writers get together, they often are caught talking not about what they write, but how they write—the long hours, the strange places, the strange inspiration, the super-duper computer or software just bought.

This is true for any level of writer—even established writers who get the chance to wax poetic about their solitary work. Would you not exaggerate ever so slightly if all ears were trained on your "pearls of personal writing wisdom"? I once read that a certain famous writer bragged that he wrote every single day of his adult life, and he allowed nothing to keep him from his appointed time—not weddings, not funerals, not holidays, not illness, not personal obligation of any kind. Right. That happened. Such talk is "writer posturing," a crazy one-upmanship that does not help you at all.

So, the first rule is don't believe everything you hear, especially from established writers. Remember, we all are professional wordsmiths. We probably believe everything we say, but you don't have to. You need to find your own way.

Having expressed that caveat, find that partner, that cheerleading squad, that support group who will push you forward with your writing project. Just choose well.

How do you do that? The best idea is to find someone interested in genealogy or in your personal project. Remember my suggestion at the beginning of your genealogical research? Remember "baby steps" about finding a "CIG" (a computer interest group) inside your local genealogical society to give you advice? Perhaps you can find a few partners in such a group as well. Or perhaps a family member would be a perfect choice for you and your family work. You'll know best.

Remembering Key Concepts

Quick. Can you name the narrative elements from your warm-ups in Part 4, "Creative Jumpstarts"? We'll get back to them in a minute, but right now let's discuss three more elements any writer, at the beginning of a new writing project, must understand:

➤ Audience

➤ Style

➤ Voice

The Audience Is Listening

Writers are often told that they should write for themselves first and foremost, and the rest will follow. Well, that may be true in the most creative of writing. No poet should ever listen to anything but her own inner voice, for instance. Yet what is a family history project but a work done for a very special and specific audience? You are giving your family a gift; make it special by keeping them in mind as you write.

A Relatively Good Idea

Picture all your relatives in one place, an auditorium or Great-granny Big-Bucks's front parlor. Picture them listening enraptured to your words. Keep that image in the front of your mind as you write, and you won't stray far from respecting your audience.

Baby, You Got Style

Did you know you've got *style?* I know this not from looking in your closet or asking your closest buddies. I know this because every writer has a distinctive way of writing. You may change your style to fit your audience or your mood, but someone who often reads your work can pick your work out of an anonymous pile because of your distinct style.

The Write Word

Style is a writer's manner of expressing thoughts in language.

I'll never forget how much fun it was to learn the power of personal style. After writing my first piece for an in-flight magazine, I had gone on to other projects as I awaited its publication, which was months in the future. One spring night, my husband called from a business trip to tell me that on the plane that afternoon he'd picked up the airline magazine, flipped through its pages, and saw an

'Riting Reminder

Your writing has a syntax whether you know it or not. Syntax is the way a writer puts sentences together. To be aware of your natural syntax choices for your sentences, short, long, phrases, clauses, etc., is to take the first step in controlling your creativity with words and polishing your unique style.

article on the topic he remembered I'd written about. "Someone beat her to it," he thought, not even looking at the byline. But as he began to read the article, he said he "heard me." That's when he finally looked at the byline and laughed out loud. He had recognized my style without even being aware of it.

Style is created from many writing choices you make beyond your ideas such as syntax, word choice, tone, and voice. My style and your style are acquired over years of writing, but they are essentially very personal.

Analyze your writing style. For a family history writing project, you will have no editor but yourself, at least for the beginning of your work. (Rare is the friend who will hazard getting between a writer and a writer's words.) Understanding your own style, and how you can improve it, is one of the first steps toward maturity a writer takes.

What is your style? Why does it matter for our purposes? In a project like a family history, you should always be aware of your style and whether it is appropriate for the subject matter.

Choose a sample of your writing. Analyze your own style by asking such questions as …

➤ Do you use a variety of sentence lengths and structures?

➤ Are you trying to be the next Hemingway with short, simple sentences used for effect? (Warning: That can grow very old and self-conscious in anything longer than a short story.)

➤ Do you always have the same tone for every piece you write?

➤ Do you "hear" your own tone and attempt to match the right sound to the right topic? (Warning: Using a humorous tone for telling about your great-aunt's brush with fame as Gypsy Rose Lee's understudy may tickle your funny bone, but will it tickle your great-aunt's?)

➤ How's your word choice? Do you favor polysyllabic, fancy, pretentious words? Do you use the same words over and over?

➤ Do you strive to sound like yourself, as if you were telling a story over the dinner table?

Finding Your Voice

The hub of your writing style is finding your voice, the writing style that sounds like you. If you are writing a family memoir, for instance, your whole story will be from your point of view, and your voice will come naturally. Your voice is what makes you unique on paper. When my husband read my article and felt a sudden familiar sound from its style, what he was hearing, even in an objective article about a summer festival, was my distinct voice. Think how much easier it would have been for him to "hear" me if I had written the article in the first person.

Voice comes in loud and clear when you write using "I," or the first person. It comes in more quietly with the third person, the invisible and omniscient point of view. The more distinct your voice becomes, the more it will show itself in all your writing.

Will you use "I" for your family history? How much of the time will you give to writing in first person compared to third person? Do you have to make these decisions now?

No, you don't. But you do need to let each piece of your family history writing puzzle tell you what it needs. Don't be afraid to write any of your own experiences in the first person.

When you do, read the story out loud. Listen for the elements of your style that gives it *your* voice.

The Bugaboo of "Purple Prose"

"The ravishing, languid lotus-blossom of a female named Lily lived, loved, and learned during her long, lurid life in the vast, red, arid, dust-blown, wind-swept, dry lands of the Egyptian tombs of the Pharoahs, who lived thousands and thousands of years before civilization as we know it sprang from the waters of the Great Gitchee-Goomee far beyond the Seven Seas ..."

A Relatively Good Idea

What should your written voice sound like? Read a recent passage from your journal aloud. As you read, ask yourself this one very important question: "Does that sound like me when I'm talking?" If the answer is no, then take a moment and rewrite the passage to sound like You, Oral Storyteller. That's your voice. Embrace it. And write it like you hear it.

Did you make it through that sentence? That was a sample of something called "purple prose," or a "purple passage." Sometimes when a writer is working hard to give a story importance or significance, he piles on flowery language. What happens? The very opposite of what's intended. The writing can seem overdone on purpose, even for comic effect, and the last thing you want is somebody laughing at your work when that response wasn't what you had in mind.

What if you discover that your voice tends toward purple prose? Now is as a good time as any to get rid of some of that unwanted color.

The Glory of Restraint

Remember the 2,500/500 warm-up in Chapter 18, "Telling Your Own Stories"? Trying to write long usually forces a writer into purple prose. Writing short makes purple prose almost impossible. It's very hard to cut down a 2,500-word anecdote to 500 words and still write "purple." Any time you suspect you may be writing a story a bit too lavishly, use the exercise as a way to teach yourself to trim that purple fat and keep it off. Using the adjectives-out exercise is also a good complement.

Normally, I would never suggest any sort of editing during your first writing efforts. Now, at the beginning of your writing, is the time for all-out creativity. But this is the one place I'd suggest working on some restraint, if you know you lean toward flowery language.

That Wonderful Format

By now you've chosen your family history format. What's your format choice? Circle it from the following:

➤ Narrative genealogy

➤ Ancestor's biography

➤ Family profiles

➤ Family stories/family memoir

➤ Literary snapshots

➤ Cookbook family history

➤ Your own family documentary

➤ Family journalism

➤ Pictorial history

➤ Your ancestors' choices

➤ Your own invention: _____

_____

In the next three chapters, we are going to take your format, create its skeleton, and slowly help you put flesh on those bones. And we are going to use your next secret password to do it.

What's the new password? *Outline.*

The Miracle of Outlining

Be honest, now.

Do you ...

➤ Love outlines?

➤ Loath outlines?

I loathed, detested, and resented outlines during most of my school years. My English teachers would assign research papers each year, and with each we were to include an outline. I'd write the term paper, then I'd make up a quick outline, scribble it on a piece of notebook paper, and slip it on top just before turning in the work. To call me a lazy student was an understatement. I was lazy, and—I admit it—stubborn.

My senior English teacher, Mrs. Birdsong, a big barrel-chested woman, was especially hell-on-wheels about outlines, yet she could never quite explain their function to me adequately. They always and forever seemed like a post-writing table of contents more than a pre-writing tool to me. But now I realize I hated outlines for artistic reasons. Outlines implied rigidity, formula, and structure. I was, subconsciously, even then, against all those things. It was like being asked to color inside the lines.

Coloring Inside the Lines

Then, in my junior year of college, I had to do a piece of research that wasn't perfunctory, that challenged and even excited me. I was being forced to do some actual thinking. First, my head hurt from the unusual activity, then, my mind fell into gear. I began doodling ideas on my notepad to help my cluttered mind think through how to write what I wanted to write the way I wanted to write. And suddenly I realized that those doodles were ... oh my gosh ... an outline! It was a messy one, but it was an outline, nevertheless.

My writing and my thinking were transformed. Since then, I practice and teach a free-form kind of outlining that Mrs. Birdsong would not like. Gone are the roman numerals (unless I decide I want to use them). Gone are the indentations and the lowercase a's, b's, and c's (unless I decide I should use them). In went the thinking tools of my own invention, messy though they may be and unreadable to all save me.

I now see such brainstorm outlining as part of the process, an ordering of thoughts that feels good, not a structure forced on my artistic free spirit. And therein lies the difference.

I also realized something about Mrs. Birdsong and all my English teachers before her. They could not teach the beauty of outlines, the creative "play" quality of them over the drudgery work of them, because they were not writers. They were teachers. They were told to teach the outline from a curriculum point of view without understanding its glorious function from a creative point of view. Form wasn't supposed to follow function. Form was supposed to follow form, because that was the accepted form, young lady! (To Mrs. Birdsong's credit, she did make me memorize the dagger soliloquy from *Macbeth*, which has come in very handy in my more literary moments.)

You Know the Drill

So, let's try it. You know the outline formula we were all taught in school. No need to waste time on it here. You will either love it or hate it. If you love it, use it in good writing health. If you hate it, then I am here to tell you to make up your own formula, be they squiggles, dots, dashes, numbers, or whatever.

Don't get hung up on the form; get hung up and revved up on the ideas pouring out on each new line of ruled paper or blank computer screen. The point is the ordering of your thoughts. If you are the type of person who thinks best when all is neat and in tidy rows, the standard outline form is for you. If you are the messy, creative type, then your most productive form of outlining is the one that gets your ideas down on paper any which way and leaves the ordering of thoughts for the next step.

Call it your brainstorm outline, your freeform outline, your recyclable outline, but don't ever think of it as a set-in-stone outline. The freer you feel with your outline, the quicker you will experience the miracle of outlining for your writing.

Create your own nonoutline outline form. To make outlines work for you, create your own symbols that don't get in the way of your brainstorming. You can print out a few (or more than a few) blank outlines that will help you in the brainstorming process. This way you don't have to sweat formatting your quick notes as you try to keep up with your ideas.

There's nothing intimidating about outlines. Yet they will never work for you unless you reinvent them in your own image. Use Xs, check marks, squiggles, or even roman numerals, but never forget that the outline is a means to an end, a thing to reinvent dozens of times during the writing of your book, something nobody will ever see but you.

Your Format and Your Outline

Let's create an imaginary first-draft cookbook family history format:

➤ Granny's homemade stuffing
  ➤ Christmas at Granny's
  ➤ Uncle Albert's false teeth in the Jell-O
  ➤ Bologna Thanksgiving
➤ Great-Aunt Cissy's Manhattans
  ➤ Great-Aunt Cissy's flapper years
  ➤ Great-Uncle Joe's move to the big city

➤ Thankful Perkins' Scratch Biscuits

> ➤ Civil War heroes
>
> ➤ Covered wagon pioneers
>
> ➤ Great-grandparents' love story
>
> ➤ Hard scrabble farm life
>
> ➤ Eastland, Texas, reunion stories

Note that the ideas, the information, and how you order them, are what is important, not the form. The form is to help you understand each entry's importance and placement.

Your turn. Open your journal to a new page. List three—just three—topics under which you could place several of your family or ancestral facts or anecdotes. Now list those things under each topic.

Stop and look at your handiwork. This is the beginning of your first of many working outlines. When you're ready to reorder your thinking again, this will be the brainstorm outline from which you'll create all your more detailed versions.

Your Outline—Where Are You Going?

Time to start your outline. Open your journal. If you think better in front of your computer, then open a new file.

At the top of the page, write the type of format you have chosen for your family history. Have your master of master lists where you can see it well. And open this book to Chapter 20, "Time to Structure," to stoke your memory about the specifics of your chosen format. On the blank page, in no exact order for the moment, list all the most important sections you want to cover, leaving at least one blank line between each. Are you writing a narrative genealogy? Then list the decades or the ancestors you want to cover. Are you writing a family profile? Then list all the interviews you know you will definitely use, deciding on either chronological order or familial order.

Now, make a scribbled mess of your page—a jumble of thoughts in some semblance of order. This is a brainstorm more than an outline. Choose an order that makes sense considering your format. Make sure to leave plenty of space between items. Here, in the lines you've left blank, is where you'll scribble more specific stories, facts, and figures under each heading, as appropriate.

How far did you go? Did you fill a page? Half a page? Two pages? Whatever it is, it doesn't matter. You've begun.

Do It Again

Take a nice, long look at your scribbles. Not bad, eh? Smile, take a deep breath, and then turn to a new page. If you're working on computer, print out your scribbled mess. Set it where you can see it.

And now start again, using the scribbled mess to guide you. That's right. Start again, on your second draft of the jotted mess we are calling your first-draft outline.

The more detailed your outline, the easier the writing will be. Get used to this pattern. A good outline will go through dozens of drafts during the writing process. Each new brainstorm will need room in the next revision of your outline. And don't be surprised if the final product looks nothing like this first effort. A good outline is a work in progress, a creative playground. Don't ever forget that.

Hushing Your Internal Nitpicker (for Now)

What's that I hear? Ah, yes, your internal nitpicker, that noisy little devil. I bet it's already causing you problems. Some writers call that voice their "internal editor" and allow that irritating inner voice to stop them at every turn by judging every piece of work and every idea before its time. Sometimes, this inner voice is so overpowering that it can stop writers from writing altogether.

There will be times—later on in the editing process—when you will cherish your internal nitpicker, letting that little hard-to-please persona have free rein over all your work in hopes of making it better. But now is not the time. Now is the time for being creative without constantly checking yourself for errors. So, gag that inner editor, and enjoy this time of pure creative energy.

Progress Report

How far have you gone with your outline so far? Try to make three versions, each one longer and more detailed, brainstorming as you go. After you've done three versions, then either copy what you have onto a clean page, or onto your computer screen. (Do you have outlining capability with your software? You might want to use it. If you do, save each old outline as you make new versions, at least for a while. You may want to go back and look at some of your old thinking later.)

The Least You Need to Know

➤ Outlining, your own way, is the skeleton for your writing endeavor.

➤ Keeping your audience, your family, always in mind as you write will keep you on track.

➤ Creating your own writing time and place is pivotal to a successful writing project.

Chapter 22

Imagining the Telling

In This Chapter

➤ Analyzing your research for "imagining" purposes

➤ Writing about lesser-known ancestors

➤ Imagining the telling: putting flesh on bone

You have your format, and you have begun your outline. The next step is to begin to imagine. Each of your stories and genealogical facts waiting to be woven together can fit into a format and an outline. But before they can become real to your audience, you'll have to begin to imagine the telling. You have to begin thinking how you'll breathe life into each character.

This may seem like an enormous undertaking, but in fact, you are primed and ready to do this. Let me show you.

Reviewing Your Research

By now, you have a good idea of what's in your stash of family history. It's time to decide what you will use and how.

Get out your brainstorm outline, and your master of master lists of all your work.

Notice that you have several categories of information. You have …

➤ Genealogical facts and figures.

➤ Genealogical anecdotes.

➤ Interviews and family stories.

Imagining the telling of the genealogical anecdotes, facts, and figures is your major undertaking. You have to weave all you have together in some interesting narrative. On the other hand, the stories from your relatives should be told as close to how they were shared with you as possible. That may seem to not leave much room for imagination, but that's not altogether true. You still have to decide exactly how and where you want your stories told.

Analyzing your data can help. Using your rough outline and your master of master lists, answer these questions:

➤ How many are lists of facts?

➤ How many are anecdotes?

➤ How many people do you have to—or want to—include?

➤ What sort of natural order does the information fall into?

➤ What natural beginnings do you see?

➤ What are your most exciting stories?

➤ What information could or should be left out?

➤ How many gaps are there, and how should you handle them?

Take some time to answer these questions thoughtfully. See this as part of your outline work, jotting notes to yourself about your answers on your outline sheet.

Flesh on Bone

Your master of master list and your brainstorm outline are what you are using to give your book-to-be its basic structure—like a body's skeleton. Using that metaphor, imagine the telling is like putting flesh on bone. As an exercise, let's try a little bit of fleshing out. Imagine how you might write the bare-bones information for the following "list of a life" from, say, your genealogical research. Your sources for this information were courthouse records, cemetery records, and your relatives' memory of family lore:

Lois Lou Lane Schmoe

Born June 8, 1865.

Married Delroy Dumas Schmoe, May 13, 1883.

Rode a horse from Tupelo, Mississippi to husband's new farm in Oklahoma.

Had six children.

Farmer husband died at age 38.

Lois Lou moved into town and opened boarding house and stables.

Married sheriff.

Had four more kids.

Famous for her pecan pie, horse trading, and choir-singing.

Second husband died at age 48.

Married undertaker.

Died at age 78.

Buried in Baptist cemetery by husband.

How might you start a paragraph about Lois Lou? Perhaps with a summary statement about the type of woman Lois Lou was—about her many marriages, or about the times she lived in the boarding house. Or perhaps with the most interesting piece of information first?

Your Turn

Now take a "list of a life" from your own work and do the same thing in your journal. But this time, review Chapter 18's narrative element warm-up to practice incorporating them. Take out your journal and write at least the first four sentences, then see if you can finish the whole thing with a bit of narrative flair.

That Wonderful Format

After you've fleshed out one of the many lives of your ancestors, the next step is to plug that work into your format. What is your format? Is it the cookbook? The family profiles? The family documentary? Where does this one episode fit best in your outline? Wherever that is, put it into your line-up. (Are you using a computer? Then cut and paste your work right into the outline.)

Let's take an example—your important anecdote about Granny LaRue's childhood in Harlem is the story you've fleshed out. You've turned all your research and family stories about her into a two-page profile of fun and interesting points about Granny LaRue. In your rough outline, you've listed Granny LaRue's Harlem Childhood as Entry #3 in your family documentary format. So, now, you would place the whole, fully told story into the outline at that point, right before Entry #4, which is about Granny LaRue's trombone-playing husband Leon.

Now all you have left to do is multiply this effort by 100 or so, and you have a book.

Okay, that's not funny, but in a very real way it's true. Treat each effort individually, reaching for the right placement, the right tone, the right length, the right treatment of facts, and the right transition and reflection, and voilà! You have a book.

Let's discuss a few ways to treat each of your writing efforts individually, then as part of your larger outline and format whole.

The Boon of Reading Historical Nonfiction/Fiction

By now, you've read many old books digging up your family's past. Have you considered reading some history of the times as well? I've mentioned how reading about a time can give you the sound of the language for the time period. But reading such books to help with imagining the telling of your specific stories is also a good idea. What sort of books do I mean? The bookstores and libraries abound with well-written accounts of history, from best-selling scholarship about Civil War generals, to diaries of men and women pioneers. Ask your librarian for ideas. There are some specific books just for this kind of research such as *The Writer's Guide to Everyday Life in the 1800s*. It will give you far more information than you'll ever need about your ancestors' settings.

The Bane of Reading Historical Fiction

Do you like historical fiction? In a certain way, it can also give a boost to your imagining, considering that fiction is imagination on a foundation of history.

But beware, o lover of historical fiction. As with all things in life, there is good and there is bad when it comes to such writing. Most writing teachers encourage students who want to be writers to also be readers. But there's a reason teachers usually pick certain books for these aspiring writers to read. The reason you, as one of those aspiring writers, should always read the kinds of the things you want to write (beyond the commonsense reasons), is that we are a very impressionable bunch. What we read all day will be what we hear in our ears, feel through our fingers, and pour onto the page.

In other words, if you enjoy a good bodice-ripping gothic romance, and that is all you are reading as you begin to write your family history accounts, then you may find yourself telling Great-granddad Leroy's story about his first meeting with Great-grandma Lois Lou with a tone that sounds more like a romance novel than Leroy and Lois Lou's true adventure.

The moral? Read. But choose well what you read.

Putting Words into Your Ancestor's Mouth

A family history is a long project, and as the facts fly by, you will keep the whole narrative more readable by sprinkling those family anecdotes throughout, as often as you can. These anecdotes will automatically tie us in historically to the time as you continue to lead us through the years. The task that will remain is to tie in your ancestor, by imagined words from his mouth, to the story.

Of course, part of imagining an ancestor or relative's story is also imagining what they might say, since rare is the anecdote that doesn't include some dialogue. But you and I both know that writing dialogue for such a story is teetering on the wrong side of truth. Unless you have the person's diary or a newspaper quote or someone else's account of your ancestor's life that includes the ancestor's very words, how could you know what he or she actually said?

Because of the lack of direct quotes, you're going to have to make some leaps of logic, and do this very type of imagining. When Cousin Bernie tells the story how Great-granddad Leroy and Great-grandma Lois Lou met, you can leave such accountability up to Cousin Bernie by quoting him exactly as he told you. But there will be a few moments as you tell story after story in your family history when you will be forced to put words in at least a few of your ancestors' mouths. The trick, if you recall, is not whether you will do it, but how you will keep from making them all sound alike.

'Riting Reminder

Review your dialogue warm-up exercise in Chapter 18. Can you incorporate any of your experiences with that exercise into your current work?

Allegedly, He Said

You can also take a cue from the newspapers. You can add the word "allegedly" or "supposedly," or the passive "It was believed that ...," or other such red flags to the reader that what is being said might or might not have been put this way in real life. This is, to use a couple of well-placed clichés, a nice way to pass the buck and to have your cake and eat it, too.

The trick, again, is to make your ancestor's voice sound different from your own voice. Remember that if you have conflicting versions—Aunt Edna telling a story about her father one way and Aunt Cissy telling it another—you'll tell both stories, explaining why. It's the same technique you employ in using the word "allegedly" to introduce an ancestor's unsubstantiated story or words.

Imagining a Life

Some of your ancestors will offer you quite a bit of raw material to create a narrative around, such as Lois Lou Lane Schmoe in the preceding example. Some, though, will only have a few tidbits, good or bad, to offer you. How many ancestors and relatives do you have in your master of master lists to include? What are you going to do with family members about whom you have only a small portion of information? Will you be including them in your family history writing, and if so, how?

Example: Thomas Jefferson Schmoe, your ancestor, was born in 1787. You know from your research that he was born and raised in a tiny village in Delaware that no longer exists, served in the War of 1812, and then came home to sire a dozen kids with the Baptist minister's daughter. But that's all you know.

How might you write this account as fully as possible, imagining his life and his connection to your family today? How much background do you have on the life and times of Colonial America? How much information do you have on the tiny village? How much do you have on the dozen kids? Answering such questions will help put flesh on ancestors' bones for your readers.

Choose one of your early ancestors. Use these questions to imagine his life from the research you've done:

➤ Who will it be?

➤ What facts do you have to include?

➤ Which facts inspire your imagination?

>   ➤ What did the ancestor look like? (Do you have pictures? Describe the photos.)

>   ➤ What was she known for?

>   ➤ What was the defining point of her life?

>   ➤ Where did she come from?

>   ➤ Where did she go?

>   ➤ Why?

Soon, you will be in the habit of imagining your ancestors' lives, whether you have lots of research to work with or just a smidgen, by asking such questions about each and every one you want to include in your family history. The trick is to use your own curiosity—the same curiosity that has fueled all your genealogical research. Now you are asking yourself to take your curiosity a step farther and mix it with your logic and your creativity and your historical background research to imagine the life you've uncovered.

Imagining Your Ancestor's Diary

Let's try a very interesting exercise that you may or may not use for your family history volume. Let's write a piece of creative writing, imagining what your ancestor's diary might sound like if you happened to find one.

> Dear Diary:
>
> I am indisposed this evening after a horrid bout with Le Grippe, a monumental sickness that has forced half the village to take to their beds. It has already claimed 20 souls here, and our doctor, who abides in the next village, seems to have no remedies to stay the tide. What shall we do? What shall I do if this sickness claims me? Oh, how I would miss my little Annie Lee if I were to be taken to heaven. I cannot leave my dear Leroy now that he has finally found some peace with the success of our dry goods endeavor. I must pray to God to spare my life, as well as my dear family's.

Your turn. Just for the fun of it, choose an interesting ancestor from your pedigree chart, and then using your master of master lists, knowing all your anecdotes, facts, and figures about that ancestor, imagine a diary entry about one of those interesting tidbits of life as that ancestor.

As you imagine what he or she might have been thinking, your ancestor should come to life for you. If not, then study your historical background of the ancestor's era a bit more to get the flavor and sound of the times, and try again. (Remember: This is just an exercise to give you a feeling of imagining dialogue and inner thoughts. In your family history, you would only use a sentence here or there for the dialogue, not a fully told diary entry, which would sound too made up.)

Ready for a little test? In your "diary entry," find and circle all these elements:

➤ Description
➤ Characterization
➤ Tone
➤ Tense
➤ Point of view
➤ Dialogue

How did you do? Do you see any characterization? Any description? Tone? Tense? Point of view? Keeping these in mind while you write will double the quality of your first few drafts.

Related Facts

Several audio and video products can also add fascinating visual and aural input to your imagining. *Ride With Me* is an audiocassette series designed to give the interested driver a historical context to the passing scene. A video program called *Flikbacks* is one of the many resources for film footage of the past by decades. Ask your librarian for other ideas.

How Much Freedom?

How much freedom in writing your ancestors' thoughts should you really give yourself? How much of this imagining is too much?

You should continue to ask that question, of course. It will keep you from overdoing your imagining. And when you do create such dialogue, then you should be upfront about it, mentioning it in your writing.

It's the rare family history research that leaves no questions unanswered and no gaps unfilled. Allow yourself to make logical assumptions about your ancestors' lives, and encourage your reader to do the same as they read what you offer them about your common ancestors. Sometimes part of the wonderful intrigue of a family history are the questions that can never be answered. You can write to these questions, by posing solutions and thoughts, as if you are doing it along with your family readers. Always, though, be careful not to abuse your freedom to imagine.

Progress Report

By now, you've imagined the telling of several of your ancestors' stories. Evaluate your efforts. Are the selections the kind of writing you want in your family history? If so, what about them do you like? Try to identify those aspects, then write one more profile of one more ancestor from your work, choosing perhaps a granny about whom you have very little information, imagining what her life was like, and use these successful aspects liberally.

The Least You Need to Know

➤ Analyzing your research for imagining purposes will help your creative thinking.

➤ Lesser-known ancestors are still important to your family history and deserve to be included.

➤ Imagining the telling is the first step to putting flesh on your family history writing skeleton.

Chapter 23

How to Start

Okay, no more delays. You have ideas, you're all warmed up, and you know what to avoid and how to imagine. You have brainstormed your outline and chosen a perfect format for your work.

It's time to start thinking about the most important piece of writing you will do for your entire project: the book's opening.

And You're Off—Beginnings

Have you ever noticed the way people decide to make a book purchase in a bookstore? Someone once took a survey of book buyers and found that each book's cover and cover copy has three seconds to grab the attention of the average potential purchaser. If all that grand artistic design and masterful copywriting have done their work and lured the potential book buyer to open the book to the first page, then there is nothing left but the first few paragraphs of your writing to hook them into taking the book home.

So, whether we writers like it or not, if we care about people reading our work, the most important part of our book is the opening. Short of personal recommendation by television hosts' book clubs or your buddy down at the coffee shop, a book must have an enticing opening page, or the rest of a writer's wondrous work may never be read.

"Oh, but the best part of my book is on page 42!" you might say. I've had plenty of students say the equivalent. My response? If it's that good, then move that part to page one. Impossible? Nothing is impossible when you're dealing with your work's "hook." After all, you're the author. You have license to do anything you want.

Hooks

The idea of a story's *hook* really is the parlance of journalism, as in the hook of the news story. But it works well for any sort of writing, because the dynamic is the same. Hook 'em in the beginning or lose 'em for the rest of the piece. For example, journalists are taught to pack all the good stuff into the beginning of their news stories and trail off to the less important information at the end. Why? Because, considering the nature of a daily newspaper, an editor may have to lop off the last few paragraphs to make the news story fit into the space provided.

The Write Word

A **hook** is an idea designed to "hook" your interest at the beginning of a piece of writing.

Not so with your work, of course, but packing the opening with the good stuff should still be something you do. But take heart! There are ways to create an enticing beginning without giving away the whole load! There really are ways to tease the reader with what's in store in the pages to follow if they are wise enough to keep reading. When this is done well, no reader can resist a hook based on such curiosity. It's the kind of enticement that makes a book a "page turner," creating a sort of suspense so the reader wants to know what happens next.

Some of the techniques you could use to open your family history interestingly and enticingly could be a vivid image, a fascinating tidbit, a creative family take on "Biblical Begats," a true-life diary excerpt from an ancestor, or even a black sheep's profile. All these things can whet a reader's curiosity to read on. A family history project can't help but offer an array of terrific hook possibilities. Let's look at a few in more detail to help you choose the one you want to use.

Going for the Vivid Image

Glance over your master of master lists. After a quick glance, ask yourself this question: What was the most vivid image you see in your mind from all the research and interviewing you've done? In all of your writing, you should be trying to create "word pictures," mental images of your colorful clan from the information you've compiled. This kind of vivid image could be an opening that will excite your family readers.

Most Interesting Ancestor

One of your ancestors led a remarkable life, over and beyond all your other kin. He was part of the Lewis and Clark Expedition. She was born on the Chisolm Trail. He was Abraham Lincoln's tailor. She was a member of the Nazi resistance in Poland. Let's say you open your family history volume with a short intriguing snapshot of such an ancestor. What sort of message does that convey about your brood? Your reader will probably infer that there are more interesting profiles to follow, and read on. Don't you think?

So, take a second to reflect. Who is your most interesting ancestor? Who might come in a close second?

Cliffhanger—the Most Exciting Ancestral Moment

An offshoot of the "Most Interesting Ancestor" would be the "Most Exciting Ancestral Moment." Have you uncovered an adventure that one of your ancestors experienced? Why not write it like a cliffhanger, as television soap operas do so successfully? While you might not want to use the tone of a soap opera, you could certainly use the idea. Begin your book with the first few moments of a story about your ancestor who rode up the San Juan Hill with Teddy Roosevelt, and then stop, keeping the reader in suspense about whether he rode down the other side, until later in the book.

> **Deep Thought**
>
> *Think about the vivid image that popped into your mind. Why do you think that vivid image above all others from your research pops into your mind? What does it say about you? About your creativity? About your own picture of your family? How might that influence the writing of your history?*

Summary Statement

A summary statement could use the vivid image idea to introduce your personal take on the most exciting discoveries or insights your family history work has uncovered, ones that the reader would surely be fascinated to learn if they'd read the rest of the book.

This is the kind of opening amalgam of images, though, that would take lots of massaging to include just the right wonders and just the right tone without overdoing it. This could also be used well in combination with other hook ideas. For example …

➤ The ancestor who ran the first newspaper in Missouri

➤ The ancestor who fled the Irish Potato famine and landed in New Orleans

➤ The granny who entertained the celebrities of her times in New York City, including Mark Twain and Lily Langtry

➤ The ancestor who sired 13 children during four marriages in pioneer days

Ancestor's Diary or Letter

Are you lucky enough to have uncovered an ancestor's diary or letters? What a great hook the right excerpt from one or the other could be. Who doesn't like to sneak a look into someone else's diary or take a peek at someone's personal correspondence? To offer a snippet of such personal writing as a teaser at the beginning of your work could be a hook no one could resist. The trick, of course, would be to choose the right excerpt, set off at the beginning by quotes, and then follow it with a good opening explanation, referring to the excerpt.

'Riting Reminder

Don't disregard other people's musings from your ancestor's time. Reading actual diaries of an ancestor's time period, even if your own ancestor never put pen to paper, is still invaluable for adding flavor to your own fledgling writing attempts at capturing your ancestors' lives.

Begats Begat Begats

Was your family a Sunday-go-to-meeting group? Chances are, if you were born anywhere in the Bible Belt, your world was influenced by Sundays spent at church. If so, a fun way to open your book might be a personal take-off on "Biblical Begats." This would be even better if your ancestors had unusual names, or the same family names which would be repeated over and over up to your generation.

Of course, such a list would also give a wonderful feeling of continuity, of roots; a sneak preview of what your research has uncovered about your special family tree.

Try this out in the following space or on a blank page of your family history journal. List one significant ancestor from each generation you researched chronologically up to the current generation. Then, when you hit this living generation, include all your relatives, as well as yourself, since they are your audience and will enjoy seeing their names. That way you can decide if it seems like a fun hook for your family history.

_____ begat _____ who begat _____

who begat _____   who begat _____

who begat _____   who begat _____

who begat _____   who begat _____

who begat _____   who begat _____

Get the picture? Give it a try!

Smack Dab in the Middle

> John Jacob Schmoe found himself surrounded by Apache braves. He had wandered from the wagon train in search of his horse ....

Think that might catch a relative's attention? A time-honored literary device is opening a story smack dab in the middle of the action and then backtracking to tell the full tale.

The literary term for this writing device is *in media res*. Why would you choose this option? Starting off in media res allows you to choose an exciting moment in the middle of an ancestor's life, even if it's an imagined one, and open with it. By doing this you will be pulling your reader into the thick of things ancestrally.

The Write Word

The phrase **in media res** means "beginning in the middle of things."

For instance, Ulysses Lincoln Schmoe, one of your ancestors, was at Gettysburg. Unfortunately, even with all of your research efforts, you know little about his personal struggle there except for the confirmed fact that he lost his life during the last day of battle. What you can do is paint a prose picture of what Gettysburg must have looked like for your ancestor (and your readers' ancestor) by drawing from background research about that Civil War battle in general. This lets you imagine the event through your ancestor's eyes and offer that sight to your family members as homage to your ancestor. Doing so would have your reader connecting with your ancestor's tragic death in a way you might find incredibly moving, as will your reader.

Do you need to tell the whole tale if you know it? Not at all. Save it for later. Just give an opening salvo, enough to entice the reader to find the full account of poor old Ulysses Lincoln Schmoe, everybody's great-great-great-great-uncle, by reading on.

Modeling "The" Ancestor

Have you noticed that many of your ancestors had similar traits, talents, features, or backgrounds? Maybe it would be fun to write a composite ancestor, using the best of your ancestors. That could be quite a unique way to begin your family history book. Your readers would get a taste of their whole family tree, as well as a hint of themselves, which they might want to explore further.

A summary transition statement after the composite that leads you into the rest of the book would be needed. For example ...

> "Such is the strange and wonderful pioneer stock we are all made from. And there is so much more that tells us about ourselves ..."

Your Personal Hero/Black Sheep/Royalty

Do you have a six-shooting bank robber in your background? Do you have a hero to be proud of? Do you have a link to royalty to brag about? Why not mention them right here at the beginning? Again, don't tell the whole tale of your hero/black sheep/royalty. Just entice the reader with a statement of fact and a bit of an anecdote. Make them turn the page to know more about their unusual ancestor.

The Quintessential Family Story

No family get-together is complete without somebody retelling that insane story about Crazy Aunt Edna and the tent revival evangelist. Or the one about your pioneer pappy who won his bride in a poker game. Or your Irish granddad who "went the distance" with heavyweight champion boxer Joe Louis.

That quintessential family story all your family members would instantly recognize could be a good way to open a family history book. Each family member would read that well-known anecdote for the first time as written history—instead of oral history—and realize that much more, through the power of the printed word, is in store with a turn of the page.

A Relatively Good Idea

A good exercise to test using the quintessential genealogical moment as your hook would be to ask a few friends to read your personal anecdote. Then, after they do, ask the same people to read one of your best attempts at another of these hook ideas to compare. Ask for honesty. Remember that if the opening is not the place for the personal anecdote, another part of the book will be.

The Quintessential Genealogical Moment

Of all the experiences you had during your genealogical diggings for your family history writing, several moments must be forever etched into your mind. Might one of these be something you could use for an opening?

The right one might offer your reader a voyeuristic moment, grasping the exhilaration you felt at certain moments in your research. Perhaps it was a road trip on which you uncovered a famous Revolutionary War ancestor's grave and felt his presence. Perhaps it was uncovering, with the help of a gruff old graveyard caretaker, a whole branch of the family no one knew about. Maybe it was the ancestral marriage certificate signed by Annie Oakley as witness. Perhaps it was the moment you found your original American ancestor and unearthed the saga of his voyage to these shores.

The last thing you want to do is interject yourself too much into your family history unless, of course, you are writing a personal family memoir rather than a family history. (See the section, "Them, Not You—

Avoiding Self-Indulgence," later in the chapter.) But if the moment is more about your discovery than you, you could have a winner.

Your Family's Place

Does your family have deep roots in a certain place? A house? A farm? A region? A state? We are such a mobile society, forced or privileged to move here, there, and everywhere to "get ahead," that we all cherish a sense of past roots. For example, I may not live in Texas, but I cannot escape the reality of "Once a Texan, always a Texan." Each word out of my mouth, delivered with my inescapable accent, betrays my origins. Yet where I live now, thousands of miles away from my home state, I secretly revel in the lore of Texas. And since both sides of my family have been Texans for over a century, before my generation's wandering ways, creating something "Texan" to open my family history volume might not be a bad idea.

Do you have similar feelings that you share with other family members? Does your ancestral past show decades of residence in a certain place that might echo with meaning for others in your family tree? A vivid description of such a place could be an excellent introduction to your family history.

Startling Statement

If you were forced to make a startling statement about your family, what would it be? Answer one—or all—of these statements to get you thinking:

➤ "We are a family of _____."

➤ "Our family was always _____."

➤ "Could any family be more _____ than ours?"

➤ "Family can mean warmth and coldness. It can mean a battle of wills and a place of comfort. Our family _____."

➤ "Some families have underachievers, some have overachievers. Some have the good, the bad, and the ugly. Ours _____."

Finishing such statements should get your thoughts bubbling about crafting your own startling statement mixed with an interesting tidbit of family research. Here's an example of a startling statement taken from a very specific, but important, piece of family history:

> "If John Jacob Schmoe had not fallen in love with the wrong woman and been banished from the old family home, you and I would not be reading this from the freedom of our American homes ...."

You get the picture. The more startling the statement, the better the hook.

'Riting Reminder

If you write an open letter to your family, remember to keep it short and vivid, offering them just a taste of what's in store, as well as why you're writing this important family history for them. If it is too long, you'll lose them before they even get past page one.

Your Open Letter

Have you thought about writing an open letter to your family for your opening? Perhaps this is better suited for a preface or forward to your book, but if you weave in lots of teasers from your research, this could be a very touching and very interesting start.

For instance, using the summary statement idea from the previous section, try fashioning parts of some of the other ideas into your open letter.

Open your family history journal and jot down a rough draft of a letter to your living family about the significance of your research, why it was worth your years of work, and how you hope it will affect them, either now or in the future. (This is also a good, all-around exercise to focus your energy for the writing ahead, whether you use it for your opening or not.)

Them, Not You—Avoiding Self-Indulgence

This is the perfect time for a very big caveat: Never forget that the primary audience of your book is them, not you. While this has been the personal excavation of your own roots, unless you have written it just for you, then at all costs avoid self-indulgence as you begin. How do you do that? By continually keeping that reader in mind, as if you are telling stories over the kitchen table, sharing what you've found about your common ancestors.

Editing Your Genealogical Slide Show

Editing mentally as you create your opening is a very good way to stay on the "them" track and off the "you" dead end. Here's a good, practical image to help you: The concept is somewhat like showing your vacation slides to company or extended family—some are semi-interested, while others are outright bored. Picture your family history as such a slide show and your family members as sitting on your sofa watching. You may be ecstatic about your adventure, but you had better come up with the most incredibly interesting slides possible for this audience.

Throwing out the second, third, and fourth slide of your spouse standing in front of Old Faithful is the first positive step in keeping the attention of the other family members sitting on your couch sharing the adventure with you. And whenever you can throw in slides of people they know or who remind them of themselves, the better the experience for all.

Ending the Beginning

Now that you've experimented with several of these beginnings, it's time to choose one. Is it an easy choice? Is there a clear winner? If not, keep working and experimenting. But if so, your next question has to be, "How do I end it and move into the rest of the book?"

One overly simple answer is a page break. Just finish your opening, leave a few spaces, and start following your outline as you begin the prose again. What is the first thing on your outline at this point? Whatever it is, it's there because you thought it was the most important. Trust your instincts and dive in.

Another, more common answer, and one you will use throughout the book, is the use of transitions, phrases, or thoughts that connect different parts of book together for the reader. This will be discussed at length in Chapter 24, "Getting It on Paper."

What Lies Ahead

What lies ahead? In the next chapter, you'll find out that the next step is the big one—what lies beyond the end of the beginning. What lies ahead is getting all those great ideas and stories from your outline to pages and pages full of prose: the creation of the rest of your manuscript.

Progress Report

Which of these opening appeals to you most? Unless you've already chosen one and are ecstatic—as well as energized—by your choice, then go back and experiment with at least two other hook ideas. Your opening should be something that has you so excited you can actually see the outline coming to life and the book rolling out before your eyes.

When you think you have that probable winning hook, then move on to the next all-important chapter, but not before. Never underestimate the power of your hook to even hook yourself. Check your energy level. If it seems a little low, then open your journal and re-read some of your narrative warm-ups or your beginning exercises until you feel your excitement rising.

The Least You Need to Know

➤ A great opening is essential to a successful book.

➤ A family history project offers many great ideas of creative openings.

➤ Keeping them (your readers) instead of you in mind as you write will help prevent self-indulgent writing.

Getting It on Paper

The moment is here. You have your beginning, you have your outline, you have exercises, and you have piles and piles of research ready to be sorted, analyzed, juggled, and massaged into a book. So why do you feel so … well … overwhelmed?

Whether that describes your feeling as if you are standing on your "real" writing precipice, or whether words like "confused," "scared," or "excited" are more accurate, all those feelings are absolutely natural. So now what? Well, how about some "insider" tips?

After the Beginning—What?

Most writers' experience has taught them some mental writing steps. Mine all hinge on having, first and foremost, a good beginning. This may sound crazy, but when I start a new piece of writing, I worry only until I figure out what my beginning will be. Once I've been able to work out my beginning, somehow, I find that I can relax because I can see in my mind's eye the rest of it. I know that all I have left to do is just write it. Of course, writing it may take weeks, months, or even years, but the confidence I feel knowing I have that beginning keeps me rolling.

I have worked this bit of mental magic so much that it is second nature now, and I will admit it gives me a great deal of comfort—a commodity that any writer needs in starting a project of any size, but especially one the size of a family history.

What is your comforting thought to help the words start flowing onto your paper? If you don't have a few bits of magic of your own, why not create some right now? Let me give you a few more tricks for jumpstarting your writing.

The Miracle of Outlining, Revisited

Once I have a beginning for a writing project, all I feel I have to do is rely on my messy brainstorm outline to clean itself up. I continue to trust that if I just keep working on that outline, the rest will fall into place when I need it to.

Can you do that? Of course, you can. All you have to do is re-create the concept of the outline into your own image and make massaging your outline your daily writing work for the first few weeks of your writing efforts.

Then, as your outline begins to gel, you'll spend less time reworking the outline and more time on the chapter chunks your outline has directed you to begin writing. And that is truly getting it down on paper.

It's Over When It's Over

When do you think the outline is finished? The answer is never, really. There's an unspoken rule about real writing—it's always in transition. As Yogi Berra once said, "It ain't over until it's over."

'Riting Reminder

Writing is rewriting. Your words are always in the act of becoming what you want them to become until the moment they are in print. Only the beginner (and a lazy one at that) believes that a first draft is a finished draft.

If you let the outline work for you instead of you working for it, then you will be changing it until the very last minute. And that's the real key to my concept of comfort. I never think I'm finished planning what I'm going to write. I know my outline and my first attempts at writing from it are always in flux, as long as the creativity is flowing.

Writing Parts of the Whole

After you have your good start on your outline and your beginning, the next step is to start writing—anything. Sometimes the best way to start writing is to just start writing.

A family history project lends itself easily to this writing trick: Choose anything—and I mean anything—on your outline—perhaps one of your favorite unearthed ancestor stories—and decide to begin to flesh it out in narrative form right now—today. Is the anecdote about Uncle Albert losing his false teeth in the Christmas Jell-O salad a family story that makes you laugh every time you think about it? Then why not go ahead and write it out? Are you incredibly excited about your Civil War colonel ancestor you researched? Write about him. It will energize you, I promise. The act of writing in itself will get your prose juices going and help you start getting it all down on paper.

Ready, Set, Write Something

Let's try it. Choose one of your favorite interviews on your outline, find your transcripts of it, then sharpen your favorite pencil.

➤ Mark up the transcripts, underlining what you think is worthy of keeping and crossing out what you think needs to go.

➤ Sit down in front of your computer or with your family history journal and rewrite the best parts of the interview into a piece of prose worthy of your family history.

➤ What form should you use? Will it be in conversation form, as in "An oral history conversation with Aunt Edna"? Or will you take the best remembrances from your elderly relatives and make them into separate profiles for each ancestor remembered? Or both?

> ### A Relatively Good Idea
>
> A good way to flesh out your work without feeling any pressure is to work inside your outline. Under the outline entry "Cousin Bernie's Mustache Tale," try writing out the story. Afterward, if you don't like it, it's easier to delete since it's only part of your rough outline. But if you like it, keep it. By doing this, your outline will grow and grow until it's time to cut and paste the best of your work onto a blank page and begin your real writing.

Gagging the Internal Nitpicker

I can hear that nasty internal nitpicker now. It's grousing in your ear that you're not up to the task, that you can't write that outline, choose the right stories, and certainly not write them vividly enough to make them as exciting and interesting as you think they are.

Recognize these other internal nitpicker favorites?

➤ "I'm great at the research, but I may not be as good at the writing."

➤ "Mrs. Thistlebutt, my eighth-grade English teacher, was right. I'm awful at grammar and spelling, so how can I expect to ever write well enough to write a book?"

➤ "Everything I write seems good when I write it, but later I can see just how bad it really is."

➤ "I'll never get all of this in an interesting order. There's just too much."

Hushing the internal nitpicker may no longer be enough. You may have to gag that loudmouth. Ignore any inner voices that make you doubt yourself. No one feels confident starting a new project, especially a big one. Again, keeping the faith is the answer. Trust. Keep working on your outline as you begin to write parts of the whole, and believe that you'll be able to do what it takes to get it on paper. Small steps, remember, are the key.

Time and Place, Revisited

Since it's so important for your writing process, now is a good time to check up on whether you've chosen your special time and place. Have you figured out where and when your creative juices are at their juiciest? If not, now is the time to do so. Why not take an inventory? In your journal, begin to jot down when you notice you are at your best.

Whenever you spend time writing during the next month, write down this information in the margin of the piece you're writing:

➤ When you wrote it (time of day)

➤ Where you wrote it

➤ How long you worked on it

➤ What music was playing

➤ Who was around (or not around) when you wrote it

If you faithfully note these circumstances, you'll soon understand your best writing ambiance and gravitate toward it. As you begin to write in earnest, you'll notice a big jump in creativity, without doubt.

Avoiding Muddle in the Middle

It's easy to see a book as a beginning, middle, and end. The beginning and end are short; the middle is long and formidable, a place to get bogged down easily. This isn't going to happen to you, of course. Keep stoking your outline, adding brainstorms and flurries of writing, and you probably won't have any middle muddle.

Let's explore a few ways to keep you going just in case you feel a little muddled. And let's throw in a few things you should keep in mind as you hit the middle.

The Art of Transition

Remember the last book you read that you couldn't put down? Remember the last one that you *could* put down and did? There was a reason, beyond content, that kept you reading one and allowed you to quit the other. That reason is the quality of the *transitions*. In any story, one thing follows another for a logical purpose. But if you don't learn the art of keeping the reader's eye flowing into the next paragraph, you'll be defeating that purpose.

This goes triple for a topic that has lots of parts like a family history. How do you make that leap from Great-great-grandpa Jeb the farmer to Great-Aunt Lulu the flapper? Ah, there's the art. Some people know how to do this naturally, but for the rest of us who would like a few tips, here we go.

There are several types of transitions you might use:

➤ **Conjunction transitions.** This is a matter of syntax and style. Your tenth-grade grammar teacher would probably tell you this was a no-no, but starting sentences and paragraphs with "and," "but," and "however," automatically keeps your reader reading.

➤ **Time passages.** Using something as simple as "Forty years before …" reminds your reader of the connection of the current anecdote to the past.

➤ **Question-posing.** A question at the end of a paragraph, a chapter, or a section will always keep your reader's interest.

The Write Word

A **transition** is a word, phrase, or idea that connects one part of writing to another, be it sentence, paragraph, or chapter.

Ready, Set, Write Something

Okay, time to write something again. This time, choose an ancestor at random from your outline, one whose research offers more information than anecdotes. Take the list of information and attempt to write a short profile, writing as vividly as you can with what you have.

Do you like what you wrote? Did it energize you? Remember, it's just a first draft, but let the energy you received from it inspire you to work again tomorrow on making it even better.

After you've written, reconsider its place in your outline. Where in your book's middle do you have this placed? Should it be moved to another place?

Checking Back with Your Format

And that brings us to your format. As you begin to write and work with your outline, you should continue to check back with your format to keep focused.

Are you staying true to your format? Does your outline reflect that order? If not, as you write your profiles, you can begin to manipulate your outline to make it happen.

Is your format a pictorial history? Then you will attempt to match your prose to the pictures you will be showing. Is your format family journalism? Then you will want to make sure you are planning ways to include other family members in writing articles about your family.

While there is no right or wrong way to create your family history format, your choice often suggests a certain logic in how it might be told.

Ready, Set, Write Something

Time to write something again to keep you energized. This time, don't look at your outline. Think of your favorite oral family history anecdote. If you've written notes about it in your family history journal, turn to them and use them to write the story as fully as you can. Then, go back and check where you have placed the story in your outline to see if it's still a good fit.

➤ Why is this our favorite family anecdote?

➤ Is this the favorite anecdote of other family members?

➤ Would this make a good opening to the book?

A Few Middle Muddle Ideas

Sometimes youneed a break from your outline and from your middle muddle. One way to keep writing and yet disconnect from the looming project you're creating is to write by free association.

Of course, your best form of free association can still be tied to your family history project. That way, anything you write is raw material you can plug into your family history work somewhere. That's the upside of letting yourself go a little to write on one of these topics for sheer pleasure.

Consider opening your journal, choosing one of the following topics and letting something from your research or your own memory work come into your consciousness, down into your fingers, and onto the blank pages of your family history journal. Which of these topics conjures something write-worthy?

➤ Parents and children

➤ Sisters and brothers

➤ Family secrets

➤ Family crises

➤ Family turning points

➤ Your strangest relative

➤ War stories

➤ Strange old social customs

➤ Grannies' lives

➤ All in the genes—family talents and traits

➤ Warm childhood memories

➤ Your favorite research moments

➤ Life in another century

A Few More Middle Muddle Ideas

Sometimes a bit of unusual thinking can bring up some fun family topics to write about and perhaps include in your middle. Here are some examples:

➤ **Distinctive family looks.** Does your father's side of the family have a set of ears that would make Dumbo proud? Have you noticed that half your relatives are left-handed or have a "Roman" nose? Have you seen yourself in some of those old family photos?

> **Deep Thought**
>
> *What are your favorite stories from your research? What do you think they say about you and your view of your family after all this work? Consider using these favorites in a special way in your outline and throughout your book. This is one way to make this special for yourself while also respecting your audience.*

➤ **World history shaping your family's destiny.** Did one event in world history affect your family forever? Wouldn't that be an interesting topic to comment on for your family history? For instance, if my great-grandfather's first wife had not died of what was probably a strain of the Spanish flu epidemic in the early 1900s, he would never have married my grandmother and none of my side of the family, including me, would exist today. Do you see research evidence of such momentous moments in your family's history? Think how interesting such comments might be for your reader if you are able to express them on paper.

➤ **Defining objects.** The things we buy often live on much longer than we do, hence, the heirloom. Do you have any objects in your house or in any of your relatives' houses that hold stories of your family through their very existence? A grandfather clock? A blue glass brought over from the Old Country? A musket? A locket? What stories do they tell you?

➤ **A cue from the Kennedys.** Thinking generationally is fun. How did all the Great Depression cousins fare? Or those baby boomers? Like the famous Kennedy family, most of us have lots and lots of cousins who have interesting and/or unusual life stories to tell, and we are all connected to them because we are all of the same generation. If you think of your family by generations, you might enjoy a page or two about generations instead of one after another individual ancestors' lives.

A Relatively Good Idea

Now is a good time to review your writing warm-ups in Chapter 18, "Telling Your Own Stories," to make sure you are using what you've learned about narrative elements.

'Riting Reminder

Is it time to manipulate your outline a little? Take a good look at it. If you were going to move one thing, what would it be? Why are you moving it? Why not?

Ready, Set, Write Something

Time to write again. After allowing yourself to daydream a bit from the preceding list, choose one of the topics, and imagine the telling in your family history journal. After you've written it, look back at your outline.

Do you feel good about what you wrote? Where might you use this new piece of prose?

A Jumpstart Trick for Tomorrow

Another problem writers gripe about is time wasted trying to get up to speed each time they start a new writing session, even when they are deeply and successfully into a project.

One time-honored trick to get you jumpstarted each time you sit down to write is something you do at the previous session. When you're ready to quit for the day, stop your work in the middle of something—or better yet, start a new section or thought that you wanted to pursue the next time. Whether it's stopping something old or starting something new, just stop the middle of it. You'll be surprised how your mind engages quicker when it sees that you're in the middle of a thought you already know how to finish. You'll be surprised at how that will propel you into new work with ease.

Eyes Too Big for Your Stomach

As you write, turning your research into prose on the page, you will begin to notice weak areas in your work. Is it your writing or is it your genealogical research? Should you delete this information? Or must you use every last scrap of your research because, doggone it, you worked hard to get it?

Your first inclination will be to use everything you've worked hard to acquire in your genealogical work. But some information will be better left out. What reasons could there be for not using a piece of research? Here are a few:

➤ **The information is "iffy."** It hasn't been verified to your satisfaction. Cousin Bernie gave you a pile of facts about the branch of the family who moved to Alaska, and you found very little to corroborate his story. Do you still want to use it? If so, you might mention its source as in, "Cousin Bernie Lipshultz unearthed some information about Geraldine Lipshultz Schmoe's son Harvey who purportedly moved to Alaska to make his fortune. Although unverified, Bernie's information is interesting. It seems that Harvey …"

➤ **The information is offensive to some living family member.** We'll discuss self-censorship more in the next section, but this is a very real problem you may have to face. Is the subject matter important enough in the saga of your family to include it even though it will upset a portion of your family, or could it be deleted without causing a ripple?

In the chapters ahead, you will learn all sorts of editing skills, and one of those will be how to evaluate what needs rewriting, what needs editing, and what needs to be discarded. For now, keep writing.

Ready, Set, First Draft

Within the next few weeks and months, if you put all the ideas and exercises into action, you will very soon have what any writer would consider a first draft. You have been faithful to your ever-evolving outline, and you've been true to your ever-creative format choice. You begin to notice a book taking shape.

When that happens, then it's time for you to ungag that nitpicker, teach it some manners, and call it your inner editor. That is the overriding topic of the remaining chapters in this book, and it will be what makes that first draft a final draft you can be proud to call your own.

Progress Report

How's the writing going? Can you see the direction in which you're headed? Are you following your outline? Remember that you can write whatever profile, anecdote, or interesting tidbit you want to, whenever you want to as you start, but as soon as you have half your outline roughed out, you should begin to write the rest in order. Why? It will help you get a feeling of continuity, and it will force you to practice the art of transition between each point on your outline and your format. That's when your writing project will begin to look, sound, and feel like a book to you, and you'll know you are on your way to your first-draft manuscript.

And when you have your first-draft manuscript in hand, that's when you need to turn the page and apply all the editing ideas waiting in the next chapter.

The Least You Need to Know

➤ Your outline will continue to change until the end.

➤ The way to start writing is to write anything.

➤ Learning how to craft transitions is pivotal to creating a book-length manuscript.

➤ Your inner editor should be gagged while you are writing creatively.

Part 6

Making Your Writing Sing

You've done it! You have a full manuscript of your family history. Congratulations are in order.

But wait. What about rewriting and editing? You want to make sure that what you publish won't embarrass you by looking amateurish, right? This section tackles the rewriting and editing segments of your book-length project, giving tips to help you massage your work into its best shape. In fact, it even makes a case for rewriting being more fun than first-draft writing (which most experienced writers find to be true). You'll learn how to make your words sound and look as professional as possible. Then, when you feel your manuscript finally "sings," you'll learn ways to see it in printed form once and for all.

Chapter 25

Mistakes You Won't Make

In This Chapter

➤ Avoiding the common mistakes of book-length projects

➤ Learning the secret of great writing

➤ Avoiding freezing when writing your ending

➤ Learning when to listen to your internal nitpicker

In a huge project like yours, the average writer has an obstacle course of mistakes to avoid, but you aren't going to fall for any of them. Why? Because I'm going to warn you about a baker's dozen of them, that's why. Forewarned is forearmed, as they say.

Now is a great time to check these mental stumbling blocks before we move on to the next level of the writing process. What's the next level? It's called "rewriting"—how to polish your work to a high sheen and what parts of your work you must grit your teeth and toss. In fact, let's start there. The first mistake in the rewriting process you will avoid will be the one that keeps you from throwing your work away.

Not Knowing When to Toss Your Work

"Throw my work away? After all my blood, sweat, and tears? I thought this book's author was a little off, but now I know she's loopy!"

Admit it. That's what you were thinking after reading the heading for this section. It sounds crazy, I know. How do you perfect your work by throwing chunks of it away?

The answer may surprise you if you're new to this level of writing. Making your writing perfect often means doing just that—throwing chunks of it away. Never fear, however. The chunks you throw away *need* to be thrown away. They are not up to your high standards, not worthy of being called a creation of your fertile mind. And when you throw the weaker parts out, in their stead, you will probably write something derived from your experience that will surprise even you with its brilliance.

So, yes, you will be deleting parts of your work. No, you won't mind doing it when you see the leaps in writing excellence you'll experience.

Believing Great Writers Don't Rewrite

Most of us have had an experience with English composition classes. Miss Thistle-butt, Mrs. Birdsong, and a host of other well-meaning English teachers were happy to get us to finish our essays, much less make us turn around and rewrite them. Actually, I can't fault such teachers. After I taught a few of these classes myself, I found out the writing teacher's weary secret: If you make your students rewrite, you have to re-read. Try doing that 20 times a semester with 40 students and still have a life. Good writing is hard work and so is teaching good writing, mostly due to the inescapable fact that good writing relies on rewriting in order to be good.

Too often, that integral part of "real" writing was not impressed upon us as we went about our school days studying great writing by the likes of Mark Twain, Louisa Mae Alcott, J.D. Salinger, Winston Churchill, and Emily Dickinson. That omission led us to believe that these incredible words and thoughts sprang whole from these super-humans. Such writers and thinkers were different from us. They picked up their pens and poured forth perfect, memorable, life-changing sentences without any effort.

I was in the second year of an American Literature Master's degree, slowly beginning to dream of writing for a living, before it hit me that my studies were teaching me to idolize these geniuses, to set them on pedestals of academia's making. The effect was a subtly implied attitude: To aspire to create any work of my own was ridiculous. Either you are a genius or you aren't. Either it comes easily or it doesn't come at all. Case closed.

Then, as I began to write professionally and understand the writing process, a light came on in my head. Even geniuses rethought, revised, rearranged, and rewrote their writing for the best effect, just as I did. In fact, they were probably geniuses at rewriting, if geniuses they were.

Rewriting is the secret of most great writing. As a wildly popular commercial novelist once put it, "I'm a good writer, but I'm a great rewriter." And that's the wonderful thing about writing. You have time to make it what you want it to be. Because the truth is, only when you finally get it down on paper do you really see what you were trying to write in the first place. Only then can you really get cooking.

That brings us to the next mistake you won't make.

Believing First Drafts Are Finished Drafts

There's a famous *Paris Review* quote that writers tell each other as they struggle with the revision part of writing. Upon being asked about rewriting, Ernest Hemingway claimed to have rewritten the last page of *Farewell to Arms* 39 times. What was the problem? "Getting the words right."

This may be the deadliest mistake most inexperienced writers make: to think their first-draft thoughts are finished ones, and that their stories are well-told with just one try. You may *tell* a story orally once and feel you've done it perfectly, but the spoken word is ephemeral, gone with the breath used to speak it. The next time you tell it, you may fail miserably and be mighty glad it wasn't recorded. But your *written* word will be there for decades to come, speaking of you and your literary finesse. You have to make it as perfect as possible. That means taking at least as long as the average experienced writer, if not as long as Hemingway.

Not Listening to Your Internal Nitpicker

> **Deep Thought**
>
> *Who was the great writer you first thought wrote perfectly without rewriting? Why? Your answer should be revealing.*

For several chapters now, I've told you to hush your internal nitpicker and when that wouldn't work, to gag the ornery inner voice. Now, though, the nitpicker becomes respectable. Now that ornery nitpicker becomes the inner editor, a worthy writing companion who isn't second-guessing your first draft choices but keeping you from making embarrassing gaffes in coherence, usage, spelling, and grammar. Your nitpicker can make your writing look like you know what you are doing. It can make your form invisible—no glitches to take a reader's notice—so your reader can see nothing but your content. After all this work, the last thing you want your readers to fixate upon is a grammar goof in Aunt Edna's interview instead of her terrific family anecdote.

If you don't ungag your internal nitpicker and invite that inner voice into your revision process, your writing will be the poorer for it. And Aunt Edna will never let you hear the end of it.

Forgetting the Fine Line Between Fact and Fiction

Several pages back, I spent a whole chapter on something called "imagining the telling." I made a big deal about attempting to give life to some of your ancestors' stories that were worthy of adding to your family history yet suffered from a lack of existing information beyond some interesting basics. I gave you ideas about how to enliven the tale to make your ancestors spring off the page without disrespecting their memory by creating caricatures of them. With a little imagined dialogue inspired by real-life events, you could also give your reader a break from paragraph after paragraph of text. These are all good things.

But as with most things in life, good things can turn sour when overdone. A lot of self-restraint is in order when it comes to what television shows call "re-creation" of events. You may have no other choice but to put words in an ancestor's mouth. You do have a choice as to how many words those are, and what kinds of words they are. The fine line between fact and fiction should always be uppermost in your mind when you begin to imagine any telling. Did you write 10 lines of dialogue? Cut them down to five. Did you write five? Cut them down to two.

A Relatively Good Idea

Plan to do a check of dialogue throughout your manuscript. Go through the pages that have dialogue, and be deadly objective. Ask yourself, "Do I really need this piece of made-up dialogue? Does it advance the story and augment the ancestor's character? Is it based in truth?"

You may enjoy the idea of writing a fact-based fictionalized version of some of these incredible stories (and what better place for fiction ideas than these great stories?), but such writing belongs in another book, not this one. Remember that your family history volume is a book devoted to preserving the past for the future. Your mission is to make it readable, yes, but also to always keep an air of truth about these important anecdotes. Yielding to the temptation to go overboard in your imagining will only hurt your whole effort. So be creative, but be ever-watchful.

Choose six lines of dialogue you've created for one of your ancestors and write them down. Now force yourself to cut them to only three lines. Why did you make the choices you made? Want to reevaluate? If so, remember, you still can't have more than three lines. The fewer words you put into your ancestors' mouths, the more power they'll have, and the truer quality they'll convey.

Forgetting Your Audience

That brings us again to your audience. You are writing, remember, for your ancestors, your descendants, and along the way, your living relatives, too, as each of them grows in their interest of their own roots. Don't miss the chance to be your family's hero. Continue to imagine all these family members, living, dead, and yet-to-be, in a big living room, a long Thanksgiving dinner table, or a cozy auditorium, listening to you read your work to them.

Being Self-Indulgent

You have worked hard. You think your part of the story and the way your effort at researching these people has uncovered your own family truths adds to the family history saga. Should you add yourself into your family history?

I discussed this in an earlier chapter, if you recall. You should be careful of interjecting yourself too much or else your family history volume will become a memoir. A memoir is a good thing, but don't get the two formats confused, because what may seem okay in a memoir will come across as deeply self-indulgent in a family history.

Again, it's all a matter of moderation. If your cross-country trek following the family pioneers' migration through the Cumberland Gap to their new life in the American wilderness tells as much about the brave ancestral pioneers as your air-conditioned, cruise-control vacation, then it will make a welcome addition to your family history book. If every chapter holds such a story about your research, however, then your reader may lose interest.

Of course, if you have a dozen of these stories and you can link them all to interesting profiles of each relative you were researching, then you have a wholly different book. Anyone reading it will be expecting to learn about your personal experiences, which will not seem self-indulgent at all. Keep focused on your original family history intent, and pursue other options after the fact.

Forgetting That Less Is More

A first draft is fat and in dire need of lots of trimming. Like a Thanksgiving turkey, the best parts are the juicy parts, not the clumps of fat that are thrown down the garbage disposer (although your dog might disagree).

Remember as you cut that you are not cutting for cutting's sake. You are cutting to find the juicy parts trapped inside all that undesirable fat. Knowing what to throw away marks you as a good editor. Remembering that less is more while you rewrite marks you as a serious, efficient writer.

A Relatively Good Idea

Revisit your 2,500/500 warm-up exercise from Chapter 18, "Telling Your Own Stories," to remind yourself how vibrant your writing becomes when you pare down your work to the one perfect verb or the exact, brilliant adjective. Try the exercise with something "finished" in your first draft.

Straying from Your Outline

You've been working on that outline from the moment you began to write. Actually, that's not true. You've been working on that outline since long before you began to write. The idea of straying from it probably seems silly, considering all the emphasis I've put on its power to keep you focused and professional.

Yet it's so easy to digress by adding information that may not be on the outline but surely is in your pile of research. Don't let yourself stray too far, but if you do catch yourself straying and you like the direction you're taking, then incorporate it into your outline. (But you knew I was going to say that, didn't you?)

Being Flexible About Your Format

At this point, you probably feel that your chosen format is set in stone, and you wouldn't think of making drastic changes to it. But interestingly, that very mindset may work against your creativity as you rewrite. You may look at large chunks of your format and wonder if they work exactly the way you intended.

The mistake many writers make is not thinking creatively about everything until the last minute. Your format is just as malleable as your outline. Be open-minded, ready for any flashes of creativity that may add another dimension to your format. Yes, you need to stay within your basic format, but no, you do not have parameters beyond that outside border of the format idea. Revise it during the rewriting process in any way that enhances your work.

In other words, your words, sentences, and paragraphs aren't the only things that need your rewriting efforts. You need to be able to step back and reevaluate your work as a whole as well, being confident you are up to any challenges. (Because you are. Don't you dare let your own format or outline intimidate you.)

Stumbling at the Start

Beginnings are so hard to get "just right," to quote Goldilocks. They are so important that I spent a whole chapter offering suggestions on creative ways to approach your opening. During your revision process, you should reevaluate the hook you attempted.

Any runner knows that stumbling at the starting blocks will probably affect the whole race. Don't let that happen to you. Take the time to experiment with other hook ideas from Chapter 23, "How to Start," before settling on a final choice. In fact, let's do it now. Ask yourself some serious questions about the opening you chose. Answer these questions in your journal:

➤ What kind of opening did you choose to write?

➤ Does it offer a good taste of the rest of your family history?

➤ Does it still grab you like it did when you first wrote it? Why or why not?

➤ Why did you choose this one over all the other ideas offered in Chapter 23?

➤ Do you consider it one of your best pieces of writing?

Now, take three other ideas from Chapter 23 that appealed to you and try them now. Finished? Then it's time to sit back and evaluate which of the four attempts you think is the strongest and the one that will ensure no stumbles at the start of your book.

Being Reference Sloppy

What do I mean by "reference sloppy"? You have just spent months, maybe years piling up research on your family's genealogy. You've taken great care to notice sloppy research, knowing inexact genealogical work could mean that ancestors are gone forever and someone else's ancestors are taking their place. You were certain not to make such a detrimental blunder. And yet, when it comes to setting down lots of specific information in print, the task of being meticulous can be a little overwhelming.

To make matters worse, many family history projects are self-published or published by a press whose sole editorial input may be to check your spelling—if you're lucky.

Your research will be your responsibility, no matter how you publish your work. A good example of the problem is the article in my home county history that listed my grandmother's given name wrong. My generation will know the mistake; the next generation will not. Oral correction will only last as long as the last person who remembers to pass on the knowledge of the goof. The printed goof is eternal.

What to do? Your last responsibility, after you feel you've written and revised your family history to perfection, is to double-check, then triple-check, your names, dates, facts, and figures, for any typos or misprints. Don't let your eyes glaze over any errors. Be meticulous.

A Relatively Good Idea

Why not bring in another family member to help double-check your facts and figures? Bribe them if you must, but don't let any of your hard work be printed inaccurately.

Forgetting to Make Form Work for You

In an episodic work such as your family history, the reader needs a little help keeping up with your subject matter. Even writers could use help. Creating chapters is certainly the most common solution. Using your outline to create chapters for your work is one of the first ways to make form work for you. After that, outlines only do so much; in the "trenches" of that text-heavy page, any writer can benefit from some organizational help and eye-breaks. That's where other forms can work for you.

Paragraphing, subheads, and page breaks can be your family history helpers in keeping everything straight inside your chapters, making your text "easy on the eyes," and moving your work along efficiently. Make friends with all three.

Paragraphing

"Graphs," as journalists and editors call them, should be a matter of form as well as content. There are two reasons to use paragraphs—to designate the beginning of a new idea and to give the reader's eyes a break. In English class, you learned that every paragraph should have a topic sentence and contain a whole thought. You moved on to a new paragraph only when you finished that thought and not before.

With apologies to the Miss Thistlebutts of our school days, that "ain't necessarily so." It's a good rule to begin with, but in a book-length work, sometimes your thought goes on and on and on. When it does, your reader needs a break. Think about how you feel when you try to read a whole page that's one long block of prose without a visual break of any kind. It looks like a big gray blob, doesn't it? You'll notice that your eyes get a little tired of it after a while.

Subheads

Another even better example of using form to help your reader find their way through all your material is subheads. Your book is falling nicely into your chosen format, but inside each of the chapters, you can keep your reader's eye traveling along by using subheads.

For instance, let's say that you have a chapter on the Schmoe family branch that lived in St. Louis in the 1920s. That clan had five outstanding ancestor stories as well as lots of facts and figures on other relatives. Two of those were Lois Lane Schmoe and your Great Aunt Lula Schmoe, the flapper who wrote your grandmother that letter you found in the trunk during Chapter 1. Each of these five stories should have subheads inside the St. Louis Schmoe's chapter. They might look something like this:

Lois Lane Schmoe, Independent Woman

(her summary profile)

Lois's Many Husbands

(interesting information uncovered about her three marriages)

Lois's Many Family Tree Branches

(detailed information created by her three different sets of offspring)

Next would be Great Aunt Lula. You could easily segue into her story by using another subhead or two:

Lula, the Flapper

(her profile introduction)

Her Bathtub Gin Days and Her Farmer Girl Past

(juicy extra information you uncovered)

Use your outline to create interesting subheads that will catch the eye of your reader, as well as help them get the most out of your work.

Page Breaks

Sometimes, inside your subheads, you'll need some further organization. Let's say you are writing along about Cousin Augustus the Army Scout. You have told about his early life, and now you need segue into his Army accomplishments. These are both subheads. But under the Army accomplishments, you have two very distinct anecdotes you've uncovered, one about his receiving a commendation and another about how he met his wife on one of his Army scouting expeditions. How do you handle this without having to use another subhead? (You can get too overloaded with subheads, you know.)

You use a page break. Just leave three or four spaces between the ending of one of those stories and the beginning of the other. Be sure to use a good transition sentence to link them, such as "Another escapade the family has retold through the years landed him a wife …"

Note that the word "Another" links the second story to the first. We'll discuss form more in Chapter 28, "Publish or Perish?" but these three ways of dividing and controlling your work will help you as you rewrite. The alternative is page after page after page of unbroken prose, and that only works for novels and other extended narratives.

Freezing in the End

How do you end something as grand as your family history? Often, writers end well, then keep writing for another paragraph or page. Will you be able to tell if this is the case with your own writing? Will you be able to find that "true" ending? Or have you yet to truly end, freezing over the prospect of pulling all this work into some monumental summary of your whole family's saga.

Don't sweat it. You have time. One of the best ways to unfreeze your attempts at ending your long work is to remember that a short ending is the best ending. Of course, to get a vivid, short ending, you will probably have to write lots and lots of words and cut most of them out. But that's called rewriting. It's also the way to say exactly what you want to say in the exact way you want to say it. Surely that sentiment expresses how you feel about the ending of your family history.

So relax. Think of your audience again. Think of all the months and years your work has been spread over. Think of the people who will read your work after you are long gone. What would you want to say to these family readers who have now come to know the same ancestors you've come to know so well? How would you sum up your relationship with these people from the past through whom you (and all your living kin) exist? Write your thoughts, then write more of your thoughts, and enjoy this last moment of expression. No need for freezing. This is your moment.

Progress Report

How many of these "mistakes you won't make" had you considered before seeing this list? Are there others I haven't listed? By now, you may have your own list and know what mistakes you're prone to committing. If you could name one, what would it be? Write it and any others that come to mind in your journal, and consider what you should do to circumvent them, as well as those I've discussed.

The Least You Need to Know

➤ Many common mistakes are made in large book projects.

➤ Every writer rewrites, especially the great ones.

➤ Use form to help create reading ease.

Chapter 26

Writing Is Rewriting

In This Chapter

➤ The joys of rewriting

➤ The dead give-aways of an inexperienced writer

➤ Relaxing in your rewriting

➤ Using rewriting self-tests

"How do I know what I think, until I see what I say?"

—E.M. Forster

Rewriting, rereading, reviewing, rethinking, repairing, restructuring, reevaluating, tightening, rearranging, sharpening, deleting, transposing, expanding, condensing, pruning, polishing, perfecting.

Rewriting is all of these and more. It is the secret weapon of the professional writer, the thing that separates the real writers from the "wannabes," the acceptable writing from the incredible writing, the average book from the page-turner. Rewriting is revision. This is the moment in your writing in which you can make your work sing.

And the secret weapon's best-kept secret is … fun.

Free from That Whirling Dervish

If you take your writing seriously (and considering your subject matter, of course you do), then the purpose of your writing is to communicate with your special group of readers. The revision part of your writing project ensures that you bridge the gap between you and your readers in the clearest possible way. You are no longer being rushed by the whirling dervish of your creativity to get it all down on paper. Now you can work at leisure to make it perfect.

Most writers soon learn the joy of the rewriting part of the writing process. This is your chance to make the words and ideas match the images in your head. You don't have to keep worrying about all that still remains to be written or how it should be organized and expressed. Now you can play around with ways to make what you have better.

There's another little secret about revision that few people learn in the classroom. In the act of playing with your first draft, you will think of new ideas, fresh inspirations, that can make all the difference in your final draft. It is a leap that happens when a person continues to make writing a part of everyday life. One day, you notice that you like the whole process; in fact, you embrace it. And it's a good thing, because the first draft is only the very beginning of that process. As Gertrude Stein once put it, "To write is to write is to write is to write is to write is to write." A writer's reaction to rewriting is usually the tip-off to how experienced the writer is.

Dead Give-Aways

What are other ways to tell the experienced writer from the inexperienced writer? There are some dead give-aways that you want to avoid at all costs. After all this work, you want to look great on paper. Here are a few of the amateur mistakes you could make.

Quantity vs. Quality

"Inside every fat book there's a thin book trying to get out."

—Unknown

Experienced writers expect to always write too long in their first drafts. After all, it's better to have too much to work with than too little, and they know that revising saves them from their first-draft wordiness.

But an inexperienced writer looks at the volume of his or her output and puffs up with pride. Quantity is quality to this unenlightened writer, who perhaps is not so much a writer, but a typist. (That reminds me of the classic literary put-down. Supposedly, a famous literary writer said, on seeing the 1,000-page book published by a rival, "It was certainly an impressive display of typing.")

A well-written, short sentence beats a long, boring one any day. Respecting the reader is part of the battle. Respecting your own potential to make the leap from typist to writer is another.

Being Married to First-Draft Words

An inexperienced writer becomes wedded to the first way he or she expresses a thought and cannot see other ways of saying the same thing better. The experienced writer knows that first draft words are more about the rush of ideas than the beauty of choosing exactly the right words to express the ideas. You know you're on your way when you look forward to transforming your rough, first-draft efforts into your second draft and beyond. This truth leads into the next give-away.

'Riting Reminder

What's the difference between writing too long and writing just right? Like Goldilocks, you'll know, with some experience.

Inability to Switch Hats

There are several hats hanging on the hat rack in your office. One is labeled "First Draft Whiz," another is labeled "First Class Rewriter," and another is labeled "Inner Editor." An essential part of the experienced writer's process in producing a piece of work ready for publication is to know when to switch hats and how to switch hats without stripping mental and psychological gears (if you'll allow a mixed metaphor).

There is no way to teach you how to make these transitions, except by telling you that you must allow a "cooling off" period to readjust your perspective. Doing so, and doing so with aplomb and determination, is a sign of an experienced, above-average writer at work.

Hyper-Sensitivity to Constructive Criticism

"I love the way you've structured this, but the opening just doesn't grab me like it should, especially considering you open with your ancestor who out-wrestled Davy Crockett."

Ouch. Someone you trusted to give you feedback didn't love every word exactly the way you first wrote it. How do you respond? If you respond by recoiling, grabbing the manuscript out of the reader's hand while screaming, "You are not worthy of experiencing the glory of my work I have deigned to share with you!" then you have a little problem with criticism.

Most writers wouldn't respond that extremely (even if we felt like doing so), but each and every one of us takes a big risk when we ask someone to give feedback on our

349

A Relatively Good Idea

Between your first draft and your second draft, you should have a cooling-off period to let your mind shift gears. How long do you wait? No less than a week and perhaps more like a month. If you allow this time away from your work, you'll pick it up and see it with new eyes.

writing. You know you've taken the leap from inexperienced writer to experienced writer when you can hear constructive criticism constructively. Instead of flinching and feeling self-defensive, you recognize partial truths in the suggestions the reader is offering.

Inability to Discern Good vs. Bad Feedback

This is the second technique in accepting constructive criticism. What happens if you ask another reader to give you feedback on the same piece of work? Surprise, surprise, the second reader thought it was quite good just the way it is. Which do you believe? You want to listen to the one who believes you are the best writer this side of the closest library. But after the compliment's glow wears off, which feedback is really the most helpful?

The danger here lies in putting too much stock in either response. One way has you foregoing any rewrite, the other has you rewriting perhaps more than needed. The answer is to learn how to discern the quality of your own drafts, knowing that with each draft you can come closer to your real potential and the potential of your subject matter. This takes the right amount of self-confidence—not too much, not too little.

Such self-awareness may take years to achieve, but you can start now by taking everyone's feedback, not as either drivel or gospel, but as "take-or-leave" information. Take a little—the parts that sound right to you, and leave the rest. No piece of writing exists that couldn't be improved by more rewriting. As Hemingway reportedly expressed the tension, a writer "abandons" a book finally rather than even finishing it. The postscript to this, of course, is learning how to let go, which brings us to the next point.

Not Knowing When to Quit

The date: Twenty years in the future.

The situation: You are still working on your family history project, now in its 79th revision.

What is wrong with that picture? You can't let go. You don't have the confidence to give your work to "the world." You don't know when to quit. Anyone can continue forever trying to make a project perfect, anyone anal retentive, that is. The experienced writer knows, like Hemingway did, that nothing is ever finished, it's abandoned. The experienced writer is prepared to accept when the time seems right to abandon a work, while the average amateur writer ignores it again and again. The result? Your descendents finding the revised-to-death, yellowed manuscript in your belongings after you're gone, instead of the finished, published product you so wanted to leave them.

Overuse of the Exclamation Point!

If you ask any editor who reads hundreds of assorted manuscripts on a monthly basis what would be the quickest editorial tip-off that a work under consideration is amateurish, a good answer would be the over-use of exclamation points. One on a page may be passable in the context of dialogue; two is questionable in any context; three exclamation points and the manuscript is probably half-way to the "circular file" under the editor's desk that gets emptied every night. Overuse of the exclamation point shows a lack of confidence in the power of one's writing to convey the right excitement. Lack of confidence is a sign of amateurism, which is the last thing you want your writing to exude.

An editor once told me that all writers, at the beginning of their careers, should be given three, and only three, exclamation points to be used any time and any place they want to. I think that says it all. (For now.)

Your Writing Process

The writing *process* is a term bandied around by writers. But what exactly does it mean? Essentially, it is a term used to describe all the stages a writer must go through to get an idea on the page in its finished form.

Actually, when you think about the term "writing process"—which every writer seems to spend a great deal of time analyzing (e.g., "My process seems to be writing my best after my fifth pot of coffee at the kitchen table after watching *The Late, Late Show*")—you might be reminded of what working with words on a computer is popularly called—*word processing*. If you think about it like that, writing is processing words. The art of writing is processing the right ones. Rewriting is processing the words over and over until they are just right. To accept this about the writing life is to make the leap between average, first-draft thinking and expert "wordsmithing."

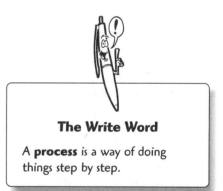

The Write Word

A **process** is a way of doing things step by step.

When put in outline form (which you are now trained to do, of course), the writing process that helps create your family history book might look a little like this:

1. Idea
2. Research

3. Free-form outlining

4. First-draft dreaming

5. First-draft writing

6. Cooling off

7. First rewrite

8. Second rewrite

9. Third rewrite

10. Fourth rewrite

11. Rewrite, rewrite, rewrite

   ...

38. Rewrite, rewrite, rewrite

39. Editing

40. Finished manuscript

And that's just to get to your own "finished" manuscript. Next is outside editing, which almost always calls for another rewrite or two. If that explanation didn't put you off writing forever, then you will do just fine as the experienced writer you aspire to be.

Cooling Off

We've gone through the first five steps of the writing process in the pages preceding this chapter. Cooling off deserves your attention now. You should take this part of the process seriously. You've been in the heat of the whirling, creative dervish as you created that first draft. You need to give yourself time to cool down, not just for your body temperature and blood pressure, but for your mind to make the transition from creative demon to practical, logical rewriter.

This can only happen if you let your work go for a while. You literally need to set the manuscript on the far corner of your desk and leave it alone. Don't fiddle with the format or the outline or even the boxes of research material that have been piled up around you for all these months. You need to close the door and go outside and look at the real world for a change.

Worried about withdrawal? That might happen, but you'll live. Then, when you've cooled down, your gears have had time to switch, your perspective has changed, and you'll find you can look at your work in a different way. You'll know the feeling. That's the time, and not before, to begin the revision stage of your work.

New Eyes, Revise

Got your new eyes focused? Now you're ready to revise. I suggest you take your manuscript (including the last revision of your outline), and sit in a different place than the desk and chair you used to write the manuscript. Again, this will help the feeling "switching hats" from writer to rewriter.

Relaxing in Rewriting

The trick to rewriting is to relax into it. To *revise* takes a calm, objective, fix-it mindset. As mentioned, the optimal word in this transition into rewriting is "fun." Now you are no longer in the grips of getting it down on paper. You now have it on paper. The goal at this point is to make what's down on paper very, very clear, very interesting, very well-written, and very good.

You have all the time in the world for this. You are going to be a wordsmith now, molding, shaping, and massaging your own words until you know you have crafted your best effort.

Relax. Have a good time. This is part of being a writer, a writer with something important to convey and the power to convey it superbly.

The Write Word

To **revise** means to look at and alter over again in order to correct or improve.

Some Self-Tests

Any rewriter, however relaxed, needs some touchstones, some self-tests to help in making that glorious rush of first draft words worthy of the printed page. Here's a short list of things to watch for as you sculpt your work into its finished form.

Redundancy

Redundancy consists of superfluous words that haunt everyone's first drafts—words that can be eliminated without changing the meaning.

➤ **Example:** Granny was known to be a drill sergeant-type mother.
➤ **Better:** Granny was a drill sergeant-like mother.
➤ **Better yet:** As a mother, Granny was a drill sergeant.

➤ **Example:** He strode onto the ship in a confident manner.
➤ **Better:** He strode onto the ship confidently.
➤ **Better yet:** He strode confidently onto the ship.

Be watchful for redundant phrases that spread like germs through our writing, such as, "appears to be," "like a," "seems to be," "as though," and "like that of." These are like "hem-haws" in your writing, as if you aren't confident in your statement enough to go ahead and make the statement. And we are all guilty of using them. The trick is to see them and delete them.

➤ **Example:** The musket made a sound like that of a thunderbolt.

➤ **Better:** The musket made a sound like a thunderbolt.

➤ **Better yet:** The musket sounded like a thunderbolt.

You can write a list of these useless phrases yourself. Here's a partial list to help you begin thinking about them in your own writing. All the following words could be replaced with "because," "about," or "now" without spilling a drop of meaning:

➤ Based on the fact that

➤ Inasmuch as

➤ In light of the fact that

➤ In the neighborhood of

➤ A number of

➤ In regard to

➤ On account of the fact that

➤ In the matter of

➤ At this point in time

➤ At the present writing

'Riting Reminder

Obfuscation is a big word with a big, negative effect on writing. It means "to make obscure," and it is every writer's enemy.

If some of these phrases remind you of the language of lawyers, there's a reason. Our legal language suggests that the more stuffy words you throw at a problem, the better the chance you'll have of matters being handled properly. Your research into old wills and estate documents certainly underscores the conviction that legal talk has always leaned toward the wordy and stuffy. *Obfuscation* is the result, not clarity. A lawyer friend of mine once admitted she had once thought about being a writer, but realized after years of writing legal documents, she had utterly lost the ability to write any other way than in fuzzy legalese.

In the same way, a person intimidated by having to write an important piece of prose, even a letter, for instance, can reach for these kinds of "sentence-stuffers" in an attempt to sound serious and formal, i.e., "smart." Don't let this be you. The idea of great rewriting is to create the most vivid image with the fewest words.

Sentence Stuffers

For the worst "sentence-stuffer" offenders, there are some fancy names. Let's look at several of them that you'll want to keep in mind.

Tautology is the word used for saying the same thing that's already been said. It's taking the "hem-haws" previously mentioned and spreading them to otherwise normal words.

➤ **Example:** Joe Schmoe the actor was very popular with his fans.

➤ **Better:** Joe Schmoe the actor was very popular.

➤ **Example:** The reason it happened was because our ancestor lived a long life.

➤ **Better:** The reason it happened was our ancestor lived a long life.

➤ **Better yet:** Why did it happen? Our ancestor lived a long life.

Other tautological terms to watch for are …

➤ Free gift

➤ False facts

➤ Few in number

➤ Usual custom

➤ In addition to … they also

➤ At a distance of

As you become aware of the problem, you'll see your own tautology well. By the way, some tautology has become part of our language and are now considered figures of speech, such as "kith and kin," "way and means," and "safe and sound."

Ah, but wait, there's more. *Verbosity* is wordiness in writing. It is the stepchild of *purple prose*. One familiar form of it is *circumlocution,* which is saying a simple thing the long way around. If this is your first draft's big problem, it's hard to cure—hard but not impossible. Revising wordiness takes a different frame of mind, and a willingness to start over in creating a sentence. My best suggestion on how to do that would be to reread the examples I gave above, and study why the "better yet" examples are truly better than the other two.

So, can you express why the "better yet" examples below are better than the other two examples? When you can actually see why, then you will do it in your own writing naturally. Take a look at each of the following examples, and see if you can put your finger on what was changed for the "better yet" example.

➤ **Example:** He strode onto the ship in a confident manner.

➤ **Better:** He strode onto the ship confidently.

➤ **Better yet:** He strode confidently onto the ship.

➤ **Example:** Granny was known to be a drill sergeant-type mother.

➤ **Better:** Granny was a drill sergeant-like mother.

➤ **Better yet:** As a mother, Granny was a drill sergeant.

➤ **Example:** The musket made a sound like that of a thunderbolt.

➤ **Better:** The musket made a sound like a thunderbolt.

➤ **Better yet:** The musket sounded like a thunderbolt.

So, we've covered wordiness and repetition, but just as taking too long to express something is a danger, you also need to guard against including things that don't support your subject. When you're cooking you know that there's a definite possibility of, let's say, adding too much salt. You can overpower a perfectly good meal with a seasoning. For writers, this translates into *prolixity*.

Prolixity is using more words than are necessary. This is a good one for the family history writer. It's like the vacation slide show analogy used in Chapter 23, "How to Start." You don't really need to see six slides of Uncle Harry standing by a cactus to know that Harry visited the desert and saw a cactus. You don't really need to know that Great Uncle Leroy was born on a Tuesday at 8:01 A.M. and weighed 8 lbs. 2 oz. Only if something is noteworthy about the information, such as the fact that he weighed 13 lbs. 11 oz., for instance and held the record for big babies, or that Tuesday was the day World War I was declared, would there be any interesting reason to mention such information.

Be careful here. You have so much research to use that sometimes you can't see the forest for all those information-laden trees, while striving to pack all the good stuff into that first draft. Rewriting will help you reevaluate which trees are the ones to keep and which are just blocking the view.

While you're looking at all the things not to do, it is crucial that you maintain *importance of subject.* Did you know that you are telling your reader what is important in many different ways beyond coming right out and saying so? Here are the ways you do it:

➤ **Length.** The longer you write about a topic, the more important your reader will think the topic is in the grand scheme of your book.

➤ **Position.** Where you place an item or a thought also indicates how important it is. Put it at the beginning of a paragraph, and you are signaling the reader to take notice. Put it at the end of a paragraph, and the reader won't consider it worthy of anything more than a quick read-through. But, interestingly enough, when it comes to sentences, whatever is at the end of the sentence gets the most attention.

➤ **Repetition.** Okay, so I said earlier that repetition in the form of redundancy isn't a very good thing. File this under that old adage that says you can break the rules after you have mastered them. Of course, this definition of repetition is unlike our explanation of repeating an idea through superfluous words. In this context, repetition of ideas through chosen words and phrases emphasizes whatever you want the reader to remember.

For instance, what if you wanted your reader to remember Cousin Silas, who was the progenitor of your branch of the family tree, as well as a War of 1812 veteran. You might write the point several times, giving the information in various ways (but always adding a little the reader didn't know before), and even refer to him in other places.

Before you get discouraged, remember that we're covering all of these "don'ts" so that your story can shine. Another "don't" to watch for is the use of *deflators*. These are bad habits that take the power from your writing. The exclamation point as we discussed earlier in this chapter is one of them. Using an exclamation point anywhere but in dialogue on the printed page calls so much attention to itself that the reader won't see anything else.

Passive voice is another deflater. Can you pick out your passive voice? Usually, the dead give-away is the presence of "was," "were," "are," or "is" directly preceding an otherwise very active verb. Example: "The train was seen by the crowd," instead of "The crowd saw the train."

Get it? The answer is to flip the sentence around, and delete the "auxiliary verbs." (That's the fancy name for those passive verbs, "was," "were," "are, and "is.") Voilà, your sentence is now powerful and active again.

Take a look at these examples:

➤ **Passive:** Joe Schmoe the politician was jeered by the hometown crowds after the scandal. (Notice the "was" in front of the usually vibrant verb "jeered"?)

➤ **Active:** The hometown crowd jeered Joe Schmoe the politician after the scandal.

'Riting Reminder

Every writer has a few style mistakes they commit over and over. What are yours? Once you are aware of them, then, and only then, can you avoid them.

Deep Thought

How can the very instrument of communication, which creates bridges of understanding and enlightenment, also create a word-laced smoke screen? The power of the printed word cannot be overstated, be it positive or negative power.

Finally, you will have to exercise great restraint to not use *hyperbole* when writing about anything as important and personal as your own genealogy. Why, your great-granny had to be the best cook in the county! Your great-grandpa was the best banjo player in the state! We all know that! Seriously, be careful here. If your point is humor, exaggeration is an ally. If your point is truth, then hyperbole will throw your work into question. (And obviously, adding an exclamation point in the mix does nothing but make the problem worse!!!)

The Write Word

Hyperbole is an extravagant exaggeration of a thought or fact.

Your Ancestors' Eyes

Want another helpful hint for keeping on track with your revisions? This one is a special one meant only for those who hazard writing a family history. While you work, as you are striving to make each ancestor's story shine as bright as their lives, you should keep a mental image of your ancestors' eyes upon you. Never forget that you are the reason these people will be remembered. That should keep you honest, shouldn't it?

Beginning, Middle, End

A good way to end a discussion on the revision process is to suggest you step back from the words. You've been zooming in; now zoom out. Look at the entire project. Turn your pair of new eyes to your outline and behold your work as a whole. See it as a beginning, a middle, and an end. Do the three tie together well? We've discussed the beginning at length; we've discussed ways not to get muddled in the middle, but how about that ending?

You may have attempted an ending to that first draft, but odds are during revision you will chuck it, or, at the very least, rewrite the dickens out of it. Why? The ending is your last chance to make the entire project connect. Everyone likes to feel that any book they decide to read will end with things wrapped up nicely, and your family is no exception. How will you do that?

This may sound strange, but you do that with what you already have. In other words, a good ending just summarizes in a fresh way what has already been said. Maybe along the way you've found the perfect statement by an ancestor that sums everything up for you, and you know instinctively that you will use it for your ending.

Maybe you've had some new thoughts about family yourself, about how this genealogical work has changed you, and while you've hinted at these thoughts in the preface or an open letter at the beginning of the book, now you explain your feelings in detail.

Those ideas are just two ways to end. However you do it, you'll know when you've done it right. Rewriting allows you the time to reflect on just how to make it right. Take advantage of the time to ponder your special ending for your special project.

Who Do You Trust? (Feedback)

Now is the time, ready or not, for someone to read the whole manuscript and give you feedback. This may sound scary. If not done right, you could lose a friend over it, not to mention your own self-image. But as mentioned, this is one of the differences between the inexperienced writer and the experienced writer (see Chapter 25). It also calls on your own self-confidence and skills of discernment in finding the right person and trusting his or her judgment.

The best advice I can give you is to choose wisely. Don't choose someone who loves to criticize for criticism's sake. On the other hand, don't choose someone who is worried about your feelings to the point that honesty will be a problem. Don't choose someone who has no interest in your subject (unless you're willing to pay for their work—then go right ahead). Bottom line? Choose well.

> ### *Deep Thought*
>
> *When you picture an ancestor's eyes on your work, what ancestor do they belong to? Why do you think that ancestor is the special one?*

Progress Report

Do you have your "First Class Rewriter" hat on? How does it fit? Name the one item from all the topics covered that should be your first rewriting priority. Name a second one. Now, pick up that manuscript, and begin this next step in your writing process—your rewrite. It's a deeply important step. Remember to take your time and enjoy shaping your rough words into pearls of your very best writing.

> ### The Least You Need to Know
>
> ➤ Rewriting can actually be fun.
>
> ➤ You can avoid the dead give-aways of an inexperienced writer.
>
> ➤ Keeping your ancestors in mind as you write is a helpful way to stay on track.
>
> ➤ Choosing a trusted reader for feedback is crucial.

Chapter 27

Editing— Unleashing Your Internal Nitpicker

> **In This Chapter**
>
> ➤ Valuing your inner writer/editor's voice
>
> ➤ Avoiding the mark of an amateur—grammar, spelling, and usage mistakes
>
> ➤ How to choose a trusted proofreader and why

After a few revisions of your work, your thoughts will turn to worrying about a more mundane, yet deeply important, part of the writing process—catching your writing "goofs." You'll begin to feel an urge to edit as you revise, and that's a good thing, because the more times you check your work—it's called proofreading—the smaller chance you'll have of being very embarrassed by mistakes in your final version.

Such mistakes will mark your work, fair or not, as amateurish, and the reader will discount *all* your work at the first sight of glaring grammatical errors, not just your skill with the English language. In other words, conveying your message in correct English may be the last hurdle for you, but it's the first hurdle between your work and your reader.

So, it's time to not only unleash your internal nitpicker, but to invite that picky inner voice into your work with open arms.

Your Internal Nitpicker (a.k.a. Your Inner Editor)

Your internal nitpicker is worried about the nits, the small things—grammar, spelling, punctuation, usage—that are really not that small. Your internal nitpicker can make your writing look as expert as its content. After all this work, you certainly don't want your readers to see anything but the printed family heritage you've crafted for them. So, now is the time to give that ornery "presence" your ear. Your internal nitpicker, now more respectfully referred to as your inner editor, can save the day.

You Are the Camera

Here's a handy image. Imagine that you've given your inner editor a fancy camera with a big lens, the kind that can zoom in. Several things will happen:

1. The first thing your inner editor does is stand back, zooming out as far as possible, in order to gain a new perspective on all your work. How's the cohesiveness of thought, it asks. How does everything fit together?

2. Then, your inner editor jiggles the zoom a little and zooms it the opposite way—closer to look at specific chunks of the work. In the context of each chapter, are there sentences that serve no purpose? Paragraphs that could be cut out and never missed? Could a profile of an ancestor be more interesting if some of the "dead wood" information was taken out? (Remember our 2,500/500 exercise in Chapter 18?)

3. Your persnickety inner editor now leans near, zooming in ever nearer. What phrases and words are poorly thought-out? What poor sentence structure can be remodeled? What can be changed to make images more meaningful?

4. Your picky inner editor sets the zoom lens on macro the setting and looks at punctuation, at the quality of word choice, at grammar goofs, and bad usage, being picayune enough to make any persnickety English teacher deliriously happy. (And trust me, you'll be deliriously happy, too, when your dear inner editor makes you look like a pro on the page.)

Then, after all that zooming out and zooming in, working to get all those words picture-perfect, your inner editor finally snaps that shutter.

You have work to do before that shutter can be snapped. We can't cover all your editorial needs in this chapter, nor will we try. I've listed some good editing resources in the appendixes. Most writers of book-length works refer to the *Chicago Manual of Style* on matters that can't be settled with common sense and common knowledge. So, I refer you there, too. But we can hit some highlights for your special project. Let's go over some tips for your inner editor to use during all that zooming.

A Relatively Good Idea

Another useful image for your inner editor is a magnifying glass. Choose any paragraph at random in your work. Imagine you are using a magnifying glass set to the "nth" degree as you read it. Odds are you'll find at least three things that need attention. What are they?

Nits Needing Picked Checklist—Going Beyond Spellcheck

Far too many writers give their work what I consider a "kiss and a promise" when it comes to editorial work. This is especially true of writers who consider themselves adept with grammar, spelling, and usage. Sometimes all such writers will do is hit the spellcheck button on their computer software and call the work "edited."

But every writer can benefit from a refresher on the basics, the "usual suspects" as well as the more sneaky offenders. This goes double if you don't have a professional editor to back you up on your family history writing.

The Usual Suspects

If you call yourself a writer, you know most of these guys very well, having heard about them in every writing class you ever had. Ready for a little review?

Sentence Fragments

This is a sentence:

> He rode his horse into town, too late to save the day.

This is a sentence followed by a sentence fragment:

> He rode his horse into town. Too late to save the day.

Unless you're writing advertising copy, or know exactly what you are doing, every one of your sentences needs a subject and a verb. Do that and you won't have any sentence fragments.

Run-On Sentences

Run-on sentences are exactly what they sound like. They are two sentences put together without any punctuation. Such as:

> He rode his horse into town he was too late to save the day.

Comma Splices

"Splice" is a nice image, one of putting two things together that don't really match. Comma splices are two stand-alone sentences put together with only a comma between them. Such as …

> He rode his horse into town, he was too late to save the day.

Double Negatives

This is a very incorrect double negative sentence:

He doesn't never wear underwear when he's riding a horse.

These are two single negative sentences that are both correct:

He doesn't wear underwear.

He never wears underwear.

Double negatives—the use of two negatives (no, never, not, isn't, aren't, don't, doesn't) in the same sentence—is a no-no.

Those Hidden Homonyms

Especially tricky to a computer's spellchecker are the words it will miss because it doesn't have your brain to understand the word's context. The best examples of this are *homonyms*. If you type in a homonym of the word intended in your first draft haste, no spellchecker is going to catch it. After all, you probably spelled it correctly.

Homonyms are tricky with or without a computer. Often, a writer sees his/her own prose the way it should be and not the way it is. Homonyms are one of the best grammatical reasons to have someone else proofread your work.

The Write Word

Homonyms are words that sound alike but have different meanings, such as "your" and "you're"; "their," "there," and "they're"; "it's" and "its"; and "write" and "right."

Misspellings and Spellcheck

Whether you are a great speller or whether you are "spelling-challenged," like many great writers of the past, you probably rely far too much on your computer's spellcheck program. This is a big mistake, and everybody makes it at one time or another, writers and nonwriters alike.

For example, a friend of mine was sending a query letter to an editor whose last name was Kenny. She ran her spellcheck, and punched the automatic replace button, which means she didn't check the spelling one word at a time. Being the trusting (and lazy) soul she is, she then popped the letter in the mail without another glance. But when she got home, a look at the letter open on her screen made her heart jump into her throat. She saw that the spellcheck had changed Kenny to Kinky. As you might imagine, she never heard from that editor.

Use your software's spellcheck like any other computer program—as a tool. Use it, but have patience. Check each questionable spelling one at a time so you can see any suggested changes and be the one to decide to make any "kinky" changes, instead of your mindless computer.

Common Wrong Word Goofs

We all know these offenders. They can bring our writing to a dead stop while we sit, chew the end of our pencils or tap our fingers on our keyboards racking our brains for which word is right. Should you use "bad" or "badly"? "Affect" or "effect"? "Farther" or "further"? "Insure" or "ensure"? "Imply" or "infer"? Instead of offering you a list of these and the long explanations needed about which is which, I refer you to one of the excellent English language usage books in the appendixes. (Besides, you need an exhaustive one on your shelf as a self-respecting, serious writer.)

'Riting Reminder

Most of today's computer word processing software offers a "grammar check" as well as a spellcheck. As with spellcheck, such a feature is best used a tool to help you find potential problems. Never let the computer decide your changes, but certainly take advantage of its "inner editor."

Why the cop-out? Our language is a living language and what was incorrect yesterday is fully accepted today. For example, one of the quickest recent turn-arounds in a new word's acceptance is the "verbing" of the noun "impact" now being used as by everybody on the planet, as in "The future of the Internet is impacted by the acceptance of the masses." A blink of an eye ago, the only thing that was impacted was a wisdom tooth. However, would I suggest you use that word in print? No, not yet. Our language can decide tomorrow that this very same word is passé. Also, a family history project looks backward instead of attempting to sound modern. The last bastion of good usage is still the printed word in book form. Be safe. If you feel the urge to use any word that seems en vogue, resist. You'll thank me when you see your work in print.

It's/Its

Every writer has one misuse goof that drives her batty. Mine is the usage goof that seems to be everywhere, on menus, on book jackets, even on expensive billboards. What is it? It's the difference between "it's" and "its." So let me pick this nit right now. The two words are as different as apples and oranges; one is a contraction, one is a possessive pronoun. Which is which? We confuse these two spellings because of logic. As you know, the normal way to show possession is to use an apostrophe and an "s" after a word, as in "Joe Schmoe's son." So surely, we think, confusing the English language with a logical thing, that same rule would hold over with a pronoun, too. But in this case, it doesn't. Exactly the opposite is true. No possessive pronoun uses an apostrophe. Contractions, however, *always* use apostrophes. Therefore "it's" is always a contraction and can be split into two words—"it" and "is," or "it" and "has."

So, forget logic and try pure memory. Remind yourself that English is a very mixed-up language and remember this: When faced with whether you use "it's" or "its" in your sentence, ask yourself, does the word split into "it" and "is," or "it" and "has"? Then it's a contraction and should be spelled with an apostrophe. If it does not, then it's the possessive pronoun "its." Did that help? Ah, our mixed-up language. It's a language with its own logic. (See the difference in the "it's and "its" in that sentence? Now you get it, right?) Thank you for listening.

Exclamation Point Use

No need to go into this again. See Chapter 26, "Writing Is Rewriting," for my ranting on this mistake. Suffice it to say, you should never use them in serious work meant for print, unless it's in the context of dialogue. Understand?

Passive Voice

As mentioned in Chapter 26, there are a few times when passive voice is preferable to active voice, but the times are rare. (Did you notice the passive voice in that sentence?) Sometimes, the effect is just what you want, but as in most things that take skill, you need to know the rules before you break them.

> **Passive voice:** "There are many tales told about the War Between the States."

> **Active voice:** "Many people tell tales about the War Between the States."

Almost always, active voice is a shorter, cleaner, and less boring way to write a sentence. My advice to you is to go through your manuscript and circle every sentence you've begun with "There are" and "It is" and see if you can write it without those words. My guess is that you can and you'll like the sentences better after the rewrite.

Comma Goofs

To comma or not to comma. That is the question.

An editor once advised me, "When in doubt, leave it out." The editor happened to be a newspaper editor. A book editor would say something more to the effect, "Check the *Chicago Manual of Style*." Newspapers will err on the side of saving space, and their style manual reflects that. Since you are writing a book, you should err on the side of clarity.

My rule for you (beyond checking the new style and grammar book you bought) is to go easy on commas, especially being wary of comma splices. When in doubt, however, read the sentence aloud and listen for the natural pauses in the sentences. (And if you're wondering whether you put commas at the end of series, go right ahead since this is a book project. "Hot dogs, cold beer, apple pie, and Mom were what Uncle Bud believed in.")

A Few More Usual Goofs

The list goes on. Whole books are filled with explanations of more "usual suspects" in the grammar-goof line-up, so we can't cover them all in one chapter. But here are a few of the more troublesome goofs every writer should know as they rewrite. Read about them in one of the editing books listed in the appendixes before rushing into revision. You'll be glad you did.

➤ Misplaced modifiers

➤ Dangling modifiers

➤ Verb tense goofs

➤ Quotation mark goofs

➤ Semicolon and colon goofs

➤ The difference between "who" and "whom"

➤ Capitalization goofs

➤ Mixed metaphors

Some Unusual Suspects

There are also some *un*usual suspects to keep in mind once you get those rowdy usual suspects corralled. Here are a few of the worst repeat offenders.

How Many "That's" You Got?

A good rule of thumb is to cut all the "that's" from your sentences that you can. (Read that sentence and cut out the second "that" and you'll see it isn't needed.) Your writing will flow more smoothly, especially when a sentence had more than one "that."

The same can be true of substituting "that" for "which." Check this out:

➤ Great-Aunt Lulu's will mentioned part ownership in a speak-easy, which no longer existed, of course.

➤ Great-Aunt Lulu's will mentioned part ownership in a speak-easy that no longer existed, of course.

Which of these two uses sounds more natural? Trust your ear, and try to be consistent.

Million-Dollar Words

Do you lean toward using big words of the quadruple-syllable kind? You might find comfort in them, but your reader will probably lose interest after the first dozen or so. Clarity is your goal. Big words can create fuzziness, calling attention to themselves instead of what they are explaining. One big word might actually add to your clarity if it is the exact word you need for the situation, but unless you happen to be writing to scholars or the literati, don't make a habit of using them. Always keep your audience's understanding in mind. Don't write down to your audience, of course. Uncle Fred is smarter than he looks. Just don't show off your way with a thesaurus.

The Write Word

Clichés are worn out, prepackaged phrases whose time has come and gone.

Surprisingly enough, when you question your word choice, you may find yourself thinking about your writing in a whole new way. And how can that be bad for your efforts?

Clichés Ain't What They Used to Be

Checking your work for *clichés* is a good idea if you aspire to better-than-average writing form. You may not think you use them much, but clichés, by their nature are insidious little things that trip out of our mouths and fingers with surprising ease, often beyond our control. We can't help ourselves. They're everywhere.

But the experienced writer strives to create an image that's fresh, instead of familiar. The only exception to that role for your family history project would be your interviews. Let Crazy Aunt Edna use all the clichés she wants, since you're quoting her. That paints an accurate picture of Edna, as well as seeming fresh because it is creating characterization.

For the bulk of your own prose, though, ferret out those clichés and rewrite them for imagination as well as clarity. The best way to sidestep our language's cliché parade of our language is to see a few of them as you begin your editing, to help sharpen your eyes. Here's a selected list to help the cause.

➤ High as a kite

➤ Happy as a clam

➤ Easy as taking candy from a baby

➤ History tells us

➤ Generous to a fault

➤ In dire need

➤ So sharp you could cut it with a knife

➤ Easy as pie

➤ Easy as ABC

➤ Easy as falling off a log

➤ Leaves much to be desired

➤ In this day and age

➤ Faster than greased lightning

➤ Home is where the heart is

➤ Best thing since sliced bread

There are hundreds of these, if not thousands, in our repertoire. You could come up with another dozen like this list in minutes. Just keep your cliché radar turned on as you edit, and you'll save your writing from sounding like everyone else's, which is what clichés do to our language. Going for the surprise image is a lot for more fun for the writer and the reader.

You try it. Change the following clichés to something fresh and interesting:

➤ As sharp _____

➤ Faster than _____

➤ Easy as _____

➤ High as _____

➤ Home is where _____

➤ The best thing since _____

_____

However, there is one caveat to remember. Okay, I admit it. Sometimes nothing works as good as a good cliché. Now and then, offering a reader a familiar image as comfortable as an old shoe is what the doctor ordered. (If you don't mix your metaphors as I just did.) As in most things, moderation is the key. A cliché used once in a blue moon works fine; a page with six clichés on it is far and away beyond the limit, way over the line. (You get the idea.)

'Riting Reminder

Every writer should have on their shelves a good thesaurus, an up-to-date grammar and style primer, and a fat modern dictionary.

To Whom Do You Refer?

Are your pronouns clearly referenced and nicely in agreement? What I refer to here is a very common grammatical goof that the writer can't see clearly, but will quickly confuse a reader. In oral tellings, and in our conversation, we are much more tolerant of unclear references. Someone might say, "He threw the ball to him." We'd ask, "Who threw the ball to whom?" and quickly get a response. "Ed, that's who. Ed threw the ball to Joe."

But in writing, we can't afford to be so slack. Any sentence that begins with a pronoun should definitely be checked. This goes for phrases that include pronouns, too. Keep in mind that your reader will automatically search for the nearest noun for a pronoun reference. You better make it the right one. Highlight any pronouns and search for the words they refer to. Then ask yourself, "Am I being clear?"

Example: He smacked the judge with a smile on his face.

Notice the two pronouns, "he and his." our first thought is that the latter "his" should refer to the first "he," right? But between the two is the noun, "judge." So, you tell me, did he smack the judge happily or did he smack the judge who was being a little too happy for his liking? You get the idea. Follow the pronouns; check the nearest nouns, and then rewrite if you suddenly realize you've given the wrong impression.

More Nits Needing Picked—Playing in the Professional/Amateur

After you have a handle on the basic stuff, then there are some more writing nits that should be picked, things that fall between revision and editing. Thinking about these aspects now as you finish your project can only strengthen your work. It's like being entered in a professional/amateur golf tournament. Which would you rather be? The pro who is confidently hitting it down the fairway time after time or the amateur tagalong, who only hopes the ball stays out of the rough? These extra thoughts can help make you look like a pro even if you feel like an amateur. Take advantage of the extra attention that can make you look good.

Checking That Outline

Your brainstorm outline that started out so messy has probably gone through two dozen revisions by the time you have a first draft. Now is the time to check your outline one last time for coherence and cohesiveness. Everything in your manuscript should match your outline. Change your outline yet again if you must, but make your writing match your thinking, which is essentially what your outline has been.

This also gives you one last chance to rethink the position of each ancestral piece of your family history puzzle, just in case some pieces suddenly seem better suited for a different place in your family history tale. Your next step will be to create a table of contents from your outline, another reason to have a clean outline.

Digressions Aside

Speaking of your outline, two sneaky writing goofs can hide from your outline's clarity of thought. First, unneeded *digressions* in your prose are poison to your cohesive effort. In Chapter 26, we talked about how position and length of a piece of ancestral information can give it a feeling of importance, whether we mean to create that feeling or not. How important is the piece to the whole book? That's what we need to ask ourselves, and plan its position and length accordingly.

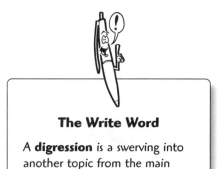

The Write Word

A **digression** is a swerving into another topic from the main topic.

Let's say you have piles of information on Aunt Sadie, but have found only a small portion interesting. If you plop the whole load into the book anyway because it took lots of your precious time to uncover it all, you do a disservice to Sadie, to the quality of the book, and to your readers. You may think you are honoring your blood, sweat, and tears by using everything you researched indiscriminately, but the opposite is the result. You should write your Aunt Sadie entry short and sweet, and move on. If you feel it's important even though it's short, then you position it more prominently.

Digressions about Aunt Sadie that are extremely boring and serve no narrative purpose should be cut out. Let's say you have her handwritten will. To include its entire contents might not be a bad idea if she died in 1823, thereby making it an interesting artifact. (Even then your reader and your book might be better served with an edited version offering just the good parts to get a flavor of the times.) But let's say Sadie died in 1941. Adding the whole boring legal document to your family history would be a very bad idea. Use your common sense and offer only the most memorable and important parts of your research.

Abrupt Turns

This is a poor cousin to digressions. In a perfect writing world, you should see warning flags of this problem in your outline, but sometimes we look at something so long, we can't see it anymore. The real question to ask as you edit is, "Do my stories all hold together?" This is partly a matter of good transition, getting from one idea and one ancestor to another without getting off track, but an abrupt turn can bury even a fantastic transition.

Sometimes, though, we become so caught up in our writing that we don't notice we've taken one of these abrupt turns in our narrative flow. You are writing a section about your ancestor who was a Rough Rider and suddenly you find yourself going off into a story about his brother who fell out of an apple tree when they were kids and was never the same again. That would be an abrupt turn without some transition, some connection to the brother's experience as a Rough Rider. What might that be? If the brother was a better rider than the future Rough Rider, yet never rode a horse again after the fall, that's a good reason to mention the apple tree incident, for instance.

A truly abrupt turn would be writing about the family tree branch who farmed in Delaware during the Harrison administration and then suddenly discussing the state of politics in this country during your childhood. Make every effort to use your common sense in piecing your work together logically. That's what your outline can and should do for your work. Check now for any digressions or abrupt turns in prose that might have slipped through the cracks of your well-built outline.

Narrative Elements

Now is the time to review the narrative elements from an editorial nitpicking angle. Remember them?

➤ Description

➤ Characterization

➤ Dialogue

➤ Tense

➤ Tone

➤ Dramatic tension

➤ Point of view

For your editorial efforts, I suggest going over these with a nitpicker's eye, double-checking them against all you learned about each one in Chapter 18's exercises. Pay special attention to point of view shifts, tense changes, and dialogue. Remember that imagined dialogue should be very sparse to work in a family history.

Who Do You Trust? (Proofreader)

Your last act as the writer of your family history is to find someone who will willingly read the whole thing to back up your own editorial efforts. Who do you know that has a gift for the minutiae of the English language? Who has experience as a proofreader? Bribe, pay, or cajole this person into doing a once-over clean-up. It can be the same person you asked to help you with your revision work, but it is probably best if it is someone else. Revising and editing are two different talents and two different duties that need to be performed on any manuscript aspiring to the professional feel and look of a printed publication.

Ask this person to mark up a copy of your manuscript with a pencil. Offer your style manuals if need be. Buy this person lunch, dinner, or whatever it takes. If you can afford it, definitely pay them for their time. As for time, make sure to give them lots of it, but suggest a time you must have it back.

Then, once their work is done and you have it back in your hands, take your *Chicago Manual of Style,* sit down with the proofed manuscript and see if you agree with the changes. Thank heaven you had such good help and input the corrections into your special labor of love.

Progress Report

Incredible. You've turned your family history into a full-length manuscript. You've revised it, you've edited it, and you've proofed it. Take the finished product in hand, read it through one last, glorious time, and smile. The feeling is great. Now is the time to begin planning your next step. Will you publish it professionally? Will you publish it at home? Will you take advantage of new options for the growing number of genealogists like yourself? Jot down your thoughts.

A Relatively Good Idea

Asking someone to proofread your manuscript is a tall order that comes with a deep responsibility. Be very careful if you choose to ask a friend or acquaintance instead of a professional. Where to find a pro? Ask your genealogical society, your librarian or even your relatives. Whatever style manual your proofreader chooses to use, ask for consistency.

The Least You Need to Know

➤ Your inner editor's voice should be heeded during this important part of the writer's process.

➤ Common grammar, spelling, and usage mistakes hinder readability and marks the writer as an amateur.

➤ Software spellchecks/grammar checks are only tools, not editors.

➤ The choice of a trusted proofreader is essential to your book project.

Chapter 28

Publish or Perish?

In This Chapter

➤ The first steps to publishing your work

➤ Why you want to create a book

➤ How to make it look like a book

➤ Creative ways to see your work in print

Now what? You've written your family history, you've revised it, you've edited it, you've enlisted family and friends alike to help you make everything as perfect as you can get it.

Do you want to publish it? Will you perish if you don't see it somehow in book form?

Don't fret. There is an interesting array of options today to see your work looking better than you could ever imagine it could. This can be true whether you sell it to a commercial publisher or spend a couple of hundred dollars at the local copy store to make your work look positively grand for your audience—your nearest and dearest relatives.

But whatever finished form it takes, we've been calling your work a book, and rightfully so. Let's explore the types of publications to determine which might be right for your specific project.

Why a Book Endures and Why You Care

This is one of those accepted truths that everybody knows and nobody expresses. You know it innately or you would not have done this mammoth amount of work. Now is the time to understand its impetus for your work. What is "it"?

The Write Word

A **book** is a set of written, printed, or blank sheets bound together into a volume or simply a long, printed composition of ideas.

I'm talking about the sociological value we place on *books*.

More than most other forms of expression, books endure. They endure because we care that they endure. Human knowledge is so valued that we even care about knowledge we personally don't care much about—if it happens to be in print. Books are special. Who among us can throw a book in the trash, even when it's about something we have no interest in at all? We don't throw books away, we give them away. Have you noticed? I once saw a person tear a section out of a book and was surprised at my own horrified reaction—and I didn't even like the book. My reaction wasn't for that book, it was for any—and every—book.

Your family history is special. By its very nature, it demands to endure. That was your plan all along. Your very first thought of this project (and ours—see Chapter 3, "What Kind of Family History Should You Write?") was probably an image of holding your finished book in your hands. You visualized it on your family members' bookshelves for decades, perhaps centuries, into the future. Your work should endure, and more than any other time in history, you have options on how to have your finished product put into printed form.

What Is Your True Purpose?

All your work has a designated audience, doesn't it? Before you began, you knew that your family was the target audience and you were writing it for yourself and for your relatives. Never forget your true purpose—recording and preserving your family history for your family.

Now that you've finished it, however, do you have other ideas? Did you uncover some historical knowledge so interesting that others beyond your family group might be interested? Perhaps you uncovered diaries, letters, and personal papers that tell an intriguing tale about a time in American history that is rarely discussed. Maybe you have a famous or near-famous ancestor about whom you have something new to say.

You could continue writing your family history by writing one (or more) of these:

➤ A special book exclusively for family and friends?

➤ A publication worthy of historical societies and museums

➤ A manuscript full of historical work that might interest a regional or academic publisher

➤ A manuscript of wide interest you might attempt to sell to a large publisher

Few family history writers will see their work of such wide interest that they find themselves choosing #4. But #1 through #3 are all viable options for your work. You never know. History is important to everyone.

My genealogist brother-in-law put together a short profile of one of his ancestors from years of research and sent it to his far-flung extended family. To his surprise, one of his relatives gave a copy to an archivist at a university library in the Texas county where the ancestor settled. The archivist was interested in my brother-in-law's work because the reasons people came to that particular vicinity in the early 1800s had been debated for years and the profile added "objective contributions to those questions."

Was it professionally published? Not at all. With the help of color copiers, scanners, binding machines, a cover designed by his graphic-designer daughter, and fancy paper, he and his neighborhood copy shop created an "outer package" worthy of its "inner content" and the result was cousins and historical museums alike taking notice.

Genealogy is such a popular hobby today that you never know where your work might take you. Another relative (after indexing every surname in the little book) donated my brother-in-law's printed ancestral profile to the Dallas Public Library's Genealogical section. Later, the powers-that-be mentioned that they might want to submit it to their biannual contest.

Such genealogical "fun" is not that unusual anymore. Contests, fairs, and other competitions to showcase and share genealogical work are happening across the country, and soon you'll have a chance to join in.

A Relatively Good Idea

Do you have a local genealogical society? Does it sponsor any seminars on publishing for its members? If not, might it know of such a seminar in a neighboring city?

Size Doesn't Matter

How long is your work? How long should it be? Did you have a vision of the thickness of your work and are disappointed that you don't have a doorstop-size family tome, after all your effort?

Listen: Size does not matter. Quality does. Whether you take great pains to beautifully bind and give away a family tree branch profile that's 50 pages long, as my brother-in-law did, or you have labored to produce a 500-page manuscript that chronicles a thousand of your closest ancestors, what you have created is unique. In fact, if you choose to create your own desktop-and-copy-shop-published work as my brother-in-law did, you may consider creating separate chunks of your work into separate volumes that work as a set. Again, the only limit is your imagination and your need.

Making It Look Like a Book

You've read lots of books in your life, so you certainly know what a "real" book looks like, don't you? Now that you have a manuscript revised and ready to roll, you'll want to create some additions to make it look like a real book for whatever publishing format you decide on.

Choose any book off your shelf. Open it. The group of pages before you get to the actual body of the book is called "front matter." This usually includes the following:

➤ Title page

➤ Dedication page

➤ Copyright page

➤ Foreword and/or preface

➤ Table of contents page

Do you have a talented family member to help design your cover? Then enlist that artist for the cause. Don't be shy. Graphic designers with computer prowess can work miracles. My niece who was enlisted to design her father's profile cover took a 140-year-old photo smeared with mouse droppings and not only salvaged it, but with her magic made it a vibrant piece of genealogical art.

Does a book cover matter? You can answer that one. You may not want to judge a book by its cover, but it's hard not to, isn't it?

Does Front Matter Matter?

Does front matter matter? Let's answer that with another question: Are you taking your work seriously? Do you want it to be taken seriously by your readers? (Okay, that's two questions. It deserved another.) Creating front matter doesn't take long and doing so will help you feel a healthy sense of respect and closure to this monumental project.

To Foreword or Preface?

The difference between a foreword and a preface you can see in this book, actually. Look in the front matter. A foreword is written by someone else, endorsing your work. A preface is something you write. For me, an interesting image always goes along with the writing of a preface. It's the image of the tired yet exhilarated author leaning back and ruminating on his or her accomplishment. It's what you, the author, want to say to help the reader understand what's to come, what you've learned from the writing of it, and why you want the reader to read the work.

Another type of preface is a prologue. While a preface is more of a rumination after writing the book that's used as an introduction, a prologue has more of a feel of being part of the beginning of the book and usually is paired with an epilogue, which appears at the end of the book. (You may find a prologue/epilogue concept more a match for your work; now is certainly the time to decide.)

Be it preface or prologue/epilogue, the only good writing rule for either is to keep it short, pithy, and full of your own excitement.

Tabling the Contents

You've been working and reworking your personal outline until the very last second of your effort. Now is the time to convert it into your table of contents. This is more than just changing the name at the top of the page from "Outline" to "Table of Contents." You should take time to reevaluate and possibly rename all your chapter titles, your subheadings, and any other elements as they relate to your manuscript. Remember to keep it as simple and as parallel in its construction as you can.

Does End Matter Matter?

Sure it matters. But what is it? Some books have end matter; most don't. You make the decision. Family histories lend themselves to additions, however. Perhaps you want to add a pedigree chart or a family tree chart. Or you'd like to add a map of all your travels or of the different locations of each of your ancestors in the book. Maybe you'd like to add a short bibliography of the works you researched. Or perhaps you uncovered a will or newspaper clipping that begs to be added. You might even want to offer an *index*, which is very helpful for such a work. These are all your decisions. You don't have to include any;

> **Deep Thought**
>
> *There's something magical about a book. Ever wonder why you feel the way you do about books? Why do you love books? Why do you want to write one?*

> **The Write Word**
>
> An **index** is a list in alphabetical order of some specific data in a book, such as names, titles, or key words, and usually is placed at the end of the book.

you may want to include all. You might even want to add a personal "last word," an epilogue, as mentioned.

These are the options for end matter:

➤ Appendixes

➤ Epilogue

➤ Index

➤ Bibliography

Magazine Publishing

Remember those genealogical magazines you studied, and maybe subscribed to, during your genealogical research? They were packed with articles about discoveries in this or that family tree, some you found helpful, some you wouldn't find interesting unless that family tree happened to be yours. But they all have one thing in common. They have all been written by genealogists just like you.

A Relatively Good Idea

Why not create a time line of your ancestors you cover in the book? A time line is different from a pedigree chart since it focuses on the time in history your ancestors lived instead of to which branch of the family each belongs. It's easy to create and is a wonderful visual aid for your readers.

Let me ask you a very good question: What's stopping you from making an article out of a chapter or two of your work about something interesting you uncovered that could be of interest to others on the genealogical trail, and sending it to a magazine for possible publication?

Nothing is stopping you. As with all writing for magazines or journals, you should read several copies of the one you'd like to submit your article to. Then study the masthead, choose an editor—usually an articles editor or the managing editor—write an effective cover letter for your article, and send it in. All you are risking is a rejection slip that usually has nothing to do with you. ("Doesn't fit our needs" on a rejection slip really does mean that it doesn't fit their needs at that time.)

Earlier in this book, we discussed several of the better-known genealogical magazines. For a vast array of such potential publication places, visit your local library, or better yet, your closest genealogical library.

Related Facts

An editor is not always an editor. The editor you need to contact is not always the one you'd suspect from his or her title. Contributing editors, for example, are not really editors. They are regular writers who have been given that honorary title. So be sure to send your query letters to the correct editors—i.e., managing editor, senior editor, or articles editor.

Want to Try the Big-Time?

Think your book manuscript may be something that would interest a "real" publisher? There are few ways to test the waters before you dive into such a big sea. You don't want to waste your time splashing around if the big sea isn't where you should be swimming. If you find this possibility intriguing, do your homework first, and then "play the game" of submissions correctly to lessen your chance of wasting time. Taking the following steps will help your chances of catching an editor's eye.

Check Out Your Competition

Use your library, your bookstore, your computer, and your head to get an educated edge. These four steps will give you a good idea of your chances.

➤ Spend time in the library to see what other types of family histories have been published recently. Check out a few, read them, and compare your work to them.

➤ Talk to the manager of your favorite bookstore. See what sort of books he or she has sold in this genre. Ask for suggestions for comparison. (Remember that most of the "family histories" that are commercially published are more along the lines of memoirs. Evaluate whether your work is closer to a memoir than to a family history.)

➤ Check online for published family histories to compare.

➤ When you do find good examples, check the copyright dates and the publishers. Look up the publishers' addresses in *Literary Marketplace*, *Writer's Digest*, or some similar publications. Write for catalogs and for current editorial staff names.

Writing That Query

After you do all your homework, if you still feel courageous enough to approach a big-time publisher, university press, or regional publisher, then craft a one-page query letter to send to one of the editors you've researched. This is truly testing the waters. How well you write this query is just as important as the content of the book you want to sell them. So take time with it, explaining what makes your family history different from everyone else's. There is an art to a well-written query letter. Many good writing manuals exist that teach this art, along with other skills needed for publishing your work. Your time and money spent buying a good writing manual will be worth it. (See Appendix A, "BookMarks—for Further Reference.")

Self-Publishing

The vast majority of family history writers with a manuscript of any length will find creative ways to get their work published for their special readership. Let's talk about three of the best options.

Desktop Publishing

Today's software options are so varied and easy to use that you—that's right, I said you—can easily transform a "working manuscript" into what anyone might think was, as printers and publishers call it, "camera-ready copy." Most word-processing programs, no matter what kind of computer you are using, offer a choice of professional-looking fonts and the capability to create page headers and footers that mimic the printed page to the letter. In fact, you can even go so far as placing your whole manuscript into a desktop publishing program and actually creating camera-ready copy for a printer. Some of you have these programs as part of your computer setup or you have friends who do. Take advantage of them (the programs, not the friends).

'Riting Reminder

Today's computer scanners enable you to have your cherished photos part of your bound self-published book.

Whether you print out your work on your home laser printer and create your family history volume at your neighborhood copy shop or you are paying a printer to self-publish your book into a beautiful, bound creation, you can save money at the same time you are controlling quality by finding out why they call it "desktop" publishing.

Subsidy Publishing's Good, Bad, and Ugly

Scrawled across seemingly every genealogical Web page and on every page of every genealogical magazine's back pages are advertisements for presses willing to publish your family history book—for a fee. "Subsidy publishing," it's called. As with all things in life, you'll find the good, the bad, and the truly ugly among this motley assembly. How do you choose?

Since this is the option for many family history writers who want their family to have a bound copy of this important, yet specialized work, you need to be careful. I have seen beautifully produced work from what once was called "vanity publishers," and I have seen work to make even a granny turn up her nose.

Here are some questions to ask of the many (and you should research many) publishers you interview for your important project:

1. What is your lowest print run? (The answer may be 250 to 1,000. The fewer books, the higher the cost of printing each.)

2. Who does your artwork, page design, and cover art, and how much extra does it cost? (It should be part of the per-book cost, not a separate expense. Ask to see samples. Ask to have approval control.)

3. Are your offices local? (There's less chance of any shady dealings if you can work with them face-to-face.)

4. Can you give a list of satisfied customers? (Ask for people you can meet, along with the chance to view their recently published books.)

5. How long will it take to see a finished product? (The answer should be in months, not years, with contractual back-up and payment in installments.)

6. Are there contracts involved? (There'd better be.)

Like any good consumer, you will want to do your research, but also rely as much as possible on word-of-mouth. The best endorsement is a friend's endorsement. Ask for recommendations at your local genealogical society, for instance.

Scrapbooks of the Future

Have you noticed? Today's scrapbooks are nothing like the big, bulky, thick-papered things into which we crammed our high school memories for posterity. My sister mailed me my high school scrapbooks recently after finding them in yet another round of cleaning out our childhood home. The pages were yellowed, the ribbon used to bind the scrapbook had all but disintegrated, and something had been nibbling at some of the memorabilia I had glued inside with Elmer's glue 30 years ago. (But that candy valentine heart was so special!)

The same week, I discovered I was living in a whole new scrapbook world when a friend asked me to a "Creative Memories" party in the same tone used for an invitation to a Tupperware party or one of those sexy lingerie parties. (Now there's a concept: "Pass the cookies, please, and also that adorable lace G-string!") Translation: "I am inviting you to my house so you can buy stuff from me." She was my friend, so I went.

What did I see? Since the last time I bought a scrapbook someone must have received their very own box of high school scrapbooks from a family member (or so I've imagined), and were so upset that those treasured mementos entrusted to dime store-quality scrapbooks were in horrid condition, they were moved to action. Perhaps the scrapbooks were discovered the same moment someone invited them to a Tupperware party, but somehow, someway, a new industry was born, and our future mementos need never fear disarray or discoloration—and especially not disintegration—ever again.

Acid-free paper, plastic envelopes for displaying treasured photos, bindings to rival items housed in the Library of Congress—these are just a few of the wonders in scrapbooking today. That's what it's called, by the way: "scrapbooking." And the "parties" have found the interest so high for such quality products for our memorabilia, you can now find these materials in retail stores as well.

Why is this important to you? Scrapbooking with these modern products is a viable option to formal publishing and even desktop publishing. If you have lots of mementos to go along with your prose, you will want to seriously consider consulting someone who sells this new wave of scrapbook materials to see if they fit with your family history format.

The family photo album format lends itself to this new wave of scrapbooking, for instance. Also, if you are blessed with dozens of irreplaceable photos, ticket stubs, and important documents, this could be an answer to preserving your important original memorabilia. With the help of today's affordable color-copying, you could make copies of these wonderful bits of history and then add your writing to create a handful of unique family history albums for your family history, either as a complement to a printed book or as the family history itself. If this format intrigues you and you only have a small number of family members you are writing for, consider this concept. As always, the limit is your own imagination.

Be Proud; Say It Loud

Now what? It's up to you, but whatever you do, don't hesitate to show everyone your work, no matter what your publishing decision is. Every day more people take up genealogy as a hobby. The number is in the millions now, especially with the Internet as a mind-bogglingly helpful tool. And with those numbers—this is America, after all—comes a plethora of opportunities and options, some hoping to make money from your interest. You've already noticed lots of them, including computer software and dozens of new genealogical magazines and journals hungry for interesting work.

Because genealogy is a labor of love, though, you'll also find many free ways of expressing your passion for genealogy with others who share that passion. Look for these. Check with your local genealogical organizations and online genealogical chat groups. As mentioned, historical museums, genealogical societies, and even libraries offer contests and fairs to showcase your work, as well as chances to see what others are doing with their family histories. Keep your eyes open as you enjoy your family's response, and be proud enough of your work to take advantage of any and all chances for "sharing and showing" that you can.

Be proud. Say it loud. You've done a marvelous piece of creative research, which will become more of a family treasure as the years go by.

Progress Report

What is your publishing decision? Are you feeling intimidated by this final step of your family history endeavor? Consider thinking of this part of your work in the same way you did its writing. Bring all your creative energy to seeing this finally in print.

Your labor of love deserves its completion, and the pride you'll experience when you hold the finished product in your hands will also be the pride and gratitude of ancestors you've forever immortalized.

The Least You Need to Know

➤ There are many ways to publish your work.

➤ You can make your manuscript look like a book by creating front and end matter.

➤ You should be proud of your work and find outlets for sharing it beyond your family and friends.

BookMarks— for Further Reference

Genealogical BookMarks

Arksey, Laura. *American Diaries: An Annotated Bibliography of Published American Diaries and Journals, 1492–1980.* Detroit, MI: Gale Research, 1983–1987.

Bentley, Elizabeth Petty. *Directory of Family Associations.* Baltimore, MD: Genealogical Publishing Company (latest edition).

Bentley, Elizabeth Petty. *The Genealogist's Address Book, Third ed.* Baltimore, MD: Genealogical Publishing Co., 1995.

Colletta, John P. *They Came in Ships: A Guide to Finding Your Immigrant Ancestors' Arrival Record.* Salt Lake City, UT: Ancestry Publishing, 1993.

Drake, Paul. *"What Did They Mean By That?" A Dictionary of Historical Terms for Genealogists.* Bowie, MD: Heritage Books, Inc., 1994.

Everton Publishers. *The Handy Book for Genealogists, Eighth ed.* Logan, UT: Everton Publishers, 1991.

Filby, William P. *A Bibliography of American County Histories.* Baltimore, MD: Genealogical Publishing Co., 1987.

Guide to Genealogical Research in the National Archives, Washington, DC: National Archives Trust Fund Board, 1982.

Hansen, James. "Research in Newspapers," *The Source: A Guidebook of American Genealogy.* Salt Lake City, UT: Ancestry Publishers, 1997, pp. 414–438.

Kemp, Thomas Jay. *International Vital Records Handbook, Third ed.* Baltimore, MD: Genealogical Publishing, Co., 1994.

Kirkham, Kay. *How to Read the Handwriting and Records of Early America.* Logan, UT: Everton Publishers, Inc., 1981.

Mills, Elizabeth S. *Evidence! Citation and Analysis for the Family Historian.* Baltimore, MD: Genealogical Publishing Company, 1997.

Neagle, James C. *The Library of Congress: A Guide to Genealogical and Historical Research.* Salt Lake City: Ancestry Publishing, UT, 1990.

Neagle, James C. *U.S. Military Records: A Guide to Federal and State Sources, Colonial America to the Present.* Salt Lake City, UT: Ancestry Publishing, 1994.

Rose, Christine. *Nicknames Past and Present, Second ed., revised.* San Jose, CA: private publisher, 1995.

Rose, Christine, and Kay Germain Ingalls. *The Complete Idiot's Guide to Genealogy.* New York: Alpha Books, 1997.

Szucs, Loretto Dennis, and Sandra Hargreaves Luebking. *The Source: A Guidebook of American Genealogy.* Salt Lake City, UT: Ancestry Publishers, 1997.

Charts and Forms Sources

American Genealogical Lending Library
P.O. Box 329
Bountiful, UT 84011

Everton Publishers, Inc.
P.O. Box 368
Logan, UT 84321

Computer Programs

Family Tree Maker
Broderbund Software
P.O. Box 6125
Novato, CA 94948

Reunion
Leister Productions
P.O. Box 289
Mechanicsburg, PA 17055

The Master Genealogist
Wholly Genes Software
6868 Ducketts Lane
Elk Ridge, MD

Census Microfilm Rental

American Genealogical Lending Library
P.O. Box 244
Bountiful, UT 84011

National Archives Microfilm Rental Program
P.O. Box 30
Annapolis Junction, MD 20701
www.nara.gov/

Magazines

The American Genealogist
P.O. Box 398
Demorest, GA 30535

Everton's Genealogical Helper
P.O. Box 368
Logan, UT 84323

Genealogical Computing
266 W. Center Street
Orem, Utah 84057

National Genealogical Society Quarterly
4527 Seventeenth Street North
Arlington, VA 22207-2399

National Genealogical Society's Computer Interest Digest
4527 Seventeenth Street North
Arlington, VA 22207-2399

Reunions Magazine
P.O. Box 11727
Milwaukee, WI 53211

Web Sites

Internet genealogical resources are expanding. Every day there are new sites. Keep checking; keep looking. These well-established sites will help you get started:

GEN-NEWBIE-L Home Page
www.rootsweb.com/~newbie/

Cyndi's List of Genealogy Sites on the Internet
www.oz.net/~cyndihow/sites.htm

Allen County Public Library Historical Genealogy Dept.
www.acpl.lib.in.us/departments/genealogy.html

LDS Family History Centers
www.genhomepage.com/FHC/

Family History Library
www.familysearch.org

The Newberry Library
www.newberry.org/

National Archives and Records Administration
www.nara.gov/

Newberry Library
www.newberry.org/nl/genealogy

Also check:

"1998 Top 20 Web Sites" *Everton's Genealogical Helper.* (November–December 1998): 52–64.

Writing BookMarks

Edelstein, Scott. *Manuscript Submission.* Cincinatti, Ohio: Writers Digest Books, 1999.

Macy, Debra Hart. *Proofreading Plain and Style.* Franklin Lakes, NJ: Career Press, 1997.

O'Connor, Patricia. *Woe Is I.* New York, NY: Riverhead Books, 1996.

O'Connor, Patricia. *Words Fail Me: What Everyone Who Writes Should Know About Writing.* New York, NY: Harcourt Brace and Co., 1999.

Ross-Larson, Bruce. *Edit Yourself.* New York, NY: W. W. Norton, 1996.

Strunk and White. *Elements of Style.* New York, NY: Allyn and Bacon, 1978.

Zinsser, William. *On Writing Well.* New York, NY: Harper Perennial, 1998.

Sample Forms

Pedigree Chart

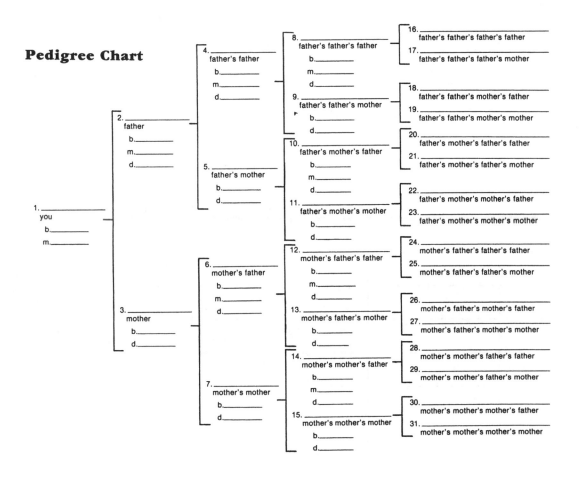

Correspondence Log

Date Sent	To Whom	Request	Reply Date	Results (Positive, Negative, Burned)

Family Group Record

HUSBAND [Full name]			SOURCES: Brief listing.	
BORN	AT		No.	
CHR.	AT		No.	
MAR.	AT		No.	
DIED	AT		No.	
BURIED AT			(Complete source citations on reverse)	
FATHER		MOTHER [Maiden Name]		
OTHER WIVES				
RESIDENCES			RELIGION	
OCCUPATION			MILITARY	
[Use separate forms for each marriage]				
WIFE [Full maiden name]				
BORN	AT			
CHR.	AT			
DIED	AT			
BURIED AT				
FATHER		MOTHER [Maiden Name]		
OTHER HUSBANDS				

Sex Children		Day-Month-Year	City/Town County State	REF. No.
1.	b.		at	Ref.
Spouse:	m.		at	Ref.
	d.		at	Ref.
2.	b.		at	Ref.
Spouse:	m.		at	Ref.
	d.		at	Ref.
3.	b.		at	Ref.
Spouse:	m.		at	Ref.
	d.		at	Ref.
4.	b.		at	Ref.
Spouse:	m .		at	Ref.
	d.		at	Ref.
5.	b.		at	Ref.
Spouse:	m.		at	Ref.
	d.		at	Ref.
6.	b.		at	Ref.
Spouse:	m.		at	Ref.
	d.		at	Ref.
7.	b.		at	Ref.
Spouse:	m.		at	Ref.
	d.		at	Ref.
8.	b.		at	Ref.
Spouse:	m.		at	Ref.
	d.		at	Ref.
9.	b.		at	Ref.
Spouse:	m.		at	Ref.
	d.		at	Ref.
10.	b.		at	Ref.
Spouse:	m.		at	Ref.
	d.		at	Ref.

PREPARED BY	OTHER MAR. OF CHILDREN
Address	Use reverse for additional marriages
City and State	Zip
Date Prepared:	

b.=born   m.=married   d.=death   ch.=christening   List references at top and use ref. numbers on items. Use reverse if necessary.

Glossary

abstract   A summary of a legal document.

administration   An estate that is intestate—with no will.

ancestor   A person from whom you are a direct descendant, i.e., parent, grandparent, great-great grandparent, etc.

anecdote   A short account of a personal or family experience.

black sheep   A family member or ancestor with a questionable reputation.

book   A set of written, printed, or blank sheets bound together into a volume; a long, printed composition of ideas.

census   An official, timely count of the country's population that includes a wealth of peripheral personal family information.

characterization   The transformation of life into a character through action and description.

circa   A word used to mean "approximately" in the context of dates and time. Abbreviation: "ca."

clichés   Worn out, prepackaged phrases whose time has come and gone.

collateral relative   A relative with whom a person shares a common ancestor, but not the same ancestral line, i.e., your ancestral aunts, uncles, and cousins.

deed   Legal document used to transfer a title of land.

description   An attempt to paint a word picture of a scene, a person, or an adventure.

dialogue   The direct words of a person in a story, as in a conversation, usually set off by quotations.

digression   A swerving into another topic from the main topic.

dramatic tension   The created suspense that drives the story forward.

emigrant   A person who departs one country for a permanent residence in another.

estate   All of a person's earthly possessions usually enumerated in a legal inheritance document, such as a will, after death.

et al.   A phrase after a person's name in a deed means "and others."

et ex.   A phrase after a man's name in a deed means "and wife."

family group chart   A form used to record a specific family's genealogical information.

gazetteer   A sketch map of homes, farms and businesses in a specific township, county or state during a certain time period.

genealogy   The investigation of ancestry and family histories.

given name   A person's first name, also called "personal name" or "Christian name."

heirloom   Something of special value handed down from one generation to another.

homonyms   Words that sound alike but have different meanings, such as "your" and "you're"; "their," "there," and "they're"; "it's" and "its"; and "write" and "right."

hook   An idea designed to grab your interest at the beginning of a piece of writing.

hyperbole   Extravagant exaggeration of a thought or fact.

immigrant   A person who arrives in a country to establish permanent residence.

in media res   A phrase that means "beginning in the middle of things."

indentured servant   A person who enters into a contract for some sort of service in exchange for passage to the new world.

index   A list in alphabetical order of some specific data in a book, such as names, titles, or key words, usually placed at the end.

intestate   To die without a will.

journal   A notebook in which one keeps an account of his thoughts or creative writing.

manumission   The name given to the act of, and the document created, giving official freedom to a slave before the Civil War's Emancipation Proclamation.

memoir   A first person narrative composed from personal experience.

memory   A recollection, an incomplete story waiting to be formed.

mug book   Colloquial term for a file in a local library containing personal history on past residents.

narrative   Writing that tells a story.

onomastic evidence   Genealogical evidence based on the similarity of name.

outline   A preliminary account of a writing project.

pedigree chart   A family tree worksheet that starts with you, then moves back through time showing your ancestors.

point of view   The position from which a story is told.

primary source   Information received from firsthand knowledge.

process   A way of doing things, step by step.

profile   A concise biographical sketch.

psychobiography   The attempt to capture a person's interior life.

revise   To review in order to correct or improve.

SASE   Abbreviation for "self-addressed stamped envelope," which should be included in all your correspondence out of courtesy and expedience.

story   The narrating or relating of an event or series of events, either true or fictitious.

style   A writer's manner of expressing thoughts in language.

surname   A last name held in common by members of a family.

tense   The "time" in which you create a story, as in present tense, past tense, or future tense.

testate   To die with a will.

tone   The attitude that the writer brings to a story.

transition   A word, phrase, or idea that connects one part of writing to another, be it sentence, paragraph, or chapter.

vital records   Birth, death, and marriage certificates required by law to be kept by the prevailing local government.

will   A legal document declaring a person's wishes for the division of his estate after his death.

Index

Y-Z